TH
AMERICAN
MAGAZINE
WRITING

2009

THE BEST AMERICAN MAGAZINE WRITING

2009

**Compiled by
the American
Society of
Magazine
Editors**

Columbia University Press   New York

Columbia University Press
Publishers Since 1893
New York   Chichester, West Sussex
Copyright © 2010 Columbia University Press
All rights reserved

Library of Congress Cataloging-in-Publication Data
ISSN 1541-0978
ISBN 978-0-231-14796-5 (pbk.)

Columbia University Press books are printed on permanent and durable
acid-free paper.
This book is printed on paper with recycled content.
Printed in the United States of America
p 10 9 8 7 6 5 4 3 2 1

References to Internet Web sites (URLs) were accurate at the time of writing.
Neither the author nor Columbia University Press is responsible for URLs
that may have expired or changed since the manuscript was prepared.

Contents

Chris Anderson

Introduction

I s print dead?" Sigh. Hardly a day goes by when I'm not asked this. As a magazine editor, it drives me crazy (I try not to let it show), but these are the times we live in. Digital distribution is so good for so many things that we start to wonder if it's best for everything. The grinding decline of newspapers, reported in their own dwindling pages, doesn't help.

But there is more to print than newspapers, with this book and the original sources of the stories in it as a prime example. Print is alive and well; it's just changing. It remains strong where the Web is weak, of which more later. But first, let's just remind ourselves what "print" means.

There is still a dizzying array of paper-based media. Starting with frequency, there are daily newspapers, weekly newspapers, weekly newsmagazines, biweekly, monthly, and quarterly magazines, and then books. In distribution there is the full range from community to globe. In audience, there are mass, niche, trade, and enthusiast. In business model, there is everything from high-price subscriptions with no ads to free with lots of ads.

Newspapers are struggling, to be sure, but most of the other forms are not. Last year, there were nearly 500,000 different books published in America, an all-time record. In the same year there were 7,400 different magazine published here, the highest numbers since the dot-com boom of 2000. While 54 magazines were closed, 628 were launched. Average circulation remained near all-time highs.

But surely the headlines are full of tales of cutbacks and crises? Yes, but don't confuse the advertising climate with the appetites of readers. For many magazines (including my own) readership is at an all-time high. People still want what we make—we're just trying to figure out how to pay for it. There are worse problems.

When I watch the media-consumption habits of my children (five kids twelve and under), I see some radically new behavior along with some things that haven't changed a bit from my own childhood. They'd rather watch videos on YouTube than on TV, and rather play videogames than either. Given a choice between a computer and food, drink, or sleep, they'll pick the computer. Active beats passive, and they crave to interact with their screens.

But when it comes to print, almost nothing has changed. They love books, and between the girls curling up in bed with a novel and the boys and their comics, print plays as much as role in their lives as it did in mine. They also love magazines, and are as thrilled by the arrival in the mail of *National Geographic Kids* or an Xbox magazine as I was by *Boy's Life* and *Popular Mechanics*.

So some print is doing fine. What's the difference between the struggling sectors and the thriving ones? That is the key question of our industry as we navigate the digital age.

I'd argue that my job, like that of nearly everyone else in the media industry, is to add value to the Internet. The online world is a given; it is the water we all swim in, the air we breathe. The question is, what can print still do that the Web cannot?

What the Web did was to break the hold over distribution that commercial media held by democratizing publishing, broadcast, and communications. The quasi monopoly of mainstream media over consumer attention derived from ownership of the means of production—the factories (multiblock printing plants), fleets of delivery trucks, newsstand leverage, and the money necessary to clear forests and blanket the world with broadsheets. In broadcast, meanwhile, you needed transmission towers and FCC licenses, studios and engineers. The barriers to entry were high and the competition, just other media giants. Don't pick a fight, as was often said, with someone who buys ink by the barrel.

Now that monopoly is broken; the media's problem is infinite competition. Any blogger can get the same digital distribution as the editor of the *New York Times*, and anybody with a camera phone can broadcast as well online as the chairman of NBC. Remember the handwringing about "media consolidation" and concentration of power in the hands of a few tycoons? They wish! Now owning a media conglomerate is about as attractive as running GM, and those tycoons, fortunes evaporating, inspire pity more than fear.

So where does that leave print, not as a business but a medium? Doing well what the Web does poorly: long-form journalism, narrative, photography, and design. In short, offering depth and immersion, complementing a Web better suited for immediacy and breadth. Newspaper readers are shifting online because that sort of short, newsy, writing works better on the Web, where it needn't wait twelve hours for the presses and trucks and the ink doesn't get on your fingers. But for the print media that's less tied to the frenetic pace of the news cycle, the time required for production is increasingly an asset, not a liability. It forces its creators to think in terms of months, not hours. It both requires and rewards invention, original thinking, and deep research

Take my own magazine. We put all of our content online, but HTML does it few favors. The 6,000-word article that represents six months of research, writing, and editing turns into twelve screens that must be clicked through. The photographs, themselves a feat of talent, planning, money, and logistics, are reduced to thumbnails. The design, which is the work of fully half of my staff, is lost entirely; browsers have no place for the fluid art form of full-page synthesis of typography, illustration, anarchic geometries, and playful filigrees, the very things that make the print form of the magazine a visual feast.

So my job (at least the print part of it) is to continue to do what the best magazine editors have always done, using paper to its fullest to create immersive, addicting, exuberant celebrations of people, ideas, events, and places. To tell stories and create art; to draw readers in and to transport them to a different place, guided by the writers' voice, even just for a few minutes. To create a sustained experience that offers depth in a world of 140 characters and fast-flip screens. Rather than being on the trailing edge of the news cycle, to be on the leading edge of the ideas cycle.

This is why print isn't dead. The very things that appear to be the disadvantages of print are equally its virtue. It is expensive, can't be changed, and takes a long time to make and deliver. But what that requires is that it be used well. Editors must be discriminating about what makes the page and select only the best of what they have. Writing is fact-checked and edited to ensure that it's right. And freed from the instantaneous demands of the Web, writers can spend months really researching and reporting their stories, finding that sweet spot between the screen and the book, the writing that's feels both of the moment and for the ages.

The articles that follow demonstrate the best of this. Some of these stories you need to read. Others you'll just want to read. Although I enjoyed all of them, I'm just going to mention one: "Papa," a report from the frontlines of the battle over James Brown's estate. It was written by Sean Flynn and appeared in *GQ* (a sister publication, although that's not why I picked it!). It is the very model of a great magazine story: deeply researched, beautifully (and hilariously) written, and full of telling details that only months of work can reveal. This is magazine making at its finest.

What's fascinating about the story is that it came out a year and a half after the Godfather of Soul's death. There is no special peg; no effort to make news. Instead, it is a twelve-page (in the magazine) exploration of a story that actually got more interesting *after* it left the daily headlines. This is the second draft of history, the draft that has the benefit of time, thought, and the candor of people living their lives after the spotlight has passed. Yet you won't be able to put it down; Brown's life is told best by his afterlife, where the people who knew him fill the vacuum he left. And it took a magazine to tell their story.

It's worth noting that the Brown feature in the magazine also has riveting photography and a delightful family-tree-gone-wrong illustration, which I'm afraid you'll just have to imagine. The articles reprinted here are, sadly, not always the full experience; book publishing does not lend itself to the photography and design and makes the glossy magazine page such a spectacle. But they were chosen to blow your mind just the same. Take a break from the screen and dive in; I think you'll emerge, many pages later, no longer worrying about the future of print.

David Willey

Acknowledgments

One of the most striking things I heard during this past year of media upheaval was when Eric Schmidt, the CEO of Google, referred to the Internet as a "cesspool." That's a pretty strong word coming from the guy in charge of the Web's most sea-changingly successful company. Schmidt was referring to the morass of information on the Web and how most of it is inaccurate, untrustworthy, biased, poorly written and edited, myopically self-indulgent, or just plain vulgar—and sometimes all the above. Schmidt later said he believes the solution to this problem is the guidance of trusted, authoritative "brands," especially those of magazines. (Caveat: He was speaking to a roomful of magazine editors trying to get a read on the growing chorus of print-is-dead prognostications, so it's possible he was trying to make us feel better.) Given that a magazine's authority and credibility are only as good as the work it produces, I heard in Schmidt's comments a full-throated endorsement of the power and importance of journalism.

Not that the head of Google is particularly bullish on the future of print journalism. He isn't. But now that Chris Anderson has articulated a more optimistic view of the *life* of print in his introduction to this book, I'll just concur and add this: Whether we want our journalism delivered in pixels or on paper, we need—perhaps more than ever—reporters, writers, and editors, as well as publications that give great stories the time, money, and space they demand and deserve. Another way of saying this is, we need magazines, which remain dedicated to the enduring power and delight of great writing, enterprising reporting, illuminating commentary, and vivid storytelling. Why? Because people don't want to be merely informed by a trusted source. They want to be surprised, deeply educated, entertained, and moved—and a great magazine story does all the above.

The seventeen pieces collected here were originally published in ink-on-paper magazines. That means they were rigorously fact-checked and artfully edited, which can't always be said for something you read on a screen. The stories were later selected as finalists (and in some cases, as winners) of the 2009 National Magazine Awards administered by the American Society of Magazine Editors (ASME) in association with the Columbia University Graduate School of Journalism. Often called the Oscars of the magazine industry (but really more akin to the Pulitzer Prizes), the National Magazine Awards are celebrated in New York City every spring, with twenty-five Alexander Calder–designed stabiles, known as "Ellies," going to the winners—which ranged this year from *The New Yorker* to *Reader's Digest* to *Field and Stream*. It's a fun, dramatic evening, but I've always thought the prelude to that celebration, while not as glitzy, has always been just as memorable. I'm talking about the three days of judging, when the best editors, photo editors, and art directors in the industry gather in New York to immerse themselves for three days in thousands of magazines and stories in search of the very best. It's a rejuvenating reminder of just how much terrific work is being done out there, sometimes in places you wouldn't expect.

On behalf of ASME, I would like to thank the 275 judges who gave so much time, energy, and advocacy to that process. Thanks also to Laura Manske and to ASME's Sid Holt and Nina Fortuna, who organized the entries before judging, and to Nicholas

Lemann, dean of Columbia's "J-School." We are grateful to our book agent, David McCormick of McCormick & Williams, and our publisher, Columbia University Press, for remaining as committed to magazine journalism as we are. Chris Anderson, the editor in chief of *Wired*, who walked away with two of those bronze elephants this year, is one of the most innovative editors in the business—and also one of the most forward-thinking commentators on technology and its impact on our culture. We are grateful he has written the introduction to this book.

And thanks most of all to Marlene Kahan, ASME's executive director, who edited this tenth annual edition of *The Best American Magazine Writing*. Marlene selected the stories included here with the same care and respect she has for all magazines and for the people who work with great skill, passion, and ingenuity to bring them very much to life.

THE BEST
AMERICAN
MAGAZINE
WRITING

2009

GQ

When James Brown, the "Godfather of Soul," told the world he was a "Sex Machine," he wasn't kidding. Brown may have fathered as many as fourteen children. But his five-page will didn't leave money to any of them. In "Papa," Sean Flynn draws a portrait of a cold, petty man whose personal life belied his on-stage abandon.

Sean Flynn

Papa

The day he buried his mama in the big cemetery on Laney Walker Boulevard, in the row where he'd buried his daddy and his third wife, too, James Brown draped an arm around Roosevelt Royce Johnson's shoulders and pointed at a plot of unturned earth.

"Well, Mr. Johnson," he said, "that's my spot right there. What you gonna put on my headstone?"

Johnson grunted. Mr. Brown talking foolish, headstones and all that. Like he might actually die someday. What's a man supposed to say to that?

He'd known Mr. Brown almost his whole life, since he was a boy, twelve years old, fetching coffee for the disc jockeys at WJMO 1490, a soul station in Cleveland. The jocks knew Mr. Brown because Mr. Brown made it his business to know the people who could play his records on the radio and keep making him rich. He'd check in with them when he came to town, hang out for a while. Easy promotion, just James Brown working, always working, at being James Brown.

That's how Roosevelt met Mr. Brown, through the deejays, in the mid-'60s. They told him they were going to meet a man, take him shopping, asked Roosevelt if he wanted to come. He thought it was odd when the jocks drove out to Burke Lakefront Airport. No stores out there. But there was a private plane. The hatch opened, and a little man with an improbable swoop of hair climbed down the steps. A black man. Blew Roosevelt's mind. *A black man with his own plane.* Damn.

Mr. Brown asked him his name, and he said, "Roosevelt, sir."

"Oh, you got manners," Mr. Brown said. Manners were important to Mr. Brown.

Then they all went to King's Menswear so Mr. Brown could buy some silk shirts. "Stay with me," he told Roosevelt, "and hold my coat." Which he did. Mr. Brown gave him four twenty-dollar bills that day, and whenever he came back to Cleveland to play Gleason's or the arena downtown, he'd send someone to find that polite kid who'd held his coat. That's what Roosevelt Johnson did for years, hold Mr. Brown's coat.

When he got older, Mr. Brown put him on a Greyhound with a crate of records to hump around to R&B stations, and when he got older still, Mr. Brown took him on tour. ROOSEVELT ROYCE JOHNSON, his business cards read. PERSONAL ASSISTANT TO MR. BROWN. Johnson would lay out Mr. Brown's pajamas at night and iron his clothes in the morning and make sure he had an aspirin with his breakfast and fifty milligrams of Viagra before every show. ("It wasn't a sex thing," Johnson says. "He thought it gave him extra energy.") He bought Mr. Brown weed in Amsterdam, and he brought Mr. Brown Gatorade when his legs cramped in the morning. He traveled the world with Mr. Brown and sang backup, too, right onstage with the Godfather himself.

By the time Susie Behling Brown was laid to rest in the winter of 2004, Johnson had been with Mr. Brown for forty years. Mr. Brown was an old man by then, almost seventy-one. His hair was bone white under the black dye, and he had cancer on his prostate and sugar in his blood. But he was still working, still touring, still paying Johnson $3,300 every week on the road.

What you gonna put on my headstone?

"I'm not gonna put nothin' on it," Johnson said. "I'm gonna let you put something on mine, 'cause I'm gonna leave *you* behind."

Which didn't happen, obviously, because Roosevelt Johnson is still here to tell stories about Mr. Brown, who up and died not quite three years after his mama, on Christmas Day 2006. But there's nothing on his headstone, because there is no headstone. Mr. Brown is not buried in the big cemetery on Laney Walker Boulevard, nor is he in the shade of the oak trees next to his South Carolina mansion or in the red clay on the slope above his pond.

More than a year after he passed, Mr. Brown is in a temporary crypt surrounded by a fence outside the house in South Carolina where one of his daughters lives. "Like a pet," Johnson says. "That's something you do with a dog—put it in the backyard."

Except Mr. Brown is actually in the front yard. A minor point. But really, it's been that kind of year.

.   .   .

James Brown was not expecting to die when he did. He was seventy-three years old, with a wheezing chest and swollen feet, but the man wasn't ready to retire. He was going back on the road: New Year's Eve at B. B. King's place in Manhattan, then up to Ontario, west to British Columbia, down to Anaheim in February. Before the tour, in late December, he went to get a new set of bottom teeth screwed into his jaw, but a doctor heard that wheeze and sent him to the hospital. Thirty-six hours later, before dawn broke Christmas morning, his heart petered out.

Yet Mr. Brown was not wholly *unprepared* to die, either. Several years earlier, in August 2000, he'd drawn up a will in which he bequeathed his "personal and household effects"—his linens and china and such—to six adult children from two ex-wives and two other women. He was very clear, too, that those were the only heirs he intended to favor. "I have intentionally failed to provide for any other relatives or other persons," he wrote in the will. "Such failure is intentional and not occasioned by accident or mistake."

Everything else he owned, including his sixty-acre estate in Beech Island, South Carolina, and his catalog of 800 or so songs, was to remain in a trust, which in turn was divided into two funds: one to educate his grandchildren (seven among those six named children, plus the daughter of his son Teddy, who died in 1973) and a much larger one to pay tuition for "financially needy" students who attend school in South Carolina or Georgia. How much is that trust worth? Hard to say, because Mr. Brown's best assets are of a sort that can be marketed and managed in perpetuity as opposed to simply liquidated for cash. But the lowball estimate is $20 million, which, with proper promotion, could be multiplied many times over for many years to come. Elvis has been dead for three decades, after all, and he's still pulling eight figures annually.

In other words, Mr. Brown left a fortune to poor strangers.

Fifteen months later, none of those poor strangers have seen a nickel. Nor *will* they for months, and more likely years, to come, by which point there may be little left, after the creditors and the lawyers are paid. The first attorney was hired barely thirty-six hours after Mr. Brown died, and the first legal challenge was initiated less than two weeks after that. The lawsuits and lawyers rapidly multiplied—there are now more than thirty lawyers suing in three different courts—which has had the predictable result of resolving . . . precisely nothing.

For such a simple little will—all of five pages, and mostly boilerplate at that—there are a stupefying number of issues to resolve.

Mr. Brown's ostensible widow and the mother of James Brown II wants at least a third and perhaps half of his riches—though, as a matter of law, she is almost certainly not his widow nor, as a matter of human physiology, the mother of his biological child. Five of the six children named in the will want the trust dissolved and the will invalidated, which would entitle them to equal shares of the entire estate; that puts them at odds with the sixth sibling, Terry, and his boys, Forlando and Romunzo, who want the will and educational trusts to stand. At least two other daughters whom Mr. Brown never acknowledged also want a share of the pot, as well as eighteen years of back child support. Four more potential children—Jane and John Does I, II, III, and IV in the court records—might have similar claims. The three men Mr. Brown named as trustees have resigned, though two of them, Albert H. "Buddy" Dallas and Alford Bradley, want to be reinstated, because they say a judge bullied them into quitting. That same judge, Doyet Early, wants to put the third former trustee, David Cannon, in jail for not repaying $373,000 in misappropriated funds. Cannon says he can't afford it, which looks bad considering he spent almost $900,000 in cash to build a house in Honduras last year. State investigators are working a criminal case on Cannon, too. The two special administrators Judge Early appointed to replace those three men, meanwhile, are being sued in federal court by Forlando Brown, who argues that they were illegally put in charge and are improperly attempting to shift assets from the trust to the estate, from which their $300-an-hour fees could be paid. The administrators, Adele J. Pope and Robert Buchanan, have in turn sued Bradley, Cannon, Dallas, entertainment lawyer Joel Katz, his firm (Greenberg Traurig), and Enterprise Bank in state court, alleging a years-long conspiracy to swindle millions from Mr. Brown. All of those people have lawyers, and many of them have more than one. Tomi Rae Hynie, the widow who's probably not technically a widow, has five. Her son has his representative, a guardian ad litem, and the guardian ad litem has his own lawyer. Pope and Buchanan have lawyers. Even the anonymous beneficiaries of the trust, all those needy and deserving would-be students, have a lawyer—the attorney general of South Carolina—and they used to have two until Judge Early tossed out the Georgia attorney general.

And those are the relatively dignified legal proceedings.

Outside the courtroom, the family has bickered over absolutely everything, including the disposition of Mr. Brown's body, which for a time was kept in a gold-plated coffin inside a climate-controlled room in his house. When it was finally decided that the corpse would be put in a crypt in daughter Deanna's yard in early March, daughter Yamma nearly missed the private ceremony because police in Atlanta had arrested her the night before for stabbing her husband in the arm with a butcher knife. Since then, Forlando Brown has accused those two aunts, Deanna and Yamma, of swiping mementos, checks, and tens of thousands in cash from his grandfather's house, and in court he called their lawyer—who used to be *his* lawyer—a liar and a forger, or at least an accomplice to forgery. Yamma, Deanna, and half-brother Daryl accused the former trustees of hunting for "certain assets" when the trustees photographed the woods around Mr. Brown's house, an obvious reference to cash Mr. Brown is believed to have buried in the yard. Tomi Rae Hynie, who prefers to be called Mrs. Brown, was locked out of the house, and she insists someone—the adult children or the former trustees, or a combination thereof—shredded more recent wills, which she believes left half of Mr. Brown's assets to her and her son, and took all of her jewelry and most of Mr. Brown's clothes. "They looted everything," she says. "You're dealing with nothing but liars and thieves and cheats who would throw a widow and a six-year-old child out on the streets." She also believes, along with several other people, that Mr. Brown was killed, though by whom and how neither she nor anyone else will say. "I can't comment on that right now," she says, "for the safety of myself and my son." Even the lawyer who drew up the will and trust that are now being contested is a tawdry little sideshow: He's in prison for the 2006 murder of a strip-club manager who'd bounced him for nakedly masturbating while waiting for a $300 lap dance.

Wait, there's more.

There are claims against the estate from creditors and would-be creditors. The funeral home wants $17,995 for the programs it produced for the services. One of Mr. Brown's managers wants a $200,000 cut of royalties he was promised. Buddy Dallas would like $624,876 in fees he says he was shorted over seven years. The Pullman Group, to which Mr. Brown mortgaged his royalties in 1999, wants $31 million (the refinancing of that deal is the subject of yet another lawsuit). A doctor wants $8,500 to reimburse her for, among other things, all the times she packed Mr. Brown into a limo to rehab in Atlanta; she'd like an additional $14,000 for two African carvings he never returned to her, or failing that, the carvings. Roosevelt Johnson, too, would like to get paid. "We were always told by Mr. Brown we would be taken care of should anything happen to him," he wrote in his claim. "We, meaning myself, and his group should have at least got two weeks severance pay. Myself for over thirty years of faithful service should get 2.5 million for a lifetime of service as he promised."

Maybe Mr. Brown did make that promise. But he never put it in writing, and it probably wouldn't have mattered if he had. Somebody surely would've sued.

·   ·   ·

Buddy Dallas met James Brown in 1984 at a political reception in Augusta, Georgia. It was a brief and unremarkable encounter—Dallas mostly remembers that his two-year-old daughter liked the little man with the funny hair—but the next day, the phone rang in Dallas's office. It was Mr. Brown.

"Mr. Dallas," he said, "I need you to represent me."

"But Mr. Brown," Dallas replied—it was somehow automatic that James Brown was *Mr. Brown*—"I don't know anything about the entertainment business."

"That's all right," he said. "I'll teach you about the entertainment business. But I need you to represent me now."

Mr. Brown's immediate problems didn't involve entertainment. Mainly, he was broke. He hadn't broken the Billboard 100 in seven years, and he was playing shows for $7,500 that cost him $9,500 to produce. The IRS wanted $20 million in back taxes and penalties, the phone company had cut his line, and the founder of the Sacramento chapter of his fan club was after him for child support. "Mr. Dallas," he said a week after they'd met, "I hate to ask you this, but I really, *really* need some money."

So the first thing Dallas did as Mr. Brown's lawyer was give him $12,000, two grand in cash, the rest in checks paid to his creditors. Less than a year later, Dallas put up his own Lincoln as collateral for another $18,000.

The second thing he did was straighten out the child-support mess in Sacramento. "Mr. Brown," Dallas told him when the paperwork was settled, "you're going to have to be more careful."

"Well, Mr. Dallas," he said, "we're not going to have to worry about that no more."

What he meant was there wouldn't be any *future* paternity suits: Mr. Brown told at least six people he'd had a vasectomy earlier that year. But that was too little and much too late: One reason his estate is such a disaster is that he left so many heirs who could lay claim to his wealth.

His first wife, Velma, bore three sons in the 1950s, of whom two survive, and a backup singer had a fourth boy. Another singer gave birth to a daughter in 1965, and his second wife, Deidre, had two girls, one in 1968 and the other in 1972. The fan-club woman in Sacramento had her son in 1968.

That's seven children from five women.

And those five women are like grains of sand on a very wide beach. Mr. Brown had an insatiable appetite for women that was at least as pathological as it was sexual. "You'd have to grow up in a whorehouse to understand how James Brown felt about women," one of his confidants says, which is apt because Mr. Brown did, in fact, grow up in a whorehouse. His mother walked out on his father when he was four, and two years later, he was sent to live in his aunt Honey's brothel in Augusta. He shined shoes for the soldiers from Fort Gordon, danced for nickels and pennies they'd flip at his feet, watched them shamble into Aunt Honey's to fuck the women, watched them shuffle back out.

When Mr. Brown grew up, when he was a famous performer touring the world forty, fifty weeks a year, he fucked a lot of women. That is a deliberate term, *fucked*, because Mr. Brown was not a man who *made love* or even *had sex*. Mr. Brown fucked. "He did not know about *the soft*," a longtime friend says. A lot of times, he'd let one of his cronies deal with the preliminaries, make small talk with a girl, get her a drink, keep her company. "She ready?" he'd ask. "I ain't got no time now. Make sure she ready." He'd hop on, roll off. Straight missionary, straight to the point. He never saw a reason for much else. "Why's a white man eat a woman?" he once asked a white friend. "What's he get outta that?" Hell, the man was in his sixties before he discovered doggy style on the Playboy Channel. He called up Roosevelt Johnson at three in the morning to tell him about it. "You sittin' down, Mr. Johnson?" he asked, which is what he always said when he had an astonishing new fact to report. "Black man don't know nothing. Black man don't know a *damned thing*. A white man, he get up in his woman from *behind*." Johnson pretended to be surprised by that. ("You had to go there with him," he says, "because you didn't know *anything* Mr. Brown didn't know.")

So how many women? How high can you count? Mr. Brown always kept a few girlfriends on the side, some for decades, and he always found a woman or two in whatever city he happened to be playing. "There'd be times, literally, when one would be coming in the front door while another one was going out the back," says Buddy Dallas.

Naturally, some of them got pregnant.

In 1961, there was a groupie named Ruby Mae Shannon, from Houston, who gave birth that December to a daughter, LaRhonda.

In 1968, there was a pretty white seventeen-year-old hippie named Lea Mernickle. She was standing in line to buy a photograph after a show in Vancouver when Mr. Brown sent one of his men to go fetch her. "Do you want to meet Mr. Brown?" he asked. Which was a silly question, because really, who *didn't* want to meet Mr. Brown? She followed the man backstage, and Mr. Brown greeted her warmly. "He seemed to be smitten with me," she says. He invited her to fly to Los Angeles with him that night. She said no—her mother would've killed her, disappearing like that—but when he asked her a few days later to fly to Denver, she went. "I was always thinking the best of people," she says. "And my head was in the stars. I was going to hang out with *James Brown.* How groovy is that?" And it was, except for, as she puts it, "the part I wasn't particularly thrilled about." She flew home pregnant and in October had a baby girl with skin the color of cinnamon, which is what she named her, Cinnamon Nicole Mernickle.

In 1970, there was a woman named Christine Mitchell, whom he culled from the audience at a show in Miami. She gave birth to yet another daughter, Jeanette.

That's ten children so far. Four more—*at least* four more— are awaiting DNA results. The laws of probability suggest there are others ("Let's hope this thing doesn't spread to Europe," Dallas says), but how many, nobody knows. "My dad would send his hounds to pay women to get rid of the babies or pay them not to talk about it," says LaRhonda, Ruby Shannon's daughter. "My mom wouldn't settle for it. I used to ask her why, and she would say, 'Because he's a friend.' "

. . .

One of Mr. Brown's hounds intercepted Lea Mernickle backstage in the summer of 1968, when he was in Vancouver for another show and she was obviously pregnant and trying to find him to tell him. The man—maybe a lawyer, maybe a bodyguard—asked a lot of questions, "accusatory questions," about her baby. Was she sure Mr. Brown was the father?

"The only thing I want to know," she told the man, "is does he want to know his daughter, does he want to see her, does he want a relationship with her?"

No.

She got paid a couple of thousand dollars, and because Lea was a minor when she got pregnant, her mother signed an affidavit saying Lea had never had sex with Mr. Brown or anyone in his entourage. And that was it.

Not long after Cinnamon was born, Lea married a man of Danish descent and moved to the Okanagan Valley, east of Vancouver, where she had three sons, all blue-eyed and blond. And when she was young, Cinnamon—who was called Nikki as a child and now Nicole as an adult—believed she was Danish, too. "If you'd asked me," she says, "my ancestors were Vikings."

But the white kids in the valley—which would have been all the kids in the valley—were merciless. They made fun of her hair, the kinks she combed out with Vaseline. They said her brothers couldn't be her *real* brothers, and when she asked her mother if that was true, Lea admitted it was. "Your real father was a famous singer," she said. Maybe she said James Brown, but Nicole had never heard of him. Later, though, when an uncle gave her a copy of *Papa's Got a Brand New Bag*, she would stare at his face on the cover. She knew that man was her daddy.

Not that it made her feel any better. "I was different, and being different sucked," Nicole says. The white kids said she was black, and when one black family finally moved to town, those kids said she wasn't black enough. In the fifth grade, one of those black girls yanked Nicole off her bike and slapped her. "Stop lying," she said. "James Brown ain't your daddy."

The problem, she decided, was that James Brown simply couldn't find her. That had to be it. Why else would a man abandon his little girl? "I was believing he didn't know I was alive," she says. "He just needed a message, and then he would come and rescue me." He never did, though, even after Lea's marriage broke up and she moved her children to Vancouver and had to collect welfare to get by.

So what's that worth, now that he's dead, all those years of being different and feeling abandoned? Is there a debt owed? One that is even possible to repay?

Nicole never asked for anything while Mr. Brown was alive. But in the mid-'90s, after she'd been divorced and had two children of her own, she did try to meet him. She started making phone calls, which eventually led her to Buddy Dallas. She told him she didn't want money, only to meet her father. It took a while, but Dallas arranged a conference call between himself, Mr. Brown, and Nicole.

Mr. Brown was polite when he answered. Always with the manners. Nicole got to the point: "Do you have any doubt that I'm your flesh and blood?"

"Yeah, I have doubts," Mr. Brown said. "You ain't my child. Somebody lyin' to you, 'cause I ain't your daddy. If you is my daughter, I'd want to hug you and tell you I love you and meet your kids. But you ain't my child."

The conversation lasted all of three minutes. She never spoke to him again, and she saw him only once, from the eighth row of a Vancouver auditorium in 2004. The way she tells it now, there was a moment, in the middle of "It's a Man's Man's Man's World," where he seemed like he saw her in the audience, like he was staring at her from the stage. "He just had this mean look," she says. "Like, *I hate you.*"

Probably just her imagination. James Brown wouldn't have recognized his daughter. And maybe that's why Nicole saw a man who looked so mean. He never gave her a reason to see anything else.

.   .   .

And what about LaRhonda? Does she have anything coming?

She was four years old, playing mud cakes in the yard, when her mother called her inside and put her in front of the TV. "I want you to see something," she said. There was a black man singing on the screen. "That's your daddy."

"That ain't my daddy," LaRhonda said. Then she went back to her mud cakes.

For years after that, whenever Mr. Brown played Houston, Ruby Shannon would dress up her daughter and take her to the arena, LaRhonda grousing the whole time about having to see some old man's show. She never believed that man was her daddy. For a long time, she wasn't even sure Ruby was her mother, what with the woman working two jobs to pay the bills, leaving LaRhonda to be raised by her great-aunt.

Then, when LaRhonda was eleven, her mother dragged her to yet another show, and she stood outside afterward, by the stage door, waiting for an autograph. It was late, two in the morning, maybe three, before he finally came out, because Mr. Brown had to wipe off the sweat and put on fresh clothes and roll his hair all over again before he'd walk outside. The man liked to stay in character, and the character always looked good.

He recognized LaRhonda in the crowd from seeing her at all those other shows with Ruby. He went straight to her, asked where her mother was. LaRhonda pointed off to one side. She watched Mr. Brown go to Ruby, watched him pick her up and twirl her around. And for the first time she thought, Maybe he *is* my daddy.

Ruby died in 1975 at forty, a heart attack after surgery. LaRhonda tried for months to tell Mr. Brown. She finally tracked him to a hotel in Birmingham and got through the switchboard by saying her name was Ruby Mae Shannon.

Mr. Brown got on the line. He was sweet. "Hey, baby," he said. "What's goin' on?"

LaRhonda started sobbing. She told him who she was, told him Ruby was dead.

"What you calling me for? I ain't your daddy."

He said that, Mr. Brown did, to his thirteen-year-old daughter.

"That daddy I always thought was gonna come home," LaRhonda says now, "that was gonna come running and pick me up and hug me and kiss me, that daddy I thought was gonna be like, 'Okay, her mom's passed, I'll take her in'—that daddy never came."

But LaRhonda kept coming back. "Like a canker sore," she says. She'd go to his shows in Houston, find someone to let her backstage. The first time, she was sixteen, and Mr. Brown just stared at her. He warmed to her as the years went by, or at least thawed some. "Me and your mama was friends," he told her once. "Your mama was built like a Coke bottle," he told her more than once. When she was nineteen, she took her own daughter, Ciara, backstage, and Mr. Brown held the baby on his lap and called her his granddaughter.

"If she's your granddaughter," one of his backup singers said, "then who's her mama?"

Mr. Brown scowled. "Ain't nobody asked you nothin'." He turned to the Reverend Al Sharpton, who was close to Mr. Brown in those days. "Reverend, you're a man of the cloth. Tell the truth: She look like me?"

"I am a man of the cloth," Sharpton said. "And she looks like you spit her out of your mouth."

Sharpton doesn't recall the conversation, but he says it sounds plausible (especially since LaRhonda does bear a gobsmackingly obvious resemblance to her father). More important, he remembers her clearly. "You mean Peaches?" he says when asked about the daughter in Houston. That's what everyone calls her, Peaches. Her father gave her that name. "She's a Georgia peach," he told Ruby years ago.

And maybe that's the worst thing: LaRhonda was never a stranger to the people around Mr. Brown. She knew most of her half siblings, held some of their children in her arms, and she found out Mr. Brown had died when his son Daryl called. "Pop's dead," he told her. Even Tomi Rae Hynie, the (maybe) widow, knows Peaches. "And Peaches," she says, "is his daughter."

So again, what's that worth, now that he's dead and LaRhonda has a letter from a DNA lab that says there is a 99.99 percent probability that James Brown is her father? Is there a debt owed?

Perhaps. If the trust stands, both LaRhonda's and Nicole's children would appear to be legitimate beneficiaries of the grand-children's educational fund. If the will and trust are invalidated, they might be in line for a fraction of what's left after the creditors and lawyers are paid. Their own lawyers have filed for back child support—though ironically, if the will *is* valid, that likely would be futile, since almost all of Mr. Brown's assets would be in the trust, not the estate. Blood from a stone and all that.

Mostly, though, there is the name: James Brown. Because that name represents both validation for his children and a rebuke toward their father. To have that name says that lawyers and lab techs did in his death what James Brown would not do in his life: acknowledge his children. "And I want people to know," Nicole says, "that he did not acknowledge me."

All things considered, that is not an unreasonable request.

•   •   •

Roosevelt Johnson's request, on the other hand, is not at all rea-sonable. He would like $2.5 million, which is a number he ap-pears to have pulled out of his hat.

It's an unfortunate number, too, because it makes Johnson look greedy when he is merely desperate. The man's broke. A few months ago, he would've been content with a lousy $1,200, enough to get his landlord off his back and keep his small apartment in a shabby tower on the Lake Erie shore. He's sold his cars and his jewelry, and he's been trying to find work, any work. "But people look at your résumé and what you've been doing for the past forty years, and they think, This guy doesn't really want a job," he says. "Yeah, I do. My job died."

He never saw it coming, either. When Johnson stood in the big cemetery on Laney Walker Boulevard in the winter of 2004, part of him really believed he'd be the one leaving Mr. Brown behind. Yes, he was twenty years younger than his boss, and he knew Mr. Brown aged like any other man, but Mr. Brown, the flesh-and-blood mortal, was not the same as *James Brown*, the Hardest-Working Man in Show Business, the character and icon. *James Brown* was—is—immortal. Any man could confuse the two, the person and the persona, and not even know his mind was playing tricks on him.

Mr. Brown came from nothing, a poor black son of the Depression South. His father made a pauper's living slicing trees for sap he could haul on his back to the turpentine plant in Bamberg, and little James's clothes were so raggedy, the teachers sometimes sent him home from school. He started stealing so he could buy something decent to wear, and when he got caught breaking into cars at fifteen, a judge gave him eight to sixteen years in prison. But he had a gift. The other inmates called him Music Box on account of his voice, his ear for harmonies and chords, the way he could arrange a gospel quartet into a sound so sweet men would weep. He told the parole board he'd sing for the Lord if they'd let him loose, which they did in 1952, three years and a day into his sentence.

That's how it started, a nineteen-year-old ex-con singing gospel in a little town called Toccoa in the hills northeast of

Atlanta. He charted his first hit, "Please Please Please," in March 1956, another hundred by April 1974, and twenty-eight more before his last, "Living in America," reached number four on the pop charts in 1986. He sold tens of millions of records and earned hundreds of millions of dollars, and yet his commercial success was less remarkable than his cultural influence. James Brown changed modern music. He put the beat on the One, birthed funk from gospel and soul, laid the foundation (and countless sample tracks) for hip-hop and rap. Long after the hits stopped coming, even after he got busted for smoking angel dust and punching women, people still paid to see him because he was still *James Brown*. In 2005, when his statue was set on the promenade in the middle of Broad Street in Augusta, near the intersection of James Brown Boulevard and not far from what would become James Brown Arena, Sharpton whispered to him, "You know, Mr. Brown, you've built a brand so high even *you* couldn't tear it down." He was still Mr. Dynamite, still Soul Brother Number One, still, and always, the Godfather of Soul. *Only four B's in music,* he liked to say. *Beethoven, Bach, Brahms . . . and Brown.*

Roosevelt Johnson was a part of that phenomenon for forty years. And what's he got now? A job with James Brown didn't come with a pension plan. There was no junior executive waiting to step up, keep the company running. Mr. Brown *was* the company. Everyone else was merely support staff, temp workers until the boss died.

So here's what he's got now: One of Mr. Brown's combs. A partial bottle of Mr. Brown's Viagra. A few hundred snapshots of himself with famous people. Some digital recordings of concerts Mr. Brown gave him that might be worth something. And he has a few stories to tell. He peddled one to a tabloid last year about Tomi Rae Hynie supposedly being a lesbian (which she denies). Forty years with a legend and that's what he's reduced to: selling scraps of another man's fame.

•   •   •

And why shouldn't he? A dead man's celebrity is a commodity, a resource for anyone willing to stake a claim to it. And a lot of people are. Take, for instance, Tascha Houston, a charming lady of a certain age whom Mr. Brown hired in 1966 as one of the original J. B. Dancers. She uses that exact phrase many, many times. As in, "Mr. Brown told me, 'I want you to keep your part of the legacy alive as one of the original J. B. Dancers.'" As in, "As long as I live, even if I'm in a wheelchair, I will always try to carry on the legacy of the original J. B. Dancers."

She is not at all insincere. She clearly adored Mr. Brown. He was her best friend and her mentor, she says, and then she has to stop talking because she has begun to cry. She's brought her manager with her, Mr. Marlowe ("Just put Mr. Marlowe," she says. "That's respect"), as well as a few photos from the day she laid a wreath on the James Brown Bridge in Macon, and a folder of official documents from mayors in five cities—Atlanta, Augusta, Philadelphia, Chattanooga, and Lithonia, Georgia—proclaiming various dates to be Tascha Houston Day, primarily in honor of her being an original J. B. Dancer. "I have a person who works on that, to make sure I get the recognition," she explains. "The minute you say *James Brown*, everyone jumps on it."

The reason she wants that recognition, of course, is that she still performs. She dances for a James Brown impersonator, and she's choreographed what she calls a one-woman tribute to the Godfather of Soul. "I would like to get it on Broadway," she says.

LaRhonda, meanwhile, would like to be on TV. "You just don't know," she says. "I am *so* destined to do a reality show." She has put a great deal of thought into this. All the Brown children, the acknowledged and the alleged, would be sequestered in a big house on an island, where they would wait, one by one and week by week, for a lab technician to compare their DNA to Mr. Brown's. At the end of each episode, one potential heir would be called to a sterile room, where the results would be revealed. "And when they find out they're not his child," she says, "it'd be like, 'Papa's got a brand new bag! Now get your things and get on outta here.'" She jerks her thumb over her shoulder when she says that last part; every decent reality show needs a gesture to go with the catchphrase.

One sibling she knows would not be kicked off the island is her half sister Nicole. LaRhonda calls her often, and they have exchanged photographs, but she has not traveled to Vancouver, and Nicole has not come to Houston, which genuinely frustrates her. "I can't wait to meet my sister," she says. "On the reality show. Or like, on *Oprah*. Oh, that'd be one of those moments." And then she's quiet while she dabs the tears out of her eyes.

A few weeks after LaRhonda sketched her reality show, a woman she calls Auntie Fannie arrived at the Park West Theater in Chicago, where the Chicago Music Awards were being dispensed, wearing a full-length white fur coat with tawny streaks and trailed by two men from Shine On TV, in Augusta, and a filmmaker named Harrison Starks. Fannie had been invited to receive an Award of Honor because, as the program noted, she used to perform "alongside her famous brother, 'The Godfather of Soul' James Brown" and because she is now "sending a positive message through the music she wrote with James Brown before his death."

The lady at the podium finished announcing the award, and then Fannie Brown bounded onto the stage and began lip-synching to a single she recorded with a few musicians who used to back Mr. Brown. It is called "He's the God Father of Soul, How We Love Him So," and it is obviously not one she wrote with Mr. Brown because it's about him being dead. During the chorus, Fannie did the Robot, and she ended the number by repeating, over and over, "my brother" and "I love you so."

Then, in quick succession, she plugged her Web site, two other sites where her CDs can be purchased, and *I Got Soul*, the film Harrison Starks is making.

Perhaps Fannie does love Mr. Brown. She is clearly distressed by the mess that is his estate. "If he'd left it to me, Michael Jackson, and Prince, we'd never let him down," she says. She lets that hang there while she fans herself, sweaty from the performance. Then: "The love that Michael and I have, oh, from when we was babies . . ."

Fannie Brown Buford (she appropriated the name) is not, however, Mr. Brown's sister. He did not have a sister. Still, she's been calling herself that since at least 1993, when she was mentioned in a photo caption in *Jet*. Yet she is referenced in neither of his autobiographies, and none of Mr. Brown's longtime associates remember her as anything more than an occasional background performer, if that. "You mean the souvenir girl?" one of them says. Yes, the souvenir girl. Fannie says so in her song: *I'm loud-talking Fannie / Selling James Brown souvenirs / From Japan to Miami*. Also, she sold them at his funeral in Augusta: "Cold Sweat" washcloths, "Hot Pan(t)s" pot holders, that sort of thing.

As Fannie tells it, she met Mr. Brown when she was eleven, in 1967, when he played the Regal Theater in Chicago. "He was sliding onstage, and I was sliding in the aisle," she says. "He did the splits, and I did the splits *and* a backbend." She caught his eye, and he let her come to wherever he was playing on the weekends during the school year, as much as she wanted when classes were out. She says Mr. Brown essentially raised her (which would make her the only child he raised). And the sister thing? Not her doing. "*He* said I was his sister." Or *like* a sister. Or something.

She believes Mr. Brown's story needs to be told and told properly, which is why she is writing a book and working with Harrison Starks on the film, about which he will reveal very little. "What I'm really worried about is all these phony people like Spike," he says. Starks means Spike Lee, who has for years planned an authorized and well-publicized biopic and who, in matters of black cultural icons, is generally not referred to as phony. "A lot of people don't know the real history," Starks says. "I do. And the real question is, Who killed James Brown?"

Fannie Brown is nodding her head. Apparently that is indeed the question.

"Ain't no one can tell his legacy but me," she says. "He never did anything without talking to me about it." Why bother asking anyone else? "You won't get anything, because everyone you dealing with is liars and druggies. How will you get to the truth when all those people heroined-up and cracked-up and coked-up?

"History will find the truth," she says. "And when I can find someone to pay for my story, I'm gonna tell the truth."

•   •   •

The truth? No one knows the truth about James Brown, not the whole truth, because Mr. Brown never let anyone close enough to reveal the full measure of himself. He could make you *believe* you were close, make you *believe* that you, and only you, had been blessed with a glimpse of his soul. But that's merely charisma. Or manipulation.

"People were his confidant in that area of his life where he was dealing with them," Sharpton says. "All of us—*all of us*—were consequential to his self-image."

And that's from a man who was closer than most to Mr. Brown. He toured with him in the 1970s, lived with him for a while in the early 1980s, wrote the introduction to his autobiography. He's called Mr. Brown his surrogate father, and Mr. Brown likened him to a son. Yet he has no illusions, either. He knows he was also a useful prop, a gifted black preacher Mr. Brown could mold and brand as a protégé, help smooth the friction with the civil rights establishment (Mr. Brown, after all, endorsed Richard Nixon). "He saw me as his answer to Dr. King," Sharpton says, and then he drops into a pretty good impersonation: "I'm gonna make my *own* Dr. King."

(Decades later, Mr. Brown still saw his reflection in Sharpton. "One of the proudest moments of my life," he told the reverend in 2004, "was when you walked out at the Democratic National Convention with that James Brown hairdo and brought James Brown into mainstream national politics.")

For all that, Sharpton doesn't claim to have known the total man. "Only tell people what they need to know, Rev," Mr. Brown told him long ago. "And anybody want to know anything outside their lane, don't trust 'em." Mr. Brown trusted Al Sharpton because he stayed in his lane.

Everyone saw in Mr. Brown only what he let them see. A mistress saw a frustrated old man trying to get hard while whacked out on PCP. His pastor in Augusta saw a spiritual man who quoted Scripture, especially Matthew: "Verily, I say unto you, inasmuch as ye have done it unto one of the least of these, my brethren, ye have done it unto me." Forlando Brown saw a grandfather who read through his college applications and checked his grades every semester. Buddy Dallas saw a captivating performer, an astute businessman, and more than that, a man who survived poverty and prison and drugs and the IRS. *We rather die on our feet / Than keep living on our knees / Say it loud / I'm black and I'm proud*. That's what Buddy Dallas saw.

But none of them saw it all. Indeed, you can tell how close someone was to Mr. Brown by how readily they admit that fact.

"Mr. Brown was an exceptionally slick, conniving, brilliant man," says Charles Bobbit, his friend for forty years and his manager from 1966 to 1977 and again from 2000 until Mr. Brown died. "And he made sure—*made sure*—he was misunderstood."

Yet there was one matter on which he clearly wanted to be understood: his legacy.

Mr. Brown told people for twenty years how he wanted to be remembered. A few small details would change now and again, but his general wishes were consistent.

For instance, he didn't want his children getting his money. Why depends on whom he was talking to and what his mood was at the time. Partly, he was a detached father. Blame the constant touring, blame the multiple divorces, blame whatever demons crawled around his head. "He was never much of a family man," Bobbit says. "But I guess you got that." Sometimes he'd say that being James Brown's child was enough of an inheritance, that the name alone was worth more than anything he had growing up. He worked for his wealth, and they could, too. If he was in a foul mood, he'd be blunter: "They ain't gettin' rich off my back," he told at least four people over the years. "They ain't gettin' a damned dime."

And that was before two of those children sued him. In the 1970s, when Deanna was six and Yamma was three, he gave them writing credits on two dozen of his records, including "Get Up Offa That Thing," which went to number four on the R&B chart. It was a low-rent scam, a way for Mr. Brown to hide money from the tax man by giving it to his daughters. Twenty-seven years later, Deanna and Yamma wanted their cut of the royalties and demanded $1 million in federal court. (The case was eventually settled for far less.)

When the suit was filed, Mr. Brown went to the Reverend Larry Fryer, his pastor in Augusta, and the preacher held him while Mr. Brown wept. "He boohooed big time," Fryer says. "Mr. Brown hated that. You can write that: He *hated* it. 'Cause you suing your daddy. You don't sue your daddy."

"My daddy never forgot that," says Terry Brown, the son who wants the will left intact. "He said, 'I'll forgive them, 'cause they're my kids and kids do stupid things. But I won't forget.' And you can believe that."

Or maybe he never forgave. Bobbit says he tried to get him to reconcile with his daughters. "They'll stab you in the back," Mr. Brown said. "Don't trust 'em." Tomi Rae says she tried, too, even gathered them all together for dinner. "I used to beg him," she says. "I used to say, 'Baby, please,' and he'd say, 'Baby, I'll do it for you. But they don't even like you, and they'll stab you in the back.'" When dinner was served, she says, "he got his plate and left the table."

He was still bitter in late 2006. Four days before he died, Emma Austin, the wife of Mr. Brown's childhood friend Leon, took him a pot of her vegetable soup because she knew he was coughing and swollen and weak. She left it at the guardhouse at the top of the drive, and by the time she got home, Mr. Brown was calling to thank her. They talked for a long while, like they always did, and the conversation drifted to Deanna and Yamma. "Sis"—he always called her Sis—"I will never forgive and I will never forget."

"Well now, Bro, we're getting to that age where we have to forgive," she said. "We can't get over to the other side holding grudges and not thinking well of people."

"Sis, I love you," he said. "And I hear you. But I will never forgive."

.   .   .

Rather than give his money to his own children, Mr. Brown wanted to leave it to poor kids. He might have been a lousy father, but he had an almost visceral empathy for kids who didn't have decent clothes or enough to eat. Which isn't difficult to understand, because he never forgot what it was like to be one of those kids.

He never wanted to forget, either.

The slope above the pond on the east side of his property is barren, an ugly scar of red clay about the size of a football field. Buddy Dallas was always telling him he should get it land-scaped, put in some bushes or lay some sod, pretty it up. "Nah, Mr. Dallas," he'd say. "Leave it alone." Instead, he'd send one of the grounds crew up there every so often to drag a harrow over it. The rain would wash the loose dirt into his fishing pond and make an awful mess, but Mr. Brown liked the smell. "Reminds me where I came from," he'd say.

"He understood the pain of poverty," Fryer says. "How it feels, how it looks. What other people say about you. How hard it is to get out and make something of your life." Fryer is a large man who lives in a small house in a worn Augusta neighborhood not far from the Red Lobster on Walton Way, where he introduced himself to Mr. Brown in 1991, shortly after Mr. Brown got out of prison for running from the police high on PCP. The reverend invited Mr. Brown to church and was his pastor until he died. Fryer was with him when Mr. Brown handed out turkeys and toys, thousands of them, to poor folks at Thanksgiving and Christmas, and he prayed with him at the turkey giveaway in 2006 when Mr. Brown looked so sick the reverend feared the Lord was ready to take him.

"I don't mean to do Scripture with you," Fryer says. "But I'm a pastor. You knew I would. And Scripture says, what profits a man if he gains the world but loses his soul? That's how it was with me and Mr. Brown. The evidence of his life is that he did not lose his soul."

And that evidence goes back years. The idea of a trust—specifically, the I Feel Good Trust, which is what the fund meant to send poor kids to college is called—dates at least from 1988, when Mr. Brown performed a charity concert in Augusta to benefit a local children's hospital. The woman who produced the show, a songwriter and singer named Jacque Hollander, made a video about one of the sick kids at the hospital, a little girl with cancer. Near the end of that tape, after Hollander had made a wrenching case for a worthy cause, she announced the creation of "the I Feel Good Children's Trust Fund." Hollander was not acting on a whim. "This was discussed with Mr. Brown and with Buddy Dallas," she says now. "I mean, it was *there*."

Well, almost there. Papers to establish the trust were never filed. Yet around the time the tape was made, she sat in an office with Dallas and listened as Mr. Brown outlined his plan for it. "I want everything to go into that trust," he said. "My house, my royalties, everything."

"Mr. Brown," Dallas said. "You've got kids . . ."

"Dammit, I ain't giving them a stepping-stone to make history," he snapped. "They all got education. I been supporting them. I ain't givin' them a dime."

Dallas remembers that conversation almost verbatim, which is notable because Hollander didn't speak to him for twenty years after it took place. And Hollander certainly has no motive to soften Mr. Brown's image now. In fact, she says he raped her later that same year, drove her deep into the woods, high on PCP, and told her to take her clothes off. When she refused, he said, "I'm not going to ask you again. And if you don't, I'm gonna." Then he put a shotgun in her face. "He told me, 'If you try to run away, I'll kill you,'" she says. "He told me he owned me. He told me he was giving me a blessing." (She never brought criminal charges, but she later passed two polygraphs, including one administered by a twenty-seven-year veteran of the FBI.)

Also, she's glad he's dead. "His death was the most unbelievable Christmas present God could have given me," she says. "Is that a horrible thing to say?" Not really, considering. But she does like to believe that Mr. Brown called his fund the I Feel Good Trust because he remembered the first one, that he chose that name to cleanse his sins.

.   .   .

In the summer of 2003, Mr. Brown positioned a lawn chair on his front porch, sat down, and told his grandson Forlando to get the broom from the pool house, the blue one with the tattered yellow bristles.

Then he told him to sweep the lawn. Which Forlando did. Mr. Brown had a way of making people do stupid, humiliating things, like not speak when he was in the room or be cowed into letting him pick their meals in restaurants. Once, when Forlando answered a question with "yeah" instead of "yes, sir," Mr. Brown glowered and pointed toward another room in the house. "Get up," he said. "Go there." Forlando was seventeen years old, but he sat in that room, alone and quiet, for three hours. "He demanded respect, and if he didn't get it, you weren't a part of his life," Forlando says.

So he swept the lawn. Hours passed before Mr. Brown told him to stop. "Now, boy," he said, "that's why you gotta get an education. Because if you don't, people gonna make you do senseless stuff like that. You ain't nothin' without an education."

Mr. Brown felt that he'd been blessed, that God had given him a voice and rhythm and the charisma to use them. But he never got past the sixth grade. So what if he hadn't been blessed? He probably would have done his full sixteen years for breaking into cars and not much else after that.

Which is why the I Feel Good Trust was set up as an educational fund. The cause wasn't new to him—"Don't Be a Dropout" broke the top fifty way back in November 1966—but he began to formalize it as his legacy on February 24, 1999. He met that night at his office to sign a will and trust drawn up by H. Dewain Herring, who, before he shot up a strip club and was sent to prison, was a respected South Carolina estate lawyer. Mr. Brown brought a tape deck with him, which he used to record four and a half minutes of musings about his eventual demise. He rambled a bit, but he made three important points:

> Hopefully the legacy will serve as a mentor for young people to make it in all walks of life. This is . . . let me say this: My intention is not just to go to black kids; this is to go to poor children. And they're not going to limit no color. We've had

that, enough of that in America already, and now we're going to begin to move over.

And then:

All the things that I have ... I'm James Brown twenty-four hours a day, and that's been proven, even in litigations that I suffered, even in my home, 'cause I was James Brown. So let's not not be James Brown now, now that I'm being paid. I want everything to go down this way.

And finally:

When you get my age, you don't think about nothing but what you can do for people. It's like, it's not what your country can do for you, but what you can do for your country. And I think this is true, which is to the country and mankind throughout the world. That I made it, from God's blessings, in spite of all obstacles, all the ups and downs we had as people, yeah, He's taken me to a point that I can give back, like I prayed before I come here. Nothing is mine anyway; it's all given to me by God. So whatever I do with it, I hope I'm doing His will. Thank you.

For whatever reason, he didn't sign those documents until June 15, 1999. A little more than a year later, in August 2000, he signed a revised version. The only significant change was that he made the trust irrevocable.

·　　·　　·

The people who are fighting over Mr. Brown's riches all agree, oddly enough, that he would want much of his wealth to benefit the poor.

What they disagree on is who is best suited to control Mr. Brown's assets and, more to the point, how much should be given away and who should get the rest. It's all become very nasty and would appear quite complicated, considering the forests of pulp trees slaughtered for legal briefs in the first year alone. But it is really, boiled down, a family feud fought on three fronts.

One front is Forlando Brown, who wants his grandfather's will and trust left exactly as written. He would then like a group of investors he has assembled to buy out the assets in the trust for a fair-market, court-approved price, which he suspects would be anywhere from $60 million to $100 million. It is not a wholly altruistic offer—the investors, though not Forlando, intend to make a profit—but it would be efficient. Professional marketers could wring more out of Mr. Brown's image and songs than some court-appointed administrator, and they would return a percentage of their annual gross to the trust. The I Feel Good Trust, then, would be flush with cash and would require only the services of a competent money manager.

Another front is Tomi Rae Hynie. She is suing as the "omitted spouse," which is a legal term meaning Mr. Brown never got around to changing his will to include the woman he married after it was written. Of course, she claims he *did* revise his will to leave her half of everything, but she can't prove it because she also claims those documents were shredded before she could get into the house to retrieve them. Yet on at least one occasion, in 2006, Mr. Brown had a codicil drawn up by an attorney named Jay B. Ross that would have left her 17 percent. That document also bequeathed 5 percent each to her son, to Roosevelt Johnson, to Mr. Brown's son Daryl, and to his housekeeper and property manager, David Washington. A percentage of *what*—all of his assets? his royalties?—wasn't clear, except in the case of Charles Bobbit, who was to receive 10 percent of the damages expected from a pending lawsuit against the photo agency Corbis.

Johnson and Bobbit watched Mr. Brown initial every page and then sign the last. He gave the papers to Bobbit, who put them in his briefcase. A few hours later, Mr. Brown asked for them back. No one ever saw those papers again. Bobbit figures he probably got mad at Tomi Rae and tore them up, which sounds reasonable. Mr. Brown got mad at Tomi Rae a lot. He used to call David Washington from the road, all worked up, saying, "Mr. Washington, pack her clothes. Get her outta there." Then Washington would wait a few hours for him to call again. "Nah," Mr. Brown would say. "I think she gonna be all right. Put her clothes back."

The real problem Tomi Rae Hynie has, though, is proving she was ever legally Mrs. Brown. She met him in 1997 in Las Vegas, where she was working as a Janis Joplin impersonator, and on June 11, 2001—seventeen years after his vasectomy—she had a son, whom she named James Brown II. Six months later, Mr. Brown married her. Bobbit asked him if he was sure, if he knew what he was doing.

"When you go home, Mr. Bobbit, there's someone waiting for you," he said. "When I go home, I'm all alone. So yes, I know what I'm doing. I love her, and I'm gonna marry her."

Unfortunately, Tomi Rae had married a Pakistani man in 1997. She says she was a dupe in a green-card scam, that the marriage was never consummated, and that she tried to get it annulled almost immediately when she discovered her groom had three other wives in Pakistan. But she didn't. Which meant her 2001 marriage to Mr. Brown was invalid, and he never remarried her after she finally did get the annulment in 2004.

The third front is the five children to whom Mr. Brown left only trinkets. They want the will invalidated and the trust dissolved, arguing in court papers that Mr. Brown was tricked into signing them by Cannon, Dallas, and Bradley. Coupled with the suit filed against those men by the special administrators, Adele Pope and Robert Buchanan—which notes prominently that Mr. Brown "had a limited formal education and relied heavily upon his trusted legal and financial advisors"—it seems to dredge up all those old, ugly images of shady white guys (though Bradley is black) stealing from a dumb black song-and-dance man.

To be fair, Mr. Brown did, on occasion, lapse into utter lunacy. He was terribly paranoid, convinced the government had bugged the armoire in the den, placed tiny cameras in the curtains, pointed satellites through his window, even wired up the yard. "See them trees," he'd say when the wind blew and the branches swayed. "That's them. They watching me." And he would occasionally flat out lose his mind. "Motherfucker was *crazy*," says Gloria Daniel, a girlfriend he kept on the side for forty years. "It was the drugs."

Mr. Brown smoked his drugs—PCP, until that got hard to find, then cocaine—mixed with tobacco from his Kools. "You sitting there rolling tobacco out of a cigarette—that's a woman's job—and you sitting there naked so he can look at you 'cause he getting ready to fuck you," she says. "Yeah, right." She rolls her eyes. The drugs, to say nothing of the diabetes and the prostate cancer, made him impotent. "He tried like hell, though," she says. "He'd wear you out. That man died trying to come."

One night in the summer of 2001, after he'd slathered her in Vaseline ("He liked you all greased up," she says. "Like a pork-chop") and wore her out trying to come, he gave up and left the room, and Gloria dozed off. When she woke up, Mr. Brown was standing at the foot of the bed in a full-length mink coat over his bare chest, a black cowboy hat, and silk pajama pants with one leg tucked into a cowboy boot and the other hanging out. He had a shotgun over his shoulder and a white stripe of Noxzema under each eye. "I'm an Indian tonight, baby," he announced. "C'mon, let's let 'em have it." Then he dumped a pickle jar of change on the floor, told her to get a machete, and went out to the garage. He took the Rolls, drove ten miles to Augusta, weaving all over the road, clipping mailboxes, smoking more dope, and screaming about being an Indian. Gloria kept thinking she should flag down a cop, say she'd been kidnapped.

Like she says, motherfucker was crazy on drugs.

When he wasn't high, though, Mr. Brown was firmly in control of his affairs. That's another point upon which all the warring parties—his kids, Tomi Rae Hynie, Forlando—concur. He was suspicious of everyone and kept an eye on all of his business dealings and the people handling them on his behalf. Bobbit used to wonder if he had ESP, the way Mr. Brown could read people. "I can't see how Mr. Brown would know everything going on around him and not know who was ripping him off," he says.

And if Buddy Dallas and the rest tricked Mr. Brown into signing a bad will and trust, why? "Pretty slick," Forlando says drily, "conning my grandfather into giving his money to poor kids." The alleged motive is that the trust, as well as Mr. Brown's earlier dealings, was structured in such a way as to guarantee enormous commissions to the trustees. But if they were going to steal his money with a bogus will, why not just name themselves beneficiaries and avoid all that paperwork? As for Dallas, whose financial records have been examined, "If there was such a grand conspiracy, why am I worrying about my credit card bills every month?"

But there's one more thing, and it's important. Buddy Dallas loved James Brown, Mr. Brown loved Buddy Dallas, and there is a long line of people who will testify to that. "Mr. Dallas is a good man," Mr. Brown told Bobbit. "Mr. Dallas didn't even know me, and he gave me $30,000."

"He always said he'd never forget what Mr. Dallas did for him," David Washington says.

The courts will maybe, probably, eventually sort all this out. And Dallas will be sitting there, like he was in February and Forlando Brown was on the witness stand. "None of us in this room," Forlando said, "not one of us sang and danced for James Brown. He did that. And I don't think it's right for any of us . . ."

His voice broke. "For any of us to tell my grandfather what to do with his money."

Dallas was in a chair against one wall, just inside the bar rail, and he had his head down, weeping for his dead friend and the mess his legacy has become.

·   ·   ·

The tour after Christmas was going to be the last one. Mr. Brown would play his final show in Anaheim, then pack it in after fifty-seven years. "When we finish this little thing, we going on a vacation," he'd told Bobbit. He was going to take Tomi Rae and go to San Francisco, a few other towns, spend some money. "Then we going to Vegas, and I'm gonna marry her again. She's my wife, I love her, and I ain't gonna punish her no more."

But first they had to do the shows, and for that Mr. Brown needed new teeth. Getting implants screwed into the jaw is a brutal procedure, and Mr. Brown didn't think he could stand the pain. He wanted to be put under. But the man was sick. His knees were shot and his feet were swollen, his stomach hurt all the time, he was constipated and couldn't pee too well, either. Now he had a bad cough, and he was losing weight.

Bobbit was waiting for him when Washington drove Mr. Brown to the dentist in Atlanta. Bobbit had a physician with him who gave Mr. Brown the once-over and then told him he might not ever wake up from anesthesia. He checked him into the hospital that Saturday, December 23. He rested all night and the next day, the doctors checking him, trying to clear out the pneumonia. Bobbit and Washington stayed with him. And then, late Sunday, just before midnight, Mr. Brown told Washington to leave the room.

"I'm gonna leave here tonight," he said.

"If you're talking about what I think you're talking about," Bobbit said, "that's a trip I can't make with you." He was trying to lighten the mood, not ready for Mr. Brown to die, not believing he *could* die.

Mr. Brown stayed serious. "I want you to look out for my wife, if you can," he said. "And I want you to look out for Little Man, if you can. And look out for Reverend Sharpton."

He always called Tomi Rae's son Little Man. He knew he wasn't his son, but whenever someone told him to get a DNA test, he said no, not while he was alive. Because he loved Little Man, loved him as his own, almost as if he was finally going to be a proper father, make up for all those years and all those other children. Bobbit thought that's why he called him Little Man. "It was his ego," he says. "Like, 'Look at him, look at that little man—he's just like me.' "

Bobbit settled into a chair at the foot of the bed. Mr. Brown lay back and dozed. Then he bolted upright, grabbed at his chest. "I'm on fire, I'm on fire," he said. "I'm burning up. Burning up." He flopped across the bed, and his gown rose up, exposing him. Bobbit got a blanket to cover him up. He was leaning down, his face close to Mr. Brown, still holding the blanket. He heard Mr. Brown take three short, weak breaths, saw his eyes open wide for an instant, then close. "As God is my witness, I don't know why," he says, "but I looked at my watch and it was one twenty-four."

The doctors worked on his body for another twenty-one minutes, but James Brown was already dead.

•　　•　　•

Some nights, when David Washington is asleep, Mr. Brown comes to him. He doesn't like to talk about this, because people tend to think you're crazy when you talk about a dead man visiting you in your sleep. But it's true. It's just the two of them, like it was all those years, Mr. Brown in his bed, Mr. Washington in the chair, watching an old Western on the television.

"Mr. Washington," he says, "go fix me some corn and bacon." And Mr. Washington gets up and goes to the kitchen and makes the food, puts salt and pepper and butter on the corn, the way Mr. Brown likes it.

He started working for Mr. Brown in 1994, part-time on the grounds crew after pulling twelve-hour shifts at the textile mill. Mr. Brown found him in the yard one afternoon, asked if he was smoking dope, asked if he was drinking on the job. "No, sir, Mr. Brown."

"Then why your eyes all red?"

"I just came from my other job, sir."

Mr. Brown told him to quit the mill, come work for him full-time. A man shouldn't have to work two jobs, wear himself out like that.

For the next ten years, Mr. Washington did almost everything for Mr. Brown. He cooked his meals and laundered his clothes and drew his bath. It wasn't always easy, because Mr. Washington never knew what kind of mood he'd be in. "You got used to it," he says. "Don't talk. Just, 'Yes, sir,' 'No, sir.'" He was supposed to be there from nine to five, but he'd stay late, listen to Mr. Brown talk, buy him a carton of cigarettes in the middle of the night, watch *Jeopardy!* and *Wheel of Fortune* with him. Mr. Brown didn't have many friends who'd watch TV with him. Mostly, he had people from whom he demanded respect, which isn't the same as a friend at all.

"He told me a long time ago, all the friends he got he could count on one hand," Mr. Washington says. That's hard on a man, makes him lonely. Sometimes Mr. Washington almost pitied him, though he'd never use that word, because Mr. Brown wouldn't take pity. "He was, like, missing something," Mr. Washington says. "He had everything in the world, but it was like . . . just something missing. Some kind of happiness."

Mr. Washington was his friend. And Mr. Brown took care of him, bought him a bedroom set and a burgundy Lincoln, paid for the burial when Mr. Washington's brother died. He told Mr. Washington he was going to buy him a house and maybe a couple of acres on Johnson Lake. Mr. Washington isn't sure where Johnson Lake is, exactly, and it doesn't matter now, anyway.

He still works at the house. Keeps the place cleaned up, looks after the grounds. Mr. Brown always said he wanted 430 Douglas Drive to be another Graceland, a shrine to the Godfather of Soul. But he's been dead sixteen months now, and Mr. Washington is one of very few people allowed past the gate without a judge's permission.

Mr. Brown came to him there once, too. About a week after he died, Mr. Washington saw him as he came up the driveway. He was sitting on the front porch, his hands folded in his lap, and Mr. Washington thought, *Mr. Brown, get yourself back in the house. You got the pneumonia.*

The driveway sloped down toward the pond, and Mr. Washington lost sight of the house at the bottom of the hill. He climbed the rise on the other side, and Mr. Brown was still there. Then he started to fade, and when Mr. Washington got to the house, it was empty and he was all alone.

The house is still empty now, and Mr. Brown is in a crypt in his daughter's front yard, lying there like somebody's pet.

The Atlantic

FINALIST—REVIEWS AND
CRITICISM

With a rare combination of intellectual vigor and unpretentious wit, Sandra Tsing Loh abides no sacred cows in her biting pieces for The Atlantic. *Whether she's writing about public education or the impact of the women's movement, Loh has an uncanny ability to make readers question their most basic assumptions, the mark of a true cultural critic.*

Sandra Tsing Loh

I Choose My Choice!

As you may have heard, some fifty years after Betty Friedan sprang us from domestic jail, we women . . . seem to have made a mess of it. What do we want? Not to be men (wrong again, Freud!), at least not businessmen— although slacker men, sans futon and bong, might appeal. In these post-Lisa-Belkin-*New-York-Times-Magazine*-"Opt-Out" years, we've now learned the worst: even female Harvard graduates are fleeing high-powered careers for a kinder, gentler Martha Stewart Living. Not only does the Problem Have a Name, it has its own line of Fiestaware!

And what are our fallen M.B.A. sisters of Crimson doing? Kvells one Harvard-grad-turned-stay-at-home-mom, on the subject of her days:

> I dance and sing and play the guitar and listen to NPR. I write letters to my family, my congressional representatives, and to newspaper editors. My kids and I play tag and catch, we paint, we explore, we climb trees and plant gardens together. We bike instead of using the car. We read, we talk, we laugh. Life is good. I never dust.

Is the mass media to blame (again!) for pushing women out of the workplace? Not so much. On our zeitgeist-setting TV shows, it's only the housewives who are desperate. Work is fun! The Manhattan working gals of *Sex and the City*, whose days revolve chiefly around dishing over cocktails, are essentially '50s suburban housewives, trophy wives of (in this case) glamorous if emotionally distant New York jobs—skyscraper-housed entities with good addresses and doormen that handsomely fund their lifestyles while requiring that they show up to service them only infrequently, in bustiers and heels. I want a vague job like the one Charlotte has, in the art gallery she never goes to; or the lawyer job Miranda has (charcoal suits and plenty o' time for lunch with the gals); or Samantha's PR gig, throwing SoHo loft parties and giving blow jobs to freakishly endowed men (actually, that's the one job I don't want); I want to spend my days like "writer" Carrie, lolling in bed in her underwear, smoking and occasionally updating her quasi-bohemian equivalent of a MySpace page.

In real life, female journalists (particularly sex columnists) have frightening stalkers, dour editors who begin phone conversations with "This is not your best," and paychecks so thin they trigger not just an amusing episode in which some Jimmy Choos must be returned but years of fluorescent-lit subway rides to a part-time job teaching ESL at some community college on Long Island. In an ugly if typical turn, one's column is suddenly moved from the Manhattan section to the North Jersey "auto buy" section because of the arrival of a younger, hotter writer. In real life, workmen would unceremoniously peel Carrie's ad off the side of the bus and replace it with an ad touting the peppy new relationship blog of Miley Cyrus.

·   ·   ·

An assault on the flaccid, pastel-hued *Real Simple* values of today's overeducated, underperforming homebound women, Linda Hirshman's marvelously cranky *Get to Work . . . And Get a Life, Before It's Too Late* drew an Internet hailstorm. (Those stay-at-home mothers—like AARP members, they've got time to type.) Short, biting, funny, and deliciously quotable (Hirshman is like an old-guard feminist Huckabee), *Get to Work* is a great value in terms of making the most of your limited reading hours. (Susan Faludi's *Stiffed* ran 672 pages; my galley of *Get* was a slim 94.)

Hirshman's thumbnail review of recent feminist history makes for prickly, entertaining reading. "Just over thirty years ago," she rails, "the feminist movement turned from Betty Friedan, the big-nosed, razor-tongued moralist," to Gloria Steinem. Not only did the honey-tressed blonde clearly have a smaller nose, as Hirshman implies, but "Gloria was nicer than Betty." The pliant undercover Bunny shepherded in a "useless choice feminism" of soft convictions and "I gotta be me" moral relativism. Hirshman quotes *Sex and the City*'s hapless Charlotte, who, when given flak for quitting her job to please her smug first husband, can only wail plaintively, "I choose my choice! I choose my choice!"

Hirshman fires with both barrels (Faster, Pussycat! Kill! Kill!) at today's mommies, who are so busy sniffing the Martha Stewart paint chips that they have forgotten Friedan's exhortation to get out and change the world. In reference to the NPR-listening, tree-climbing Harvard grad quoted above, Hirshman acidly notes:

> Assuming she is telling the truth, and she does live in the perfect land of a Walgreens' ad, is not all this biking and tree climbing a bit too much of the inner child for any normal adult? Although child rearing, unlike housework, is important and can be difficult, it does not take well-developed political skills to rule over creatures smaller than you are, weaker than you are, and completely dependent upon you for survival or thriving. Certainly, it's not using your reason

to do repetitive, physical tasks, whether it's cleaning or driving the car pool. My correspondent's life does have a certain Tom Sawyerish quality to it, but she has no power in the world. Why would the congressmen she writes to listen to someone whose life so resembles that of a toddler's, Harvard degree or no?

Ouch!

Not afraid, in her own big-nosed, razor-tongued way, to alienate everyone (or at least half of everyone), Hirshman considers all stay-at-home mothers fish in her barrel (think fish pedaling tiny aquatic bicycles). No target is too small: Hirshman even tears mercilessly into the sleep-deprived new mothers who've made the unfortunate decision to share their rambling thoughts on something called Bloggingbaby.com. (Really, aren't there any blogs over which the Web should draw its gentle curtain? Apparently not.) But in fact, Hirshman insists, the problem starts well before motherhood. It begins when young women enter college and violate Hirshman's No. 1 rule of female emancipation: "Don't study art."

Why aren't the women who are outnumbering men in undergraduate institutions leading the information economy? "Because they're dabbling," she snaps. Here's yet another Problem That Has a Name: Frida Kahlo.

> Everybody loves Frida Kahlo. Half Jewish, half Mexican, tragically injured when young, sexually linked to men and women, abused by a famous genius husband. Oh, and a brilliantly talented painter. If I was a feminazi, the first thing I'd ban would be books about Frida Kahlo. Because Frida Kahlo's life is not a model for women's lives. And if you're not Frida Kahlo and you major in art, you're going to wind up answering the phones at some gallery in Chelsea, hoping a rich male collector comes to rescue you.

As Woody Allen's own Whore of Mensa would sigh and pencil in the margin, "Yes, very true!" And don't we all know them, those defiant, dreadlocked young lovelies with their useless degrees in studio art, experimental fiction, modern dance, and gender studies, lactose-intolerant and unemployable: "I choose my choice! I choose my choice!"

Of course, Hirshman, with that somewhat unlovely, censorious tone, is being a tad simplistic. She leaves aside the matter of whether women driven to make piles of money are the same ones likely to incite meaningful social change. If the Harvard stay-at-home mom walked away from an attack-dog corporate-lawyer job with Exxon, I, for one, would rather see her playing tag and climbing trees. And although Hirshman did work as a lawyer (lawyer, along with doctor and judge, is the kind of high-degree, socially relevant job she approves of), she then became a professor of philosophy and women's studies. (Call the White House! We have a professor of philosophy on the line!)

Not that being an academic isn't a hell of a lot of fun; in fact, its very pleasantness contributes to a bias peculiar to members of the thinktankerati. So argues Neil Gilbert, a renowned Berkeley sociologist, in *A Mother's Work: How Feminism, the Market, and Policy Shape Family Life.* According to Gilbert, the debate over the value of women's work has been framed by those with a too-rosy view of employment,

> mainly because the vast majority of those who publicly talk, think, and write about questions of gender equality, motherhood, and work in modern society are people who talk, think, and write for a living. And they tend to associate with other people who, like themselves, do not have "real" jobs— professors, journalists, authors, artists, politicos, pundits, foundation program officers, think-tank scholars, and media personalities.

Many of them can set their own hours, choose their own workspace, get paid for thinking about issues that interest them, and, as a bonus, get to feel, by virtue of their career, important in the world. The professor admits that his own job in "university teaching is by and large divorced from the normal discipline of everyday life in the marketplace. It bears only the faintest resemblance to most work in the real world." In other words, for the "occupational elite" (as Gilbert calls this group), unlike for most people, going to work is not a drag.

Indeed, what does Linda Hirshman know about "work"? (It's a veritable WWE Smackdown of Academics!) Parries Gilbert:

> Linda Hirshman claims that "the family—with its repetitious, socially invisible, physical tasks—is a necessary part of life, but allows fewer opportunities for full human flourishing than public spheres like the market or the government." Many people would no doubt find unpaid household chores less interesting than Professor Hirshman's job. . . . But walking up and down the supermarket aisle selecting food for a family dinner is a job that has more variety and autonomy than the paid work being done by the supermarket employees who stack the same shelves with the same food day after day, and those who stand in a narrow corner at the checkout counter all day tallying up the costs of purchases, and the workers next to them who pack the purchases into paper or plastic bags. That space in the market is a bit cramped for human flourishing.

To be sure, attacking feminist criticism as being the extended whine of a privileged, educated upper class is as old as . . . well, as bell hooks's 1984 critique of Friedan's *Feminine Mystique*: "[Friedan] did not tell readers whether it was more fulfilling to be a maid, a babysitter, a factory worker, a clerk, or a prostitute than to be a leisure-class housewife." It's a point that keeps having to be made, though. And hooks's list doesn't even include the legions of colorless office jobs that most women endure, "real" jobs that trap them from eight to five in a cramped cubicle under hideous lighting. During the course of a *Sex and the City* workday you're likely to encounter Mr. Big, but at a "real" job you're far more likely to be thrown in with the pimply, fright-wigged characters of *Dilbert* or with Dwight Shrute from *The Office*, the show whose name is synonymous with tedium, idiocy, and despair.

The eight-to-five routine entails quite a few repetitious, socially invisible physical tasks (think Rob Schneider's Richmeister on *Saturday Night Live*: "Makin' kahpies!"). Research suggests that such drudge work holds no special lure even for (free at last!) females. Citing a survey of 909 employed women on how they had felt during 16 different daily activities, Gilbert notes:

> Employed women expressed a higher degree of enjoyment for shopping, preparing food, taking care of their children, and doing housework than for working at their jobs—an activity that was ranked at the next-to-lowest level of enjoyment, just above commuting to work.

Further, in a development that would shock only today's most radical feminists (where are those last two hiding? Buffalo?):

> When it came to interactions with different partners, the women ranked interactions with their children as more enjoyable than those with clients/customers, coworkers, and bosses.

But aren't women at home subject to the oppression of their chauvinistic, soul-crushing husbands? As if a mere human could compete with clogged freeways and Sisyphean paper pushing (or its more up-to-date equivalent, paperless pushing) and burnt-coffee-laced afternoons counting the acoustic tiles in stale conference rooms, and the hours spent arguing over the wording of a memo that within minutes after its dissemination will be dragged into the now-two-dimensional circular file. Unless he's an abusive alcoholic or something similar, to be more oppressive than a "real" job, a husband would have to possess tireless text-messaging thumbs: "Where's my dry cleaning?" "Did you pick up my dry cleaning?" "Where are you shopping right now?" "No! No! I told you—no butter lettuce from Safeway, only Whole Foods!" (Come to think of it, this may be a fairly accurate bit of communication between a privileged mother and a micromanaged nanny.) Even providing a chilled martini at six o'clock and roast beef at seven to the legendary suburban alpha male of yore allowed most of one's day to be fairly flexible. As for today's poorer husbands, many of them are likely too tired from their job's repetitious, socially invisible physical tasks—such as makin' kahpies!—to continually oppress their wives.

But surely women's economic independence is worth it? Oy. Wrong again. Here Gilbert launches into an exhaustive and rather depressing analysis of how far we've come since the 1970s. It's a long way, baby . . . if chiefly in terms of the accessibility of appliances. Seventies luxuries—air conditioners and clothes dryers—are of course the new millennium's necessities. Although more than half of all households were hanging their clothes on a line or schlepping them to a laundromat in 1971, for instance, by 2001, the majority of even poor households owned dryers. And now we all require goodies like cell phones and 900 channels of cable unheard-of thirty years ago—by 2001, eight out of ten low-income households owned VCRs/DVD players. No question, getting moms a paycheck has been very good for the U.S. consumer-electronics market, not to mention fast-food vendors, child-care providers, and—despite all those clothes dryers—the dry-cleaning industry.

However, while the economy benefits, for working-class families with young children, so much of a second income is eaten up by child care and taxes and other costs related to holding down a job that, after purchasing the microwave—now necessary to produce hot meals in the ten minutes left for food preparation—and the de rigueur DVD player, the second wage earner might as well have stayed at home. Gilbert concludes, then, that financial need is not the force behind women's shift in the past fifty years from work in the home to work in the marketplace; rather, it is the desires of those who have made out like bandits in this new order, the tiny minority (3.5 percent in 2003) of women who earn $75,000 or more. Members of this occupational elite have created a host of cultural norms by which their far less privileged sisters— who, again, make up the vast majority of working women—feel they must abide. For Hirshman's doctors, lawyers, judges, and professors, work has been terrific, so it's no wonder they've advocated social change, imposing on society between the 1960s and the mid-1990s "new expectations about modern life, self-fulfillment, and the joys of work outside the home."

They've gotten results: fathers in the United States now spend more time with their children and do more of the household tasks than their counterparts did, and Congress and employers both have made market-friendly provisions, such as parental leave, designed to encourage mothers of young children to take up paid employment. The society that has emerged, in which equality between men and women supersedes equality between social classes, may therefore be seen as "the triumph of feminism over socialism." Never mind the social costs, we now have an army of consumers and a vast labor pool—what could be more market-friendly? Indeed, since the late 1990s, so-called family-friendly policies in Europe have been, as the Oxford sociologist Jane Lewis observes, "explicitly linked to the promotion of women's employment in order to further the economic growth and competition agenda." Women have achieved the freedom to join men on a more or less equal footing in the marketplace, which strengthens the notion that the only thing ultimately of value is one's ability to turn a buck. The triumph of feminism, Gilbert reminds us (echoing those socially conservative men of the left, George Orwell and Christopher Lasch), has served the culture of capitalism. As he sums up the whole darn tangle:

> The capitalist ethos underrates the economic value and social utility of domestic labor in family life, particularly during the early years of childhood; the prevailing expectations of gender feminists place too high a value on the social and psychological satisfactions of work; and the typical package of family-friendly benefits delivered by the state creates incentives that essentially reinforce the devaluations of motherhood prompted by the capitalist ethos and feminist expectations.

• • •

All of which brings us, finally, to Sweden. (And doesn't a shot of raspberry Absolut sound good at this point?) The debate about mothers and work: it always ends—doesn't it?—with Sweden. Oh, if America could only be like Sweden—such a humane society, with its free day care for working mothers and its government subsidies of up to $11,900 per child per year. The problem? One hates to be Mrs. Red-State Republican Bringdown, but yes . . . the taxes. Currently, the top marginal income-tax rate in Sweden is nearly 60 percent (down from its peak in 1979 of 87 percent). Government spending amounts to more than half of Sweden's GDP. (And it doesn't all go to children, given Sweden's low fertility rate.) On the upside, government spending creates jobs: from 1970 to 1990, a whopping 75 percent of Swedish jobs created were in the public sector . . . providing social welfare services . . . almost all of which were filled by women. Uh-oh. In short, as Gilbert points out, because of the 40 percent tax rate on her husband's job, a new mother may be forced to take that second, highly taxed job to supplement the family's finances; in other words, she leaves her toddlers behind from eight to five (in that convenient universal day care) so she can go take care of other people's toddlers or empty the bedpans of elderly strangers. (As Alan Wolfe has pointed out, "The Scandinavian welfare states which express so well a sense of obligation to distant strangers, are beginning to make it more difficult to express a sense of obligation to those with whom one shares family ties.")

I'm pretty sure that changing diapers of all sizes isn't the kind of women's work Betty Friedan had in mind, nor Linda Hirshman. The bottom line (and this fact will become more so as humans live longer): there's a whole lot of caregivin' goin' on. We all fantasize about work that uses our creativity, is self-directed, happens during the hours we choose, and occurs in an attractively lit setting with fascinating people—you know, jobs like women have on TV. Oprah's job! However, since in reality—even in Sweden—so many roads lead to a wet wipe, I myself feel grateful and lucky to be here in California while I type this essay . . . which I am actually doing in bed, clad in my sweatpants rather than in high heels and a bustier (as, fortunately, I am not a fantasy character on television—not unless they did a *Sex and the City* "lumberjack" edition). Later, I will feed the cats for my single, working-gal neighbor, who has a real office schedule, complete with commute. Perhaps I'll also fling Popsicles at my latchkey children in the next room, mesmerized by a Princess video. (How much money have I earned while running Princess videos? I should pay Disney! Well, maybe not.)

Work . . . family—I'm doing it all. But here's the secret I share with so many other nanny- and housekeeper-less mothers I see working the same balance: my house is trashed. It is strewn with socks and tutus. My minivan is awash in paper wrappers (I can't lie—several are evidence of our visits to McDonald's Playland, otherwise known as "my second office"). My girls went to school today in the T-shirts they slept in. But so what? My children and I spend seventy hours a week of high-to-poor quality time together. We enjoy ourselves. As that NPR-listening, tree-climbing mother said: "We read, we talk, we laugh. Life is good. I never dust." Perhaps our generation of mothers can at least offer an innovation that the early radical feminists never had. I think of Linda Hirshman approvingly quoting Pat Mainardi's angry political analysis of the hidden tally of unrewarded "women's" housework:

> Here's my list of dirty chores: buying groceries, carting them home and putting them away; cooking meals and washing dishes and pots; doing the laundry; digging out the place when things get out of control; washing floors. The list could go on but the sheer necessities are bad enough.

Wait . . . she washed the floor?! Time to redefine "necessities," Pat. Say what you will about them, those radical feminists were tidy housekeepers. What I'd say to them over a distance of thirty years is (*Ching*! There's the microwave!) . . . you *can* have it all—if you run your house like a man.

Esquire

Taking us backward in time from the burial of Sgt. Joe Montgomery to the battlefield on which he fell, Chris Jones's "The Things That Carried Him" is a heart-rending, virtuoso account of the fate of not just one soldier but ultimately of all those who have lost their lives in Iraq.

Chris Jones

The Things That Carried Him: The True Story of a Soldier's Last Trip Home

Part One

Indiana, The End

Don Collins stood in the sun and mapped out in his mind a rectangle on the grass, eight feet by three feet. He is forty-nine, wears a handful of pomade in his hair, and no longer needs a tape to take the measure of things.

Indiana state law dictates that the lid of the burial vault be two feet below the surface. That meant Collins had to dig down five feet, ultimately lifting out about a hundred cubic feet of earth. He wouldn't need a tape to measure that, either. Since 1969, his father, Don Sr., has owned the Collins Funeral Home, just up Elm Street, just past the little yellow house with the two yellow ribbons tied to the tree out front. As a boy, Don Jr. had lived upstairs with the spirits and the rest of his family, over the chapel. He and his younger brother, Kevin, would later work with their dad in the back room, embalming the bodies of their neighbors at three o'clock in the morning, and he still assists his father in his capacity as coroner. But Don Jr. has had enough of bodies in back rooms. He likes it better outside, in the sticky air, working with the earth.

Now he pushed a slick of bangs off his low forehead and lifted a square-bladed shovel out of the back of his pickup truck. It was the second to last day of May, but it was already summer hot, and he moved slowly, surveying again his imaginary rectangle. Satisfied that it lay parallel to the path, the hedgerow, and the train tracks beyond it, Collins made his first cut into the grass.

He set aside the sod and then eased a small Kubota backhoe off his trailer and onto a couple of large sheets of plywood he'd laid down to protect the surrounding ground and the vaults beneath it. The plywood creaked when he anchored the machine and pushed the teeth of the scoop into the dirt. Normally he would have left a pile beside the grave and covered it with a tarp, but as he thought about tomorrow, pictured it in his mind, he decided to haul the earth to a far corner of Scottsburg Cemetery.

The next day, Thursday, May 31, 2007, he sat in the heat on a distant tombstone, waiting until he could finish the rest of his work. Just after twelve o'clock, the first people arrived: a vanload of nine honor-guard soldiers up from Fort Knox, dressed in their green Class-A uniforms, with knotted ties and berets. Collins had seen them practicing and pointing at various spots in the grass when he dug the grave. Now seven of them stacked their M16s in one of those spots. Each gun held three rounds; Sergeant Aaron Huber, a broad-backed thirty-one-year-old veteran of the war in Iraq, had taken care to polish his ammunition to a high shine. Six of the soldiers, including Huber, then assembled in two rows between the grave and where they knew the hearse would park. The extra rifleman remained with the weapons, and the noncom in charge, thirty-seven-year-old Sergeant Kenneth Dawson, stood at attention nearby. The ninth man, Specialist Robert Leatherbee, a boy-faced twenty-six-year-old from Massachusetts, took his place about forty feet away. With his buzz cut and iron-crisp uniform, he looked like a soldier, but there seemed something smaller or gentler about him, at least compared with the others. Maybe it was just that he was holding a trumpet instead of a gun, his fingers tender on the brass.

The funeral motorcade was taking a more circuitous route than the soldiers had from Scottsburg United Methodist Church. After Sergeant Dawson had wheeled the flag-draped casket down the church's aisle and his men had carried it outside and loaded it into the hearse, they had traveled directly to the cemetery, less than five minutes away. The hearse, however—driven by seventy-one-year-old Don Collins Sr., dressed in black with a wide-brimmed black hat—led the long procession through the people-lined streets of Scottsburg, population 6,000.

Around one o'clock, it finally passed through the cemetery gates, which were flanked by dozens of flag-toting members of the Patriot Guard Riders, civilian motorcyclists who have made it their habit to attend military funerals, standing at rigid attention even in the early-afternoon heat.

The soldiers from Fort Knox removed the casket from the hearse and set it on the lowering device over the openmouthed burial vault. The vault was made by a Chicago company, Wilbert Funeral Services, Inc., designed specifically for soldiers killed in Iraq: The Operation Iraqi Freedom vault is made of precast concrete lined with Trilon, and its lid is adorned with a lithograph depicting scenes from the war in Iraq, including Saddam's statue falling. Earlier, the lid had been propped up on display for the mourners, who included fifteen or so young men wearing Nine Inch Nails T-shirts. Now the soldiers withdrew and, along with the attending rifleman, picked up their weapons from the stack. The crowd filled in the spaces around the casket and hushed.

The Reverend Doug Wallace offered a brief prayer, and then a band of kilted bagpipers played "Amazing Grace." (A freight train passed nearby, but the engineer left his finger off the horn at the crossing.) Three recorded songs were played over loudspeakers, including "Hurt," by Nine Inch Nails, before Reverend

Wallace said a few more words, and then Dawson gave his men the signal.

The seven soldiers stood in a stiff line and fired three volleys each. This is a part of the ritual they practice again and again. The seven weapons should sound like one. When the shots are scattered—"popcorn," the soldiers call it—they've failed, and they will be mad at themselves for a long time after. On this day, with news cameras and hundreds of sets of sad eyes trained on them, they were perfect. After the final volley, Huber bent down and picked up his three polished shells from the grass.

Leatherbee wet his lips before he raised his trumpet. That was the first indication that he was a genuine bugler. There is such a shortage of buglers now—ushered in by a confluence of death, including waves of World War II and Korea veterans, the first ranks of aging Vietnam veterans, and the nearly four thousand men and women killed in Iraq—that the military has been forced to employ bands of make-believe musicians for the grave-side playing of taps. They are usually ordinary soldiers who carry an electronic bugle; with the press of a button, a rendition of taps is broadcast out across fields and through trees. Taps is played without valve work, so only the small red light that shines out of the bell gives them away.

Now Leatherbee, using his lungs and his lips to control the pitch, played the first of twenty-four notes: G, G, C, G, C, E. . . . Taps is not fast or technically difficult, and even if it were, most true Army buglers, like Leatherbee, are trained at the university level, possessing what the military calls a "civilian-acquired skill." They have each spent an additional six months in Norfolk, Virginia, for advanced work in calls. But there are still subtle differences that survive the efforts at regimentation—in embouchure, volume, and vibrato, and in how they taper the notes—and there is always the risk of a cracked note, whether due to cold or heat or the tightness that every bugler feels in his chest.

"You always run into the question," Leatherbee said later, "do I close my eyes, so that emotion won't be involved, or do I leave them open, so that more emotion will be in the sound? In my opinion, you can't close your eyes. There's a person in a casket in front of you. You want to give them as much as you can."

After Leatherbee lowered the trumpet from his lips, the six men who carried the casket to the burial vault returned to fold the flag. For some soldiers, that can be the hardest part. "Because you're right there," said one of the riflemen, Sergeant Chris Bastille. "You're maybe two feet from the family. And the younger the soldier is, the younger the family is."

"He had a few kids," Huber said.

First, the soldiers folded the flag twice lengthwise, with a slight offset at the top to ensure that the red and white would disappear within the blue. "Their hands were shaking," Dawson would remember later. "I could see that they were feeling it."

Then they made the first of thirteen triangular folds. Before the second fold, Huber took the three gleaming shells out of his pocket and pushed them inside the flag. No one would ever see them again—a flag well folded takes effort to pull apart—but he took pride in having polished them.

After the final fold, Bastille tucked in the last loose flap and passed the flag to Dawson for inspection. Dawson then passed it to the fifty-two-year-old woman with the general's star standing next to him.

The Army's Chief of Staff has directed that a general officer, randomly assigned, will attend every funeral of every soldier killed in Iraq or Afghanistan. Brigadier General Belinda Pinckney had flown in the night before from Washington, D.C., after she received a request via e-mail. "You're never not available," said Pinckney, an African American with short hair and a kind face, her eyes expressive behind her glasses. She didn't know how many funerals she had attended—"I don't like to keep count"—but she remembered flashes of each of them, certain faces in the crowd, what the weather was like. Here, she would remember especially the wife, Missie, young and pretty.

"Before the service, I noticed that she had been keeping her distance. She had this look on her face," Pinckney recalled. "And in my mind, she was not dealing with the death of her husband, so I decided to approach her. I went up to her and said, 'How are you doing?' And with a straight face, she said, 'Fine.' I said, 'Missie, look at me. You're not fine. It's okay not to be fine.' That's when she started crying, when I told her it was okay to cry. And we just pulled into each other. I just hugged her, it's okay, it's okay, it's okay. That was her letting go. And I wanted that. I wanted to connect with her."

Now Pinckney approached Missie again, this time dropping to her knees in front of her.

"I was just telling myself, You have to be strong when you're doing this," Pinckney said. "Because it is emotional. I was saying to myself, When I give them this flag, they have to know it's coming from the heart, that you really mean it, and that you're there with them. Especially because these funerals are for young men and women, and being a mother, I say to myself, It could have been my son—Andre, he's twenty-seven years old—or I say, It could have been me. I try to imagine what they're going through. I try to relate to them to say that I know these are hard times. Because no one expects to get that phone call."

The meaning behind the flag folding is lost mostly to myth— the thirteen folds supposedly represent the thirteen colonies, the triangle the lines of George Washington's cocked hat—but its architecture makes it ideal for being clutched to a widow's chest, the points across her shoulders. That's how Missie held the flag when Pinckney gave it to her and said:

"This flag is presented on behalf of a grateful nation and the United States Army in appreciation for your loved one's honorable and faithful service."

Now the service was over, the end of this journey home. As the bagpipes played, the mourners left in groups. The nine honor-guard soldiers returned to their van, exhaled, and pulled onto the highway, bound for Fort Knox. General Pinckney prepared to fly back east. And Don Collins Jr. helped his father lower the casket and seal the lid on the burial vault. They were the last in a long line of men and women who, beginning late one night nine days earlier, had carried this soldier to this place.

Don Jr. began hauling back the dirt from the far corner of the cemetery, the first scoopfuls landing on top of the lithograph, burying Saddam along with the soldier. After he had tamped down the last of the earth, he replaced the sod he had cut loose the day before, doing his best to knit the seams. Finally, he placed a temporary metal marker from the Collins Funeral Home at the head of the grave, because there had not been time yet to carve a tombstone. It read:

SGT. JOE MONTGOMERY
1977–2007

·   ·   ·

A few hours earlier, Gail Bond had sat in the front row of Scottsburg United Methodist, her church, and dried her eyes. She was sad and she was angry, even her happiest memories having suddenly gone spoiled. Robert Joe Montgomery Jr. had been among the first group of babies baptized in this church, days after it opened in the fall of 1977. His name is inked in the records book there in careful cursive, top of the first page. Gail could still remember so clearly holding him that day, his little head poking out the top of his blanket. Now Joey was in the flag-draped casket in front of her, new memories stealing away from the old.

Over the following hours, Gail would need a lot of things that she wouldn't get, but she would get a cigarette. She had smoked a lot over the last nine days, and she had already smoked plenty in her sixty-eight years. She has a kit—a little black leather bag to hide the ugly warnings on the cardboard pack, linked by a brass chain to another little black leather bag that holds her lighter. There was something touchingly ladylike about the kit, and there was something touchingly ladylike about her whenever she pulled it out, sparking up another brandless smoke at her round kitchen table, between bouts of tears and cans of Bud Light. She had thought a lot about quitting, but whenever she had built up enough nerve, something happened that made it impossible for her to put the kit in a drawer and close it.

When she was sixteen, Gail's nine-year-old brother, Frederick, had died of rheumatic fever. Her first husband, Joey's father, Robert Joe Montgomery Sr., had been killed in a car wreck during their seventeenth year of marriage. She had taken to calling Joey "my miracle baby," because she had learned she was pregnant with him the day after his father's funeral. Her parents died on consecutive days in 1999. Five years later, her second husband, Joey's substitute father, Don Bond, to whom she was married for twenty-three years, drowned after his pickup truck slid on a patch of black ice and into a swollen river. Somehow, Gail had weathered all of it, even when people's eyes followed her down the street—she hated their pity—but now she had lost Joey, and that was enough to make her scream at God in the night.

She looked across the front of the church at those who had survived her love. Her oldest son, Micah, forty, a master sergeant and an Army lifer, who had come home from his own deployment in Iraq to attend his little brother's funeral. Her daughter, Mindy, who has red hair and freckles like Joey did. Her brother, Bill Graham, the mayor of Scottsburg for twenty years. Her baby sister, Vicki Wells, Aunt Vicki, A.V., the two of them identical in their sad, tired eyes. Missie, Joey's wife, twenty-nine, too young to know what Gail knew, and Missie's children, Gail's grandchildren, nine-year-old Skyla, seven-year-old Robert Joe, and two-year-old Ella. There they sat, huddled in a row, and behind them hundreds of mourners, with them but without. There were so many that the church had opened an overflow room downstairs, and more people were standing in the parking lot outside.

A lot of them had come because they knew the mayor and were sorry that he'd lost a nephew. More came because they knew Gail, because she had helped them plan for their retirements at Edward Jones, and they were sorry for her, too. And many had come because Joey was the first of them—the first man or woman from Scott County—to die in Iraq. The truth is, not many of them knew Joey, and hardly any of them knew Sergeant Joe Montgomery, and they would learn only a little about him that morning in the church. There was no eulogy to tell them what they should think of him, as though the family had grown tired of sharing their grief and wanted to keep something of Joey for themselves. The strangers would be left to fill in the blanks on their own.

Looking at the faces of Joey's family, they could know that he was loved. Looking at his friends in their black concert T-shirts, they could guess that he really liked Nine Inch Nails. Looking at his Aunt Vicki, standing behind the pulpit and holding it together just long enough to read one of Joey's poems, they could learn that he liked to write. Looking at his flag-draped casket, they could be certain that he was a soldier. Looking at General Pinckney, giving Missie both a Purple Heart and a Bronze Star and promoting Sergeant Montgomery posthumously to staff sergeant, they could deduce that he was a brave one. They may have believed that he became a soldier because he had loved his country, but they could not have known that before he was a soldier he had been ashamed that his jobs in the steel forge and running cable for security systems had left his young family living in a bad part of town in a rented house with holes in the floor. They couldn't have known that he became a soldier because he wanted to make his older brother proud, and that he wanted even more to make a better life for his wife and his kids, this second generation of fatherless Montgomerys.

.   .   .

Joey had lain at the Collins Funeral Home since Tuesday evening, when the brothers David and Tim Barclay, state troopers on black motorcycles, had led the procession from the airport, Freeman Field in Seymour, Indiana. They had worked traffic all day and then got a call late that afternoon, May 29, that the body of a dead soldier would need an escort down the I-65 to Scottsburg. They didn't know Joe Montgomery or his family, but they knew his hometown, and they knew Seymour, and they knew best of all the stretch of highway in between. It was about twenty-three miles, a straight shot, north to south, four lanes, divided.

When they arrived at the airfield, sweat-soaked, the brothers were taken aback by the number of cars waiting in a line. There were scores, maybe hundreds, as well as about sixty members of the Patriot Guard Riders and their motorcycles, decorated with American flags flapping in the early-summer breeze. The procession would be three miles long.

"We've done a few of these, and it was by far the biggest we've seen," Tim Barclay said. They decided to shut down the highway, the main route between Indianapolis and Louisville, for as long as it took to cover the ground to Scottsburg. They would speed forward to block the on-ramps, and they told the ride captain of the Patriot Guard, Tim Chapman—they knew him from way back—to bring up the rear and not let anyone pass.

The Patriot Guard was formed a few years ago in response to the threat of protesters from the extreme-fundamentalist Westboro Baptist Church, in Topeka, Kansas, who sometimes disrupted the funerals of soldiers killed in Iraq. There were rumors the church intended to hold up signs along the highway like, GOD HATES YOUR TEARS and THANK GOD FOR DEAD SOLDIERS. Gail Bond stayed up the night before for a lot of reasons, but partly because she was worried about how her family and friends might react, how she might react, to such taunts. But now she saw the men on their Harley-Davidsons, with their long hair coming out the backs of their helmets, and she didn't worry anymore.

The Barclay brothers moved out, lights flashing, with Don Collins Sr. right behind them, piloting his black hearse. In the seat beside him was Sergeant Charles Dunaway, a twenty-nine-year-old paratrooper from Alabama. He had become friends with Micah Montgomery in jump school and had volunteered to come down from Fort Richardson, Alaska—where Joey had been based before he was deployed to Iraq—to be Joey's official escort on these last legs home. On his lap was the paperwork that confirmed the details of Sergeant Montgomery's death, as well as the medals that would be presented to Missie at the church. Dunaway isn't much of a talker, and sometimes he struggles to find the words. "I consider it an honor," he said of what it felt like to sit in a hearse with a flag-draped casket in the back and a dead soldier's medals in his hands. "It kind of hits home for you."

Behind the hearse, Gail sat in the car with her brother, Bill, the mayor, who was at the wheel. "It's hard to drive and cry," he said. The tears began flowing as soon as they pulled out of the airport and onto the main road in Seymour, bound for the I-65. Traffic had stopped. Townspeople lined the sidewalks, holding their hands over their hearts, waving flags, whispering to their children.

"It breaks your heart when you drive through and you see people and they're crying for you," Vicki said later. She was especially struck by the nameless mechanic in his coveralls, black with oil. He had crawled out from under a car, out of the pit, and he stood in front of the garage, perfectly straight, perfectly still, saluting the hearse, and lines formed under his eyes in the oil on his face.

When Joey worked at the steel forge, he would come home to the trailer that he and Missie shared, and he would be black like that mechanic. He worked the hammer in the forge, using tongs to hold strings of molten metal, and the hammer would clang down loud enough that you could hear it from the parking lot. Once, Joey had nearly done his thumb in—it got crushed between the handles of the tongs when the hammer came down— and it was scarred enough years later to look almost transparent.

In the last car of the procession, Ryan Heacock, Joey's best friend, was having trouble seeing, he was crying so hard. His fiancée, Kayla, sat beside him; he tried to focus on the car in front of him, scared that he would drive into it through his fog; his rearview was filled with motorcycles and flags. Ryan had recently e-mailed Joey in Iraq and asked him to be the best man at his wedding the July after next. "Of course," Joey had written back, and Ryan had hoped the commitment would bring Joey back home to stay. "To say that he was my brother doesn't do it justice," Ryan said one evening, sitting at Gail's kitchen table, where he sat often, a can of beer in one hand and a smoke in the other.

They became friends in high school. "We were kind of the outcasts," Ryan said. "We didn't quite fit in. We weren't hard enough to ride with the tough crowd, and, you know, we were a little bit rough around the edges for the squeaky-clean crowd. So we were something in the middle."

Together Ryan and Joey rode their skateboards on the street, and they grew their hair long—except around the back and sides, which they shaved with dog clippers—and they talked about what they wanted for themselves. Joey wanted to meet Missie, who was in Ryan's freshman math class, and Ryan helped her with her homework to set them up. Ryan wanted to go to college to study art, and he did, at Indiana University Southeast. Joey helped Ryan along, the way Ryan had helped Joey.

"Every once in a while I'd be hard up and I'd sell my painting to him for twenty bucks or whatever. I think, of anybody, Missie's probably got the biggest collection of my stuff."

Ryan eventually found work at Fewell Monument in downtown Scottsburg. Out front, there are rows of tombstones for sale. And inside, at his desk, Ryan is designing Joey's.

Now they pulled onto the I-65, this great long string of mourners and their memories. They were surprised to see every overpass—U.S. 31, Commiskey Pike, the 250 to Uniontown, 600 South—lined with flags and signs welcoming Joey home. Volunteer fire departments, dressed in full uniform, stood at attention in front of their shining trucks. Farmers drove across their fields of baby corn and soy to reach the shoulder and stood in the beds of their old pickup trucks. As reports of the procession spread— traffic helicopters joined in, flying overhead—and long-haul truckers shared the news over their radios, they pulled over and climbed out of their rigs, and cars filled with families did, too, all of them standing and saluting from across the grassy median, the northbound lanes stopped nearly as completely as the southbound.

"I can't even tell you what that meant to our family," Bill Graham said.

There had been hard times for Joey after he finally finished high school in his fifth year. He got a tattoo on his arm of an eye with an anarchy symbol for a pupil. He broke up with Missie. And then Gail and Don kicked him out of the house. "He would sleep all day and play all night," Gail said. "And I knew something was wrong—you don't do that. I put up with it and put up with it and put up with it, and tried to talk to him and, didn't work. So, tough love. Find another place to live, you get a job, you get a job and obey the rules, and you can stay here. And if not . . . So for probably a year, Joe was what he considered homeless. A lot of it was right around here, and I know my mother helped him out a lot. But you could see him walking up and down the road."

Eventually, Joey went down to Jacksonville, Florida, where his sister, Mindy, was living with her husband. "He was the sweetest boy," Mindy said. "I loved Joey to death. He was very sensitive, very creative. He had some troubles, but it made him turn out to be a better person in the end."

Mindy struggled to right Joey, until Ryan came to Jacksonville to visit. Maybe that was enough for him to be pulled back to Scottsburg.

"I'll never forget when he called me and asked me to bring him home," Gail said. "He wanted chicken and noodles. And I said: Joey, Dad and I aren't over this yet. So I think you need some time to think about it. Because when you get home, you gotta work, you gotta obey the rules if you're gonna live with us, that's just the way it is."

Joey did come home, he obeyed the rules, and he went to work, turned black at the steel mill. He also became a father. While he was in Florida, Missie had found herself another boyfriend, and now she was pregnant. She and Joey got back together, and Ryan remembers riding with Joey back from the hospital in 1998 with the baby, Skyla, and she was his from that moment on.

Two years later came Robert Joe, and Joey's work at the mill wasn't making ends meet. He began work running cable, first for other security companies, and then on his own. A lot of people didn't pay their bills, and then Missie was pregnant again, and Joey decided that he wasn't going to scratch through the rest of his life. In January 2005, he joined the Army.

"He always thought a whole lot of Micah," Ryan said.

It fit Joey nearly as well. He liked the Army, and he liked Alaska. It was a fresh start, a break from their old life, looking ahead to something new, out over the mountains. He rose through the ranks, and they lived in a townhouse on base—516A Beluga

Avenue—and Joey built a swing set for the yard, and they put some money away, and they finally felt as though the constant wobble in their lives was smoothed out, like they had been properly aligned for the first time.

Gail last saw her son at Christmastime, 2006. He had been in Iraq for only a few weeks, and it would be the only midtour leave he would receive—he would have to spend more than a year straight at war—but he wanted to see his kids. Ryan took a picture of the entire family then, Joey smiling his crooked smile, his hands on Robert's shoulders, Missie smiling and holding Ella on her hip, Skyla in front of them both, shining. Gail would put that picture on the front of the thank-you cards she would send out, after. At the end of Joey's leave, she took him to the airport in Louisville, hugged him tight, and said goodbye.

"When he got ready to go on the plane, I thought, You're standing so tall, you like yourself, you're proud of yourself," she said.

And now Joey was coming home, over the Muscatatuck River, the procession pulling off the highway and into Scottsburg, the streets lined there, too, shoulder-to-shoulder, the storefronts decorated, the fire trucks out, their ladders raised and making a triangle over the road. Between them, an enormous flag had been strung. The family drove underneath it on their way to the Collins Funeral Home. There, the local police chief, Delbert Meeks, and his men met the hearse, and they carried Sergeant Montgomery's casket inside—"I'd known Joey all his life," Chief Meeks said—and placed it on a pedestal in a corner of the chapel.

Alone, Don Collins Sr. and Sergeant Dunaway peeled back the flag like a bedsheet and opened the casket. There was Joey, carefully dressed in his Class-A uniform with white gloves and polished boots, his badges and cords in place, and his face serene. It was mostly unmarked, and the two men agreed that even though the Port Mortuary in Dover, Delaware—where every soldier killed in action is prepared for burial—had advised against a family viewing, Joey looked good enough for the Montgomerys to see him if they would like.

"I needed to do that to believe it was him," Gail said. She, Missie, and Micah stood over Joey for a long time that Tuesday evening. They touched him and spoke to him gently. Gail and Missie hadn't seen him in months, and war had changed him, or maybe it was their memories of him that had changed, and now their eyes took him in, every inch of him, as though he'd been long lost.

It was Micah who noticed that his ring was missing. Joey was a Mason, and the ring was a chunk of steel that he wore on the middle finger of his right hand, a gift from Gail that last Christmas to replace the one that had been cut off him before he deployed, his finger swollen with infection. Now Micah took off his own Mason's ring, and he leaned down to slip it onto Joey's right middle finger, over his white glove. That's when Gail began to shake; the gloved finger folded in on itself, empty but for cotton and carefully rolled strips of gauze.

•   •   •

Jim Staggers, an army chaplain, father of two young sons, and frequent reader of the Book of Job, had needed to find a quiet place to hide at Freeman Field earlier that afternoon. He had already changed into his dress blues in the airport office, and even in there, in that relative privacy, the curious and concerned had asked him about the small plane due to come in. But he didn't know more than anybody else—he had watched plenty of dead soldiers leave in the bellies of C-130s, lifting over the brown Afghan hills, but he had never before been on the receiving end, at least never in a place like this. Across the tarmac, the doors of a white hangar were open, and an empty church cart waited out front. Inside, workers had set up chairs and laid out a table of refreshments. Everybody was moving carefully, and everybody spoke in whispers. Any building can be turned into a church, Staggers thought.

He had come down to Seymour from Indianapolis in the van with the rest of the funeral detail, those Indiana National Guardsmen who had seen Sergeant Montgomery's name written on the whiteboard in their office. There were several different marker colors used on that board, but black—the color in which Sergeant Montgomery's name was written—was the most significant. That usually meant an active-duty soldier killed in action, and that meant Specialist Andrew Schnieders and Sergeants Capricia Gerth and Flor Snell-Rominger and three other pallbearers—take them out of uniform and they might look like lifeguards or college students—would be asked to carry someone very much like themselves from the plane to the church cart and into the waiting hearse. "Honorable transfer," they call it, the last in a series of military handoffs, when the Army finally turns over a dead son or daughter, husband or wife, to his or her family.

Staggers stole away behind the hangar to read his Bible. He had confronted grief for most of his adult life, but he had to get his head straight. He had somehow seen this future for himself while standing at the lip of a mass grave in Bosnia a decade ago, had seen it in the faces of two hundred men, women, and children massacred and thrown in a pit. "That was a spiritual moment," he said. "That's when I said I will follow this calling that you've been pestering me with, God, for all my years." Since then, he has worked as a sheriff's chaplain, and alongside one of the Army's casualty notification officers, and in the trauma room of a city hospital. Most recently had come his tour in Afghanistan, where he had missed the birth of his youngest son to pray over the bodies of the sorts of men he hoped his son might one day become.

Today, though, was new and it was different: It was not a farewell but a return. Today would be about framing a reality that was only now coming home. "I was thinking, What would I

want for my wife and kids if I were the one not to make it back?"
Staggers said. "I would want someone to give them 100 percent
of their attention and preparation."

When Sergeant Montgomery's family arrived from Scottsburg
a short time later, and after Don Collins Sr. had parked his hearse
and opened the door, Chaplain Staggers introduced himself and
did his best to prepare them for what they were about to see. He
went over the mechanics of the ritual, but he also tried to steady
them for the emotion that would follow. There might have been
times over the past week when they felt like they were in a movie,
actors playing parts. That feeling would end this afternoon.

The guardsmen had carried enough caskets to deduce, from
what their arms told them as they grasped the handles and lifted,
something of the person inside. They know if the dead soldier
was big or little, and they can also make a good guess at how he
died, whether he was killed by small-arms fire or a helicopter
crash or an IED. Sometimes they'd lifted caskets and been surprised by the weight of them—wooden caskets are heavier than
metal, and that combined with a strapping young man can make
for a considerable burden, several hundred pounds—and sometimes there was barely any weight at all, and they knew that inside the casket was a pressed uniform carefully pinned to layers
of sheets and blankets, between which might be nestled only
fragments of a former life, sealed in plastic.

They had also learned how not to betray a hint of this sudden
knowledge. Sergeant Montgomery's casket was lighter than they
were expecting, but they kept what they call their "game faces."
They'd learned to train their eyes on one place, focusing usually
on a point in the distance, the way sailors settle their stomachs
by looking at the horizon.

On that short march from planeside, Schnieders stared at the
logo on a police car parked nearby. Gerth accidentally caught
sight of tearful children and scrambled to find somewhere else
to look. Snell-Rominger whispered to her to look at just this one

girl in the hangar—not at her face but at her pretty dress, which had flowers on it. "Pick out a flower," she said, and both of them stared at a flower on that girl's dress until they had set the casket on the church cart.

The pallbearers withdrew in formation. Staggers took their place and stood alone with the casket, pausing for a moment. He looked at Missie and the children, and he couldn't help thinking again of his own wife and children. "God is our refuge and our strength," he began. "Therefore, we will not fear."

He finished with a reading from the Forty-sixth Psalm—*The Lord maketh wars to cease unto the end of the earth*—and invited the family to approach the casket. Gail was the first to step forward, followed by Missie and Micah and then the children.

Missie folded her arms on top of the flag and put her face into them and wept.

"Daddy's here," Gail said, bending down and clutching her grandchildren from behind before she reached out to smooth a corner of the flag.

And Staggers put the flat of his right hand in its white glove onto the flag as well, over the stars, and he gave up trying not to cry.

"You can't deny your humanity," he said. "You can put up the wall for so long, but it always crumbles. It crumbles."

After a few minutes—there is no protocol for this, only feel— he signaled the honor guard that it was time to march forward and lift the casket to their waists again, and to carry it to the back of the hearse.

As the state troopers, the Barclay brothers, led the funeral procession south toward Scottsburg, the honor guard turned north, heading back to Indianapolis. They talked about what they did right and what they did wrong and how they could be better next time.

A few months later, two of the people in the back of that van, Sergeant Edward Blackburn and Lieutenant Matthew Mason, would join more than three thousand members of the Indiana National Guard bound for Iraq.

Part Two

Dover Air Force Base

Steve Greene picked up the phone in late November 2006. It was the Pentagon.

Greene, a burly guy with a nicotine-stained mustache, works for a company called Kalitta Charters out of a hailstone-dented trailer at the airfield in Morristown, Tennessee. Kalitta's head office is in Ypsilanti, Michigan, and much of its business had been staked on flying parts for the auto industry. But with Detroit scaling back production, Greene had been talking to the Air Force about chartering his fleet of white-and-burgundy Falcon 20s, reliable, low-cost twin-engine jets with decent range and an oversized door for large cargo. "I thought, There's a niche somewhere for this plane," Greene said recently. "Of course, this was the furthest thing from my mind."

Not long ago, and for decades, the remains of soldiers were shipped like parcels in the bellies of commercial planes. That practice began to end on November 15, 2005, when a twenty-one-year-old medic with the 101st Airborne named Matthew Holley was killed by a roadside bomb in Iraq. His parents, John and Stacey, had also served with the 101st Airborne; now they were told that their only child would arrive home in San Diego as freight in the hold of a US Airways flight, ferried to the family by baggage handlers.

After lodging a complaint with the Army and receiving help from California senator Barbara Boxer, the Holleys saw their son met by an honor guard instead. Still angry, they began a campaign to change the way all military dead would be delivered. California representative Duncan Hunter, then chairman of the House Armed Services Committee, wrote legislation that eventually became known as the Holley Provision to the 2007 Defense Authorization Act. It directed that the bodies of fallen soldiers, sailors, airmen, and marines would no longer be booked passage on US Airways, Delta, Northwest, or Continental but would be flown on military or military-contracted flights and met by honor guards.

The Air Force had already auditioned Kalitta: In June 2006, two soldiers, Privates Thomas Tucker and Kristian Menchaca, had been kidnapped, executed, and mutilated in Iraq, and their bodies needed to be flown from Dover Air Force Base to Redmond, Oregon, and Brownsville, Texas, respectively. "It was a high-profile thing," Greene said. "And I guess because it was so high profile, they didn't want to use the air carriers like they had been doing. I told them there was no reason we couldn't do it, and we did."

Now, just weeks before its January 1, 2007, deadline, the Pentagon was on the phone once again. Greene was asked if Kalitta's pilots could do for every soldier killed in action what they did for Tucker and Menchaca. He said they could. He was given a statement of work and a flight estimate—"Thankfully, we have not had to fly the number of missions they anticipated," he said—and Kalitta agreed to station four of its Falcon 20s and flight crews at Dover full time. After company mechanics worked through Christmas designing and building a portable electric lift and outfitting the jet interiors with ball mats and roller strips, room for two caskets each, the pilots flew themselves into place on New Year's Eve. The next day, they were back in the air.

The crews were assigned randomly out of Kalitta's ranks. One of the pilots was a low-key, goateed twenty-eight-year-old from Michigan named Greg Jones; one of the copilots was a seventy-two-year-old Alabaman named Royce Linton, an Air Force veteran, soft-spoken and sinewy. They had each worked for Kalitta since September 2003—flying car and washing-machine parts, organs for organ transplants ("Four hours for a heart, two days for a liver," Jones said), golfers to Pebble Beach, and Kid Rock to Vail. Now they would work two weeks on, one week off, hauling bodies in caskets.

"Once you're in the plane, you're just flying," Jones said. "You just keep your eyes forward."

Jones and Linton have flown some routes so frequently they could fly them blind, because not all towns have lost in equal measure. The thumbtacks stuck into their mental maps are in bunches. Boise, Idaho, has suffered more than most, and so has Little Rock, Arkansas. Then there are the gaps, entire states having escaped their touching down. Jones has never flown into Vermont; by fluke of scheduling, Linton has somehow avoided his home state of Alabama.

Before the afternoon of May 29, 2007, neither man had flown into Seymour, Indiana. Their manifest that day included two deliveries. They stopped first for fuel in Ypsilanti en route to Fargo, North Dakota, where they set down Sergeant Jason A. Schumann, twenty-three, of Hawley, Minnesota. His nickname was Tuba, after the instrument he played in his high school band; he was killed south of Baghdad by a roadside bomb. After topping up the fuel tanks, Jones and Linton charted course southeast, with only Joe Montgomery's metal casket now tied down in the back. Sergeant Dunaway sat in the jump seat between the pilots, Sergeant Montgomery's paperwork and medals on his lap. As they approached Freeman Field, Jones and Linton circled, high in the bright blue sky. From the ground, it looked as though the pilots were offering a sweeping final salute. They were only getting their bearings.

After they touched down and taxied toward the open-sided hangar, they took stock of the waiting crowd. This is going to be tough, Linton thought. "It just seems the smaller the town, the bigger the turnout," he said later.

"Absolutely," Jones said. "Always."

Back in January, their first flights had ended in echo chambers. Linton flew a boy to Stockton, California, where the soldier's parents, divorced, were fighting over the funeral arrangements, and neither showed up. "I want to tell you, it made me mad," Linton said. Jones had a similar experience. His first assignment was a flight to Atlanta, and the dead soldier's father had insisted on accompanying his son, sitting in the cockpit jump seat. ("They have that option, but it doesn't happen very often," Jones said.) After touchdown, the honor guard was nowhere to be found, and Jones had to enlist airport personnel to help him carry the casket. "I was pissed," he said. "I'm like, this is pathetic, especially with the father there. That was the worst one. They got better after that."

By the end of May, everybody involved was more practiced, and the crowds had grown bigger, at least in small towns. The Ypsilanti-Fargo-Seymour leg was in the middle of a particularly busy, brutal run, coming with the troop surge in Iraq. Jones and Linton would log eighty-five hours of flying time in a single two-week stretch.

They unbuckled themselves from their seats, readied the lift, unlatched the door, and immediately felt the heat radiating off the tarmac. Sergeant Betty Clarett, the Indiana National Guard's designated "plane dawg," because she's little, climbed on board. She checked the paperwork to make sure the name matched the name on the office whiteboard, and that the flag on the casket hadn't slipped or been damaged in flight. After Jones had unloaded and readied the lift, Linton bent down to push the casket onto the ball mat.

Inside the hangar, Sergeant Montgomery's family had been waiting for what felt like years. Chaplain Staggers might have tried to warn them, but they still had to live through the moment. Jones and Linton had seen it often—the moment when the family is hit by the truth, when the nose of the casket finally pokes through the door. That's when the air comes out of them and the place they're in, as it did that afternoon in Seymour. The hangar emptied with a gust that buckled men's legs.

"I think that was the hardest part of this whole thing," Gail would say later, before stopping, unable to say anything more.

Linton pushed the casket the rest of the way off the ball mat onto the lift. Jones pressed a button to lower it to pallbearer height. During his first few flights, Linton had stayed in the open door, but that was before an immigrant family in California whose son had been killed in Iraq rushed the casket when it was still on the lift. The family had angrily opposed their son's decision to enlist, and now they let loose on him, beating the sides and top of the casket and screaming at him through their tears. Linton didn't want to turn his back to their suffering, and so he stood statue-still in the door for five minutes, ten, and then fifteen, watching from above while this family aired their last grievances with their rebel son. On the flight back to Dover, Linton told Jones, "I'm never standing there again," and he never has. After he centered Sergeant Montgomery on the lift, Linton stepped back into the shadows inside the plane.

Sometimes, Steve Greene said, the phone rings in his trailer and he hears from dispatch that the pilots need a little extra time before they lift back into the air, although that happens less than it once did. Now they have delivered hundreds of dead soldiers back to their families, and their recollections of the flights have begun to run together. But some Jones and Linton remember more clearly than others. They can remember the thirty-year-old father of five they brought in south of Omaha and seeing the dead man's youngest son, maybe two years old, toddle up to the casket and twist the bottom bar of the flag in his tiny hand. They can remember dropping out of the low clouds over Juneau, Alaska, on their way to Fairbanks, and seeing the light reflecting off the mountains and the water. And they can remember their approach to Seymour, Indiana, when they circled in the sky and there were so many people below, waiting in a hangar in the heat, including a girl in a pretty flowered dress.

.   .   .

The first time Major Cory Larsen entered the Port Mortuary at Dover Air Force Base in Delaware, in 2006—and saw what he has seen nearly every day there since—he went back outside into the sunlight and gulped down the fresh air and resolved to call his mother more often.

By 0800 on Friday, May 25, when he arrived for his shift, Larsen, a thirty-two-year-old Air Force reservist with a shaved head and hooded eyes, had completed two tours within the building, officially called the Charles C. Carson Center for Mortuary Affairs. There were only twelve permanent staff, including four licensed morticians; the rest of the fifty or sixty people who worked within the building were ordinary airmen and reservists, like Larsen, who had been pressed into tours that spanned four months. Many of them, like Larsen, had worked as many as seventy-five days in a row without a day off. Many, like Larsen—who worked in the unit that catalogs incoming remains—volunteered to return.

"Some people are broken here," said Karen Giles, the director of the Carson Center. "But there are a lot of repeaters. We're very protective of each other."

Giles has served here since 2003, when the building opened that fall, the world's largest mortuary, she said, 72,000 square feet of stainless steel and tile. She is small, with a short haircut, and she dresses modestly, in a golf shirt and cargo pants, but she is a presence in the room: She has seen things that she will never discuss, but she isn't shy about what must happen here.

It is a long, low building with broad stretches of tinted glass; surrounded by parking spaces, it looks a little like a shopping mall. The original facility, which opened in 1955, was one-third the size and looked like a warehouse—too much like a warehouse, some people thought after September 11, 2001, when the men and women killed at the Pentagon were brought here for processing. Now, behind the front doors, there is an atrium with plants and a fountain. DIGNITY, HONOR AND RESPECT reads the motto on the stone wall, above a sweeping display that commemorates moments in history that ultimately ended here.

It includes, in part:

VIETNAM: 21,693 DECEASED . . . MASS SUICIDE, PEOPLES TEMPLE CULTISTS IN GUYANA: 913 DECEASED . . . TERRORIST BOMBING OF MARINE HEADQUARTERS IN BEIRUT, LEBANON: 237 DECEASED . . . CRASH OF THE SPACE SHUTTLE *CHALLENGER*: 7 DECEASED . . . OPERATION DESERT SHIELD/DESERT STORM: 310 DECEASED . . . BOMBING IN NAIROBI, KENYA: 11 DECEASED . . . PENTAGON, 9/11: 188 DECEASED . . . CRASH OF THE SPACE SHUTTLE *COLUMBIA*: 7 DECEASED . . .

And for Operation Iraqi Freedom—every soldier, sailor, airman, and marine killed in action to date, including number 3,431: Sergeant Robert Joe Montgomery Jr., of Scottsburg, Indiana.

When Larsen arrived that Friday morning, Sergeant Montgomery was still in his aluminum transfer case, packed in ice, inside a large refrigerator, along with the remains of the twelve other active-duty soldiers and marines who had arrived at Dover with him. He would spend five days here, being readied for the trip home.

Like every transfer case, Sergeant Montgomery's was carried first into the E.O.D. Room, or Explosive Ordnance Disposal Room. Its foot-thick, steel-reinforced walls are built to withstand a blast from a pound of C-4. Sergeant Montgomery was scanned for unexploded bombs, ammunition, booby traps. . . . None was found.

He was then unpacked from the case, which would be cleaned and shipped back to Baghdad to be used again. He was still zipped inside the black body bag, cold and wet to the touch. His remains were lifted out onto a metal table and digitally photographed and archived. Besides the photographic record, the bodies—and parts of bodies, if separate—and their personal effects are bar-coded to make sure nothing is lost. "You can't make a mistake here," Giles said. "You make one mistake, you've automatically made two." Deliver the wrong wedding ring to one wife and another wife is left longing.

No personal effects were found on Sergeant Montgomery's body. Had there been, they would have been taken to another room, where they would have been cleaned and placed in a clear plastic bag for return to his family. The staff assigned to the personal-effects detail are never asked to work with human remains; personal effects turn the bodies, sometimes unrecognizable, back into men and women.

In the atrium, there are two doors, labeled COUNSELING and MEDITATION. They are used by families on rare occasions—such visits aren't encouraged—but most often by those assigned to cleaning and cataloging dog tags, wallets, packs of cigarettes and gum, photographs of baby girls, and envelopes that still smell like perfume.

"If I'm shoulder to shoulder with them, working with them, that's where the conversation starts," said David Sparks, one of the chaplains here. He is retired military, a civilian now, a unit unto himself: tall, with gray hair and a bit of a belly held in check by a New England Patriots belt buckle. He was first called to the Port Mortuary during the days following September 11, and he never left.

"The chaplains are back there with us every single day," Larsen said. "Everyone appreciates that."

When Sergeant Montgomery arrived, like all the dead when they arrive, he carried "believed to be" status; identity can be confirmed only here. The fingerprints of his left hand were examined by experts from the FBI; dental and full-body X-rays were made; DNA samples would be compared with those on record, obtained before deployment with a blood sample. Only then was the body on the table officially given his name.

Then the autopsy began. (Sometimes it's made complicated by the work of doctors and medics in the field: ribs cracked open, hearts bruised from massage, holes from IV lines up and down pale arms.) The gross causes of death—explosion, automatic-weapons fire, falling bricks—may be obvious, but the medical examiners set out to chart both specific causes and the mechanisms and pathways of death. They do so, they say, because they are as interested in predicting the future as in documenting the past. Earlier in the Iraq war, for example, they began to notice a disproportionate number of deaths caused by small shrapnel wounds to the neck. They recommended that soldiers on the ground start wearing armored collars, which have significantly reduced the number of fatal neck wounds dissected at Dover.

At Sergeant Montgomery's autopsy, it was noted that he had suffered traumatic injuries consistent with proximity to an explosive device. There was massive blast and burn trauma to his legs, and he was missing most of his right hand. His torso was intact, and his face was unmarked, except for a single blemish on his forehead. But death would have been instantaneous. It was also noted that his remains were incomplete. (Not long after, as is customary, someone from the Army would call Gail at home in Scottsburg and ask: If more of her son were discovered and subsequently identified at the Port Mortuary, would she like those missing pieces returned to her? She declined.)

Once Sergeant Montgomery's wounds were documented and recorded in the mortuary's database, he was moved to the embalming suite to be prepared for burial. He was placed on top of one of about a dozen workstations, marked by an American flag on the wall and spools of wire to close skull fractures. This is difficult, painstaking work; few of the men and women brought here have died from natural causes or in their sleep, which means that most of them died with their eyes open. Sergeant Montgomery's eyes were blue. Only here were they finally closed, two gloved fingers delicate on his eyelids. For the morticians, that is almost always the first step.

What remained of Sergeant Montgomery's bodily fluids was replaced by preservation agents. Strong solutions are employed, because the morticians don't know where the body they are working on might be sent. In some cases, when injuries are too extensive, no reconstruction is attempted. Instead, the remains are wrapped in absorbent gauze and sealed in plastic; they are then tucked inside crisp white sheets, closed with safety pins, one inch off the crease, the head of every pin facing the same direction; a green blanket is wrapped around the entire cocoon, and a full uniform is pinned on top.

But the presumptive goal of the morticians and their staff is what they call "viewability"—to give the family at least part of their son or daughter back as they remember them. (In the end, the families of about 85 percent of those killed in action are able to hold at least a partial viewing.)

The mortician assigned to Sergeant Montgomery put him back together as best he could. He built a right hand out of gauze and cotton and similarly stuffed the legs of his uniform pants. He paid particular attention to Sergeant Montgomery's face, which, with the help of the airmen stationed alongside him, he washed and shaved and layered in makeup.

Chaplain Sparks tells a story he heard from one of his fellow chaplains. He was on the floor, watching an airman who was tenderly washing the blood and sand out of a young soldier's hair. He would later comb it carefully into place, but for now he concentrated on cleaning the dead man's hair, rinsing it, and washing it again, the water running through it and his fingers and into the sink. The chaplain asked the airman about that, and the airman said, "His mother washed his hair the first time, and I'm washing it for the last time."

"It's very intimate," Sparks said. "Preparing remains is a very intimate thing. This is hands-on."

Then, like Sergeant Montgomery, the bodies are placed in caskets—wood or metal, it's up to the family—and dressed. The mortuary contains a full uniform shop, the most complete in the country, including every size of uniform shirt, jacket, and pants of every branch of service—every badge, every insignia, every cord, every bar, flag, and stripe. Sergeant Montgomery was dressed in his Class-A uniform. His three stripes were stitched to his sleeve, and his Airborne wings were pinned to his chest, along with a freshly made plastic badge that read MONTGOMERY, white on black.

Karen Giles tells a story about another young airman, who was polishing the brass on a dead soldier's uniform jacket. He was using a little tool, a kind of buffer, to make sure that every button shined. A visitor complimented him on his attention to detail. "The family will really appreciate what you're doing," the visitor said. But the airman replied, "Oh, no, sir, the family won't know about this." The airman told him that the family had requested that their son be cremated, and just a short while later, he was.

The flag comes last. They hang by the dozens on a rack on the wall beside a rollaway door, through which a beige van will carry the caskets back to the tarmac. The flags are pressed in the uniform shop, so they are creaseless. And they are longer than a standard flag—nine and a half feet long by five feet wide, a different proportion from the more usual eight by five—to ensure that they cover the ends of the casket; a polyester elastic braid is wrapped around the casket, close to the bottom edge of the flag, to keep it in place until it's folded and given to the family. The flags are always draped the same way, with the stars over the soldier's heart.

•   •   •

Major General Richard P. Formica is stout, with a high-and-tight haircut and a voice that sounds custom-built for giving orders—but now he was sitting in a boardroom in the Pentagon, choking on his words.

The Army Chief of Staff ordered that not only must a general officer attend every funeral of every soldier killed in action, but also that a general officer must greet every plane landing at Dover with dead soldiers in its hold. This is because the return of the dead to American soil is viewed as more than just another leg in their journey; it also serves to remind the corps of generals of the personal cost of war.

It had been Formica's turn on that Thursday evening, May 24, when a Boeing 747—chartered by Transportation Command from an Oregon-based freight company named Evergreen International Aviation, and bearing the remains of Sergeant Joe Montgomery—taxied across the tarmac at Dover. This particular 747, tail number N47OEV, was sometimes converted into a supertanker, dropping thousands of gallons of retardant onto forest fires. But when it touched down a little after 5:30 P.M., just a bit more than forty-eight hours after Sergeant Montgomery had been killed, it carried only the bodies of fourteen men in flag-draped aluminum transfer cases. Thirteen of them had been flown separately out of Iraq by Air Force cargo planes—including Sergeant Montgomery, whose point of departure was Baghdad International Airport—and assembled at Camp Wolf in Kuwait. Ten of them were soldiers; two were marines; one was classified as "disassociated portions"— incomplete remains that were not yet identified. The group was then flown to Ramstein Air Base in Germany, where they were transferred onto the Evergreen jumbo jet and locked to the cargo-hold floor for the flight over the Atlantic Ocean. At Ramstein, the fourteenth case, containing the body of a retired veteran who had died in Europe and was being given passage home, was also loaded on board.

Waiting for the plane were honor guards from the Army, Air Force, and Marines, including Major Larsen, Chaplain Sparks, a representative of the base commander, a Marine colonel, and General Formica. They waited together in the passenger terminal, where volunteers from the local branch of the USO had put out their usual spread of soup and sandwiches and chips; the waiting can weigh on the men and women inside the terminal, rolling in their hands the "incoming sheets," long lists of the dead.

"I remember many nights sitting there with someone from the base, talking about what his religion says to him about all of this," Chaplain Sparks said later, "and maybe there are things that are deeper, not that religion's not important, but maybe there are things that are deeper than that. And I'm born and raised religious, that's my job, that's what I do. But a lot of what religion has to offer doesn't speak very well to fourteen transfer cases. Is that an awful thing to say?"

After the pilots shut down the plane's four huge engines, the K-loader—a large truck with a platform on top that can be raised and lowered like a scissors lift—pulled up to the cargo door, just behind the wing. On base, the K-loader is called the Red Carpet; a length of red carpet had been rolled across the platform.

The honor guards marched out in order (Army first, because it's the oldest branch of service), followed by the general-officer party, including Formica and Sparks. The Air Force detail had already boarded the plane and prepared the transfer cases, unlocking them from the floor. Now the others followed them into the belly of the jumbo jet.

Sometimes there is a single case waiting there in the semi-darkness. The worst planeload Sparks can remember—he has administered to more than seven hundred of these flights—contained the bodies of forty-two men and women, a flying cemetery. "It never becomes old habit," he said. "When I walk up on the back of a plane, it takes my breath away, as much as it ever did."

The Air Force honor guard moved only one case at a time and, as is their protocol, whenever a case was moved, no matter the distance, it was given a three-second salute, present arms. The airmen carried each case onto the Red Carpet, placing them carefully in neat rows of three. When the last case was in place in front of the cargo door, the general-officer party stood at attention before it, and Sparks said a prayer. He writes a different prayer for every flight he meets. In the case of Sergeant Montgomery's return, Sparks wrote the prayer on the incoming sheet that afternoon, during the wait. Now he looked at the cases in their rows and prepared to speak.

Sparks has a beautiful, rich voice, a tenor's voice. On the night when he'd spoken to the forty-two dead, his voice had failed him. "I walked up on the ramp and opened my mouth for the prayer and nothing would come out," he said. "It took some seconds before I could get control to be able to speak at all."

But on this evening, his voice was strong and clear:

"It is the dream of all people that we may live together without fear, without prejudice, without hopelessness. We thank you this night for giving to us these so brave and courageous. We are saddened by the overwhelming and devastating loss of these young men who will now never see the fulfillment of the dream for which they died . . .

"We are proud to welcome home these fallen heroes, to share the grief of their families, and to offer our honor and respect.

"Now, as always, we pray for a time when we are not cursed by terrorism and when young men and women do not die in war.

"This we pray in the name of the Prince of Peace.

"Amen."

Formica and the others returned to the ground to watch, but Sparks stayed in the plane, in the empty space. The lift was lowered, and the honor guards took turns carrying the cases off the lift and into a pair of trucks. There was no way for them to know which body was in which case, so the Army might have carried a marine and vice versa; sharing the load was also a practical matter, because the cases can weigh as much as five hundred pounds each. After the first group had been moved—again, one at a time, again saluted—the Air Force detail lifted each remaining case forward. The process was repeated, as it is repeated, exactly, for every flight, until the Red Carpet was empty and the trucks were full.

"This is the most important thing I've ever done," Sparks would say later of his job here. "I may never do anything more important."

Back in the boardroom near his office in the Pentagon, Formica would pause before talking about that day. "This is personal for me," he said. "Every one of these chokes me up. When I'm performing this service, my most conscious thought—especially when that door closes and the truck drives away—I always think about what these families are going through, waiting for their son or daughter. Please tell them that they were welcomed home with dignity and respect. Please let them know that."

Once the trucks were loaded, Sergeant Montgomery and the others were driven away toward the Port Mortuary, where their transfer cases would be carried inside, placed in the refrigerator, and guarded until eight o'clock the following morning, when it was time to go to work.

Part Three

Forward Operating Base Falcon

Staff Sergeant Terry Slaght sat in a helicopter two days earlier, facing backward, looking down at the body of his friend lying across his boots. He stared at the green Army blanket that had been draped over the body bag and stretcher; the blanket replaced the American flag that had covered Sergeant Montgomery overnight, because it was heavier and wouldn't blow off in the rotor's wash. Slaght is twenty-five, a nice kid from Prairie du Chien, Wisconsin, with red hair and oversized features. He had known Monty for a long time, since 2005, when both men were among the first to join Charlie Troop, 1st Squadron, 40th Cavalry Regiment, 4th Brigade Combat Team, 25th Infantry Division, based at Fort Richardson, Alaska. He had a hard time believing that his friend was the shape under the blanket.

Slaght had been up all night arranging the flight—angel flights, they call them—from the moment he had first heard the letters KIA crackle over his radio at Forward Operating Base Falcon, eight miles outside the Green Zone, in south Baghdad. He had been up late planning the next day's mission, mapping out the path the platoon would walk to the next house, the next palm grove, the next weapons cache. At first, he had heard his men calling for a medevac, urgent surgery, but his stomach turned over when the calls became less urgent and the men said they didn't need a medevac anymore. KIA, they said, and they said it again, KIA, as though they couldn't quite wrap their heads around it.

Then Slaght had found out that it was Monty who was dead, through a kind of radio code: Charlie Echo Mike (for Montgomery), and the last four digits of Sergeant Montgomery's social security number, his battle-roster number. Slaght had pushed through his trembling and made new plans for tomorrow; now they included himself as courier. He'd summoned a pair of Black Hawks—they always fly in pairs—to touch down at Falcon at 0600 and lift him and his friend into the early morning light, dust-filtered and thin.

He hadn't put on the headphones, because he didn't want to listen to the chatter between the pilots and the two gunners perched over his shoulders. He just listened to the thrum of the helicopter, and he stared at the blanket, and he began to feel guilt well up inside of him. Slaght had been promoted while in Iraq, which meant that he was no longer out on hump with the rest of the guys. Instead, he helped direct their footsteps from the relative safety of Falcon, and one of those footsteps had killed Monty. I should have been there, he thought. I should have been out on that road in the tall grass in the dark.

Baghdad's low-rise sprawl opened up before him, the sun rising on this May 23, just about halfway through Charlie Troop's tour in Iraq. It wouldn't take long, maybe fifteen minutes, to reach the tarmac outside the makeshift Mortuary Affairs building, draped in brown camouflage, at Baghdad International Airport. As the helicopters touched down, a single bread truck backed up toward them, its doors open.

Slaght, the helicopter gunners, and a three-man detail from Mortuary Affairs grabbed the stretcher's poles and carried Sergeant Montgomery into the truck. It drove through a rollaway door into the two-room plywood building. After, Slaght sat in the office, waiting for another helicopter to take him back to base, trying not to think about what was being done to his friend on the other side of the wall.

Over there, Sergeant Montgomery's body was examined for distinguishing features to help confirm his identity, and note was taken of the tattoo of an eye on his left forearm; his pockets were cut open to make sure no personal effects had been overlooked; he was zipped back into his body bag, placed in an aluminum transfer case that was stamped HEAD at one end and FOOT at the other, and packed in ice.

Sergeant Montgomery would be in the air to Camp Wolf in Kuwait six hours later; Slaght would wait in the office for more than twelve. Mostly, he watched TV—ESPN was on, beamed via satellite from some distant, make-believe universe—and he watched the day turn into night before he finally got a tap on his shoulder: time to go. The helicopters dropped soldiers off at bases all over Baghdad, up and down and up again, four or five stops before Slaght was finally back at Falcon. He had been awake for nearly forty hours. He dropped onto his cot, pulled up his blanket, and forced himself to sleep.

. . .

Micah Montgomery, who had visited his little brother outside Baghdad only the week before—unknowingly posing for their last photographs, his big arm draped around Joey's shoulders—was now among the first to learn he was dead. Micah had been shaken awake in his cot by someone with word from the in-country grapevine. After a few minutes, his shock was pushed aside, at least for the moment, by worry for his mother. He knew it wouldn't be long before two grim strangers, a notification officer and an Army chaplain, would receive their orders and make the short drive north from Fort Knox, through Louisville, to knock on her door. Looking at his watch, Micah subtracted the hours—it was a little after two o'clock in the morning on Wednesday, May 23, in Baghdad, but still Tuesday evening in Scottsburg—and feared that they might arrive in the middle of the night. He imagined Gail standing in the open door in her nightgown and her heart giving out.

Micah decided to call his uncle, Mayor Bill Graham, but couldn't reach him. Next he called his Aunt Vicki, who was just home from work in nearby Sellersberg. It was still light outside.

"Hi, A.V. It's me, Micah."

"I know . . . Why are you calling here?"

Unlike his brother, Micah rarely called home from Iraq and never called Vicki. Her heart had begun to pound.

"It's about Joey."

"What about Joey? Is everything all right?"

"No," he said.

Then Micah asked Vicki to go to Gail's house—not to tell her, please don't tell her, but to be with her when the soldiers walked up her driveway, up to the little yellow house, past the tree with the two yellow ribbons tied to it.

At Fort Richardson, Alaska, where it was only mid-afternoon, dread suspicions were first raised by a communications blackout at Falcon, which was never good. Word spread through unofficial channels that one of Charlie Troop's wives would be finding out that she was now a widow. As was the practice, women began to gather together so that one of them would not be alone when she found out. Three of the candidate wives—Britany, Tawnya, and Katie—gathered by chance at Missie Montgomery's place, 516A Beluga Avenue. The group of them had formed a kind of surrogate, extended family, first when they were new in Alaska and now in the absence of their husbands. Every Sunday, before the deployment and during, they would get together for cookouts in the courtyard behind Joey and Missie's house. They would rent an inflatable playground for the kids to bounce around in, and they would set up volleyball nets, and they would eat hot dogs and drink beer. Britany, a twenty-eight-year-old from Mississippi with three kids the same ages as Missie's three kids, was especially close to them. "We knew something was wrong," Britany said later. "But we didn't know what or who."

They sent their kids to play at a neighbor's house, sat down in Missie's living room, in a circle, and began an interminable wait, looking at one another and wondering if one of them would need to be caught. They didn't know how the news would travel or how fast: whether the phone would ring with information about another of the wives; whether they would hear crying from a neighbor's yard; whether someone would knock at Missie's door, looking for one of them.

Back in Scottsburg, Vicki pulled up in her truck behind Gail's house. From inside her kitchen, through the small window in the back door, Gail saw her sister get out of her truck, and she saw that Vicki was shaking. Gail opened the door.

"No, no, no, no, no, no . . ." Gail said, beginning to cry.

Vicki began to cry, too.

"Which one?" Gail asked.

Vicki could only mouth the word: "Joey."

And Gail began to scream, "Not my baby! Not my baby!" Neighbors started coming out onto their front steps, and it wasn't long before phones across Scottsburg began to disturb the early-evening wind-down, at the mayor's office, at the church, and at Ryan Heacock's house, where an ordinary day suddenly ended.

"I heard sooner than I should have," Ryan said later, his cigarette drawing down to his fingers. Too soon, because his first instinct had been to pick up the phone and call Missie, who was still sitting in that circle in her living room.

Her phone rang, and Missie answered.

"Missie," Ryan said, "I'm so sorry."

Then Ryan heard the clatter of the phone on the floor.

Britany picked up the phone and asked Ryan what he knew, which wasn't much. She hung up. The women hugged and cried and began a second round of waiting. Minutes turned to hours, afternoon to evening, and a kind of helplessness set in. There wasn't much to say—what could be said? Someone did the dishes. Someone else did the laundry. The calculations went unspoken, but the women knew that Missie and her kids would be leaving for the funeral, and that the funeral would be in Indiana, which was hotter than Alaska. Britany quietly began digging out the children's summer clothes.

Around dinnertime, they came, two men from the base, friends of Joey's filling the door. "I can still see those men standing there, every night," Britany said, and she cried, remembering. "Missie, she just put her face into the wall."

After the men had left, friends blocked out the empty spaces in the house and bags were packed. The same sort of gathering was taking place at Gail's house in Scottsburg. People brought chicken dinners wrapped in tinfoil, cases of Diet Coke, cartons of cigarettes. Joey's boyhood friends—Ryan and the rest of "the guys" who had spent so much time on Elm Street; "I raised them all," Gail said—erected a flagpole on her lawn in the dark and roped an American flag halfway up. Soon a small stone bench arrived, and a photograph of Joey, and a Bible, and a wreath, something new for just about every person who stopped by. The house was full to bursting until late that night, when Gail was finally bundled into bed, and everybody else cleared out except for Mindy, who lay awake in the next room.

At four o'clock in the morning, there came the knock at their door.

•   •   •

Sergeant Joe Montgomery was riding shotgun earlier that night, May 22, 2007. The platoon was heading in a convoy, six Humvees on a string, from Falcon to Patrol Base Red, a drive that could take anywhere between twenty minutes and forever. To pass the time, Sergeant Montgomery had rigged up his iPod to the headsets that he and his team wore so they could talk over the noise of the engine. Now he cranked up "B.Y.O.B," by System of a Down, its ironically melodic chorus filling the night, lit by only a sliver of moon. *Everybody's going to the party have a real good time.*

A kid from Parker, Colorado, Private Kaylon Ross, twenty years old, was driving the truck. He bounced his head to the music. In the backseat, the platoon leader, Lieutenant Eric Rudberg—twenty-five, a stocky Arizonan who for some reason sounds like he's from Boston, the sort of guy you would want leading you into battle—monitored the radios. The team was rounded out by the gunner, Specialist Ron Gilliland, twenty-three, from Butler, Pennsylvania. Sometimes he shivered uncontrollably, his hands seized by tremors on the grip of the machine gun. But the loud music helped. It gave him something to think about other than snipers shooting at him from rooftops or the truck rolling over a pressure plate and liquid copper darts firing through the floorboards.

Sergeant Montgomery was quieter than usual, perhaps thinking about the conversation he'd just had with his wife and kids, his weekly morning phone call—night for them in Alaska, twelve hours behind. Skyla and Robert got on the line first, as they usually did. This time, Skyla had a question for him. Who knows how a nine-year-old's mind works, when she was going to sleep or out on the swings, but she had been thinking that she would like her name to be Skyla Montgomery from now on. She sounded almost shy when she'd asked her dad whether that would be all right. Sergeant Montgomery had promised that they would sign the papers as soon as he got back from away.

Then he'd asked to speak to Mom. They hadn't been on the phone together long before Missie heard an explosion. That wasn't unusual—explosions interrupted their conversations as often as doorbells—but this blast sounded closer than most.

"Oh, my God, I've got to go," Joey had said, and he'd hung up.

These were always anxious waits. Skyla had filled this one, excited about her new name, until a short e-mail landed. Joey had wanted to let Missie know that everything was all right before he hit the road.

"I'm okay," it read.

Now the trucks turned onto Senators, heading east toward the Tigris River. The route between Falcon and Patrol Base Red was not a straight shot; straight shots were death in Iraq. But driving remained dangerous, because there were only so many roads, and it was easy to predict American traffic. Pack an IED into what looked like a curbstone, wait in the bushes for the convoy to drive by, trip the circuit with a cell phone, and a planeload of dead soldiers would be on its way to Dover.

The music changed up, "Friends in Low Places," by Garth Brooks. The convoy turned right onto Red Wings—on Army maps, the roads in Baghdad's southeast were named after hockey teams. They were approaching the edge of the city, near an affluent collection of Sunni farms stretching between rows of irrigation canals and fish ponds. Rudberg hated the canals, because canals meant bridges, and bridges were too easy to bomb. Charlie Troop had eighty men in it; on a patrol like this, the platoon would be carrying between twenty-two and thirty packs. There just weren't enough eyes or ears between them to cover so much ground. They were too thin.

Red Wings started straight and hard-topped, but as it neared Patrol Base Red, the road began to buckle and turn to gravel and then dirt. This was the most stressful part of the drive; it was easier to hide things in dirt. The danger was worse in summer, especially on dark nights like tonight—closing in on eleven o'clock, well past curfew—when Iraqis would bed down on their rooftops to find relief from the heat. They would stir and watch the convoy, these families turned into shadows, leaning over the parapets, and it was so hard to know if they had been visited that week by men bearing threats or a small bundle of money, and if now there was a machine-gun nest where their sleeping mats had been.

At last, the Humvees pulled gratefully inside the walls at Patrol Base Red. It was a house, a mansion by Iraqi standards, once owned by a chicken farmer with a penchant for planting IEDs, so the Americans had seized it and made it into an out-post, a fort on the frontier. There were still boot marks on the front door from the first raid. Since then, the troop had built rings of defenses around it, spools of wire and T-walls, concrete slabs fifteen feet high and eight feet wide. Every window had been filled with sandbags, and firing positions on the roof were permanently manned. The platoons would cycle through in shifts: three or four days guarding the house, sleeping on the cots upstairs; three or four days, like today, shuttling between Falcon and Patrol Base Red before heading out on patrol; and then maybe two days of semirest back at Falcon, cleaning weapons and trucks, getting some proper sleep in air-conditioned barracks. The house had marble floors and chandeliers and a big kitchen with a microwave; whenever Sergeant Montgomery was posted here, he would zap the bags of popcorn that Gail sent him by the boxful and share them with the boys. It would have been all right if the generator had given off a bit more juice and there had been running water. Its absence meant that the platoon shared buckets for their bathroom, which meant that house duty sucked, but it sucked less than patrol. At least here there were walls.

Captain Derrick Goodwin—a big guy, African American, with a deep voice, who had taken over command of the troop only the week before—went inside the house with Rudberg to look at the maps on the wall and confirm the night's mission. In a few minutes, they came back out and briefed the platoon. While he listened, Sergeant Montgomery took a dip from his can of Copenhagen.

"If he didn't have Copenhagen, I don't think he would go on the mission," Ross said later.

They had a pretty good hump ahead of them that night, five clicks, there and back, nearly two hours each way. An informant had told them they should raid a farm out there, down a track called Compound Road; there were rumors that the farmer had a cache of weapons in his palm grove. The platoon would walk out, shake down the house and the trees, and walk back by early morning, before light.

Rudberg's custom was to rotate the squads—a platoon consists of three nine-man squads—through lead position. Tonight, it was first squad's turn, Sergeant Montgomery's squad. He volunteered, as he often did, to walk point. Ross would take second position; Gilliland would take third. Behind them were a couple more regulars—Specialist Jarod Meeks, a lanky twenty-two-year-old from Spanaway, Washington, and Specialist Mark Leland, a twenty-five-year-old Baptist from South Bend, Indiana. In the past week, Leland had pulled the guys aside, in ones and twos, and apologized to them for his letting Iraq change him. He had let himself curse and tell rude jokes, and now that part of his war was over. "I was being challenged in my faith, just because of the situation we were in," he said later. "I remember talking to Monty about it. He told me that he wasn't sure exactly what he believed, but he knew he believed in God."

Now they moved out, led by Sergeant Montgomery, outside the walls and down the road. The boys behind him, especially Ross and Gilliland, ribbed Monty all the time about his age. Only in the Army could a twenty-nine-year-old man be called Gramps, Father Time, Skeletor. But it was good-natured ribbing, because those boys loved him. They loved him because he was first in that line, and if he was scared—and he was almost certainly scared—he never let them see it. He told his family back home that he was scared only of the big camel spiders that scurried behind the men, keeping in their shadows for the extra degree of cool. He tried to ignore the sound of their chase, his boots crunching on the gravel, spitting out juice from his dip.

The men wore night-vision goggles, their nogs, over one eye, everything cast in a ghostly green. They had to choose whether to focus them near or far; most of the men chose to see on down the road rather than their feet. They didn't speak much, except for the occasional crackle over the radio. With about thirty feet between each man, they stretched in a great long line through the night. Goodwin, at the back of the line, was probably six hundred feet from Sergeant Montgomery. They snaked like that, between the farms and over the bridges, cursing under their breath at the incessant barking of dogs. The dogs were like spotlights in a prison yard. Plenty of American soldiers had died because dogs had betrayed their position.

They walked out of the houses and into the fields. There were no dogs here, and the barking stopped. About three clicks out from Patrol Base Red, beside them rose the ruins of an ADA, an air defense artillery site, concrete bunkers covered with steep mounds of earth. Saddam had built them everywhere around Baghdad; this one, like most of them, had been bombed into craters during the initial strike. Recently, though, there had been reports that insurgents had returned here to train. Weeks earlier, a car riddled with bullets, as though it had been used for target practice, had been pulled out from it. Now some of the men felt as though they were being watched.

Rudberg, who was tenth in line, called Sergeant Montgomery on the radio. They identified themselves by numbers. Sergeant Montgomery was number 11. "Hey, 11, take your time," Rudberg said. "We're in no rush."

Sergeant Montgomery had built a gap between himself and Ross. It closed a little when they rounded a bend. The track was soft here, loose dirt, bordered on either side by thick, waist-high grass. There was only one path to take, one foot in front of the other.

Two sounds broke open the night:

Crack, then BOOM.

It was impossibly loud, "the loudest noise I've ever heard in my life," Goodwin said.

Ross did a backflip, landing on his face. Gilliland was knocked down, too. The rest of the men dropped to the dirt and scattered to the sides of the path. In front of them, a plume of black smoke billowed, darker than the dark. It rose out of a great cloud of dust.

Ross couldn't hear Gilliland yelling at him, "Ross, are you hit? Ross, Ross!"

He staggered to his feet, his ears blasted past ringing, dirt still raining down on his shoulders. His pants were covered in blood. Gilliland thought it was Ross who'd been hurt. It wasn't.

"Then you two started screaming his name," Meeks recalled later.

"We couldn't see Monty," Ross said.

They wanted to rush forward, but IEDs were often planted in clusters, and they couldn't see anything in the dust, especially through their night vision. It was just so much green smoke.

Near the back of the line, the platoon sergeant, Bob Bostick, a skinny thirty-four-year-old Texan, was calling for Sergeant Montgomery on the radio, trying to find out what happened: "Hey, hey, come in 11, come in."

Rudberg now moved forward. He found Ross and Gilliland disoriented. "We can't find Monty," they said. Rudberg had the rest of the squad take defensive positions on either side of the path, scouting for a triggerman. He also called on the radio for the medic, who was near the back of the line. They still couldn't see for shit, but they pushed into the cloud.

Rudberg fell into the crater, dead center of the path. Gilliland fell into it, too, and he landed on Sergeant Montgomery's rifle, an M4, stripped down by the force of the blast. "That's when I got really scared," he said.

They looked all around for Sergeant Montgomery. Gilliland finally saw what he thought was a pile of dirt from the crater bending down the tall grass, about twenty feet left of the path. He reached down blindly to touch it and grabbed hold of what felt like a uniform. He adjusted his nogs, fumbling with the dials, so that he could see close-up.

That's when he saw Sergeant Montgomery. His eyes were open, but his body stopped at the waist.

"I knew he was gone," Gilliland said.

Ross staggered over and saw him, too. "There was nothing we could do. We just knew."

"I remember seeing his blank stare," Rudberg said. "It's all so surreal, too, because you have to see it with that fucking night vision."

Rudberg radioed Bostick, "It doesn't look good." He also radioed Goodwin, who radioed Patrol Base Red and then Falcon. Some of the men, including Leland, had been busy clearing a landing zone for a medevac in a nearby field, hoping somehow that Sergeant Montgomery was only hurt. Now Leland saw Goodwin walk by, saying, "KIA, KIA" into his radio to Staff Sergeant Slaght, and they stopped clearing the field.

They decided they would take turns carrying Sergeant Montgomery out. Rudberg had a poleless litter in his pack—a nylon sheet with handles, room for three carriers on each side—and together the men gathered what they could of Sergeant Montgomery and his belongings. They found his helmet, his nogs, his gun, his pack. But they never found all of him. "We didn't find his ring, either," Gilliland remembered. They laid everything on top of the litter, and they began to push out of the grass.

They stayed off the path, and they all took turns carrying the litter, including Ross, the closest of them to the blast. Everyone kept asking him if he was really all right. "It was such a big explosion, and I didn't get a single scratch," he said. "My ears really hurt, but no one believed me when I said I was okay."

The handles of the litter dug into their hands. Only Gilliland refused to be spelled. "I never let go of the litter," he said. "I just couldn't do it."

When he wasn't carrying Sergeant Montgomery, Ross put his arm around his friend. "We just kept walking," he said.

No one spoke.

Some of them were in shock.

All of them were covered in blood.

The platoon carried him like that for an hour or so, a couple of kilometers back up the track and out of the fields. About a click from Patrol Base Red, in sight of the house, one of the sniper teams met them on the road with a Humvee. They placed Sergeant Montgomery on the hood of the truck, and they drove him slowly down the road, the platoon walking flank until they were back inside the walls.

The medic later couldn't bring himself to talk about what happened next, but this is what happened next: He went through Sergeant Montgomery's pockets, and he went through his person, removing anything he thought the family might want. He found Sergeant Montgomery's wallet, his ID card, his pack of Marlboro Lights and his Copenhagen, and the laminated photographs of Missie and the kids that he kept tucked inside his helmet. The medic put them all in a bag, and then he put Sergeant Montgomery in a different bag, black with a long zipper. And then the snipers draped an American flag over it, and they placed it on a stretcher, and they laid it across the backseat of Bostick's truck.

"It felt like time was standing still," Bostick remembered. On the short, silent drive back to Falcon, in the middle of the convoy of six trucks, his mind turned to Micah Montgomery. Bostick had known him for a while, and when he had handpicked Joey Montgomery for Charlie Troop, Bostick had made a promise to his friend. "I told Micah then, I'll take care of your brother. So I had a lot of questions that night. I just kept thinking, Did this really happen? What about his wife? What about his children? What do I say to a guy who's just lost his brother?"

Bostick didn't get a chance to break the news to Micah; someone else did, and Micah was on a plane home to Scottsburg before they could talk.

The two of them didn't speak, in fact, until that July, two months after Sergeant Montgomery's death, when Bostick's own brother, Major Tom Bostick, was killed in Afghanistan. He was thirty-seven years old, with a wife and two children.

The platoon finally drove through the gates at Falcon. It was nearly two o'clock in the morning. The rest of the troop had heard, been rousted out of their cots, and they stood in straight lines, many of them in tears, and they saluted the men in the trucks.

"That's when I lost it," Meeks said.

"That's when most of us broke down," Ross said. "I've never been that emotional in my entire life."

Sergeant Montgomery was carried into the base's utilitarian morgue, laid on a rough table at the front of it. Chaplain Jay Tobin waited there. He is a big man, thirty-seven, with short black hair and round cheeks. He asked to be alone with the base doctor. He unzipped the bag, and he saw Sergeant Montgomery's blank stare, and he nodded. "This is Sergeant Robert Joe Montgomery," he said, and the doctor wrote on some papers, and then Tobin zipped up the bag and called in the platoon, red-eyed, still in their bloodstained uniforms.

He led them in a prayer. The boys bowed their heads and they cried and they prayed for Sergeant Montgomery and for his family. Leland prayed especially hard. He thanked God that he had said sorry to Sergeant Montgomery when he did.

Not many of them could sleep that night. Most of them met outside, at a burn barrel. They threw their uniforms into the fire, and they watched them burn.

·　　·　　·

The last time the platoon saw Sergeant Montgomery was later that morning, at first light. It was Wednesday, May 23. They all came out of their barracks to see the helicopters land. And these sleepless young men, from Colorado, from Pennsylvania, from Washington, they took hold of the poles of the stretcher, three on each side, with their friend from Indiana between them,

zipped up inside a black bag tucked under a green Army blanket, and they carried him into one of the Black Hawks, and they
watched them lift off into the dawn and dust, and they saluted
then, saluted the start of one journey and the end of another,
holding their salutes all the while as the birds flew away, until
they were gone over the horizon.

Bicycling

David Darlington's stirring narrative shows the devastating price paid by cyclists when the legal system and society fails to hold drivers accountable for deadly recklessness on our roads.

David Darlington

Broken

By almost any measure, Sonoma County should qualify as cycling heaven. Spanning more than a million acres from the Pacific coast to the Mayacamas Mountains, it has every kind of riding, from flat to steep to gently rolling, much of it on lightly traveled roads through quiet forests, farmland and vineyards—a pastoral landscape that, blessed by a balmy climate, amounts to a paradise for two-wheeled travel. That, no doubt, is why race organizers chose it for two stages of the 2007 Tour of California—the first one rolling up the coast and heading inland toward Santa Rosa on Occidental Road, the second passing through Sonoma and Napa Valleys via Trinity Grade, an 8.2 percent slope of chaparral.

In the United States, however, cycling heaven is a qualified concept. Five years previous to the 2007 race, Ross Dillon set off on a June training ride that reversed the peloton's eventual route. A twenty-five-year-old Cat 3 racer who had ridden with the 2007 TOC winner Levi Leipheimer on group outings from Santa Rosa, Dillon was spending the summer at his family's home on Trinity Road before starting his first year of law school at Boston College. Since graduating cum laude from Santa Clara University in 1999, he had moved to the East Coast with his girlfriend, Katie, also a B.C. law student, whom he was now planning to marry in August. In the meantime, having saved some money from a job as an investment clerk at Liberty Mutual, Dillon was taking the summer off to race and train, hoping to upgrade to Cat 2 with the Boston Bicycle Club in the fall.

"In races Ross would typically be third or fourth," says his father, Rusty, who is also a cyclist, as well as a psychotherapist and Anglican minister. "He once told me that he thought he had too wholesome a family background to be a really successful racer—he wasn't angry enough."

"He was afraid of being hurt," Rusty's wife, Betsy, elaborates. "He wouldn't go out and take risks." Among his friends, Ross was known for a funny and disarming, if stubborn, personality. When a low-intensity training ride turned into a hammerfest, Dillon would ride resolutely off the back. If somebody in the group was acting like a jerk—being overly critical of riders, or telling everyone else what to do—Ross would pedal up alongside the authoritarian and announce how honored he was to ride with him. That sort of thing made people laugh. Everybody would loosen up.

At about 12:30 P.M. on June 3, 2002, Betsy telephoned Ross from her job tutoring children with learning disabilities. He told her that he was going to ride his Land Shark into Santa Rosa, go to the bank and the bike shop, and be home for dinner by 6:30. In between, he'd do a long ride out toward the coast, heading west from Santa Rosa on Occidental Road.

Occidental, a fast, semirural two-lane road, marks the geographic transition from eastern to western Sonoma County. Although the wine industry has given this area a reputation for civilized gentility, Santa Rosa (the county seat) is becoming a congested urban grid, and the region's wooded western reaches are giving way grudgingly to different kinds of development. With the demise of dairies and orchards, wine grapes now compete for prominence with the county's other major cash crop, *cannabis sativa*. As California Highway Patrol officer Eric Nelson observes: "Those back roads that are so wonderful to ride and drive on were built for farmers in agrarian times, not for the [conditions] we have today. We're driving 2000-model vehicles on roads designed in the 1920s, '30s and '40s."

It was a 1997 Mitsubishi Mirage that Cathie Hamer was driving at 2:45 P.M. when she turned off California 116 (the Gravenstein Highway) west onto Occidental Road. She was on her regular commute route from the town of Sebastopol, where she owned a shop called Yin Yang Clothing—a boutique that sells hemp garments, jewelry, incense, and Eastern religious statuary. After stopping off at the supermarket, Hamer was headed for her home in Duncans Mills, a tourist stop on the Russian River, which was a half-hour drive away. Occidental Road isn't the most direct or well-traveled route between these two points, but that is the reason Hamer—and Ross Dillon—preferred it. As the road enters the coastal hills to the west, it gets twisty and more hazardous, but in the stretch where Cathie Hamer began to overtake Dillon, it is one of the least challenging sections of pavement in western Sonoma County.

"The road there is straight and the shoulder is wide," corroborates Travis Bland, then a sixteen-year-old student who happened to be driving behind Hamer on his way home from Analy High School. As Bland followed a few lengths behind Hamer at fifty miles an hour, he noticed that, for no apparent reason, her car was starting to drift to the right, gradually entering the bike lane behind a cyclist up the road. "I thought maybe [Hamer] knew him and was trying to scare him," Bland recalls. "I thought it might have been one of my classmates playing a joke on somebody." He could clearly see, though, that if the Mirage didn't steer back into the road right away, it was on a collision course with the bike.

At 2:50, Dale Killilea was standing on a deck at Plumfield Academy, a school a half mile to the north, when he and a few of his fellow teachers heard a "large, ugly crash." Although there had been no screeching tires or blaring horns, they thought a significant two-car collision had occurred. "[The sound] was so loud that you could feel it even where I was standing," Killilea says.

This "boom" also got the attention of Ken Fader, an oral surgeon who was headed east in his car on Occidental Road. Turning his eyes toward the source of the sound, Fader saw Hamer's Mitsubishi barreling through the grass on the other side of the road, debris flying behind it, a spandex-clad bike rider tumbling in its wake. Then the car swerved back onto the pavement, heading right at Fader before correcting direction again and speeding off to the west. Fader's first thought was that he'd witnessed an attempted murder. He likens it to a scene in a movie where an assassin runs down a victim: "It was an awful thing to see. It was bizarre—it was breathtaking. It seemed outrageous, because the cyclist was not taking any risk. He seemed to be in as safe a place as a cyclist could be."

Thinking that the Mirage was fleeing the scene, Fader pulled a U-turn to try to get its license-plate number. Meanwhile, Bland had stopped to flag down other drivers, imploring them to call 911. He also terms the incident "unreal"—when he saw Dillon's legs flailing above the roof of the car, Bland was "surprised at the height that he was thrown up into the air. It was like he was flying—but then when he hit the ground, he didn't move at all."

As Fader turned his car around to chase the Mitsubishi, he saw Dillon in a motionless heap fifty yards from the first point of impact. A trained emergency physician, Fader realized that the cyclist's survival might be hanging in the balance. "If he'd been conscious he would have righted himself," Fader says. "That twisted position would have been too uncomfortable." Fader made a decision to abandon the chase and instead administer to Dillon, whom he found turning blue. Failing to detect a pulse, he repositioned the cyclist's head to clear his airway, taking care not to worsen any cervical injuries; after he'd done this three times, Dillon coughed weakly and started drawing shallow, raspy breaths. A few minutes later, emergency technicians from local volunteer fire departments pulled up to the scene, responding to the 911 bulletin.

Unbeknownst to most of those present, Cathie Hamer had stopped her car a hundred yards up the road. When officer Nelson arrived at 3:02, he saw Hamer walking toward the spot where Fader and the firemen were attending to Dillon. Crying hysterically and holding both sides of her head with her hands, she fell to her knees as Nelson approached; when he helped her up, he felt her legs wobbling. "What happened?" she kept asking, mucous flowing from her nose.

Nelson walked Hamer back to her car and told her to wait there. He noticed that the vehicle's right front and sides were damaged—its right windshield wiper had been torn off and the windshield was smashed, including a ten-inch "intrusion" apparently caused by Dillon's helmet. There was jewelry hanging from the rearview mirror, a bunch of grocery bags in the back seat.

As Dillon was taken away in an ambulance, Nelson thought he was probably a fatality. By the time Nelson returned to talk to Hamer, she had calmed somewhat. "I was just driving along and then there was this big bang," she said. "I thought to myself that I had been hit by another car. All I saw was black, and there was glass flying everywhere. It all happened so fast. I just ended up here, and I got out and that was when I realized I had hit somebody. Did you get any witnesses? Was he in my lane? I really don't know what happened. It just went black, and I guess now I know that the black I saw was the guy rolling over my windshield."

Nelson asked Hamer if she was aware she'd drifted onto the shoulder before the crash. "I was just driving straight," she said.

"Were you talking on your cell phone, or reaching for something in the car?" Nelson asked. Hamer said that her phone didn't get reception in that area, and that she'd been looking directly ahead. Finally, Nelson asked if she'd taken any medications or drugs before driving, and she said she hadn't. As her car was being impounded, Nelson gave Hamer a ride home, during which he concluded that she wasn't under the influence of alcohol or otherwise impaired, though he didn't administer any chemical tests.

When the ambulance crew arrived at Santa Rosa Memorial Hospital, an emergency-room nurse told the operating room: "I'm not sure you have a patient." Dillon had catastrophic head injuries—a member of the trauma team said he had the biggest brain hematoma she'd ever seen—and his C-7 vertebrae was broken, but his spinal cord was undamaged and, thanks to the quick reactions of passersby and emergency personnel, he entered surgery within forty-five minutes of being hit. Over the course of his ordeal, he'd stop breathing four times—immediately after the crash, once in the ambulance, once in the operating room and once in intensive care.

Betsy and Rusty Dillon didn't learn about their son's crash until that night. When he failed to come home for dinner, Betsy telephoned the Highway Patrol, which confirmed that a cyclist named Ross Dillon had been involved in an accident. When Betsy asked where he'd been taken, she waited for several minutes on hold before learning the name of the hospital. (Later she realized that the CHP office probably thought Ross was in the morgue.) By the time the Dillons arrived at Memorial, surgeons had already removed part of Ross's skull to relieve the swelling in his brain, and when Betsy first glimpsed him in the intensive-care unit, she was overwhelmed. "One of his eyes was yellow and swelled up to the size of a baseball," she remembers. "They had him hooked up to a bed that was moving him from side to side like a rotisserie."

The prognosis was equally bad. The Dillons were told that Ross would never be the same, and that they should prepare themselves for some very tough decisions. "People thought he might be brain dead," Betsy says. "When we got there, they started talking to Rusty about donating Ross's organs." By the next day, Dillon's condition had stabilized, but he remained in critical condition and in a coma. Six days after the crash, a neurosurgeon friend of the Dillons rated his chances for future improvement at 5 percent.

Upon receiving all this news, Rusty telephoned Kate Moore, a family friend whose son had grown up with Ross. "My beautiful boy is broken," he said.

One week after the crash, CHP officer Eric Nelson called Cathie Hamer with a few clarifying questions. She told him she had nothing new to add, and that her attorney would have to participate in any further discussions. Nelson said that he understood, but also wanted to let her know that a "possible" bag of marijuana and rolling papers had been found in the glove compartment of her car. (The examiner who evaluated the material described the results inconclusively, saying they'd partially changed color in a chemical test.) Hamer gasped, telling Nelson that the bag contained "herbs" to help her quit smoking cigarettes.

Ultimately Nelson would conclude in his report that, just before she ran into Dillon, Hamer realized she was on the last straight stretch of Occidental Road before the miles of twists and turns, decided to get something out of one of the grocery bags in the back and, in the process, unwittingly steered onto the shoulder at fifty miles an hour.

In other words, it was just an accident. Hamer was distracted— she wasn't impaired. Because she hadn't killed Dillon, she couldn't be charged with manslaughter, and because she wasn't weaving or braking erratically, she couldn't be charged with reckless driving. There was never any argument about who was at fault; multiple witnesses testified that Dillon was in the bike lane. It was just his tough luck to be biking on Occidental Road when Cathie Hamer got hungry.

Dillon would remain in a coma for four months, a vegetative state for ten. Two months after the crash, he underwent surgery to drain fluid from his brain and repair a previously undetected fracture in his skull, after which he developed pneumonia and septic shock. He was subsequently moved to a subacute pulmonary ward where his doctors remained pessimistic. During that period, however, his parents began treating him with acupuncture and, unknown to hospital authorities, smuggled an unauthorized TENS (transcutaneous electrical nerve stimulation) unit into his room, hiding it under a splint on his wrist to stimulate his brain through his right arm—a treatment developed in North Carolina by orthopedic surgeon Edwin Cooper, whose son happened to be a friend of Lance Armstrong's. Soon after that, Ross began moving his head in response to voice commands, and on January 29 he mouthed his first word since the crash. As a tracheotomy tube to his throat was being suctioned out and changed, Betsy thought she heard him say, "Shit!"

Based on such unexpected developments, in March Dillon was moved to a rehabilitation center in Marin County. Over time, however, the insurance company judged his progress inadequate for continued coverage; treatment had been funded by a COBRA policy he'd taken out upon leaving his job at Liberty Mutual, but the designation of his condition as subacute meant that professional nursing care was no longer medically necessary. Rather than warehouse him in a facility without active therapy, his parents decided to bring him home on June 7, 2003—almost exactly a year after the crash. The Dillons thus became financially responsible for their son's rehabilitation and equipment, which would come to include a power wheelchair, a hospital bed, a wheelchair-accessible van, a full-time live-in attendant, and regular physical, occupational, and speech therapy.

Cathie Hamer's $25,000 liability insurance had likely been used up by Ross's emergency care before Betsy and Rusty even learned he'd been in an accident. They later got a note from

Hamer, "obviously concocted by her attorney," to avoid any admission of guilt, says Betsy. The letter said Hamer "couldn't believe" what had happened. At one point Hamer left the Dillons a tearful telephone message declaring, "You don't know what this has done to me." Hamer's husband sent the Dillons an e-mail saying there hadn't been a carefree day in their house since the crash.

"I used to believe the one thing worse than this would be if Ross had done it to someone else," Betsy admits. Still, she feels there's a difference between Hamer's remorse and acceptance of responsibility for what happened. Although it might seem like splitting hairs, it doesn't sit right with Betsy that Hamer never simply said she was sorry. (Such a statement could be used against Hamer in court if the Dillons filed a civil suit, but they say they'd abandoned that notion after learning that she had no assets.)

Part of the reason the Sonoma County district attorney's office declined to pursue charges against Hamer was its expectation that a jury would identify and sympathize with her, a common occurrence across the country. In that light, Rusty unintentionally describes not only Hamer and her spouse but also the American populace in general when he says: "Their sorrow doesn't seem to be empathic. It's always about how bad *they* feel."

. . .

As cyclists we accept the fact that our pastime can be dangerous. We recognize that riding among automobiles is a risk, we know we're the equivalent of sitting ducks, we're aware that drivers don't pay much attention, we've seen cars do all kinds of crazy things, and we've had our lives repeatedly threatened by clueless or outright hostile jerks. Still, we pride ourselves on our skills and instincts, confident that we're alert enough to recognize danger developing and sufficiently skilled to elude it. But none of us has any defense against what happened to Ross Dillon. As the now-twenty-two-year-old Travis Bland (who resorted exclusively to mountain biking after witnessing the crash) reflects: "The only thing that might have helped him is if he'd had a mirror. But even then, he would have had only a second or two to react."

Dillon's story is a nightmare, its lack of legal accountability an abomination. But it's only one of many such incidents that have occurred throughout the United States. "Barely a week goes by when you don't hear of a cyclist being killed, the behavior of the driver being outrageous, and the response of law enforcement or the penalty passed on to the driver being woefully inadequate," says Andy Clarke, executive director of the League of American Bicyclists. "The kinds of crashes we're talking about almost always involve a motorist who was hopelessly distracted or out of control—speeding, taking corners as they shouldn't, talking on a cell phone, or reaching for a CD. Most are avoidable and preventable, but the response is so feeble. It's an intensely frustrating feeling of powerlessness."

As with Cathie Hamer, the law—or, more accurately, the lack of it—often stands in the way of penalizing inattentive drivers. Gary Brustin, a California personal-injury attorney who specializes in bicycle cases, says that a typical response he encounters among district attorneys is: " 'Give us some ammunition— some teeth in the law.' Juries are filled with people who aren't cyclists, and a driver's behavior has to be far beyond negligent for a criminal case—there have to be aggravating circumstances to make it vehicular manslaughter or murder. If there aren't, [drivers] usually go to jail for less than a year, or get a suspended sentence."

"When the intent is not there to kill or harm someone, the offenses aren't there to prosecute," Clarke agrees. "When a cyclist is killed by a driver who was text-messaging someone, you read as much in the paper about how awful the driver feels.

We've made driving so easy, accessible and convenient—and the system is so forgiving—that people can drive distracted at great speeds and mostly get away with it. But we've seen conclusively that not paying attention will cause bad things to happen; studies have shown that distracted driving is just as dangerous as driving drunk. We should be penalizing those people the same way that we treat drunk drivers."

Clarke observes that while cyclists are uniquely vulnerable, society tolerates traffic fatalities in general. "Despite seat belts, anti-lock brakes, air bags, crumple zones and any number of silver-bullet devices, 43,000 people are killed in crashes in the United States every year," he says. "I worked for four years as a highway contractor for the Federal Highway Transportation Department, which always said that safety was its number-one priority. But if that were true, we wouldn't kill so many people, including 5,000 pedestrians and 700 cyclists per year. In other countries, they've been more active about taking those words seriously."

The United States has the highest traffic-death rate (15 per 100,000 residents) of all developed democratic countries. Several European nations—for example, Austria, Belgium, France, Germany, the Netherlands and Switzerland—have slashed their annual traffic-fatality figures over the past few decades, largely through "traffic-calming" measures that forcibly reduce the speeds of motor vehicles. In places such as Germany and the Netherlands, traffic regulations are actually biased in favor of cyclists and pedestrians—in the event of a bike-car collision, the legal burden is on motorists to prove that they weren't at fault, and Dutch drivers are financially liable even if cyclists are at fault.

But that's the Netherlands, where almost half of all local travel is done by bicycle. Dutch and German children are schooled in safe cycling practices and, when they grow older and learn to drive, are taught how to avoid vehicle collisions even with lawbreaking cyclists. In the United States, by contrast, drivers aren't trained to expect bikes on the road; as bicycle lawyer Brustin observes, after a car runs into a bike, "the number-one statement [of motorists] is 'I didn't see him.'"

"That's just unacceptable," declares Christine Culver, executive director of the Sonoma County Bicycle Coalition. "Having stuff hanging from your rearview mirror isn't worth somebody's life. We can all relate to what it's like to be in a car and do something stupid, but as a result, people are reluctant to punish [distracted drivers]. They think, 'If someone's dead, what good is it going to do?' It used to be that way with drunk drivers, too. We need to put more responsibility on what it means to drive an automobile. It's criminal not to be in control of your car, and there should be consequences for it. We've done an amazing job protecting people inside the car with seat belts and air bags; we need to put an equal emphasis on protecting people outside the car."

The Sonoma County Bicycle Coalition was founded in 1999 by Janice and Mike Eunice, a retired librarian and a high-school teacher who came to the area because they thought it "the best place in the world to ride a bike." But after moving to Santa Rosa, the Eunices were disheartened by what they perceived as a bike-unfriendly atmosphere—its lack of bike lanes or cycling facilities, plus the occasional bottle or epithet hurled by a passing motorist. Looking for ways to improve things, they attended a League of American Bicyclists rally in Eugene, Oregon, where they learned that hundreds of millions of federal dollars were available for local bike projects; but when they sat in on meetings of the Santa Rosa Bicycle and Pedestrian Advisory Committee, they were told that, as a public agency, it wasn't permitted to lobby for change.

"The staff members recommended that we form an independent advocacy group," Mike says. The Santa Rosa Cycling Club, of which he was a board member, feared that getting involved in politics would be divisive for a recreational organization. But with $200 donated by the club, a few interested individuals began holding regular meetings and producing a quarterly coalition newsletter. With board members including a mayor, a transit planner, an air-quality expert, a bike-shop owner, an accountant, an attorney and an advocate for the poor, the group contained a formidable collection of skills, and within a year, it had implemented a bicycle-parking program and promoted a Bike to Work Week. In time it would grow to include more than 750 members, representing cyclists at government meetings, attracting hundreds of millions of dollars in set-asides for traffic planning, partnering with the city of Santa Rosa to establish a Share the Road campaign, implementing Street Skills for Cyclists and bicycle-education classes for traffic-ticket holders. It has also created at least one new bike lane and bike path per year, sold thousands of cycling maps of Sonoma County, obtained 501(c)(3) nonprofit status and in general, according to Christine Culver, "explained that bikes belong on our roads—even the most narrow road—and that people need to be in control of their cars. It comes down to everyone needing to take a breath and relax—and it's made a huge difference here. Now we're contacted by cities and the county when they have questions about implementing a bicycle project."

A former collegiate and pro mountain bike racer (she won the national downhill championship in 1989), Culver got involved with the Coalition in 2001. She'd been riding her bike to work at Aussie Racing Apparel one morning in Petaluma, south of Santa Rosa, when a driver stopped and motioned for her to cross while she was waiting on the shoulder.

"There wasn't any crosswalk," Culver remembers. "The guy stopped in the middle of the street. If I got hit in that situation, I would have been at fault—so I waved him on, and suddenly he started yelling at me to get off the road. Apparently it angered him that he'd made this effort and I hadn't taken his offer. A lot of people don't think it's even legal for cyclists to be on the street."

As soon as she got to work that day, Culver did a Web search for "Sonoma County Bicycle Coalition." She didn't even know if such a group existed—she'd never been a member of any organization in her life—but she'd noticed the effectiveness of the San Francisco and Marin County coalitions next door. "Marin had done a fantastic job promoting Safe Routes to School," she says. "San Francisco got bike lanes put in throughout the city and opened the Golden Gate Bridge to bicycles twenty-four hours a day. It showed that bikes are a transportation mechanism just as valid as cars, and it gave me the idea that we could make a change."

Culver started going to SCBC meetings and volunteering at the group's public-information tables. "I'd been working in sales and bike shops for fifteen years," she remembers. "Now I was going to council meetings and trying to figure out the system—who was making policy decisions, who were the bicycle-friendly politicians, where the money for bike projects came from." She turned out to be a fast learner: Culver was elected to the coalition's board of directors that same year and became its executive director in June 2002—the same month that Cathie Hamer ran into Ross Dillon.

At the time, Culver says, she didn't know how to support a family in the Dillons' circumstances. "I didn't want to intrude on their grief," she says. "Their focus was on Ross, and it seemed so trivial to say, 'I want to go after this woman.' I tried to get more information, but the police wouldn't release the accident report to me because I wasn't family. I kept running into roadblocks and didn't know how to get around them."

As part of her education in two-wheeled politics, Culver also attended educational retreats staged by the Thunderhead Alliance, a national coalition of local and state bicycle groups working to influence legislation and advance bicycle safety. She started to learn how to deal with the media, raise money and connect with public officials. "A lot of it is networking and long-term relationships," she says. "Now I have contacts I can call in local law enforcement. I've also learned that families like the Dillons need the support of the cycling community—people with the background to pressure the D.A. and see that justice is done."

Unfortunately, after two years of on-the-job learning, Culver would get a chance to put her new skills to the test.

.   .   .

On Easter Sunday of 2004, Alan Liu and Jill Mason embarked on a bike ride from Santa Rosa. They'd been dating for about six months since meeting on the master's swim team in Mountain View, south of San Francisco. Liu, thirty-one, was the team's head coach; a graduate of MIT and Stanford, he was employed by Applied Materials, a semiconductor-equipment manufacturer in Silicon Valley, where he'd recently been made a manager. (He also held four engineering patents.) In addition, Liu was a successful coach: A competitive swimmer since age five, he was known for encouraging people to perform beyond their own expectations. Since taking over the 300-member Mountain View master's program in 1997, he'd expanded it to include water polo and triathlons.

Like Liu, Mason, twenty-six, was a triathlete. Growing up in the Sierra Nevada foothills, she'd been a member of the track, cross-country, lacrosse, and soccer teams at Nevada Union High School, where she was nicknamed Forrest Gump because of her surprising speed. Shorter than most of her opponents, Mason was a fierce competitor in the hundred-meter hurdles despite taking four steps between each set of barriers instead of the usual three (and thus leading with a different leg on every other hurdle). She had gone on to run marathons at Santa Clara

University, which she'd attended at the same time as Ross Dillon—in fact, she'd contributed to his rehabilitation fund the previous year. With a new master's degree in mass communications from San Jose State, Mason was working as a marketing director for an environmental and geotechnical engineering company in Mountain View, where she met Alan Liu after joining the swim team. The confident, upbeat Mason was a match for the energetic Liu, and soon the two of them were running, riding, and swimming together regularly.

They planned their Easter ride to prepare for an upcoming half-Ironman triathlon, riding thirty miles in Sonoma Valley that April 11, passing not far from the Dillons' house on Trinity Road. At 11:19 A.M., the route brought them back into eastern Santa Rosa on California Highway 12, a high-speed artery that becomes increasingly congested as it approaches the city. Local riders avoid it, but Liu and Mason were out-of-town visitors, seeking the most direct route back into town to meet Liu's mother for brunch.

As the couple pedaled west on the highway, Harvey Hereford got into his Nissan Sentra at the seniors-only Oakmont subdivision, adjacent to Highway 12. Hereford wasn't expecting any Easter visitors; on the contrary, he later said that he felt deserted by his family. A sixty-nine-year-old personal-injury attorney, he was described by neighbors as a friendly and funny guy, but his ex-wife had recently called police when she couldn't reach him, thinking he might be suicidal. Over the past fifteen years, ten federal tax liens and one state Employment Development lien had been issued against Hereford's office and former residence in San Francisco.

At 11:20, a pair of Oakmont residents, Kate Brolan and Sydney Brown, were sitting in their car on Pythian Road, waiting at a red light at the intersection with Highway 12. When the light turned green, a Nissan Sentra in front of them pulled out and turned toward Santa Rosa; within seconds, according to Brown, it was flying "like a shot out of hell," weaving all over the road as it bore down on a pair of cyclists on the shoulder. Liu was riding behind Mason, and the car hit him first, killing him instantly as it severed his brain stem. An instant later it slammed into Mason, cleaving her spinal cord, lacerating her liver, breaking her arm and traumatizing her brain. When Brolan and Brown reached her, she was sobbing and shivering on the ground.

Not unlike Cathie Hamer's Mitsubishi, the Nissan came to a stop a hundred yards up the road, where its driver was detained by a couple of passing off-duty cops. Hereford, whose driver's license was found to have expired, told the officers that he suspected something was wrong when he noticed that his windshield was broken. He didn't remember running into anybody; nor did he remember getting into his car or driving away from his house. His blood-alcohol percentage was 0.29, more than three times the legal limit.

As with Ross Dillon, doctors at Santa Rosa Memorial Hospital expected Mason to either die or remain in a vegetative state. A day after the crash, her mother and father—Joanne, a school counselor, and Larry, an adaptive phys. ed. teacher for disabled students—were given the same pessimistic advice the Dillons had received. That night, more than three dozen Sonoma County Bicycle Coalition members gathered in front of the county courthouse and rode in silence to the hospital, where they held a candlelight vigil for Mason. Among them were Betsy and Rusty Dillon, who urged Mason's parents not to give up—they said they'd received similar predictions about Ross, and that two years later he was still improving.

Sure enough, the next day Jill Mason's doctors reported that her prognosis wasn't as bad as they'd feared. But the story was over for Alan Liu, whose stepsister had been killed by a drunk driver on New Year's Day the previous year.

•　　　•　　　•

A weeklong debate about traffic safety and bicycle-car animosity ensued in the pages of the *Santa Rosa Press Democrat*. A letter complaining about cyclists who run stop signs and hog the road was printed in the paper under the headline "Educate Riders," and one week after the Mason-Liu tragedy, *Press Democrat* reporter Paul Payne published a story about "daredevil" cyclists entitled "Taking Risks on the Road." None of this negative rhetoric pertained to the behavior of Mason and Liu, who had been riding single file on the shoulder, and Christine Culver vented her outrage that day at an SCBC information table on the Sonoma town plaza. "They're trying to make this a bicycling issue when it's a drunk-driving issue," she complained to Danny O'Reilly, an SCBC member who had volunteered to park bikes at the Earth Day celebration they were both staffing.

O'Reilly, a marketing analyst at Kendall-Jackson Wine Estates, north of Santa Rosa, e-mailed Culver from work the next day. "I read the article you mentioned," he wrote. "It's just that a stupid motorist can do a whole lot more damage than a stupid cyclist. That's where the author let everyone down. All activities carry a risk to them—even sitting on your couch (radon gas under the home or formaldehyde in the insulation)." O'Reilly went on to cite a study that compared the risks, on a per-passenger-mile basis, of all modes of transportation. "Scuba diving tops the list," he revealed. "Elevator travel is the safest mode of transportation. Cycling is slightly more dangerous than driving."

O'Reilly lived twenty miles southeast of Santa Rosa in the town of Agua Caliente, where he and his wife, Patty, a dance teacher, were raising two daughters. A former fund raiser for the San Francisco Ballet, he'd taken up cycling when he couldn't continue dancing; he often made the sixty-mile round-trip to work and back by bike, showering and changing in a locker room he'd convinced Kendall-Jackson to build. O'Reilly was known as the company's "environmental conscience"—he'd spearheaded its bike-to-work and recycling programs, and on the evening of the day he e-mailed Culver, he planned to check the insulation in his attic to see if it could be made more energy-efficient. At five o'clock on April 19, he started pedaling home on Mark West Springs Road, aiming to circumvent the city on a winding back-country route called Riebli Road.

William Michael Albertson was also headed east on Mark West Springs Road in a Ford F-150 pickup truck. The forty-six-year-old, who lived in Lake County, to the north, was on probation from federal prison for battery with serious bodily injury. Clinically diagnosed as bipolar, he also had a history of alcoholism, but had been sober from 1984 to 1999. During that time, Albertson had developed a successful recording business, but in 1996 a loudspeaker had fallen on him, injuring his back. He'd subsequently become addicted to painkillers, and on April 19 he was out of drugs—he'd caused a ruckus in nearby Healdsburg when he showed up at a couple of medical facilities demanding medication, then driven on to Santa Rosa and started drinking in his truck. Eventually he'd called a girlfriend to come pick him up, but she'd responded that a DUI would serve him right. Ultimately, Albertson later claimed, he decided to check himself into a hospital in St. Helena, twenty-five miles from Santa Rosa via Mark West Springs Road.

According to the police report, Albertson rear-ended a vehicle at a red light at 4:38 P.M. He drove away, and forty-five minutes later the Highway Patrol got a call from a fireman reporting an F-150 blocking a lane of Mark West Springs Road. The truck had a broken headlight and a dented hood, and the right side of its windshield was shattered; the driver, described as intoxicated and belligerent, was resisting efforts to treat a cut on his forehead. When the police arrived, Albertson got out of his truck and blurted, "Fuck you, copper! I'm a convicted felon—what are you going to do?" He reached into the rear of his waistband and took a step toward the patrolman, who doused him with pepper spray and arrested him. Albertson's blood-alcohol level was 0.22.

As firefighters were clearing debris, they noticed a bicycle wheel on the south side of the road. Looking farther, they peered over an adjacent guardrail and saw a body 10 yards away. It was determined that Danny O'Reilly had died of a head injury, and moreover that his hair matched a sample found in Albertson's windshield. Albertson, who hadn't previously said anything about hitting a cyclist, admitted he'd sideswiped O'Reilly; he said he'd "stopped and prayed," but had continued driving, losing control of his truck at the spot where he was arrested.

"You know what I am?" Albertson sobbed to police officers who'd taken him to a hospital for a blood test. "I'm a fucking junkie. I'm an artist but . . . I killed that man and I need to pay."

．　　　．　　　．

When Christine Culver learned that Danny O'Reilly had been run over on the same day he'd e-mailed her about the risks of road cycling, she was, to put it mildly, stunned. "He was such a good person," she laments. "Danny was the kind of soul you wish this world could have more of." In light of the Mason-Liu tragedy only a week earlier, it seemed that some kind of curse had been cast on Sonoma County cyclists. The SCBC didn't react with voodoo rituals, however. A lawyer named Oren Noah, one of the group's founding members, proposed a campaign similar to one that had been waged five years earlier in Marin County, after a rider named Cecily Krone—an occupational therapist who worked with handicapped children—was killed at 9:30 A.M. on a Sunday by a drunk driver searching for a cigarette. Cyclists packed county courtrooms at every hearing related to the case, and the driver was sentenced to six years in jail for vehicular manslaughter. Noah now suggested that Sonoma cyclists follow that example, not only to draw the attention of judges and the media, but also to show the perpetrators themselves "that they killed humans with friends and robbed from the community . . .

[and to] maintain the focus where it should be: on the drunk killers."

Two nights after O'Reilly's death, SCBC members joined a group of victims-rights advocates in front of the Sonoma County courthouse. Before newspaper and TV reporters, they hammered home the message that these deaths weren't an inevitable outgrowth of a dangerous sport, but rather products of a cultural attitude that promotes impatience and irresponsibility. "If the public thinks it's just 'those crazy people' who were killed, they don't have any reason to get involved," Culver says. "We had to show that a bicyclist isn't just something in your way—it's somebody's dad, or dentist or doctor." This new alliance with the county's Victim Assistance Center (a division of the district attorney's office) gave the SCBC an ear on the court schedule, so when hearings for Hereford and Albertson were imminent, Culver e-mailed the SCBC membership, urging people to take off work and show up at the courthouse in person.

Given the narrow time span in which Liu and O'Reilly were killed, legal proceedings against the two drivers were almost simultaneous. Bill Brockley, a deputy D.A. in the homicide division, was handling both cases for the county; and when he came down the corridor for Hereford's arraignment, he was surprised to see a crowd outside the courtroom. "There were probably fifty people," Brockley remembers. "I thought it was going to be support for the defendant, but as I got closer, I saw it was people carrying helmets and wearing bicycle lapel pins." This demonstration continued throughout the summer, with cyclists filling the courtrooms even when hearings for Hereford and Albertson occurred at the same time. Reportedly, everyone who worked in the courthouse, from bailiffs to lawyers to judges, was moved by the show of support.

"You rarely get people coming to court when they don't know the victim," says Brockley, the prosecuting attorney. "It was remarkable that most of them weren't personally acquainted with the cyclists who died—they were just concerned citizens who helped the court see the seriousness and reality of the losses. When a judge has discretion in sentencing and knows that the public is watching, it really has an effect."

Hereford and Albertson both ended up pleading guilty to vehicular manslaughter and driving under the influence. At Hereford's sentencing, he was confronted by an especially effective witness: the wheelchair-bound Jill Mason, who had been released from the hospital only a few days earlier. After Hereford ran into her, Mason had remained in a coma for five days; a hole had been cut into her throat to allow her to breathe, and surgeons operated on her broken spine for twelve hours. She was fed through a tube for a month, and didn't speak for eight weeks. She had no memory of the crash, nor of Alan Liu—she found out that she'd lost a boyfriend from e-mail collected on her computer.

Today Mason can drive a car, paddle a kayak, work out at a gym and ride a hand-powered bike. She lives on her own with a roommate in Sacramento and gives PowerPoint presentations to school groups for the Every Fifteen Minutes program (named for the frequency with which someone dies in a drunk-driving crash). Short of some miraculous breakthrough in medical research, however, she'll never walk again.

Hereford, who admitted he was guilty of "a monumentally selfish act," was sentenced to eight years and eight months in prison, the maximum for his offenses. Albertson, whose punishment was aggravated by fleeing the scene as well as by his earlier felony conviction for battery, got fourteen years.

"The court does intend to send a message to the defendant(s) and to the community that drinking and driving will not be tolerated in Sonoma County," declared judge Elaine Rushing. "Bicycle riders have the same rights as automobile drivers."

Unfortunately, Rushing neglected to heed her own message. Nine months later, she was arrested for drunk driving on Riebli

Road, not far from the spot where Albertson killed O'Reilly. She remains on the bench, but no longer hears criminal cases.

. . .

For months after Danny O'Reilly died, his widow, Patty, was unable to sleep, cook, or clean. She abandoned the garden that Danny had planted and she closed her eleven-year-old ballet school in Vallejo, twenty-five miles away. What she wanted most at that point, other than getting her husband back, was revenge on his killer.

One night during this period, as O'Reilly's daughters—twelve-year-old Erin and seven-year-old Siobhan—were resisting her order to take a bath, she found herself screaming at them in a way that hardly fit their crime. "They were the last people who needed to be yelled at," she acknowledges now. "I was carrying around a lot of anger and hatred and self-pity, and in that moment it became clear to me that I had to let go of it. Otherwise, I would end up hurting not Mike Albertson, but my daughters and myself."

At Albertson's sentencing, Patty would have a chance to address him directly. Before that took place, however, she read a background report on him that revealed that, as a child, he had been raped by his own father. "If I called him the scum of the earth," O'Reilly reasoned, "he would just feel more self-pity. Then, when he got out of jail, he'd probably start drinking again and another family would be in our situation."

Albertson wept throughout his sentencing hearing, ultimately apologizing to the family and asking for their forgiveness. Sometime after that, Siobhan made a card for him that contained a drawing of her own face streaked with tears; it nevertheless said, "I'm not mad at you." Patty subsequently decided to investigate a new state prison program for "restorative justice," in which victims meet with convicts so that both can process the consequences of their crimes. Her first such excursion was to San Quentin, in Marin County, where she spoke not with Albertson but with other convicted killers. The following year, a mediator from the California Office of Victim and Survivor Services, Rochelle Edwards, arranged a meeting between O'Reilly and Albertson.

In order to take part in the encounter, Albertson had to undergo months of preparation and training, which included accepting responsibility for his crime. Over the course of these meetings, he told Edwards that, in the weeks before he killed Danny O'Reilly, he had been angry at an acquaintance of his girlfriend's, who had been urging her to end her codependent relationship. The friend happened to be a cyclist, and Albertson had developed a theory that, when he saw O'Reilly on his bike, he might have transferred his rage to Danny and hit him intentionally.

Edwards conveyed this to Patty, who, as she thought it over, doubted that the drunken Albertson would have been able to steer his truck that well. She decided she still wanted to go through with the meeting, which took place in September 2006 at a state prison near Sacramento. Accompanied by her sister Mary, O'Reilly sat across a table from Albertson and told him how much hatred she'd felt toward him; she recounted her last conversation with Danny, and she recalled the nightmare, when he didn't come home that night, of seeing a sheriff's deputy approach their house. She described the reactions of her daughters when she told them that their father was dead, showed Albertson an album of family photos, and enumerated all the things she and her children had to do without a father or husband. Still, she said, it had taken courage for Albertson to admit he might have hit Danny on purpose. "Maybe this is a chance to redeem yourself," she said.

Albertson said he'd been driven to addiction by a history of abuse. He revealed that after hitting Danny, crashing his truck, and seeing the Highway Patrol pull up, he'd pretended to reach for a gun because he wanted to be put out of his misery. He admitted, however, that nobody could repair the damage from what he had lived through. "I just have to feel it," he said.

O'Reilly told Albertson not to feel sorry for himself—that would constitute "going backward." She urged him to stay active in Alcoholics Anonymous and she gave him a bracelet that Siobhan, now ten, had made for him. As part of the restorative justice program, Albertson is required to write to O'Reilly every three months, and in their correspondence, Patty later suggested to him that, in addition to staying sober, Albertson get help for the emotional trauma that had caused him to start drinking.

A prison guard told Edwards that, until Albertson started corresponding with O'Reilly, he'd never heard an inmate admit blame for a crime. " 'Satisfying' isn't really the right word to describe it," O'Reilly says of her resulting feelings. "Mike also thanked me for saving his life, which came as a bit of a shock—I can't say I was entirely pleased to be thanked for saving the man who killed my husband. But I'm glad this process forced him to deal with issues he had chosen not to deal with."

In the course of confronting Albertson, Patty had researched the word "vengeance," which, she learned, had less to do with revenge than it did with justice. "My revenge was for him to face me across a table and get the full impact of what he did," she says. "I don't think 'an eye for an eye' was ever meant to be taken literally, but in that sense I got a life for a life. Mike is a different man now. And I've let go of the poisonous anger I felt, which has helped me and my daughters heal."

A few months after O'Reilly resolved to forgive Albertson, another ballet school came up for sale in Sonoma. Its director was retiring, and Patty decided to buy it with life insurance from Danny. She now works three miles from home, teaching children the art and discipline that first brought her and her husband together.

•   •   •

At 10 A.M. on February 20, 2007, Stage 2 of the Tour of California rolled out of Santa Rosa into Sonoma Valley. Within half an hour of the start, the race crossed Highway 12 and began climbing Trinity Road, the day's first test in the King of the Mountains competition. Partway up the three-mile, 1,320-foot climb, the riders passed a driveway where a group of friends and families had gathered, waving and clanging cowbells as the peloton passed by. In the throng, wearing a red-and-white bicycle jersey and sitting in a wheelchair, was Ross Dillon.

In the five years since he was run into by Cathie Hamer, Dillon—thanks to his family, a nationwide support network and hundreds of thousands of dollars in donations—had defied his doctors' predictions. Unresponsive and incapable of movement when he came home in June 2003 (he was still being fed through a tube), Dillon started moving his right leg the following December and swallowing pureed food in March; by July '04 he was nodding or shaking his head in response to questions, and six months later he started feeding himself with a spoon. In July '05, after seeming to mouth words silently for some time, he flabbergasted his family and live-in caregiver, Jeremiah Temo, by saying, "I love my parents and they love me" and "I don't want to die."

"My theory is that he'd been practicing," his mother Betsy says. "I've always thought there was more going on cognitively than Ross could show us."

A week before the Tour of California came by, Dillon had stood up under his own power, steadied by Temo's hand on his arm. "His therapists all say they don't see a ceiling yet," Betsy reports.

Dillon's upper body is amazingly strong—the kind of musculature you would expect from a mature athlete in his prime. Still, it's hard to watch his sixty-year-old parents struggle to reteach their thirty-year-old son how to walk and talk. Although

Dillon's spinal cord was undamaged, his brain injuries were severe, and from the waist up, his motor and cognitive skills lag far behind those of Jill Mason. Enormous effort is required for him to ambulate and communicate, and even though his stubbornness seems intact, his attention continually wanders (to be recaptured, most typically, by gummy bears, which he reliably grabs and chews).

"We had Ross as we knew him up to that instant [when Hamer hit him], and then we had another Ross," his father Rusty says philosophically. "He's still distinctly Ross, but one whose life is extremely different. At one point it was hard to believe he would be able to do one-tenth of what he does now. So we have to live according to our faith, trusting that his story isn't over yet."

Betsy offers an apt metaphor for how they cope. "We just put one foot in front of the other," she says. "My hope is that Ross will be independent—able to take care of himself, with supervision—by the time I'm gone. Usually I can be totally focused on doing what's best for him. Periodically I'm overwhelmed with grief; it takes me about an hour or so, and then I'm back in the saddle. It has to do with the juxtaposition of where he is now and where he was before—he was so vigorous and excited about getting married and going to law school. He had moved from being our child to being our friend. And he wanted to be a dad so bad."

Cathie Hamer became a mother earlier this year. She was never charged with any driving infraction, fined, ordered to perform community service, or even required to attend traffic school for running into Dillon. She and her husband subsequently moved to the Mendocino County coast, though Hamer still has a clothing shop in Sebastopol; at one point, the Dillons received a telephone message from her mother offering to donate an unspecified "portion of profits" from a sale at the store, but Rusty and Betsy declined, saying they didn t want a commercial venture to use Ross's name as advertising.

Today Betsy Dillon believes that anyone responsible for hitting another person should lose his or her license for six months and be required to work in an injury clinic or rehab facility. "I don't think [Hamer] should have gone to jail," Betsy allows, "but I think she should be doing something more than feeling bad."

"At the very least, she should be doing community service," says Christine Culver. "I have no doubt she was distraught, but people have to be responsible for their behavior. Her actions need to keep this from happening to somebody else."

It would be nice to be able to end this story by describing how much safer the Santa Rosa area is now for cyclists—how the deaths of Liu and O'Reilly, and the shattered lives of Dillon and Mason, shocked Sonoma County into realizing that, as Culver says, bicycles belong on the road and people need to be in control of their cars. In fact, last year the Santa Rosa Police Department doubled the number of speeding tickets it issued in 2005, helping reduce vehicle collisions by 10 percent and total traffic fatalities from twelve to two. But it's also true that, a year after Liu and O'Reilly were killed, another drunk driver (seventy-two-year-old Joseph Lynchard) slaughtered another innocent cyclist (forty-three-year-old Kathryn Black) on Mark West Springs Road and, the year after that, an off-duty nurse on a bike (forty-seven-year-old Kathy Hiebel) was slain by a truck driver (forty-six-year-old Reymundo Hernandez) who turned in front of her at an intersection in Santa Rosa. Lynchard, who had six previous DUI arrests, will probably die in jail—he pleaded guilty to murder in a so-called Watson decision, named for the Supreme Court finding that ignoring the risks inherent in drunk driving implies malicious intent. As for Hernandez, a police investigation found that he appeared to be at fault for killing Hiebel, though no charges have yet been filed against him.

"Is it safer?" Culver asks, pondering the inevitable question. "I don't know. It's better known now that hitting a cyclist is a serious offense, but we still have a long way to go. It's a cultural shift that needs to take place—a change in how we are in our cars. A change in TV commercials that are always pushing speed and horsepower, a change in the mind-set that racing around in a car is cool, and a change in society's understanding so we acknowledge the fact that being inattentive at the wheel of a car is criminal."

Maybe most basically, Culver believes, we need to change the language we use to describe the consequences. "Call them crashes," she says. "Not accidents."

In this tenderly drawn account, David Lipsky delicately recreates a brilliant writer's personal struggles, which drove him into depression and, ultimately, suicide.

David Lipsky

The Lost Years
and Last Days
of David Foster
Wallace

He was six-feet-two, and on a good day he weighed 200 pounds. He wore granny glasses with a head scarf, points knotted at the back, a look that was both pirate-like and housewife-ish. He always wore his hair long. He had dark eyes, soft voice, caveman chin, a lovely, peak-lipped mouth that was his best feature. He walked with an ex-athlete's saunter, a roll from the heels, as if anything physical was a pleasure.

David Foster Wallace worked surprising turns on nearly everything: novels, journalism, vacation. His life was an information hunt, collecting hows and whys. "I received 500,000 discrete bits of information today," he once said, "of which maybe 25 are important. My job is to make some sense of it." He wanted to write "stuff about what it feels like to live. Instead of being a relief from what it feels like to live." Readers curled up in the nooks and clearings of his style: his comedy, his brilliance, his humaneness.

His life was a map that ends at the wrong destination. Wallace was an A student through high school, he played football, he played tennis, he wrote a philosophy thesis and a novel before he graduated from Amherst, he went to writing school, published the novel, made a city of squalling, bruising, kneecapping editors and writers fall moony-eyed in love with him. He published a thousand-page novel, received the only award you get in the nation for being a genius, wrote essays providing the best feel anywhere of what it means to be alive in the contemporary world, accepted a special chair at California's Pomona College to teach writing, married, published another book and, last month, hanged himself at age forty-six.

"The one thing that really should be said about David Foster Wallace is that this was a once-in-a-century talent," says his friend and former editor Colin Harrison. "We may never see a guy like this again in our lifetimes—that I will shout out. He was like a comet flying by at ground level."

His 1996 novel, *Infinite Jest*, was Bible-size and spawned books of interpretation and commentary, like *Understanding David Foster Wallace*—a book his friends might have tried to write and would have lined up to buy. He was clinically depressed for decades, information he limited to family and his closest friends. "I don't think that he ever lost the feeling that there was something shameful about this," his father says. "His instinct was to hide it."

After he died on September 12, readers crowded the Web with tributes to his generosity, his intelligence. "But he wasn't Saint Dave," says Jonathan Franzen, Wallace's best friend and the author of *The Corrections*. "This is the paradox of Dave: The closer you get, the darker the picture, but the more genuinely lovable he was. It was only when you knew him better that you had a true appreciation of what a heroic struggle it was for him not merely to get along in the world, but to produce wonderful writing."

.   .   .

David grew up in Champaign, Illinois. His father, Jim, taught philosophy at the University of Illinois. His mother, Sally, taught English at a local community college. It was an academic household—poised, considerate—language games in the car, the rooms tidy, the bookcase the hero. "I have these weird early memories," Wallace told me during a series of interviews in 1996.

"I remember my parents reading *Ulysses* out loud to each other in bed, holding hands and both lovin' something really fiercely." Sally hated to get angry—it took her days to recover from a shout. So the family developed a sort of interoffice conflict mail. When his mother had something stern to say, she'd write it up in a letter. When David wanted something badly—raised allowance, more liberal bedtime—he'd slide a letter under his parents' door.

David was one of those eerie, perfect combinations of two parents' skills. The titles of his father's books—*Ethical Norms, Particular Cases*—have the sound of Wallace short-story titles. The tone of his mother's speaking voice contains echoes of Wallace's writing voice: Her textbook, *Practically Painless English*, sounds like a Wallace joke. She uses phrases like "perishing hot" for very hot, "snoof" for talking in your sleep, "heave your skeleton" for go to bed. "David and I both owe a huge debt to my mother," says his sister, Amy, two years younger. "She has a way of talking that I've never heard anywhere else."

David was, from an early age, "very fragile," as he put it. He loved TV, and would get incredibly excited watching a program like *Batman* or *The Wild Wild West*. (His parents rationed the "rough" shows. One per week.) David could memorize whole shows of dialogue and predict, like a kind of plot weatherman, when the story was going to turn, where characters would end up. No one saw or treated him as a genius, but at age fourteen, when he asked what his father did, Jim sat David down and walked him through a Socratic dialogue. "I was astonished by how sophisticated his understanding was," Jim says. "At that point, I figured out that he really, really was extraordinarily bright."

David was a big-built kid; he played football—quarterback—until he was twelve or thirteen, and would always speak like an athlete, the disappearing G's, "wudn't," "dudn't" and "idn't" and "sumpin'." "The big thing I was when I was little was a really serious jock," Wallace told me. "I mean, I had no artistic ambition. I played citywide football. And I was really good. Then I got to junior high, and there were two guys in the city who were better quarterbacks than me. And people started hitting each other a lot harder, and I discovered that I didn't really love to hit people. That was a huge disappointment." After his first day of football practice at Urbana High School, he came home and chucked it. He offered two explanations to his parents: They expected him to practice every day, and the coaches did too much cursing.

He had also picked up a racket. "I discovered tennis on my own," Wallace said, "taking public-park lessons. For five years, I was seriously gonna be a pro tennis player. I didn't look that good, but I was almost impossible to beat. I know that sounds arrogant. It's true." On court, he was a bit of a hustler: Before a match, he'd tell his opponent, "Thank you for being here, but you're just going to cream me."

By the time he was fourteen, he felt he could have made nationals. "Really be in the junior show. But just at the point it became important to me, I began to choke. The more scared you get, the worse you play." Plus it was the seventies—Pink Floyd, bongs. "I started to smoke a lot of pot when I was fifteen or sixteen, and it's hard to train." He laughed. "You don't have that much energy."

It was around this time that the Wallaces noticed something strange about David. He would voice surprising requests, like wanting to paint his bedroom black. He was constantly angry at his sister. When he was sixteen, he refused to go to her birthday party. "Why would I want to celebrate her birthday?" he told his parents.

"David began to have anxiety attacks in high school," his father recalls. "I noticed the symptoms, but I was just so unsophisticated about these matters. The depression seemed to take the form of an evil spirit that just haunted David." Sally came to call it the "black hole with teeth." David withdrew. "He spent a lot of time throwing up junior year," his sister remembers. One wall of his bedroom was lined with cork, for magazine photos of tennis stars. David pinned an article about Kafka to the wall, with the headline THE DISEASE WAS LIFE ITSELF.

"I hated seeing those words," his sister tells me, and starts to cry. "They seemed to sum up his existence. We couldn't understand why he was acting the way he was, and so of course my parents were exasperated, lovingly exasperated."

David graduated high school with perfect grades. Whatever his personal hurricane was, it had scattered trees and moved on. He decided to go to Amherst, which is where his father had gone, too. His parents told him he would enjoy the Berkshire autumn. Instead, he missed home—the farms and flat horizons, roads stretching contentedly nowhere. "It's fall," David wrote back. "The mountains are pretty, but the landscape isn't beautiful the way Illinois is."

.   .   .

Wallace had lugged his bags into Amherst the fall of 1980— Reagan coming in, the seventies capsized, preppies everywhere. He brought a suit to campus. "It was kind of a Sears suit, with this Scotch-plaid tie," says his college roommate and close friend Mark Costello, who went on to become a successful novelist himself. "Guys who went to Amherst, who came from five prep schools, they always dress a notch down. No one's bringing a suit. That was just the Wallace sense that going East is a big deal, and you have to not embarrass us. My first impression was that he was really very out of step."

Costello came from working-class Massachusetts, seven kids, Irish Catholic household. He and Wallace connected. "Neither of us fit into the Gatsby-ite mold," Costello says. At Amherst David perfected the style he would wear for the rest of his life: turtleneck, hoodie, big basketball shoes. The look of parking-lot kids who in Illinois were called Dirt Bombs. "A slightly tough, slightly waste-product-y, tennis-playing persona," Costello says.

Wallace was also amazingly fast and good company, even just on a walk across campus. "I'd always wanted to be an impressionist," Wallace said, "but I just didn't have an agile enough vocal and facial register to do it." Crossing a green, it was The Dave Show. He would recount how people walked, talked, held their heads, pictured their lives. "Just very connected to people," Costello recalls. "Dave had this ability to be inside someone else's skin."

Observing people from afar, of course, can be a way of avoiding them up close. "I was a complete just total banzai weenie studier in college," Wallace recalled. "I was really just scared of people. For instance, I would brave the TV pit—the central TV room—to watch *Hill Street Blues*, 'cause that was a really important show to me."

One afternoon, April of sophomore year, Costello came back to the dorm they shared and found Wallace seated in his chair. Desk clean, bags packed, even his typewriter, which weighed as much as the clothes put together.

"Dave, what's going on?" Costello asked.

"I'm sorry, I'm so sorry," Wallace said. "I know I'm really screwing you."

He was pulling out of college. Costello drove him to the airport. "He wasn't able to talk about it," Costello recalls. "He was crying, he was mortified. Panicky. He couldn't control his thoughts. It was mental incontinence, the equivalent of wetting his pants."

"I wasn't very happy there," Wallace told me later. "I felt kind of inadequate. There was a lot of stuff I wanted to read that wasn't part of any class. And Mom and Dad were just totally cool."

Wallace went home to hospitalization, explanations to his parents, a job. For a while, he drove a school bus. "Here he was, a guy who was really shaky, kind of Holden Caulfield, driving a school bus through lightning storms," Costello recalls. "He wrote me a letter all outraged, about the poor screening procedures for school-bus drivers in central Illinois."

Wallace would visit his dad's philosophy classes. "The classes would turn into a dialogue between David and me," his father remembers. "The students would just sit looking around, 'Who is this guy?'" Wallace devoured novels—"pretty much everything I've read was read during that year." He also told his parents how he'd felt at school. "He would talk about just being very sad, and lonely," Sally says. "It didn't have anything to do with being loved. He just was very lonely inside himself."

· · ·

He returned to Amherst in the fall, to room with Costello, shaky but hardened. "Certain things had been destroyed in his head," Costello says. "In the first half of his Amherst career, he was trying to be a regular person. He was on the debate team, the sort of guy who knows he's going to be a success." Wallace had talked about going into politics; Costello recalls him joking, "No one is going to vote for somebody who's been in a nuthouse." Having his life fall apart narrowed his sense of what his options were—and the possibilities that were left became more real to him. In a letter to Costello, he wrote, "I want to write books that people will read 100 years from now."

Back at school junior year, he never talked much about his breakdown. "It was embarrassing and personal," Costello says. "A zone of no jokes." Wallace regarded it as a failure, something he should have been able to control. He routinized his life. He'd be the first tray at the dining hall for supper, he'd eat, drink coffee dipped with tea bags, library study till eleven, head back to the room, turn on *Hawaii Five-O*, then a midnight gulp from a scotch bottle. When he couldn't turn his mind off, he'd say, "You know what? I think this is a two-shot night," slam another and sleep.

In 1984, Costello left for Yale Law School; Wallace was alone senior year. He double-majored—English and philosophy, which meant two big writing projects. In philosophy, he took on modal logic. "It looked really hard, and I was really scared about it," he said. "So I thought I'd do this kind of jaunty, hundred-page novel." He wrote it in five months, and it clocked in at 700 pages. He called it *The Broom of the System*.

Wallace published stories in the Amherst literary magazine. One was about depression and a tricyclic anti-anxiety medication he had been on for two months. The medication "made me feel like I was stoned and in hell," he told me. The story dealt with the in-hell parts:

> You are the sickness yourself. . . . You realize all this . . . when you look at the black hole and it's wearing your face. That's when the Bad Thing just absolutely eats you up, or rather when you just eat yourself up. When you kill yourself. All this business about people committing suicide when they're "severely depressed;" we say, "Holy cow, we must do something to stop them from killing themselves!" That's wrong. Because all these people have, you see, by this time already killed themselves, where it really counts. . . . When they "commit suicide," they're just being orderly.

It wasn't just writing the novel that made Wallace realize his future would lie in fiction. He also helped out friends by writing their papers. In a comic book, this would be his origin story, the part where he's bombarded with gamma rays, bitten by the spider. "I remember realizing at the time, 'Man, I'm really good at this. I'm a weird kind of forger. I can sound kind of like anybody.'"

Grad school was next. Philosophy would be an obvious choice. "My dad would have limbs removed without anesthetic before ever pushing his kids about anything," Wallace said. "But

I knew I was gonna have to go to grad school. I applied to these English programs instead, and I didn't tell anybody. Writing *The Broom of the System*, I felt like I was using 97 percent of me, whereas philosophy was using 50 percent."

After Amherst, Wallace went to the University of Arizona for an MFA. It was where he picked up the bandanna: "I started wearing them in Tucson because it was a hundred degrees all the time, and I would perspire so much I would drip on the page." The woman he was dating thought the bandanna was a wise move. "She was like a sixties lady, a Sufi Muslim. She said there were various chakras, and one of the big ones she called the spout hole, at the very top of your cranium. Then I began thinking about the phrase 'Keeping your head together.' It makes me feel kind of creepy that people view it as a trademark or something— it's more a recognition of a weakness, which is that I'm just kind of worried that my head's gonna explode."

Arizona was a strange experience: the first classrooms where people weren't happy to see him. He wanted to write the way he wanted to write—funny and overstuffed and nonlinear and strange. The teachers were all "hardass realists." That was the first problem. Problem two was Wallace. "I think I was kind of a prick," he said. "I was just unteachable. I had that look—'If there were any justice, I'd be teaching this class'—that makes you want to slap a student." One of his stories, "Here and There," went on to win a 1989 O. Henry Prize after it was published in a literary magazine. When he turned it in to his professor, he received a chilly note back: "I hope this isn't representative of the work you're hoping to do for us. We'd hate to lose you."

"What I hated was how disingenuous it was," Wallace recalled. "'We'd hate to lose you.' You know, if you're gonna threaten, say that."

Wallace sent his thesis project out to agents. He got a lot of letters back: "Best of luck in your janitorial career." Bonnie Nadell was twenty-five, working a first job at San Francisco's

Frederick Hill Agency. She opened a letter from Wallace, read a chapter from his book. "I loved it so much," Nadell says. It turned out there was a writer named David Rains Wallace. Hill and Nadell agreed that David should insert his mother's maiden name, which is how he became David Foster Wallace. She remained his agent for the rest of his life. "I have this thing, the nearest Jewish mother, I will simply put my arms around her skirt and just attach myself," Wallace said. "I don't know what it means. Maybe sort of WASP deprivation."

Viking won the auction for the novel, "with something like a handful of trading stamps." Word spread; professors turned nice. "I went from borderline ready-to-get-kicked-out to all these tight-smiled guys being, 'Glad to see you, we're proud of you, you'll have to come over for dinner.' It was so delicious: I felt kind of embarrassed for them, they didn't even have integrity about their hatred."

Wallace went to New York to meet his editor, Gerry Howard, wearing a U2 T-shirt. "He seemed like a very young twenty-four," Howard says. The shirt impressed him. "U2 wasn't really huge then. And there's a hypersincerity to U2, which I think David was in tune with—or that he really wanted to be sincere, even though his brain kept turning him in the direction of the ironic." Wallace kept calling Howard—who was only thirty-six—"Mr. Howard," never "Gerry." It would become his business style: a kind of mock formality. People often suspected it was a put-on. What it was was Midwestern politeness, the burnout in the parking lot still nodding "sir" to the vice principal. "There was kind of this hum of superintelligence behind the 'aw, shucks' manner," Howard recalls.

The Broom of the System was published in January of 1987, Wallace's second and last year at Arizona. The title referred to something his mother's grandmother used to say, as in, "Here, Sally, have an apple, it's the broom of the system." "I wasn't aware David had picked up on that," his mother says. "I was thrilled that a family expression became the title of his book."

The novel hit. "Everything you could hope for," Howard says. "Critics praised it, it sold quite well, and David was off to the races."

His first brush with fame was a kind of gateway experience. Wallace would open *The Wall Street Journal*, see his face transmuted into a dot-cartoon. "Some article like 'Hotshot's Weird New Novel,'" he said. "I'd feel really good, really cool, for exactly ten seconds. Probably not unlike a crack high, you know? I was living an incredibly American life: 'Boy, if I could just achieve X, Y and Z, everything would be OK.'" Howard bought Wallace's second book, *Girl with Curious Hair*, a collection of the stories he was finishing up at Arizona. But something in Wallace worried him. "I have never encountered a mind like David's," he says. "It functioned at such an amazingly high level, he clearly lived in a hyperalert state. But on the other hand, I felt that David's emotional life lagged far behind his mental life. And I think he could get lost in the gap between the two."

Wallace was already drifting into the gap. He won a Whiting Writers' Award—stood on a stage with Eudora Welty—graduated Arizona, went to an artists' colony, met famous writers, knew the famous writers were seeing his name in more magazines ("absolutely exhilarating and really scary at the same time"), finished the stories. And then he was out of ideas. He tried to write in a cabin in Tucson for a while, then returned home to write—Mom and Dad doing the grocery shopping. He accepted a one-year slot teaching philosophy at Amherst, which was strange: sophomores he had known were now his students. In the acknowledgments for the book he was completing, he thanks "The Mr. and Mrs. Wallace Fund for Aimless Children."

He was balled up, tied up. "I started hating everything I did," he said. "Worse than stuff I'd done in college. Hopelessly confused, unbelievably bad. I was really in a panic, I didn't think I was going to be able to write anymore. And I got this idea: I'd flourished in an academic environment—my first two books had sort of been written under professors." He applied to graduate programs in philosophy, thinking he could write fiction in his spare time. Harvard offered a full scholarship. The last thing he needed to reproduce his college years was to reactivate Mark Costello.

"So he comes up with this whole cockamamie plan," Costello recalls. "He says, 'OK, you're going to go back to Boston, practice law, and I'm going to go to Harvard. We'll live together—it'll be just like the house we had at Amherst.' It all ended up being a train wreck."

They found an apartment in Somerville. Student ghetto: rickety buildings, outdoor staircases. Costello would come home with his briefcase, click up the back stairs, David would call out, "Hi, honey, how was your day?" But Wallace wasn't writing fiction. He had thought course work would be a sideline; but professors expected actual work.

Not writing was the kind of symptom that presents a problem of its own. "He could get himself into places where he was pretty helpless," Costello says. "Basically it was the same symptoms all along: this incredible sense of inadequacy, panic. He once said to me that he wanted to write to shut up the babble in his head. He said when you're writing well, you establish a voice in your head, and it shuts up the other voices. The ones that are saying, 'You're not good enough, you're a fraud.' "

"Harvard was just unbelievably bleak," Wallace said. It became a substance marathon: drinking, parties, drugs. "I didn't want to feel it," he said. "It was the only time in my life that I'd gone to bars, picked up women I didn't know." Then for weeks, he would quit drinking, start mornings with a ten-mile run. "You know, this kind of very American sports training—I will fix this by taking radical action." Schwarzenegger voice: "If there's a problem, I will train myself out of it. I will work harder."

Various delays were holding up the publication of his short-story collection *Girl with Curious Hair*. He started to feel spooked. "I'm this genius writer," he remembered. "Everything I do's gotta be ingenious, blah, blah, blah, blah." The five-year clock was ticking again. He'd played football for five years. Then he'd played high-level tennis for five years. Now he'd been writing for five years. "What I saw was, 'Jesus, it's the same thing all over again.' I'd started late, showed tremendous promise—and the minute I felt the implications of that promise, it caved in. Because see, by this time, my ego's all invested in the writing. It's the only thing I've gotten food pellets from the universe for. So I feel trapped: 'Uh-oh, my five years is up, I've gotta move on.' But I didn't want to move on."

Costello watched while Wallace slipped into a depressive crisis. "He was hanging out with women who were pretty heavily into drugs—that was kind of alluring to Dave—skanking around Somerville, drinking himself blotto."

It was the worst period Wallace had ever gone through. "It may have been what in the old days was called a spiritual crisis," he said. "It was just feeling as though every axiom of your life turned out to be false. And there was nothing, and you were nothing—it was all a delusion. But you were better than every-one else because you saw that it was a delusion, and yet you were worse because you couldn't function."

By November, the anxieties had become locked and fixed. "I got really worried I was going to kill myself. And I knew, that if anybody was fated to fuck up a suicide attempt, it was me." He walked across campus to Health Services and told a psychiatrist, "Look, there's this issue. I don't feel real safe."

"It was a big deal for me, because I was so embarrassed," Wallace said. "But it was the first time I ever treated myself like I was worth something."

By making his announcement, Wallace had activated a protocol: Police were notified, he had to withdraw from school. He was sent to McLean, which, as psychiatric hospitals go, is pedigreed: Robert Lowell, Sylvia Plath, Anne Sexton all put in residences there; it's the setting for the memoir *Girl, Interrupted.* Wallace spent his first day on suicide watch. Locked ward, pink room, no furniture, drain in the floor, observation slot in the door. "When that happens to you," David said, smiling, "you get unprecedentedly willing to examine other alternatives for how to live."

Wallace spent eight days in McLean. He was diagnosed as a clinical depressive and was prescribed a drug, called Nardil, developed in the 1950s. He would have to take it from then on. "We had a brief, maybe three-minute audience with the psychopharmacologist," his mother says. Wallace would have to quit drinking, and there was a long list of foods—certain cheeses, pickles, cured meats—he would have to stay away from.

He started to clean up. He found a way to get sober, worked very hard at it, and wouldn't drink for the rest of his life. *Girl with Curious Hair* finally appeared in 1989. Wallace gave a reading in Cambridge; thirteen people showed up, including a schizophrenic woman who shrieked all the way through his performance. "The book's coming out seemed like a kind of shrill, jagged laugh from the universe, this thing sort of lingering behind me like a really nasty fart."

What followed was a phased, deliberate return to the world. He worked as a security guard, morning shift, at Lotus Software. Polyester uniform, service baton, walking the corridors. "I liked it because I didn't have to think," he said. "Then I quit for the incredibly brave reason that I got tired of getting up so early in the morning."

Next, he worked at a health club in Auburndale, Massachusetts. "Very chichi," he said. "They called me something other than a towel boy, but I was in effect a towel boy. I'm sitting there, and who should walk in to get their towel but Michael Ryan. Now, Michael Ryan had received a Whiting Writers' Award the same year I had. So I see this guy that I'd been up on the fucking rostrum with, having Eudora Welty give us this prize. It's two years later—it's the only time I've literally dived under something. He came in, and I pretended not very subtly to slip, and lay facedown, and didn't respond. I left that day, and I didn't go back."

He wrote Bonnie Nadell a letter; he was done with writing. That wasn't exactly her first concern. "I was worried he wasn't going to survive," she says. He filled in Howard, too. "I contemplated the circumstance that the best young writer in America was handing out towels in a health club," Howard says. "How fucking sad."

●   ●   ●

Wallace met Jonathan Franzen in the most natural way for an author: as a fan. He sent Franzen a nice letter about his first novel, *The Twenty-seventh City*. Franzen wrote back, they arranged to meet in Cambridge. "He just flaked," Franzen recalls. "He didn't show up. That was a fairly substance-filled period of his life."

By April of 1992, both were ready for a change. They loaded Franzen's car and headed for Syracuse to scout apartments. Franzen needed "somewhere to relocate with my wife where we could both afford to live and not have anyone tell us how screwed up our marriage was." Wallace's need was simpler: cheap space, for writing. He had been researching for months, haunting rehab facilities and halfway houses, taking quiet note of voices and stories, people who had fallen into the gaps like him. "I got very assertive research- and finagle-wise," he said. "I spent hundreds of hours at three halfway houses. It turned out you could just sit in the living room—nobody is as gregarious as somebody who has recently stopped using drugs."

He and Franzen talked a lot about what writing should be for. "We had this feeling that fiction ought to be good for something," Franzen says. "Basically, we decided it was to combat loneliness." They would talk about lots of Wallace's ideas, which could abruptly sharpen into self-criticism. "I remember this being a frequent topic of conversation," Franzen says, "his notion of not having an authentic self. Of being just quick enough to construct a pleasing self for whomever he was talking to. I see now he wasn't just being funny—there was something genuinely compromised in David. At the time I thought, 'Wow, he's even more self-conscious than I am.'"

Wallace spent a year writing in Syracuse. "I lived in an apartment that was seriously the size of the foyer of an average house. I really liked it. There were so many books, you couldn't move around. When I'd want to write, I'd have to put all the stuff from the desk on the bed, and when I'd want to sleep, I would have to put all the stuff on the desk."

Wallace worked longhand, pages piling up. "You look at the clock and seven hours have passed and your hand is cramped," Wallace said. He'd have pens he considered hot—cheap Bic ballpoints, like batters have bats that are hot. A pen that was hot he called the orgasm pen.

In the summer of 1993, he took an academic job fifty miles from his parents, at Illinois State University at Normal. The book was three-quarters done. Based on the first unruly stack of pages, Nadell had been able to sell it to Little, Brown. He had put his whole life into it—tennis, and depression, and stoner afternoons, and the precipice of rehab, and all the hours spent with Amy watching TV. The plot motor is a movie called *Infinite Jest*, so soothing and perfect it's impossible to switch off: You watch until you sink into your chair, spill your bladder, starve, die. "If the book's about anything," he said, "it's about the question of why am I watching so much shit? It's not about the shit. It's about me: Why am I doing it? The original title was *A Failed*

Entertainment, and the book is structured as an entertainment that doesn't work"—characters developing and scattering, chapters disordered—"because what entertainment ultimately leads to is 'Infinite Jest,' that's the star it's steering by."

Wallace held classes in his house, students nudging aside books like *Compendium of Drug Therapy* and *The Emergence of the French Art Film,* making jokes about Mount Manuscript, David's pile of novel. He had finished and collected the three years of drafts, and finally sat down and typed the whole thing. Wallace didn't really type; he input the giant thing twice, with one finger. "But a really fast finger."

It came to almost 1,700 pages. "I was just terrified how long it would end up being," he said. Wallace told his editor it would be a good beach book, in the sense that people could use it for shade.

· · ·

It can take a year to edit a book, re-edit it, print it, publicize it, ship it, the writer all the time checking his watch. In the meantime, Wallace turned to nonfiction. Two pieces, published in *Harper's,* would become some of the most famous pieces of journalism of the past decade and a half.

Colin Harrison, Wallace's editor at *Harper's,* had the idea to outfit him with a notebook and push him into perfectly American places—the Illinois State Fair, a Caribbean cruise. It would soak up the side of Wallace that was always on, always measuring himself. "There would be Dave the mimic, Dave the people-watcher," Costello says. "Asking him to actually report could get stressful and weird and complicated. Colin had this stroke of genius about what to do with David. It was a much simpler solution than anyone ever thought."

In the pieces, Wallace invented a style writers have plundered for a decade. The unedited camera, the feed before the director in the van starts making choices and cuts. The voice was humane, a big, kind brain tripping over its own lumps. "The *Harper's* pieces were me peeling back my skull," Wallace said. "You know, welcome to my mind for twenty pages, see through my eyes, here's pretty much all the French curls and crazy circles. The trick was to have it be honest but also interesting—because most of our thoughts aren't all that interesting. To be honest with a motive." He laughed. "There's a certain persona created, that's a little stupider and schmuckier than I am."

The cruise-ship piece ran in January 1996, a month before David's novel was published. People photocopied it, faxed it to each other, read it over the phone. When people tell you they're fans of David Foster Wallace, what they're often telling you is that they've read the cruise-ship piece; Wallace would make it the title essay in his first collection of journalism, *A Supposedly Fun Thing I'll Never Do Again*. In a way, the difference between the fiction and the nonfiction reads as the difference between Wallace's social self and his private self. The essays were endlessly charming, they were the best friend you'd ever have, spotting everything, whispering jokes, sweeping you past what was irritating or boring or awful in humane style. Wallace's fiction, especially after *Infinite Jest*, would turn chilly, dark, abstract. You could imagine the author of the fiction sinking into a depression. The nonfiction writer was an impervious sun.

The novel came out in February of 1996. In *New York Magazine*, Walter Kirn wrote, "The competition has been obliterated. It's as though Paul Bunyan had joined the NFL, or Wittgenstein had gone on *Jeopardy!* The novel is that colossally disruptive. And that spectacularly good." He was in *Newsweek*, *Time*, Hollywood people appeared at his readings, women batted their eyelashes, men in the back rows scowled, envied. A FedEx guy rang his bell, watched David sign for delivery, asked, "How's it feel to be famous?"

At the end of his book tour, I spent a week with David. He talked about the "greasy thrill of fame" and what it might mean to his writing. "When I was twenty-five, I would've given a couple of digits off my non-use hand for this," he said. "I feel good, because I wanna be doing this for forty more years, you know? So I've got to find some way to enjoy this that doesn't involve getting eaten by it."

He was astonishingly good, quick company, making you feel both wide awake and as if your shoes had been tied together. He'd say things like, "There's good self-consciousness, and then there's toxic, paralyzing, raped-by-psychic-Bedouins self-consciousness." He talked about a kind of shyness that turned social life impossibly complicated. "I think being shy basically means being self-absorbed to the point that it makes it difficult to be around other people. For instance, if I'm hanging out with you, I can't even tell whether I like you or not because I'm too worried about whether you like me."

He said one interviewer had devoted tons of energy to the genius question. "That was his whole thing, 'Are you normal?' 'Are you normal?' I think one of the true ways I've gotten smarter is that I've realized that there are ways other people are a lot smarter than me. My biggest asset as a writer is that I'm pretty much like everybody else. The parts of me that used to think I was different or smarter or whatever almost made me die."

•   •   •

It had been difficult, during the summer, to watch his sister get married. "I'm almost thirty-five. I would like to get married and have kids. I haven't even started to work that shit out yet. I've come close a few times, but I tend to be interested in women that I turn out to not get along very well with. I have friends who say this is something that would be worth looking into with someone that you pay."

Wallace was always dating somebody. "There were a lot of relationships," Amy says. He dated in his imaginative life too: When I visited him, one wall was taped with a giant Alanis Morissette poster. "The Alanis Morissette obsession followed the Melanie Griffith obsession—a six-year obsession," he said. "It was preceded by something that I will tell you I got teased a lot for, which was a terrible Margaret Thatcher obsession. All through college: posters of Margaret Thatcher, and ruminations on Margaret Thatcher. Having her really enjoy something I said, leaning forward and covering my hand with hers."

He tended to date high-strung women—another symptom of his shyness. "Say what you want about them, psychotics tend to make the first move." Owning dogs was less complicated: "You don't get the feeling you're hurting their feelings all the time."

His romantic anxieties were full-spectrum, every bit of the mechanics individually examined. He told me a joke:

What does a writer say after sex?

Was it as good for me as it was for you?

"There is, in writing, a certain blend of sincerity and manipulation, of trying always to gauge what the particular effect of something is gonna be," he said. "It's a very precious asset that really needs to be turned off sometimes. My guess is that writers probably make fun, skilled, satisfactory, and seemingly considerate partners for other people. But that the experience for them is often rather lonely."

One night Wallace met the writer Elizabeth Wurtzel, whose depression memoir, *Prozac Nation*, had recently been published. She thought he looked scruffy—jeans and the bandanna—and very smart. Another night, Wallace walked her home from a restaurant, sat with her in her lobby, spent some time trying to talk his way upstairs. It charmed Wurtzel: "You know, he might have had this enormous brain, but at the end of the day, he still was a guy."

Wallace and Wurtzel didn't really talk about the personal experience they had in common—depression, a substance history, consultations at McLean—but about their profession, about what to do with fame. Wallace, again, had set impossible standards for himself. "It really disturbed him, the possibility that success could taint you," she recalls. "He was very interested in purity, in the idea of authenticity—the way some people are into the idea of being cool. He had keeping it real down to a science."

When Wallace wrote her, he was still curling through the same topic. "I go through a loop in which I notice all the ways I am self-centered and careerist and not true to standards and values that transcend my own petty interests, and feel like I'm not one of the good ones. But then I countenance the fact that at least here I am worrying about it, noticing all the ways I fall short of integrity, and I imagine that maybe people without any integrity at all don't notice or worry about it; so then I feel better about myself. It's all very confusing. I think I'm very honest and candid, but I'm also proud of how honest and candid I am—so where does that put me?"

·   ·   ·

Success can be as difficult to recover from as failure. "You know the tic big-league pitchers have," his mother says, "when they know that they've pitched a marvelous game—but gee, can they do it again, so they keep flexing that arm? There was some of that. Where he said, 'OK. Good, that came out well. But can I do it again?' That was the feeling I got. There was always the shadow waiting."

Wallace saw it that way too. "My big worry," he said, "is that this will just up my expectations for myself. And expectations are a very fine line. Up to a certain point they can be motivating, can be kind of a flamethrower held to your ass. Past that point they're toxic and paralyzing. I'm scared that I'll fuck up and plunge into a compressed version of what I went through before."

Mark Costello was also worried. "Work got very hard. He didn't get these gifts from God anymore, he didn't get these six-week periods where he got exactly the 120 pages he needed. So he found distraction in other places." He would get engaged, then unengaged. He would call friends: "Next weekend, Saturday, you gotta be in Rochester, Minnesota, I'm getting married." But then it would be Sunday, or the next week, and he'd have called it off.

"He almost got married a few times," Amy says. "I think what ultimately happened is he was doing it more for the other person than himself. And he realized that wasn't doing the other person any favors."

Wallace told Costello about a woman he had become involved with. "He said, 'She gets mad at me because I never want to leave the house.' 'Honey, let's go to the mall.' 'No, I want to write.' 'But you never do write.' 'But I don't know if I'm *going* to write. So I have to be here in case it happens.' This went on for years."

In 2000, Wallace wrote a letter to his friend Evan Wright, a *Rolling Stone* contributor: "I know about still having trouble with relationships. (Boy oh boy, do I.) But coming to enjoy my own company more and more—most of the time. I know about some darkness every day (and some days, it's all dark for me)." He wrote about meeting a woman, having things move too easily, deciding against it. "I think whatever the pull is for me is largely composed of wanting the Big Yes, of wanting someone else to want you (Cheap Trick lives). . . . So now I don't know what to do. Probably nothing, which seems to be the Sign that the universe or its CEO is sending me."

.   .   .

In the summer of 2001, Wallace relocated to Claremont, California, to become the Roy Edward Disney Chair in Creative Writing at Pomona College. He published stories and essays, but was having trouble with his work. After he reported on John McCain's 2000 presidential campaign for this magazine, he wrote his agent that it would show his editor that "I'm still capable of good work (my own insecurities, I know)."

Wallace had received a MacArthur "genius" award in 1997. "I don't think it did him any favors," says Franzen. "It conferred the mantle of 'genius' on him, which he had of course craved and sought and thought was his due. But I think he felt, 'Now I have to be even smarter.'" In late 2001, Costello called Wallace. "He was talking about how hard the writing was. And I said, lightheartedly, 'Dave, you're a genius.' Meaning, people aren't going to forget about you. You're not going to wind up in a Wendy's. He said, 'All that makes me think is that I've fooled you, too.'"

Wallace met Karen Green a few months after moving to Claremont. Green, a painter, admired David's work. It was a sort of artistic exchange, an interdisciplinary blind date. "She wanted to do some paintings based on some of David's stories," his mother says. "They had a mutual friend, and she thought she would ask permission."

"He was totally gaga," Wright recalls. "He called, head over heels, he was talking about her as a life-changing event." Franzen met Green the following year. "I felt in about three minutes that he'd finally found somebody who was up to the task of living with Dave. She's beautiful, incredibly strong, and a real grown-up— she had a center that was not about landing the genius Dave Wallace."

They made their debut as a couple with Wallace's parents in July 2003, attending the Maine culinary festival that would provide the title for his last book, *Consider the Lobster*. "They were both so quick," his father says. "They would get things and look at each other and laugh, without having to say what had struck them as funny." The next year, Wallace and Green flew to his parents' home in Illinois, where they were married two days after Christmas.

It was a surprise wedding. David told his mother he wanted to take the family to what he called a "high-gussy" lunch. Sally Wallace assumed it was Karen's influence. "David does not do high gussy," she says. "His notion of high gussy is maybe long pants instead of shorts or a T-shirt with two holes instead of eighteen." Green and Wallace left the house early to "run errands," while Amy figured out a pretext to get their parents to the courthouse on the way to the lunch. "We went upstairs," Sally says, "and saw Karen with a bouquet, and David dressed up with a flower in his buttonhole, and we knew. He just looked so happy, just radiating happiness." Their reception was at an Urbana restaurant. "As we left in the snow," Sally says, "David and Karen were walking away from us. He wanted us to take pictures, and Jim did. David was jumping in the air and clicking his heels. That became the wedding announcement."

According to Wallace's family and friends, the last six years—until the final one—were the best of his life. The marriage was happy, university life good, Karen and David had two dogs, Warner and Bella, they bought a lovely house. "Dave in a real house," Franzen says, laughing, "with real furniture and real style."

To Franzen's eye, he was watching Wallace grow up. There had been in David a kind of purposeful avoidance of the normal. Once, they'd gone to a literary party in the city. They walked in the front door together, but by the time Franzen got to the kitchen, he realized Wallace had disappeared. "I went back and proceeded to search the whole place," Franzen recalled. "He had walked into the bathroom to lose me, then turned on his heels and walked right back out the front door."

Now, that sort of thing had stopped. "He had reason to hope," Franzen said. "He had the resources to be more grown-up, a wholer person."

And then there were the dogs. "He had a predilection for dogs who'd been abused, and unlikely to find other owners who were going to be patient enough for them," Franzen says. "Whether through a sense of identification or sympathy, he had a very hard time disciplining them. But you couldn't see his attentiveness to the dogs without getting a lump in your throat."

• • •

Because Wallace was secure, he began to talk about going off Nardil, the antidepressant he had taken for nearly two decades. The drug had a long list of side effects, including the potential of very high blood pressure. "It had been a fixture of my morbid fear about Dave—that he would not last all that long, with the wear and tear on his heart," Franzen says. "I worried that I was going to lose him in his early fifties." Costello said that Wallace complained the drug made him feel "filtered." "He said, 'I don't want to be on this stuff for the rest of my life.' He wanted to be more a member of the human race."

In June of 2007, Wallace and Green were at an Indian restaurant with David's parents in Claremont. David suddenly felt very sick—intense stomach pains. They stayed with him for days. When he went to doctors, he was told that something he'd eaten might have interacted with the Nardil. They suggested he try going off the drug and seeing if another approach might work.

"So at that point," says his sister Amy, with an edge in her voice, "it was determined, 'Oh, well, gosh, we've made so much pharmaceutical progress in the last two decades that I'm sure we can find something that can knock out that pesky depression without all these side effects.' They had no idea that it was the only thing that was keeping him alive."

Wallace would have to taper off the old drug and then taper on to a new one. "He knew it was going to be rough," says Franzen. "But he was feeling like he could finally afford a year to do the job. He figured that he was going to go on to something else, at least temporarily. He was a perfectionist, you know? He wanted to be perfect, and taking Nardil was not perfect."

That summer, David began to phase out the Nardil. His doctors began prescribing other medications, none of which seemed to help. "They could find nothing," his mother says softly. "Nothing." In September, David asked Amy to forgo her annual fall-break visit. He wasn't up to it. By October, his symptoms had become bad enough to send him to the hospital. His parents didn't know what to do. "I started worrying about that," Sally says, "but then it seemed OK." He began to drop weight. By that fall, he looked like a college kid again: longish hair, eyes intense, as if he had just stepped out of an Amherst classroom.

When Amy talked to him on the phone, "sometimes he was his old self," she says. "The worst question you could ask David in the last year was 'how are you?' And it's almost impossible to have a conversation with someone you don't see regularly without that question." Wallace was very honest with her. He'd answer, "I'm not all right. I'm trying to be, but I'm not all right."

Despite his struggle, Wallace managed to keep teaching. He was dedicated to his students: He would write six pages of comments to a short story, joke with his class, fight them to try harder. During office hours, if there was a grammar question he couldn't answer, he'd phone his mother. "He would call me and say, 'Mom, I've got this student right here. Explain to me one more time why this is wrong.' You could hear the student sort of laughing in the background. 'Here's David Foster Wallace calling his mother.'"

In early May, at the end of the school year, he sat down with some graduating seniors from his fiction class at a nearby cafe. Wallace answered their jittery writer's-future questions. "He got choked up at the end," recalls Bennett Sims, one of his students. "He started to tell us how much he would miss us, and he began to cry. And because I had never seen Dave cry, I thought he was just joking. Then, awfully, he sniffled and said, 'Go ahead and laugh— here I am crying—but I really am going to miss all of you.'"

His parents were scheduled to visit the next month. In June, when Sally spoke with her son, he said, "I can't wait, it'll be wonderful, we'll have big fun." The next day, he called and said, "Mom, I have two favors to ask you. Would you please not come?" She said OK. Then Wallace asked, "Would your feelings not be hurt?"

No medications had worked; the depression wouldn't lift. "After this year of absolute hell for David," Sally says, "they decided to go back to the Nardil." The doctors also administered twelve courses of electroconvulsive therapy, waiting for Wallace's medication to become effective. "Twelve," Sally repeats. "Such brutal treatments," Jim says. "It was clear then things were bad."

Wallace had always been terrified of shock therapy. "It scares the shit out of me," he told me in 1996. "My brain's what I've got. But I could see that at a certain point, you might beg for it."

In late June, Franzen, who was in Berlin, grew worried. "I actually woke up one night," he says. "Our communications had a rhythm, and I thought, 'It's been too long since I heard from Dave.'" When Franzen called, Karen said to come immediately: David had tried to kill himself.

Franzen spent a week with Wallace in July. David had dropped seventy pounds in a year. "He was thinner than I'd ever seen him. There was a look in his eyes: terrified, terribly sad, and far away. Still, he was fun to be with, even at 10 percent strength." Franzen would sit with Wallace in the living room and play with the dogs, or step outside with David while he smoked a cigarette. "We argued about stuff. He was doing his usual line about, 'A dog's mouth is practically a disinfectant, it's so clean. Not like human saliva, dog saliva is marvelously germ-resistant.'" Before he left, Wallace thanked him for coming. "I felt grateful that he allowed me to be there," Franzen says.

Six weeks later, Wallace asked his parents to come to California. The Nardil wasn't working. It can happen with an antidepressant; a patient goes off, returns, and the medication has lost its efficacy. Wallace couldn't sleep. He was afraid to leave the house. He asked, "What if I meet one of my students?"

"He didn't want anyone to see him the way he was," his father says. "It was just awful to see. If a student saw him, they would have put their arms around him and hugged him, I'm sure."

His parents stayed for ten days. "He was just desperate," his mother says. "He was afraid it wasn't ever going to work. He was suffering. We just kept holding him, saying if he could just hang on, it would straighten. He was very brave for a very long time."

Wallace and his parents would get up at six in the morning and walk the dogs. They watched DVDs of *The Wire*, talked. Sally cooked David's favorite dishes, heavy comfort foods—pot pies, casseroles, strawberries in cream. "We kept telling him we were so glad he was alive," his mother recalls. "But my feeling is that, even then, he was leaving the planet. He just couldn't take it."

One afternoon before they left, David was very upset. His mother sat on the floor beside him. "I just rubbed his arm. He said he was glad I was his mom. I told him it was an honor."

At the end of August, Franzen called. All summer long he had been telling David that as bad as things were, they were going to be better, and then he'd be better than he'd ever been. David would say, "Keep talking like that—it's helping." But this time it wasn't helping. "He was far away," Franzen says.

A few weeks later, Karen left David alone with the dogs for a few hours. When she came home that night, he had hanged himself.

"I can't get the image out of my head," his sister says. "David and his dogs, and it's dark. I'm sure he kissed them on the mouth, and told them he was sorry."

The New Yorker

FINALIST—REPORTING

In this deeply reported and insightful piece, Ryan Lizza chronicles Barack Obama's rapid ascent in the rough-and-tumble world of Chicago politics from 1991 until his victorious Senate campaign.

Ryan Lizza

Making It: How Chicago Shaped Obama

One day in 1995, Barack Obama went to see his alderman, an influential politician named Toni Preckwinkle, on Chicago's South Side, where politics had been upended by scandal. Mel Reynolds, a local congressman, was facing charges of sexual assault of a sixteen-year-old campaign volunteer. (He eventually resigned his seat.) The looming vacancy set off a fury of ambition and hustle; several politicians, including a state senator named Alice Palmer, an education expert of modest political skills, prepared to enter the congressional race. Palmer represented Hyde Park—Obama's neighborhood, a racially integrated, liberal sanctuary—and, if she ran for Congress, she would need a replacement in Springfield, the state capital. Obama at the time was a thirty-three-year-old lawyer, university lecturer, and aspiring office seeker, and the Palmer seat was what he had in mind when he visited Alderman Preckwinkle.

"Barack came to me and said, 'If Alice decides she wants to run, I want to run for her State Senate seat,'" Preckwinkle told me. We were in her district office, above a bank on a street of check-cashing shops and vacant lots north of Hyde Park. Preckwinkle soon became an Obama loyalist, and she stuck with him in a State Senate campaign that strained or ruptured many friendships but was ultimately successful. Four years later, in 2000, she backed Obama in a doomed congressional campaign against a local icon, the former Black Panther Bobby Rush. And in 2004 Preckwinkle supported Obama during his improbable, successful run for the United States Senate. So it was startling to learn that Toni Preckwinkle had become disenchanted with Barack Obama.

Preckwinkle is a tall, commanding woman with a clipped gray afro. She has represented her slice of the South Side for seventeen years and expresses no interest in higher office. On Chicago's City Council, she is often a dissenter against the wishes of Mayor Richard M. Daley. For anyone trying to understand Obama's breathtakingly rapid political ascent, Preckwinkle is an indispensable witness—a close observer, friend, and confidante during a period of Obama's life to which he rarely calls attention.

Although many of Obama's recent supporters have been surprised by signs of political opportunism, Preckwinkle wasn't. "I think he was very strategic in his choice of friends and mentors," she told me. "I spent ten years of my adult life working to be alderman. I finally got elected. This is a job I love. And I'm perfectly happy with it. I'm not sure that's the way that he approached his public life—that he was going to try for a job and stay there for one period of time. In retrospect, I think he saw the positions he held as stepping stones to other things and therefore approached his public life differently than other people might have."

On issue after issue, Preckwinkle presented Obama as someone who thrived in the world of Chicago politics. She suggested that Obama joined Jeremiah Wright's Trinity United Church of Christ for political reasons. "It's a church that would provide you with lots of social connections and prominent parishioners," she said. "It's a good place for a politician to be a member." Preckwinkle was unsparing on the subject of the Chicago real-estate developer Antoin (Tony) Rezko, a friend of Obama's and one of his top fund raisers, who was recently convicted of fraud, bribery, and money laundering: "Who you take money from is a reflection of your knowledge at the time and your principles." As we talked, it became increasingly clear that loyalty was the issue that drove Preckwinkle's current view of her onetime protégé. "I don't think you should forget who your friends are," she said.

Others told me that Preckwinkle's grievances against Obama included specific complaints, such as his refusal to endorse a former aide and longtime friend, Will Burns, in a State Senate primary—a contest that Burns won anyway. There was also a more general belief that, after Obama won the 2004 United States Senate primary, he ignored his South Side base. Preckwinkle said, "My view is you have to bring your constituency along with you. Granted, you have to make some tough decisions. Granted, sometimes you have to make decisions that people won't understand or like. But it's your obligation to explain yourself and try to do your supporters the courtesy of treating them with respect." Ivory Mitchell, who for twenty years has been the chairman of the local ward organization in Obama's neighborhood—considered the most important Democratic organization on the South Side—was one of Obama's earliest backers. Today, he says, "All the work we did to help him get where he finally ended up, he didn't seem too appreciative." A year ago, Mitchell became a delegate for Hillary Clinton.

The same month Mitchell endorsed Clinton, the Obama campaign reached out to Preckwinkle, and eventually she signed on as an Obama delegate. I asked her if what she considered slights or betrayals were simply the necessary accommodations and maneuvering of a politician making a lightning transition from Hyde Park legislator to presidential nominee. "Can you get where he is and maintain your personal integrity?" she said. "Is that the question?" She stared at me and grimaced. "I'm going to pass on that."

"Who Sent You?"

Obama likes to discuss his unusual childhood—his abandonment by his father and his upbringing by a sometimes single mother and his grandparents in Indonesia and Hawaii—and the three years in the 1980s when he worked as a community organizer in Chicago, periods of his life chronicled at length in his first memoir, *Dreams from My Father*. He occasionally refers to his time in the United States Senate, which he wrote about in his second memoir, *The Audacity of Hope*. But his life in Chicago from 1991 until his victorious Senate campaign is a lacuna in his autobiography. It is also the period that formed him as a politician. Some Obama supporters professed shock when, recently, he abandoned a pledge to stay within the public campaign-finance system if the presumptive Republican nominee, Senator John McCain, agreed to do the same. Preckwinkle's concern about Obama—that he is a pure political animal—suddenly became more widespread; commentators abruptly stopped using the words "callow" and "naïve."

Chicago is not Obama's hometown, but it's where he chose to forge his identity. Several weeks ago, he moved many of the Democratic National Committee's operations from Washington to Chicago, making the city the unofficial capital of the Democratic Party; his campaign headquarters are in an office building in the Loop, Chicago's downtown business district. But Chicago, with its reputation as a center of vicious and corrupt politics, may also be the place that Obama needs to leave behind.

Simply moving there, as he did after graduating from Harvard Law School, was a bold decision. Chicago, where the late mayor Richard J. Daley and his son, the current mayor, have governed for forty out of the past fifty-three years, is not hospitable to political carpetbaggers. Abner Mikva, who was a congressman from Hyde Park and later the chief judge on the Washington, D.C., circuit court, was one of the first Chicago politicians to successfully challenge the Daley machine, and it took him years to overcome people's skepticism about his Wisconsin roots. Mikva, who is now eighty-two, tried to recruit Obama to work for him in Washington as a law clerk. Obama turned him down, replying that he was returning to Chicago to run for office. "I thought, Boy, does he got something to learn," Mikva told me recently. "You just don't come to Chicago and plant your flag."

I met Mikva at the Cliff Dwellers, a private dining club atop a downtown office building. As we looked out over Lake Michigan, he told me a story that has often been repeated by others to capture the essence of politics in the city. "When I first came to Chicago, Adlai Stevenson and Paul Douglas were running for governor and senator," he said. "I had heard about the closed party, closed machine, but they sounded like such great candidates, so I stopped in to volunteer in the Eighth Ward Regular Democratic headquarters. I said, 'I'm here for Douglas and Stevenson.' The ward boss came in and pulled the cigar out of his mouth and said, 'Who sent you?' And I said, 'Nobody sent me.' He put the cigar back in his mouth and said, 'We don't want nobody nobody sent.'"

·   ·   ·

There was another tradition in Chicago politics, the so-called Independents, which grew up in opposition to Richard J. Daley—Boss Daley—whose reign lasted from 1955 to 1976. Anchored in Hyde Park and nurtured by the University of Chicago community, the Independents brought together African Americans and white liberals in coalitions that became the city's main alternative to the Democratic machine. The Independents arose after the Second World War to challenge the closed patronage system that controlled the city and became a serious political force in the mid-1950s. Their numbers increased with a new wave of black activists energized by Martin Luther King Jr.'s

Chicago organizing in 1966, and with white liberals outraged when antiwar protesters were beaten and tear-gassed by Chicago police during the Democratic National Convention in 1968.

Mayor Daley died in office in 1976, at the age of seventy-four. He was replaced by a reliable and ineffectual machine candidate, Michael Bilandic, whose appointment marked the beginning of twelve years of chaotic, balkanized politics, sometimes called the "inter-Daley period." David Axelrod, who has been Obama's chief strategist since 2002 and is the foremost political consultant in Chicago, was a witness to all of it, first as a political reporter for the *Chicago Tribune* and later as the chief consultant to two mayors: Harold Washington, Chicago's first black mayor and a hero of the Independents, and the current Mayor Daley, whose last name still carries negative connotations in the precincts of Hyde Park. Axelrod, who is fifty-three, is by nature subdued. He wears a mustache that curls down the sides of his upper lip in a permanent expression of melancholy. We met in a Houlihan's, off the lobby of the building that houses the Obama campaign headquarters.

Axelrod recalled the election, in 1979, of Jane Byrne, Chicago's first female mayor, which he wrote about for the *Tribune*. Byrne's campaign, assisted by snowstorms that shut down the city and showcased Bilandic's incompetence, was the first successful insurgency in modern Chicago history. "It was a great reform campaign," Axelrod said. "I then chronicled, for the next four years, her systematic abrogation of every commitment she had made to reform. She became sort of a parody of a machine mayor." In office, Byrne aligned herself with City Council officials who were hostile to the city's black leadership, pandered to the voters of the most racist wards of the city, and purged African Americans from key positions. On the South Side, there was a backlash; Washington, who had run a spirited campaign for mayor in 1977, was elected to Congress in 1980. In 1983, he was essentially drafted by a Hyde Park–based coalition desperate to unseat the disappointing Byrne. Washington won a three-way primary, with 36 percent of the vote, and went on in the general election to defeat a white Republican who ran, briefly, on the implicitly racist slogan "Before it's too late." Washington's first term was dominated by warfare with a City Council controlled by white aldermen determined to stymie every proposal. But in 1986 he took control of the council and the following year was reelected. Seven months after his victory, he collapsed at his desk, dead of a heart attack at the age of sixty-five. Axelrod saw much of this history from the inside, as Washington's strategist; Obama saw it from the perspective of an organizer who occasionally had brushes with the powerful at political events or meetings at City Hall. "He saw the jagged edges of Chicago politics and urban politics pretty close up," Axelrod said.

Obama spent three years in the city, from 1985, after he graduated from Columbia University, to the end of the Washington era. As a community organizer, he tried to turn a partnership of churches into a political force on the South Side. But the work accomplished very little.

"When I started organizing, I understood the idea of social change in a very abstract way," Obama told me last year. "It was to some extent informed by my years in Indonesia, seeing extreme poverty and disparities of wealth and understanding sort of in a dim way that life wasn't fair and government had something to do with it. I understood the role that issues like race played and took inspiration from the civil-rights movement and what the student sit-ins had accomplished and the freedom rides.

"But I didn't come out of a political family, didn't have a history of activism in my family. So I understood these things in the abstract. When I went to Chicago, it was the first time that I had the opportunity to test out my ideas. And for the most part I would say I wasn't wildly successful. The victories that we achieved were extraordinarily modest: you know, getting a job-training site set up or getting an after-school program for young people put in place."

Constructing a Network

In 1988, Obama left for Harvard Law School, returning to Chicago twice for summer stints at élite law firms, including, after his first year, Sidley Austin. (Sidley Austin is where he met Michelle Robinson, whom he married in 1992.) He returned to Chicago permanently when he graduated, in 1991. In a short period, he built a notable résumé and a network of connections. During the 1992 presidential campaign, he ran a voter-registration drive that placed him at the center of the city's politics. That year, Illinois elected the first African American woman to the U.S. Senate, Carol Moseley Braun, and Bill Clinton became the first Democratic presidential candidate to carry Illinois since Lyndon Johnson, in 1964. Meanwhile, Obama practiced civil-rights law at a firm admired in the city's progressive circles and became a popular lecturer in the law school at the University of Chicago. He was on the board of two liberal foundations that spread grant money around Chicago, and he settled in Hyde Park.

It was a neighborhood in transition when Obama arrived. The *Hyde Park Herald* serves as a sort of time capsule. It reported that crime was rising; a series of violent robberies was another reminder that Hyde Park existed as a middle-class island in a sea of high-crime urban poverty. New data showed that white enrollment was steeply declining at one local school. During the Martin Luther King Jr. celebrations, the newspaper noted in passing that Jeremiah Wright was scheduled to give a speech at the University of Chicago. Considerable coverage was given to two institutions: the local food co-op, where Obama shopped every Saturday, and the Independent Voters of Illinois–Independent Precinct Organization, or I.V.I.-I.P.O., one of the neighborhood's most influential political groups. There was a new political force in Hyde Park as well. Real-estate developers were swooping in to rehabilitate low-income housing. On more than one occasion, the *Hyde Park Herald* reported on the rise in campaign donations from these developers to South Side politicians; in 1995, it ran a front-page article about Tony Rezko, who was then a very active new donor on the scene.

While it's true that nobody sent Obama in the sense that Abner Mikva meant it, one of Obama's underappreciated assets, as he looked for a political race in the early nineties, was the web of connections that he had established. "He understands how you network," Mikva said. "I remember our first few meetings. He would say, 'Do you know So-and-So?' And I'd say yes. 'How well do you know him? I'd really like to meet him.' I would set up some lunches."

The 1992 voter-registration drive, Project Vote, introduced him to much of the city's black leadership. "If you want to look at the means of ascent, if you will, look at Project Vote," Will Burns, the former Obama aide, said. In Chicago progressive circles, Burns, who is thirty-four, is described as an up-and-coming African American legislator in the Obama tradition. Obama's refusal to endorse Burns in his primary earlier this year infuriated and mystified a number of Chicago Democrats, though Burns himself displays no bitterness and is now an adviser to the Obama campaign.

At Project Vote, Burns said, Obama "was making connections at the grassroots level and was working with elected officials. That's when he first got a scan of the broader black political infrastructure." It was also the beginning of a dynamic that stood out in Obama's early career: his uneasy relationship with an older generation of black Chicago politicians. Project Vote "is where a lot of the divisional rivalries popped up," Burns said.

In this early foray into politics, Obama revealed the toughness and brashness that this year's long primary season brought into view. As Burns, who has a mischievous sense of humor and a gift for mimicry, recalled, "Black activists, community folks, felt that he didn't respect their role"—Burns imitated a self-righteous activist—"in the *struggle* and the *movement*. He didn't engage in obeisance to them. He wanted to get the job done. And Barack's cheap, too. If you can't do it and do it in a cost-effective manner, you're not going to work with him." Ivory Mitchell, the ward chairman in Obama's neighborhood, says of Obama that "he was typical of what most aspiring politicians are: self-centered—that 'I can do anything and I'm willing to do it overnight.'"

During Project Vote, Obama also began to understand the larger world of Chicago's liberal fund raisers. "He met people not just in the African American community but in the progressive white community," David Axelrod said. "The folks who funded Project Vote were some of the key progressive leaders." Obama met Axelrod through one of Project Vote's supporters, Bettylu Saltzman, whose father, Philip M. Klutznick, was a Chicago shopping-mall tycoon, a part owner of the Bulls, and a former commerce secretary in the Carter administration. Saltzman, a soft-spoken activist who worked for Senators Adlai E. Stevenson III and Paul Simon, took an immediate interest in Obama. "I honestly don't remember what it was about him, but I was absolutely blown away," Saltzman says. "I said to several people that this guy, who is now thirty years old, is someday going to be president. He will be our first black president."

Obama's legal career helped bring him into Chicago's liberal reform community. In 1993, after he finished his work with Project Vote and was seeking to join a law firm, instead of returning to Sidley Austin he took a job at Davis, Miner, Barnhill and Galland, a boutique civil-rights firm led by Harold Washington's former counsel, Judson Miner. Miner had perfect anti-Daley credentials, routinely filing lawsuits against the city, and was a founding member of the Chicago Council of Lawyers, which was to Chicago's legal elite what the Independents were to the Democratic machine.

Working at Davis, Miner enhanced Obama's profile. "When you go work for Judd Miner's law firm, that's another kind of political statement," Don Rose, a longtime Chicago political consultant, who ran Jane Byrne's campaign, told me. Will Burns said, "I think it might have been helpful with a certain group of people that Barack may have wanted to have at his back at the outset. So you get the support of the liberals and the progressives and the reformers, and then that gives you a base to then expand to pick up other folks. And then folks would be willing to give money to the bright, shiny new candidate." Joining Miner's firm, like living in Hyde Park, was a way of choosing sides in the city's long-running political battle between the machine and the Independents. Toni Preckwinkle explained Miner's legal work this way: "They've shown a remarkable willingness to take on the Democratic organization and the Democratic establishment in this city and win. Which is why I like them and a lot of people hate them."

If Project Vote and Miner's firm introduced Obama to the city's lakefront liberals and South Side politicians, it was his wife who helped connect him to Chicago's black elite. One of Michelle's best friends was Jesse Jackson's daughter Santita, who became the godmother of the Obamas' first child. Michelle had worked as an aide to the younger Daley—hired by Valerie Jarrett, who is now one of Obama's closest advisers. (Jarrett, an African American, was born in Iran, where her father, a doctor, helped run a hospital; she and Obama formed a bond over their unusual biographies.) It was also through Michelle that Obama met Marty Nesbitt, a successful young black entrepreneur who happened to play basketball with Michelle's brother, Craig. (Nesbitt's wife, Anita Blanchard, an obstetrician, delivered the Obamas' two daughters.) Nesbitt became Obama's closest friend and a bridge to the city's African American business class.

．　　　．　　　．

Obama seems to have been meticulous about constructing a political identity for himself. He visited churches on the South Side, considered the politics and reputations of each one, and received advice from older pastors. Before deciding on Trinity United Church of Christ, he asked the Reverend Wright about critics who complained that the church was too "upwardly mobile," a place for buppies. Though he admired Judson Miner, he was similarly cautious about joining his law firm. Miner once told me that it took "a series of lunches" and hours of discussion before Obama made his decision. At the time, Obama was working on *Dreams from My Father.*

Many have said that part of the appeal of *Dreams* is its honesty, pointing out that it was written at a time when Obama had no idea that he would run for office. In fact, Obama had been talking about a political career for years, musing about becoming mayor or governor. According to a recent biography of Obama by the *Chicago Tribune* reporter David Mendell, he even told his future brother-in-law, Craig Robinson, that he might run for president one day. (Robinson teased him, saying, "Yeah, yeah, okay, come over and meet my Aunt Gracie—and don't tell anybody that!") Obama was writing *Dreams* at the moment that he was preparing for a life in politics, and he launched his book and his first political campaign simultaneously, in the summer of 1995, when he saw his first chance of winning.

Many people who knew Obama then remember him for his cockiness. He had good reason to be self-assured. A number of his accomplishments had been accompanied by adoring press coverage. When he was named president of the *Harvard Law Review,* in 1990, he was profiled by, among others, the *Times,* the *Boston Globe,* the *Los Angeles Times,* the *Chicago Tribune, Vanity Fair,* and the Associated Press. Even then, the essential elements of Obama-mania were present: the fascination with his early life, the adulatory quotes from friends who thought that he would be president one day, and Obama's frank, though sometimes ostentatious, capacity for self-reflection. ("To some extent, I'm a symbolic stand-in for a lot of the changes that have been made," he told the *Boston Globe* in 1990.)

His work for Project Vote was similarly applauded. In 1993, *Crain's Chicago Business* reported that Obama had "galvanized Chicago's political community, as no seasoned politico had before," and an alderman told *Crain's*, "Under Barack's leadership, we had the most successful, cost-effective and orderly voter registration drive I've ever been involved with." When *Dreams from My Father* was published, the reviews were overwhelmingly positive; *Booklist* included the memoir in a "guide to some of the best books of 1995."

Obama knew that Hyde Park, despite its reputation as the center of anti-machine progressives, was not exempt from other Chicago political traditions. During the first half of 1995, when he was preparing for his campaign for the State Senate, a big story in the neighborhood was a race for alderman marked by accusations of dirty tricks (endorsement flyers from a phony group of gay African Americans were distributed the day before the election, apparently in an effort to stoke homophobia) and anti-Semitism (the campaign of one of the candidates was accused of being run by "Jewish overseers").

The South Side Chooses

Obama's campaign began without much excitement. He had ties to so many of the city's elite factions that the local press described him as "a well-connected attorney." In August, the *Chicago Sun-Times* noted that Valerie Jarrett was hosting "a private autograph party" for Obama. His memoir was turning him into a figure of some acclaim. The same month, the *Hyde Park Herald*, which later called the book "a local indie hit," ran a flattering profile that highlighted a theme from *Dreams*: how Chicago helped Obama end a long journey of self-discovery, a narrative that helped defuse any notion that Obama was a carpetbagger. "I came home in Chicago," he told the newspaper. "I began to see my identity and my individual struggles were one with the struggles that folks face in Chicago."

A month later, on September 19, Obama invited some two hundred supporters to a lakefront Ramada Inn to announce his candidacy for the State Senate, and some of what he said sounded very much like the Obama of recent months. "Politicians are not held to highest esteem these days," he told the crowd. "They fall somewhere lower than lawyers. . . . I want to inspire a renewal of morality in politics. I will work as hard as I can, as long as I can, on your behalf." Alice Palmer introduced Obama, and an account in the *Hyde Park Herald* quoted more from her speech than from his; it was, after all, chiefly her endorsement that certified him as a plausible candidate. "In this room, Harold Washington announced for mayor," Palmer said. "Barack Obama carries on the tradition of independence in this district. . . . His candidacy is a passing of the torch."

Also in attendance that day were Toni Preckwinkle and Will Burns, who was then a recent University of Chicago graduate. (He went on to get a master's in social sciences; Obama helped persuade him to leave the university before he got a Ph.D., telling him, "You shouldn't be too academic.") Obama's talk of a "renewal of morality in politics," which previewed themes that emerged in this year's campaign, also tapped into a desire for generational change—similarly consistent with his current rhetoric. He was able to capture the imagination of some young African Americans frustrated by their local leadership. Burns said, "You have to understand, it's 1995. It's the year after the Republicans have taken over control of Congress, and in Illinois all three branches of government were also controlled by the Republicans. So it was a really dark point. I was looking to be engaged in something that would mean something, that would actually get something done and that was beyond symbols. Around the same time that I started up with Barack, volunteering on his campaign, I had gone to some of the old community groups and nationalist organizations. I respected what they had done, but I didn't feel like that was really where I wanted to be."

However, the campaign was no insurgency. Obama abided by the local way of doing things. He had lined up support from Preckwinkle, his alderman, and Ivory Mitchell, the local ward chairman, and Palmer's endorsement brought with it two organizational assets: local operators and local activists. The operators helped Obama get on the ballot and handled the mechanics of his election. Two key operators were Alan Dobry and his wife, Lois Friedberg-Dobry, then in their late sixties and leaders of the Independent movement. "When you go to a political meeting, and you see a couple of guys or girls at the back of the room, and they aren't glad-handing or anything, those are the operators," Alan Dobry told me recently. There was a machinelike quality to the way the campaign unfolded. Palmer's endorsement was the only signal that the Dobrys needed to start the slow, detailed organizing necessary to win a State Senate seat for Obama, whom they had never met, though they lived in his neighborhood.

Palmer's imprimatur was also helpful with a small group of Hyde Park activists, some of whom she asked to hold fund-raising coffees for Obama. At her suggestion, Sam and Martha Ackerman, who were leaders of Independent Voters of Illinois, hosted a coffee at their home. Unlike the Dobrys, they insisted on a meeting with Obama before backing him, and their support was important enough for him to spend an hour with them in their dining room, submitting to an interview. Their reaction to him was a common one. "I don't think he said he wanted to run for president, but he indicated that he was into public service for the long haul," Martha Ackerman told me. "I remember very clearly I said to Sam, 'If this guy is for real, he could be the first African American president of the United States.'"

Bill Ayers and Bernadine Dohrn, another activist Hyde Park couple, also held an event for Obama. Forty years ago, Ayers and Dohrn were leaders of the Weathermen, the militant antiwar group that bombed the Pentagon and the United States Capitol. By the time Obama met Ayers, the former radical and onetime fugitive had been accepted into polite Chicago society and had been reborn as an education expert, eventually working as an informal adviser to Mayor Daley. (Those ties remain intact in the jumbled culture of Chicago politics. When Obama's association with Ayers first became a campaign issue, Daley, whose father, in 1968, sent his police force into the streets to combat Ayers's fellow radicals, issued a statement praising Ayers as "a valued member of the Chicago community.")

Obama seemed sure enough that he would win the State Senate primary, to be held in March 1996—in Chicago, winning the primary is tantamount to winning the seat—to take time, late that summer, for a brief book tour, which started in Hyde Park and carried him as far as California. In October, he was one of the thousands of African Americans from Chicago who travelled to Washington for the Million Man March. (Obama criticized the march, telling a local alternative newspaper that it was a waste of energy.) When he returned home, he had more immediate problems. In December 1995, the South Side coalition that he had cobbled together began to fall apart. Palmer's congressional campaign was eclipsed by her Democratic-primary opponents—Jesse Jackson Jr. who had star power, and Emil Jones, a longtime leader in the State Senate. Several weeks before the primary, a group of her supporters—mostly older black activists, not unlike those Obama had tangled with when he was running Project Vote—realized that Palmer was destined for defeat and summoned him to a meeting. The *Chicago Defender* reported that Obama was asked "to step aside like other African Americans have done in other races for the sake of unity and to release Palmer from her commitment"—so that she could reclaim her State Senate seat. Obama left the meeting noncommittal.

Palmer was soundly defeated by Jackson—she got only 10 per cent of the vote—and there were more insistent demands that Obama withdraw. He refused, which angered Palmer and her husband, Buzz. Buzz Palmer was a founder of the Afro-American Patrolman's League, a reform group within the Chicago police department, and the couple had many ties to the city's black leadership. Palmer, announcing that she had been drafted back into the State Senate race, went from being Obama's most important supporter to his chief challenger; the woman who had launched his political career now threatened to end it. "That's Chicago politics," Obama told a reporter—with a sigh, the account said.

The South Side political community was forced to choose. The Ackermans went with Palmer, the Dobrys with Obama. Emil Jones announced his support for Palmer. Alderman Preckwinkle stayed with Obama. "I had given him my word I would support him," she told me. "Alice didn't forgive me, and she's never going to forgive me."

"These old nationalist guys start beating a drum—probably not the right metaphor—about how Barack should let this elder back in and how seniority's important," Burns said. "And they're writing essays in the *Defender* and *N'Digo*"—another local paper covering Chicago's black community. A comment in the *Defender* by Robert Starks, a professor of political science at Chicago's Northeastern Illinois University and one of Palmer's chief supporters, was typical: "If she doesn't run, that seat will go to a Daley supporter. We have asked her to reconsider not running because we don't think Obama can win. He hasn't been in town long enough. . . . Nobody knows who he is. . . . We need someone with experience."

But, almost as fast as the threat to his campaign appeared, Obama stamped it out. The Dobrys were surprised that Palmer had so quickly gathered the signatures necessary to qualify for the ballot. They went to the Chicago board of elections and reviewed her petitions; as they suspected, they were filled with irregularities. One skill that the Independents had mastered in the years of fighting the first Mayor Daley was the machine's tactic of challenging ballot petitions, and the Dobrys were experts at this Chicago ritual. Publicly, Obama was conciliatory about the awkward political situation, telling the *Hyde Park Herald* that he understood that some people were upset about the "conflict between old loyalties and new enthusiasms." Privately, however, he unleashed his operators. With the help of the Dobrys, he was able to remove not just Palmer's name from the ballot but the name of every other opponent as well. "He ran unopposed, which is a good way to win," Mikva said, laughing at the recollection. And Palmer said last week, "Anyone who enters Chicago politics and can't take the rough and tumble shouldn't be there. Losing the seat was just that—not the end of the world."

Instead of arriving in Springfield as the consensus candidate of his district, Obama was regarded as a troublemaker. "He had created some enemies," Emil Jones, who in 2003 became president of the Illinois Senate, said. Burns described the fallout of the Obama-Palmer race this way: "It established a reputation that 'you're not going to punk me, you're not going to roll me over, you're not going to jam me.' I think it established him as a threat. You have his independence with Project Vote, you have his refusal to knuckle under during the Alice Palmer thing, and so now you have a series of data points that have some established leaders in the black community feeling disrespected. And so the stage is now set for the comeuppance during the congressional race. That was their payback."

Illinois Turns Blue

In the political culture of 1996, two years after the ascendancy of the Gingrich Republicans, many Democrats ran as chastened and cautious politicians; among them was Bill Clinton, who turned his reelection-campaign strategy over to Dick Morris (who had worked for Jesse Helms and Trent Lott, as well as Democrats) and the militantly centrist pollster Mark Penn (the Morris protégé who helped run Hillary Clinton's primary campaign). By then, Bill Clinton had abandoned his effort for universal health care and was about to sign into law a welfare-reform bill that Senator Daniel Patrick Moynihan had denounced, saying, "For the first time since it was enacted in 1935, we are about to repeal a core provision of the Social Security Act." The bill was one of the most important factors in securing Clinton's reelection.

Had Obama not been running for office in one of the most liberal districts in Illinois, he would have drawn notice as a fairly bold Democrat. To judge by his public comments, he seemed both appalled and impressed by President Clinton's political skill. In an interview with the *Cleveland Plain Dealer*, published a few days after Clinton said that he would sign the welfare-reform bill, Obama talked about the presidential campaign, saying that Bob Dole "seems to me to be a classic example of somebody who had no reason to run. You're seventy-three years old, you're already the third-most-powerful man in the country. So why? . . . And Bill Clinton? Well, his campaign's fascinating to a student of politics. It's disturbing to someone who cares about certain issues. But politically it seems to be working."

Soon, Obama began writing a regular column—"Springfield Report"—for the *Hyde Park Herald*. In the first one, on February 19, 1997, he wrote, "Last year, President Clinton signed a bill that, for the first time in 60 years, eliminates the federal guarantee of support for poor families and their children." The column was earnest and wonky. It betrayed no hint of liberal piety about the new law, but emphasized that there weren't enough entry-level jobs in Chicago to absorb all the welfare recipients who would soon be leaving the system.

In effect, while President Clinton and the national Democratic Party were drifting to the right, State Senator Obama pushed in the opposite direction. The new welfare law was one of the first issues that Obama faced as a legislator. "I am not a defender of the status quo with respect to welfare," he said, choosing his words with care during debate on the Illinois Senate floor. "Having said that, I probably would not have supported the federal legislation, because I think it had some problems. But I'm a strong believer in making lemonade out of lemons." Perhaps the law's most punitive aspect was that it cut off aid to poor legal immigrants, a provision that Clinton, in his 2004 memoir, called "particularly harsh" and "unjustifiable." The law that Obama helped pass in Illinois restored benefits to this group. (In a continuing effort to produce lemonade, Obama's first ad of the 2008 general-election campaign says that he "passed laws moving people from welfare to work.") Obama resisted the national rightward trend of the mid-nineties in other small ways. He sponsored an amendment to the state constitution that would have made health care a universal right in Illinois and helped pass an ethics bill that reformed Illinois's antiquated campaign-finance system.

In hindsight, little of his legislative record seems controversial. Some of the bills that he sponsored, statements that he made, and votes that he cast could be caricatured in a presidential campaign. (In one 1997 column, he said, "I supported Governor Edgar's plan to raise the income tax," and in a 1999 debate, speaking of himself and his two opponents, he noted that "we're all on the liberal wing of the Democratic Party.") But 2008 is not 1988, and Republican attacks on tax hikes and calling an opponent a liberal lack much of their formerly compelling electoral power.

Obama has benefitted from impeccable timing. As the national party entered a period of ideological timidity, he was at the vanguard of a Democratic revival in Illinois that had begun in 1992, when Clinton and Braun won the state, and grew stronger when, four years later, Democrats took over the Illinois House of Representatives. It continued through 2002, when Democrats won the State Senate and the governor's office. By 2004, when Obama ran for the United States Senate, Illinois was a solidly blue state.

Not all of this was due to Democratic ingenuity; during this period the state Republican Party collapsed under the weight of corruption scandals. That is something of an Illinois tradition: four of the last nine governors have been indicted on charges of corruption, and three were convicted. As Saul Bellow once remarked, "Politics are politics, crime is crime, but in Chicago they occasionally overlap. The line between virtue and vice meanders madly—effective government on one side, connections on the other."

.   .   .

There were further changes under way in Chicago. Obama had won his first campaign by using old-fashioned Chicago machine tactics at a time when the notion of machine politics was increasingly anachronistic. As the political consultant Don Rose and his colleague James Andrews explain in a chapter for a book about the current Mayor Daley's first victory, the machine literally provided voters with access to food, health care, and a job. In most American cities, that model vanished after the Second World War; by then, the blue-collar base was leaving for the suburbs and reform movements were challenging machine politics. In Chicago, Rose and Andrews say, the elder Daley updated and preserved the system by creating a modern machine that combined "big labor and big capital, blue and white collars, and minorities"—a hybrid model that died with him.

Gradually, Chicago caught up with the rest of the country and media-driven politics eclipsed machine-driven politics. "It became increasingly difficult to get into homes and apartments to talk about candidates," Rose said. "High-rises were tough if not impossible to crack, and other parts of the city had become too dangerous to walk around in for hours at a time. And people didn't want to answer their doors. Thus the increasing dependence on TV, radio, direct mail, phone-banking, robocalls, et cetera—all things that cost a hell of a lot more money than patronage workers, who were themselves in decline, anyway, because of anti-patronage court rulings." Instead of a large army of ward heelers dragging people to the polls, candidates needed a small army of donors to pay for commercials. Money replaced bodies as the currency of Chicago politics. This new system became known as "pinstripe patronage," because the key to winning was not rewarding voters with jobs but rewarding donors with government contracts.

E. J. Dionne Jr., of the *Washington Post*, wrote about this transition in a 1999 column after Daley was reelected. Dionne wrote about a young Barack Obama, who artfully explained how the new pinstripe patronage worked: a politician rewards the law firms, developers, and brokerage houses with contracts, and in return they pay for the new ad campaigns necessary for reelection. "They do well, and you get a $5 million to $10 million war chest," Obama told Dionne. It was a classic Obamaism: superficially critical of some unseemly aspect of the political process without necessarily forswearing the practice itself. Obama was learning that one of the greatest skills a politician can possess is candor about the dirty work it takes to get and stay elected.

At the time, Obama was growing closer to Tony Rezko, who eventually turned pinstripe patronage into an extremely lucrative way of life. Rezko's rise in Illinois was intertwined with

Obama's. Like Abner Mikva and Judson Miner, he had tried to recruit Obama to work for him. Chicago had been at the forefront of an urban policy to lure developers into low-income neighborhoods with tax credits, and Rezko was an early beneficiary of the program. Miner's law firm was eager to do the legal work on the tax-credit deals, which seemed consistent with the firm's over-all civil-rights mission. A residual benefit was that the new developers became major donors to aldermen, state senators, and other South Side politicians who represented the poor neighborhoods in which Rezko and others operated. "Our relationship deepened when I started my first political campaign for the State Senate," Obama said earlier this year, in an interview with Chicago reporters.

Rezko was one of the people Obama consulted when he considered running to replace Palmer, and Rezko eventually raised about 10 percent of Obama's funds for that first campaign. As a state senator, Obama became an advocate of the tax-credit program. "That's an example of a smart policy," he told the *Chicago Daily Law Bulletin* in 1997. "The developers were thinking in market terms and operating under the rules of the marketplace; but at the same time, we had government supporting and subsidizing those efforts." Obama and Rezko's friendship grew stronger. They dined together regularly and even, on at least one occasion, retreated to Rezko's vacation home, in Lake Geneva, Wisconsin.

"Whatever Your Name Is"

Obama's subtle understanding of the way the city's politics had changed—with fund raising replacing organization as the key to victory—surely encouraged him in his next campaign. Almost as soon as he got to Springfield, he was planning another move. He was bored there—once, he appeared to doze off during a caucus meeting—and frustrated by the Republicans' total control over the legislature. He seemed to believe, according to colleagues at the time, that he was destined for better things than being trapped in one of America's more notoriously corrupt state capitals. Obama spent little time socializing with "the guys basically from Chicago," the veteran senator Emil Jones said. "He hung around a lot of the downstaters. They became good friends."

Obama's relations with some of his black colleagues from Chicago were dreadful from the beginning. On March 13, 1997, Obama introduced one of his first pieces of legislation, a modest bill to make a directory of community-college graduates available to local employers. There was a response from Rickey Hendon, a state senator from the West Side of Chicago who had been close to Alice Palmer. After Obama explained his bill, Hendon, who has dabbled in film and television work, earning him the nickname Hollywood, rose to ask a question, and the following exchange occurred:

HENDON:	Senator, could you correctly pronounce your name for me? I'm having a little trouble with it.
OBAMA:	Obama.
HENDON:	Is that Irish?
OBAMA:	It will be when I run countywide.
HENDON:	That was a good joke, but this bill's still going to die. This directory, would that have those 1-800 sex line numbers in this directory?
OBAMA:	I apologize. I wasn't paying Senator Hendon any attention.
HENDON:	Well, clearly, as poorly as this legislation is drafted, you didn't pay it much attention either. My question was: Are the 1-800 sex line numbers going to be in this directory?
OBAMA:	Not—not—basically this idea comes out of the South Side community colleges. I don't

know what you're doing on the West Side
community colleges. But we probably won't be
including that in our directory for the
students.

HENDON: . . . Let me just say this, and to the bill: I seem
to remember a very lovely Senator by the name
of Palmer—much easier to pronounce than
Obama—and she always had cookies and nice
things to say, and you don't have anything to
give us around your desk. How do you expect
to get votes? And—and you don't even wear
nice perfume like Senator Palmer did. . . . I'm
missing Senator Palmer because of these weak
replacements with these tired bills that makes
absolutely no sense. I . . . I definitely urge a No
vote. Whatever your name is.

Although the exchange was part of a longstanding tradition of
hazing new legislators, the tensions between Hendon and Obama
were real. On another occasion, Obama voted—a parliamentary
error, Obama says—to block funding for a child-welfare facility
in Hendon's district. Hendon rose and criticized Obama for the
vote. The two men became embroiled in a yelling match on the
Senate floor that looked as if it might become physical; they were
separated by Courtney Nottage, then the chief of staff for Emil
Jones. Nottage led Obama off the floor to a room that legislators
used to make telephone calls. "It looked like two men that were
having a serious disagreement and they had walked up to one
another really close," Nottage told me. "I didn't think anything
good could come of that."

Hendon told me, "*He's* the one that got mad, because he said I
embarrassed him on the Senate floor. That's when he came over
to *my* desk." Before Nottage broke them up, Obama, who had
learned to box from his Indonesian stepfather, supposedly told

Hendon, "I'm going to kick your ass!" Hendon said, "He said *something* like that." He added that more details will appear in a book that he's written, entitled *Black Enough, White Enough: The Obama Dilemma.*

•   •   •

Obama's friends were not surprised when, in 1999, he decided to challenge Bobby Rush, who has represented the South Side in Congress since 1992. Rush had run against Daley in the 1999 mayoral primary, and Obama interpreted Rush's defeat in that citywide race as a harbinger of his declining popularity in his congressional district.

The race against Rush was the turning point in Obama's political career. It started with a brilliant bit of oratory that alluded to Abner Mikva's story about the insularity of Chicago politics and sought to turn Obama's disadvantages into strengths. "Nobody sent me," Obama said at his campaign kickoff, on September 26, 1999. "I'm not part of some long-standing political organization. I have no fancy sponsors. I'm not even from Chicago. My name is Obama. Despite that fact, somebody sent me. . . . The men on the corner in Woodlawn drowning their sorrows in alcohol . . . the women working two jobs. . . . They're all telling me we can't wait." It was the best moment of his campaign.

Obama was financially outmatched. Although he raised about $600,000, sustained television advertising in Chicago cost between $200,000 and $300,000 a week, according to Dan Shomon, Obama's campaign manager at the time. A series of unusual events defined the race. A few months before the election, Rush's twenty-nine-year-old son, Huey Rich, was shot and killed, which made the incumbent a figure of sympathy, and in the final weeks of the campaign Rush's father died. Obama made a serious misstep when, visiting his grandmother in Hawaii, he missed a crucial vote on gun-control legislation in Springfield. Even worse, on the day of the vote a column by Obama about how the gun bill was "sorely needed" appeared in the *Hyde Park Herald,* under the headline "Ideologues Frustrate Gun Law." Obama protested that his daughter was ill and unable to travel, and that he saw his grandmother, who lived alone, only once a year, but the press treated the trip as a tropical vacation.

Obama lost by thirty-one points—a humiliating defeat. On Election Night, at the Ramada Inn where he had begun his political career, he sounded dejected, hinting that he might leave politics. "I've got to make assessments about where we go from here," he said. "We need a new style of politics to deal with the issues that are important to the people. What's not clear to me is whether I should do that as an elected official or by influencing government in ways that actually improve people's lives." The defeat marked not so much the beginning of a new style of politics for Obama as the beginning of Obama's mastery of the old style of politics.

Obama had misread the political dynamics of Rush's unsuccessful mayoral campaign. "He thought he would get some help from Daley because Rush had run against Daley for mayor," Mikva said. "He thought that Daley might use the opportunity to get even. That's not the way the Daleys work. It's not the way the machine works. When Barack went in to see the mayor, whom he knew slightly, Daley said what his old man used to say: 'Good luck!'"

Mayor Daley concurred. "Bobby Rush was very strong," he said. "When you lose a race, you can be strong in another avenue, and he was always strong in his congressional district. It was a learning experience when I lost to Harold Washington. The next day, I endorsed him." He added, "You learn from defeat. If you don't learn from defeat, then you go away as a sour politician—you think that people turned on you. Barack Obama understood that. The lesson from that campaign is you can't just run for any office saying you thought someone lost an election

and you thought they were weak. He realized that and he rededi-
cated himself."

The Inner Sanctum

Obama learned the exact nature of his appeal, as well as his
handicaps. Unlike Obama's State Senate district, where the University of Chicago and the multicultural Hyde Park produced
most of the votes, Rush's congressional district extended deep
into black neighborhoods where Obama was unknown. His
academic background was a burden, too. Will Burns explained,
"Even though the University of Chicago is one of the largest employers on the South Side of Chicago, it is seen by some, particularly black nationalists, as a bastion of white political power, as a
huge entity that doesn't take into account the interests of the
community, that doesn't have a full democratic partnership with
the community, and does what it wants to the community in
maintaining clear boundaries about where black people are. It's
seen as an expansive force, trying to expand into Bronzeville and
into Woodlawn"—historically black neighborhoods adjacent to
Hyde Park—"and put poor blacks out of the area. The University
of Chicago is not a brand that helps you if you're trying to get
votes on the South Side of Chicago."

Obama's fund-raising success and his professional networks
were also viewed with suspicion. Chicago is still a city of vil-
lages, and Obama was adept at gliding back and forth between
the South Side, where he campaigned for votes, and the wealthy
Gold Coast, the lakefront neighborhood of high-rise condomin-
iums and deluxe shopping, where he raised money. One day in
Hyde Park, I mentioned the name Bettylu Saltzman (the Project
Vote supporter and daughter of a Bulls owner) to Lois Friedberg-
Dobry (the South Side operator). "I don't run in those circles,"
she said. Later, over lunch with Saltzman at a café in a gourmet
supermarket on the Gold Coast, I mentioned the Dobrys and

Obama's Independent Voters of Illinois friends, and she said, "You know, the North Side and the South Side of Chicago—it's like two different worlds."

A South Side operator named Al Kindle, a large man with a booming voice, was a field operator for Obama's race against Rush. He had helped elect Harold Washington, and he saw Obama's congressional campaign from the street level. We met one evening at Calypso Café, a Caribbean restaurant that Obama has said is his favorite place to eat in Hyde Park, and Kindle described some of the worst moments in the campaign. "The accusations were that Obama was sent here and owned by the Jews," Kindle said. "That he was here to steal the black vote and steal black land and that he was represented by the—as they were called—'the white man.' And that Obama wasn't black enough and didn't know the black experience, the black community. It was quite deafening in terms of how they went after Alderman Preckwinkle and myself. People would say, 'Oh, Kindle, man, we trust you, you being fooled. Obama's got you fooled.' And some people called me a traitor."

The loss taught Obama a great deal about the components of his natural coalition. According to Dan Shomon, the first poll that Obama conducted revealed that the demographic he could win over most easily was white voters. Obama, who hadn't shown any particular gift for oratory in the race, now learned to shed his stiff approach to campaigning—described by Preckwinkle as that of an "arrogant academic." Mikva told me, "The first time I heard him talk to a black church, he was very professorial, more so even than he was in the white community. There was no joking, no self-deprecation, no style. It didn't go over well at all."

But, as he had in his 1996 campaign, Obama had attracted a young and zealous corps of campaign workers. "I remember one of the candidates in the race used to talk about how crazed our volunteers were, because they were passionate, energized," Will

Burns said. "You'd come by the office on Eighty-seventh Street and there'd be a bunch of guys with no teeth waiting to get their next Old Grand-Dad and then these Shiraz-drinking, *Nation*-reading, *T.N.R.*-quoting young black folk. It was a random-ass mix. It was beautiful, though. When I see the crowds now, they're very reminiscent of what was happening then."

Emil Jones told me that, after 2000, Obama moved decisively away from being pigeonholed as an inner-city pol. During one debate with Rush, he noted that he and the other candidates were all "progressive, urban Democrats." Even though he lost, that primary taught him that he might be something more than that. "He learned that for Barack Obama it was not the type of district that he was well suited for," Jones said. "The type of campaign that he had to run to win that district is not Barack Obama. It was a predominantly African American district. It was a district where you had to campaign solely on those issues. And Barack did not campaign that way, and so as a result he lost. Which was good." Meaning, it was good for Barack Obama.

•   •   •

One day in the spring of 2001, about a year after the loss to Rush, Obama walked into the Stratton Office Building, in Springfield, a shabby 1950s government workspace for state officials next to the regal state capitol. He went upstairs to a room that Democrats in Springfield called "the inner sanctum." Only about ten Democratic staffers had access; entry required an elaborate ritual—fingerprint scanners and codes punched into a keypad. The room was large, and unremarkable except for an enormous printer and an array of computers with big double monitors. On the screens that spring day were detailed maps of Chicago, and Obama and a Democratic consultant named John Corrigan sat in front of a terminal to draw Obama a new district. Corrigan was the Democrat in charge of drawing all Chicago districts, and he also happened to have volunteered for Obama in the campaign against Rush.

Obama's former district had been drawn by Republicans after the 1990 census. But, after 2000, Illinois Democrats won the right to redistrict the state. Partisan redistricting remains common in American politics, and, while it outrages a losing party, it has so far survived every legal challenge. In the new century, mapping technology has become so precise and the available demographic data so rich that politicians are able to choose the kinds of voter they want to represent, right down to individual homes. A close look at the post-2000 congressional map of Bobby Rush's district reveals that it tears through Hyde Park in a curious series of irregular turns. One of those lines bypasses Obama's address by two blocks. Rush, or someone looking out for his interests, had carved the upstart Obama out of Rush's congressional district.

In truth, Rush had little to worry about; Obama was already on a different political path. Like every other Democratic legislator who entered the inner sanctum, Obama began working on his "ideal map." Corrigan remembers two things about the district that he and Obama drew. First, it retained Obama's Hyde Park base—he had managed to beat Rush in Hyde Park—then swooped upward along the lakefront and toward downtown. By the end of the final redistricting process, his new district bore little resemblance to his old one. Rather than jutting far to the west, like a long thin dagger, into a swath of poor black neighborhoods of bungalow homes, Obama's map now shot north, encompassing about half of the Loop, whose southern portion was beginning to be transformed by developers like Tony Rezko, and stretched far up Michigan Avenue and into the Gold Coast, covering much of the city's economic heart, its main retail thoroughfares, and its finest museums, parks, skyscrapers, and lakefront apartment buildings. African

Americans still were a majority, and the map contained some of the poorest sections of Chicago, but Obama's new district was wealthier, whiter, more Jewish, less blue-collar, and better educated. It also included one of the highest concentrations of Republicans in Chicago.

"It was a radical change," Corrigan said. The new district was a natural fit for the candidate that Obama was in the process of becoming. "He saw that when we were doing fund raisers in the Rush campaign his appeal to, quite frankly, young white professionals was dramatic."

Obama's personal political concerns were not the only factor driving the process. During the previous round of remapping, in 1991, Republicans had created Chicago districts where African Americans were the overwhelming majority, packing the greatest number of loyal Democrats into the fewest districts. A decade later, Democrats tried to spread the African American vote among more districts. The idea was to create enough Democratic-leaning districts so that the party could take control of the state legislature. That goal was fine with Obama; his new district offered promising, untapped constituencies for him as he considered his next political move. "The exposure he would get to some of the folks that were on boards of the museums and C.E.O.s of some of the companies that he would represent would certainly help him in the long run," Corrigan said.

In the end, Obama's North Side fund-raising base and his South Side political base were united in one district. He now represented Hyde Park operators like Lois Friedberg-Dobry as well as Gold Coast doyennes like Bettylu Saltzman, and his old South Side street operative Al Kindle as well as his future consultant David Axelrod. In an article in the *Hyde Park Herald* about how "partisan" and "undemocratic" Illinois redistricting had become, Obama was asked for his views. As usual, he was candid. "There is a conflict of interest built into the process," he said. "Incumbents drawing their own maps will inevitably try to advantage themselves."

●   ●   ●

The partisan redistricting of Illinois may have been the most important event in Obama's early political life. It immediately gave him the two things he needed to run for the Senate in 2004: money and power. He needed to have several times as much cash as he'd raised for his losing congressional race in 2000, and many of the state's top donors now lived or worked in his district. More important, the statewide gerrymandering made it likely that Obama's party would take over the State Senate in 2002, an event that would provide him with a platform from which to craft a legislative record in time for the campaign.

Obama's political activity from 2001 to 2004 reveals a man transformed. The loss to Rush drained him of much of the naïveté he once exuded. For instance, when Obama arrived in Springfield, in 1996, he was still enamored of the spirit of community organizing and determined to apply its principles as a legislator. In an interview with the *Chicago Reader* in 1995, he laid out this vision:

> People are hungry for community; they miss it. They are hungry for change. What if a politician were to see his job as that of an organizer, as part teacher and part advocate, one who does not sell voters short but who educates them about the real choices before them? As an elected public official, for instance, I could bring church and community leaders together easier than I could as a community organizer or lawyer. We would come together to form concrete economic development strategies, take advantage of existing laws and structures, and create bridges and bonds within all sectors of the community. We must form grass-root structures that

would hold me and other elected officials more accountable for their actions.

Obama took at least one concrete step to turn this notion of the legislator as community organizer into a reality. In his first column in the *Hyde Park Herald*, the same one in which he addressed welfare, he announced that he was "organizing citizens' committees" to help him shape legislation. He asked his constituents to call his office if they wanted to participate. That kind of airy talk about changing politics gave way almost immediately to the realities of the job. I asked a longtime Obama friend what ever became of the committees. "They never really got off the ground," he said. By 2001, if there was any maxim from community organizing that Obama lived by, it was the realpolitik commandment of Saul Alinsky, the founding practitioner of community organizing, to operate in "the world as it is and not as we would like it to be."

In electoral politics, operating in the world as it is means raising money. Obama expanded the reach of his fund raising. Every network that he penetrated brought him access to another. Christie Hefner, Hugh Hefner's daughter, who runs Playboy Enterprises from the fifteenth floor of a lakefront building, explained how it worked. Hefner is a member of a group called Ladies Who Lunch—nineteen Chicago women, most of them wealthy, who see themselves as talent scouts and angel investors for up-and-coming liberal candidates and activists. They interview prospects over a meal, often in a private dining room at the Arts Club of Chicago. Obama's friend Bettylu Saltzman, a Ladies Who Lunch member, introduced Obama to the group when he was preparing his Senate run. Hefner, who declined to support Obama in 2000, was ready to help him when he came calling in 2002.

Not long ago, Hefner and I talked in her office; we were seated at a granite table strewn with copies of *Playboy*. "I was very proud to be able to introduce him during the Senate race to a lot of people who have turned out to be important and valuable to him, not just here but in New York and L.A.," Hefner explained. She mentioned Thomas Friedman, the *Times* columnist, and Norman Lear, the television producer. "I try and think about people who I think should know him."

The Speech

One insight into the transition that Obama was making during the short period between his painful loss to Bobby Rush and his Senate victory can be gained by comparing his reactions to the two major national-security crises of the time: the terrorist attacks of September 11, 2001, and the Iraq war. For many Illinois state legislators, September 11 was not an event that required much response. The attacks occurred just before an important deadline in the redistricting process. John Corrigan, the Democratic consultant in charge of redistricting, told me that he spent September 12 talking to many legislators, Obama not among them. "It was like nothing had happened," he said. "Everybody came in and all they cared about was their districts. It wasn't any one particular legislator from any one particular community. I learned a lot about state government. Their job was not to respond to September 11. They were more worried about making sure that they had a district that they could run in for reelection."

Obama's response to the event was published on September 19 in the *Hyde Park Herald*:

Even as I hope for some measure of peace and comfort to the bereaved families, I must also hope that we as a nation draw some measure of wisdom from this tragedy. Certain immediate lessons are clear, and we must act upon those lessons decisively. We need to step up security at our airports. We must reexamine the effectiveness of our intelligence networks. And we must be resolute in identifying the perpetrators of these heinous acts and dismantling their organizations of destruction.

We must also engage, however, in the more difficult task of understanding the sources of such madness. The essence of this tragedy, it seems to me, derives from a fundamental absence of empathy on the part of the attackers: an inability to imagine, or connect with, the humanity and suffering of others. Such a failure of empathy, such numbness to the pain of a child or the desperation of a parent, is not innate; nor, history tells us, is it unique to a particular culture, religion, or ethnicity. It may find expression in a particular brand of violence, and may be channeled by particular demagogues or fanatics. Most often, though, it grows out of a climate of poverty and ignorance, helplessness and despair.

We will have to make sure, despite our rage, that any U.S. military action takes into account the lives of innocent civilians abroad. We will have to be unwavering in opposing bigotry or discrimination directed against neighbors and friends of Middle Eastern descent. Finally, we will have to devote far more attention to the monumental task of raising the hopes and prospects of embittered children across the globe— children not just in the Middle East, but also in Africa, Asia, Latin America, Eastern Europe and within our own shores.

A year later, Obama agreed to speak at an antiwar rally in downtown Chicago, organized by Bettylu Saltzman and some friends, who, over Chinese food, had decided to stage the protest. Saltzman asked John Mearsheimer, a professor of political science at the University of Chicago—and, later, the coauthor of the controversial book *The Israel Lobby and U.S. Foreign Policy*—to speak, but he couldn't make it. "He was one of the main people we wanted, but he was speaking at the University of Wisconsin that day," Saltzman said. Then she called her rabbi and then Barack Obama. Michelle answered the phone and passed the message on to her husband, who was out of town.

Saltzman also called Marilyn Katz, who runs a Chicago public-relations firm and is close to Mayor Daley. Katz managed to get Jesse Jackson as a speaker, and handled many of the organizing details. Katz, a petite woman who was, improbably, the head of security for S.D.S. at the 1968 Democratic Convention, described what she felt the political mood was at the time of the rally. "Professors are being turned in on college campuses, Bush's ratings are 87 percent," she said. "Among my friends, there hasn't been an antiwar demonstration in twenty years. There's huge repression, Bush has got all this legislation. They're talking about lists, they're denying people entry into the country.... Bush's numbers were tremendously high, but we had no choice. Unless we wanted to live in a country that was fascist."

Despite the politics of Saltzman and Katz, Obama's now famous speech was notable for the absence of the traditional tropes of the antiwar left. In his biography of Obama, David Mendell, noting that Obama's speech occurred a few months before the official declaration of his U.S. Senate candidacy, suggests that the decision to publicly oppose the war in Iraq was a calculated political move intended to win favor with Saltzman. The suggestion seems dubious; the politics were more in the framing of his opposition, not the decision itself. As Saltzman told me, "He was a Hyde Park state senator. He had to oppose the war!"

The sensitive language of his September 11 statement was gone. Instead, Obama distanced himself from the pacifist activists who were surely present. "Let me begin by saying that although this has been billed as an antiwar rally, I stand before you as someone who is not opposed to war in all circumstances," he told the crowd. He then went further, defending justifiable wars in almost glorious terms. "The Civil War was one of the bloodiest in history, and yet it was only through the crucible of the sword, the sacrifice of multitudes, that we could begin to perfect this union, and drive the scourge of slavery from our soil. I don't oppose all wars. My grandfather signed up for a war the day after Pearl Harbor was bombed, fought in Patton's Army. He saw the dead and dying across the fields of Europe; he heard the stories of fellow troops who first entered Auschwitz and Treblinka. He fought in the name of a larger freedom, part of that arsenal of democracy that triumphed over evil, and he did not fight in vain. I don't oppose all wars." It took some nerve to tweak the crowd in this way. After all, it was unlikely that many of the protesters knew who Obama was, and in a lengthy write-up of the event in the *Chicago Tribune* the following day he was not mentioned. Yet the speech reads as if it had been written for a much bigger audience.

During this period, Obama also became more of a strategist, someone increasingly comfortable discussing the finer points of polls, message, and fund raising. According to his friends, Obama does not delegate campaign planning. Marty Nesbitt, his best friend, who became a familiar presence on the campaign trail this spring, flying in to play basketball with Obama on primary days, described the first meeting in which Obama pitched the idea of running for the U.S. Senate to his closest advisers and fund raisers. This was in 2002, and things seemed to be going his way. The incumbent Republican, Peter Fitzgerald, was unpopular, and the race was attracting a large field of Democrats.

"He didn't start telling people he was interested in running for Senate until he figured out what the road map was," Nesbitt said. "He had a good sense of the odds, and he knew there were certain things that had to happen. . . . The first thing he said was, 'O.K., nobody with approval ratings like this has ever been re-elected, so it's not gonna be him, right?' And then he said there's a bunch of candidates who can potentially run, one of whom was Carol Moseley Braun. And he said, 'If she runs, I probably don't have a chance, because there's gonna be certain loyalty within the African American community to her, even though she had some mistakes, and I'm probably not gonna get those African American votes, which I need as my base if I'm gonna win. So if she runs, I don't run.'

"Then he just laid out an economic analysis. It becomes about money, because he knew that if people knew his story they would view him as a better candidate than anybody else he thought might be in the field. And so he said, 'Therefore, if you raise five million dollars, I have a 50 percent chance of winning. If you raise seven million dollars, I have a 70 percent chance of winning. If you raise ten million dollars, I guarantee victory.'"

That year, he gained his first high-level experience in a state-wide campaign when he advised the victorious gubernatorial candidate Rod Blagojevich, another politician with a funny name and a message of reform. Rahm Emanuel, a congressman from Chicago and a friend of Obama's, told me that he, Obama, David Wilhelm, who was Blagojevich's campaign cochair, and another Blagojevich aide were the top strategists of Blagojevich's victory. He and Obama "participated in a small group that met weekly when Rod was running for governor," Emanuel said. "We basically laid out the general election, Barack and I and these two." A spokesman for Blagojevich confirmed Emanuel's account, although David Wilhelm, who now works for Obama, said that Emanuel had overstated Obama's role. "There was an advisory council that was inclusive of Rahm and Barack but not limited to them," Wilhelm said, and he disputed the notion that Obama was "an architect or one of the principal strategists."

David Axelrod, the preeminent strategist in the state, declined to work for Blagojevich. "He had been my client and I had a very good relationship with him, but I didn't sign on to the governor's race," Axelrod said. "Obviously he won, but I had concerns about it. . . . I was concerned about whether he was ready for that. Not so much for the race but for governing. I was concerned about some of the folks—I was concerned about how

the race was being approached." Axelrod's unease was war-
ranted. Blagojevich and people close to him have been tied to a
seemingly endless series of scandals. The trial of Tony Rezko revealed that Rezko used his influence in the Blagojevich administration to profit from companies seeking business with the state.
There is speculation that Blagojevich will be the next governor
to be indicted, and the Democratic speaker of the Illinois House,
Michael Madigan, has raised the issue of impeachment.

Part of Obama's political success is that he has been able to
exploit relationships with important yet ethically dubious figures
in Illinois while still maintaining his independence. In some
ways, this is an Illinois tradition. When the liberal reformer
Adlai Stevenson ran for governor, in 1948, one Democratic boss
reportedly noted that he would "perfume the ticket." The earnest
Lincoln scholar Paul Simon stood out in the Senate for his moral
rectitude and his commitment to good government even as his
state wallowed in scandal. "The political bosses knew they had to
have what they used to call in business a loss leader—the show-
casing," Don Rose, the Chicago political consultant, said. "The
car that you sold for under its value for advertising purposes.
While you had at the top of your ticket a shining star, under that
it was like turning over a rock."

Obama has said little about the scandals in his home state.
Besides the Rezko and Blagojevich cases, there have been indictments and convictions against the Daley administration con-
cerning hiring and contracting practices. Getting close to the
sullied political leadership in Illinois was probably an unavoidable cost of winning the U.S. Senate seat. Emil Jones told me that
another of the lessons Obama learned after his 2000 loss was the
importance of political sponsorship.

Jones and Obama have had a complicated history. As a community organizer, Obama led a protest against Jones, and in his
memoir he unflatteringly describes him as an "old ward heeler."

("I guess he figured I was part of the establishment," Jones told me, objecting to the description. "He didn't know too much about politics and he was very idealistic.") Years later, Jones backed Palmer over Obama in the State Senate race. But their relationship changed dramatically after 2000. When Obama praised Jones as "my political godfather," Jones began using the theme music from *The Godfather* as his cell-phone ringtone.

I spoke to Jones in his office minutes after he left a meeting with the governor, a close ally whom he has defended during the recent difficulties. Jones, who is seventy-two, is a former sewer inspector and insurance salesman; he speaks in a soft rumble and practices politics in a characteristically Chicago manner. He recently explained his support for a proposal to increase the salaries of legislators by saying, "I need a pay raise." In May, the *Chicago Sun-Times* reported that Jones "provided himself with tens of thousands of dollars in interest-free loans from his campaign fund," which, the report noted, is not illegal in Illinois but is "highly unusual." A spokesman for Jones said that Jones "has always made it a practice to pay back the loans and continues to do so."

Being in the majority has proved hard for the Democrats. They were having trouble agreeing on a budget deal, and the newspapers were filled with those murmurs of impeachment. For Jones, discussing his long history with the presumptive Democratic presidential nominee—from target of the youthful Obama's antiestablishment organizing to political patron in Springfield—seemed a welcome relief, a reminder of happier times for Democrats in Illinois.

"When he ran that race against Bobby Rush, he had no one supporting him who had political influence over others and whom people respected, so he was out there as a lone wolf in that race," Jones said. That's why, in 2002, as Obama planned his next campaign, he sought out Jones. "We never discussed it, but he had to analyze that race and recognize he had no other powerful elected officials supporting him," Jones said. "And so he felt I could be very, very key if he was going to make the run for the U.S. Senate.

"In politics, you must know who is connected to whom," Jones continued. "The mayor of Chicago and the father of Dan Hynes"—one of Obama's primary opponents—"when they were both state senators they shared an apartment together in Springfield, so there's a relationship between those two. And the governor? One of his chief financial supporters in his first run was also in the race. I work with both the mayor and the governor, so, by my jumping in strong behind Barack Obama, they didn't want to alienate me and have me upset with them, so they stayed out of the race."

In the State Senate, Jones did something even more important for Obama. He pushed him forward as the key sponsor of some of the party's most important legislation, even though the move did not sit well with some colleagues who had plugged away in the minority on bills that Obama now championed as part of the majority. "Because he had been in the minority, Barack didn't have a legislative record to run on, and there was a buildup of all these great ideas that the Republicans kept in the rules committee when they were in the majority," Burns said. "Jones basically gave Obama the space to do what Obama wanted to do. Emil made it clear to people that it would be good for them." Burns, who at that point was working for Jones, was assigned to keep an eye on Obama's floor votes, which, because he was a Senate candidate, would be under closer scrutiny. The Obama-Jones alliance worked. In one year, 2003, Obama passed much of the legislation, including bills on racial profiling, death-penalty reform, and expanded health insurance for children, that he highlighted in his Senate campaign.

One Step Ahead

Perhaps the greatest misconception about Barack Obama is that he is some sort of antiestablishment revolutionary. Rather, every stage of his political career has been marked by an eagerness to accommodate himself to existing institutions rather than tear them down or replace them. When he was a community organizer, he channeled his work through Chicago's churches, because they were the main bases of power on the South Side. He was an agnostic when he started, and the work led him to become a practicing Christian. At Harvard, he won the presidency of the *Law Review* by appealing to the conservatives on the selection panel. In Springfield, rather than challenge the old-guard Democratic leaders, Obama built a mutually beneficial relationship with them. "You have the power to make a United States senator," he told Emil Jones in 2003. In his downtime, he played poker with lobbyists and Republican lawmakers. In Washington, he has been a cautious senator and, when he arrived, made a point of not defining himself as an opponent of the Iraq war.

Like many politicians, Obama is paradoxical. He is by nature an incrementalist, yet he has laid out an ambitious first-term agenda (energy independence, universal health care, withdrawal from Iraq). He campaigns on reforming a broken political process, yet he has always played politics by the rules as they exist, not as he would like them to exist. He runs as an outsider, but he has succeeded by mastering the inside game. He is ideologically a man of the left, but at times he has been genuinely deferential to core philosophical insights of the right.

Obama's establishment inclinations have alienated some old friends. During the 2004 Senate primary, Obama sometimes reminded voters of his anti-machine credentials, but at the same time he shrewdly wrote to Mayor Daley's brother, William, who had backed one of Obama's primary opponents, asking for his support if he won the primary. As he outgrew the provincial politics of Hyde Park, he became closer to the mayor, and this accommodation, as well as his unwillingness to condemn the corruption scandals ensnaring Daley and Blagojevich, both of whom he supported for reelection, have some of his original supporters feeling alienated and angry. "I am not thrilled with Barack, simply because we elected him as an Independent, and he switched over to Daley," Alan Dobry said. Ivory Mitchell, speaking of Obama's Senate race, said, "When he won the primary out here and he went downtown, it appears as though Daley took over the campaign for him. . . . We were excluded." David Axelrod told me, in response, that some of the Independents on the South Side blame Daley for just about anything. "I think there's kind of this Wizard of Oz mystique," he said. "Daley had virtually no role in the Senate campaign."

Another transition from primary to general election is now under way for Obama, and it is causing him a similar set of problems, all of which stem from a realization among his supporters that superheroes don't become president; politicians do. Judging by the reaction to Obama's most recent decisions—his willingness to support legislation to modify the Foreign Intelligence Surveillance Act, his rightward shift on interpreting the Second Amendment, his decision to "refine" his Iraq policies—some voters will be crushed by this realization and others will be relieved. In another episode that has Obama's old friends feeling frustrated, Obama recently blamed his first campaign manager, Carol Anne Harwell, for reporting on a 1996 questionnaire that Obama favored a ban on handguns. According to her friends, Harwell was furious that the campaign made her Obama's scapegoat. "She got, as the saying goes, run over by a bus," Lois Friedberg-Dobry said.

Obama's rise has often appeared effortless. His offstage tactics—when he is engaged in the sometimes combative work of a politician—are rarely glimpsed by outsiders. Penny Pritzker, a friend and fund-raiser for Obama, remembers meeting with him at her office in 2006 to discuss his presidential campaign. Pritzker, whose family, one of the wealthiest in Chicago, owns the Hyatt hotel chain, was as crucial to Obama's next campaign as Toni Preckwinkle's was to his first. "We were talking about whether he was ready to do this or not," Pritzker told me. She was blunt, telling Obama, "As I see it, the two things that you're going to need to address are your executive leadership skills, because your résumé doesn't have that in it, and the second would be your credentials in national security." Obama returned with an organizational chart indicating how the campaign would be structured—one of his great tactical advantages over the disorganized Clinton campaign—along with a list of advisers. Pritzker agreed to become his finance chair. Obama has frequently been one step ahead of his friends and the public in anticipating his own rise. Perhaps it is all those people he has met over the years who told him that he would be president one day. The Reverend Alvin Love, a South Side Baptist minister and a longtime Obama friend, said that Obama called him in December 2006, seeking advice about whether to run for president. "My dad told me that you've got to strike while the iron is hot," Love recalls saying, and Obama replied, "The iron can't get any hotter."

Obama has always had a healthy understanding of the reaction he elicits in others, and he learned to use it to his advantage a very long time ago. Marty Nesbitt remembers Obama's utter calm the day he gave his celebrated speech at the 2004 Democratic National Convention, in Boston, which made him an international celebrity and a potential 2008 presidential candidate. "We were walking down the street late in the afternoon," Nesbitt told me. "And this crowd was building behind us, like it was Tiger Woods at the Masters."

"Barack, man, you're like a rock star," Nesbitt said.

"Yeah, if you think it's bad today, wait until tomorrow," Obama replied.

"What do you mean?"

"My speech," Obama said, "is pretty good."

The Nation

Naomi Klein's hypervigilant columns neither waste nor mince words. Whatever the topic, she delivers articulate, wide-awake commentary that quickens the pulse and the fires the synapses.

Naomi Klein

Disowned by the Ownership Society

Remember the "ownership society," fixture of major George W. Bush addresses for the first four years of his presidency? "We're creating . . . an ownership society in this country, where more Americans than ever will be able to open up their door where they live and say, welcome to my house, welcome to my picce of property," Bush said in October 2004. Washington think-tanker Grover Norquist predicted that the ownership society would be Bush's greatest legacy, remembered "long after people can no longer pronounce or spell Fallujah." Yet in Bush's final State of the Union address, the once-ubiquitous phrase was conspicuously absent. And little wonder: rather than its proud father, Bush has turned out to be the ownership society's undertaker.

Well before the ownership society had a neat label, its creation was central to the success of the right-wing economic revolution around the world. The idea was simple: if working-class people owned a small piece of the market—a home mortgage, a stock portfolio, a private pension—they would cease to identify as workers and start to see themselves as owners, with the same interests as their bosses. That meant they could vote for politicians promising to improve stock performance rather than job conditions. Class consciousness would be a relic.

It was always tempting to dismiss the ownership society as an empty slogan—"hokum" as former Labor Secretary Robert Reich put it. But the ownership society was quite real. It was the answer to a roadblock long faced by politicians favoring policies to benefit the wealthy. The problem boiled down to this: people tend to vote their economic interests. Even in the wealthy United States, most people earn less than the average income. That means it is in the interest of the majority to vote for politicians promising to redistribute wealth from the top down.

So what to do? It was Margaret Thatcher who pioneered a solution. The effort centered on Britain's public housing, or council estates, which were filled with die-hard Labour Party supporters. In a bold move, Thatcher offered strong incentives to residents to buy their council estate flats at reduced rates (much as Bush did decades later by promoting subprime mortgages). Those who could afford it became homeowners while those who couldn't faced rents almost twice as high as before, leading to an explosion of homelessness.

As a political strategy, it worked: the renters continued to oppose Thatcher, but polls showed that more than half of the newly minted owners did indeed switch their party affiliation to the Tories. The key was a psychological shift: they now thought like owners, and owners tend to vote Tory. The ownership society as a political project was born.

Across the Atlantic, Reagan ushered in a range of policies that similarly convinced the public that class divisions no longer existed. In 1988 only 26 percent of Americans told pollsters that they lived in a society bifurcated into "haves" and "have-nots"—71 percent rejected the whole idea of class. The real breakthrough, however, came in the 1990s, with the "democratization" of stock ownership, eventually leading to nearly half of American households owning stock. Stock watching became a national pastime, with tickers on TV screens becoming more common than weather forecasts. Main Street, we were told, had stormed the elite enclaves of Wall Street.

Once again, the shift was psychological. Stock ownership made up a relatively minor part of the average American's earnings, but in the era of frenetic downsizing and offshoring, this new class of amateur investor had a distinct shift in consciousness. Whenever a new round of layoffs was announced, sending another stock price soaring, many responded not by identifying with those who had lost their jobs, or by protesting the policies that had led to the layoffs, but by calling their brokers with instructions to buy.

Bush came to office determined to take these trends even further, to deliver Social Security accounts to Wall Street and target minority communities—traditionally out of the Republican Party's reach—for easy homeownership. "Under 50 percent of African Americans and Hispanic Americans own a home," Bush observed in 2002. "That's just too few." He called on Fannie Mae and the private sector "to unlock millions of dollars, to make it available for the purchase of a home"—an important reminder that subprime lenders were taking their cue straight from the top.

Today, the basic promises of the ownership society have been broken. First the dot-com bubble burst; then employees watched their stock-heavy pensions melt away with Enron and WorldCom. Now we have the subprime mortgage crisis, with more than 2 million homeowners facing foreclosure on their homes. Many are raiding their 401(k)s—their piece of the stock market—to pay their mortgage. Wall Street, meanwhile, has fallen out of love with Main Street. To avoid regulatory scrutiny, the new trend is away from publicly traded stocks and toward private equity. In November Nasdaq joined forces with several private banks, including Goldman Sachs, to form Portal Alliance, a private equity stock market open only to investors with assets upward of $100 million. In short order yesterday's ownership society has morphed into today's members-only society.

The mass eviction from the ownership society has profound political implications. According to a September Pew Research poll, 48 percent of Americans say they live in a society carved into haves and have-nots—nearly twice the number of 1988. Only 45 percent see themselves as part of the haves. In other words, we are seeing a return of the very class consciousness that the ownership society was supposed to erase. The free-market ideologues have lost an extremely potent psychological tool—and progressives have gained one. Now that John Edwards is out of the presidential race, the question is, will anyone dare to use it?

Harper's

FINALIST—FEATURE
WRITING

In a timely and haunting piece, writer Paul Reyes eloquently describes the "trashing out" of foreclosed homes in Florida, putting a human face on the mortgage meltdown.

Paul Reyes

Bleak Houses

When I ask my father what he remembers about the first houses he "trashed out"—a phrase we use to describe the process of entering a home that has been foreclosed upon by the bank, and that the bank would like to sell, and hauling all of what the dispossessed owner has left behind to the nearest dump, then returning to clean the place by spraying every corner and wiping every inch of glass, deleting every fingerprint, scrubbing the boot marks off the linoleum, bleaching the cruddy toilets, sweeping up the hair and sand and dust, steaming the stains out of the carpet (or, if the carpet is un-salvageably rancid, tearing it out), and eventually, thereby, eras-ing all traces of whoever lived there, dispensing with both their physical presence and the ugly aura of eviction—he says he doesn't remember much. It was around fifteen years ago, for one thing, well before I joined him; and since then he has trashed out so much bizarre flotsam, under such strange circumstances, that his memories of those first few houses have faded.

None of the anecdotes my father shares about his work are up-lifting. Sure, there are comedies and tragicomedies, and some plots are shot through with an absurdity that seems indigenous to Florida, where this began for us. But overall the situation remains bleakly fixed: every foreclosed house, empty or not, clean or crumbling, feels lost, no matter the neighborhood or amenities, no matter the waterfront view. Some houses are found spotless, others in a wretched degradation, and the varieties are shared among the rich and poor, the elderly and upwardly mobile. Some houses are lost before ever having been lived in. Others, abandoned long ago, provide shelter for addicts, bums, whores, snakes, strays, and low fungal kingdoms that fan out in the darkness, kick-started, maybe, by a cat turd or bowl of leftovers.

The junk left behind has fascinated me since I began working for my father ten years ago—during holidays, or between jobs, boomeranging between his home in Tampa and wherever I ended up next—tagging along with his regular crew, a pair of Puerto Rican laborers who start the day at six and call it at three. I've always been the crew's weak link, both because I flinch in places that, after a year of abandonment, have become so gloriously foul, and because I can't help but read a narrative in what has been discarded. I begin to pick, sweating nearly every item we throw away, creeping among gadgets and notes and utility bills and photographs in order to decipher who lived there and how they lost it, a life partially revealed by stuff marinating in a fetid stillness. It is a guilt-ridden literary forensics, because to confront the junk is to confront the individuality being purged from a place. My father has never been all that interested in this particular angle. He likes to keep things simple: he gets an address, the crew goes to work. Now and then I join them, but I've never been much good at keeping up.

Foreclosures are our family business. My father moved us to Florida in 1984, when I was thirteen, and after starting a small construction company, and losing it, and, after a relatively diplomatic divorce from my mother and a brief midlife crisis, marrying again, to a real estate agent this time, he began dabbling in houses—repairing them, restoring the historic ones, flipping most for a modest profit, redeeming his misery behind a desk by building things. His second wife, Mena, had been working with foreclosures for a while, and with my father now close at hand, when it came time to clean a place out, she knew who could do the job. The houses kept coming, but for every home lost, odds were that a buyer could be found: real estate in Florida was at least somewhat predictable. Even during the boom of the early 2000s, foreclosures were common but eventually became solvent properties within a matter of weeks.

By the time I flew home this spring, however, buyers had long since disappeared, and houses by the thousands—both new and old—now sat empty, beginning their slow corrosion. The crowds that once camped outside subdivision gates, hoping to snatch a prime lot, had evaporated, and the subdivisions were devouring their own value: homes built in 2006 were being repossessed within a year and by spring 2008 sold for half as much as the surrounding homes, finished just a few months earlier. Some homeowners, in a brave tactic, were simply walking away from their debt, mailing the keys to the bank. While the Federal Reserve weighed its billion-dollar pledges to the institutions that had puppeteered the biggest economic collapse since the Great Depression, the statistical damage on the ground was giving that comparison some weight: between the time Florida's housing market began to cool off in 2005 and my arrival this past spring, the rate of homes being lost had quadrupled, to more than 35,000 per month, 4,700 of which were in cities within my father's working radius—Tampa, St. Petersburg, Clearwater. The collapse was surreal in its proportion, biblical in its egalitarian reach, like an economic cleansing fire.

And yes, this spring, my father's crew and I were flush with work.

.   .   .

I landed in Tampa on a drizzly afternoon a couple of weeks before Easter, the air close and laced with salt from the Gulf. My father met me at the airport with a subtle hug and a slap on the back of the head with his folded newspaper. He'd been absorbing headlines lately: a housing meltdown, Fidel Castro's exit—his profession, his mother country both at a crossroads. He took my satchel and deferred the heavier luggage to me; his back had become unpredictable a few years ago, after a big sneeze, of all things. Now I carry the heavy luggage, and he compensates for this reversal by indulging in some old disciplinary reflexes, however useless: after gently deflecting my excitement about the news from Cuba, he looked at me and said, with no small dose of disapproval, "You need a haircut."

Out on the highway, the traffic poured from the airport and split along overpasses, blending with thicker tendrils of more traffic that flowed out toward the suburbs and sprawl. We headed east on an errand: a foreclosure on Hillsborough Lane. Whoever lived in the house had ignored the first notice my father posted, prompting a second notice, same as the first, to call Mena. As the intermediary between the bank and the owner, Mena, at the bank's request, will prepare a home to be placed back on the market. If the house is occupied, she can sometimes negotiate a less painful exit, through a cash-for-keys exchange. If the owner refuses, the bank sends a sheriff, an expert messenger of bad news and ultimatums.

My father had already visited this house once before, to see whether it was occupied. A rottweiler in the front yard was a pretty good clue, and so he left the first notice in the mailbox, on the prudent side of a chain-link fence. We knew nothing about the occupant. We almost never do at first. We are given an address and a name, and in this case we didn't even have the name. All my father had this time was the rottweiler. "Bad," he said. "Black."

"All rottweilers are black," I said.

"Well, this one was *black*."

We took the Waters Avenue exit off the freeway and dipped down to street level, rolling past the Derby Lane dog track (DOGS,

PONIES, POKER!), past the All Nations Outreach Center, past a meat market, past tall boys weaving on small bikes and girls in bathing suits ambling on the sidewalk toward the neighborhood pool, ignoring the rain, or just dressed to endure the heat. At Hillsborough Lane we turned and coasted slowly until we spotted the house's number, then squeaked to a stop. We sat still, and with the drizzle against the windshield that stillness swelled a little. I looked at the houses surrounding this one: neighbors barely keeping it together and others teetering into squalor, a mash of hasty, low architecture, single-story, pale cinder-block jobs squatting under live oaks sagged with Spanish moss. A four-by-four beam stood seven feet tall in front of the house we were after, with a pair of small satellite dishes perched on top, a ubiquitous amenity. Next to it, the plastic mailbox.

The dog was missing. The chain-link gate was swung wide open. The yard was a psoriatic patchwork of grass and gray sand. Judging by the size of the plywood doghouse, the rottweiler was indeed big. The yard reflected its temperament: blown-out pits within the ten-foot radius of a chain anchored by a dumbbell half-buried in the sand. Lizards—thick and deep-black, masculine, and, after a childhood in Florida, nostalgically repulsive to me—scuttled along the edge of the fence.

The rain thickened. The wipers dragged slowly back and forth. A FOR SALE sign leaned between the fence and the street.

"That wasn't here a couple of days ago," my father said, and humphed. "He can say he wants to sell it all he wants to, he's not going to cover the debt." The house probably wasn't even worth what the owner owed the bank. Likely, he had sucked out every penny of equity to help pay for something else, and was, in the economic lingo, upside-down. When real estate in Tampa was hot, this house had been worth perhaps $120,000, but it wasn't worth half that now.

My father pulled a notice from between the driver's seat and the armrest. Every notice he posts is the same: a photocopy of

Mena's business card with instructions to contact her. In the upper-right corner of the card is her portrait—smiling, professionally shot, the light softened a little. This style of head shot is popular among real estate agents. Maybe, under calmer circumstances, for a client who is interested in buying or selling a home, the smile evokes a sense of trust or good fortune. Ushering you out onto the street, the smile seems a bit inappropriate. But there it was, photocopied in black and white on a sheet of paper. My father laid it flat on his briefcase and began scribbling the simple instructions in pencil, in the penmanship he'd learned as a draftsman and which I've always admired for its precision but have never been able to imitate exactly—capital, architectural letters, perfectly straight, the joints of each letter bolted together, the words aligned as if written along a phantom ruler, impossible to misread: PLEASE CALL MENA. WE ARE OFFERING CASH FOR KEYS. If the house was left in acceptable condition, the bank would provide cash to help cover the cost of moving (in this case, $500)—a small amelioration, but cash nonetheless.

Normally, he would have taped the notice to the door and ducked out. But it was raining, and the rottweiler, though out of sight, might still have been napping around back, and so my father merely slipped out of the truck, shoved the notice into the mailbox, then slipped back in.

"I'm surprised you haven't been shot," I said.

"It's always on my mind," he said, and began scribbling down the FOR SALE sign's phone number so Mena could call. He slid the gear shift into drive and looked around, disappointed. That mythical black motherfucker of a dog—he had wanted me to see it for myself.

·   ·   ·

Early the next morning, in a bruise-colored light, we lurched behind a school bus as it blinked and stopped every fifty yards or so, nearly all the way to Centennial Court, where we were looking for a single-story ⅔ (two bedrooms, two baths). It was a dense neighborhood remarkable only for its anonymity, built in the postwar boom but whose homes didn't seem to embody the American dream as prescribed. At best, these were starter kits to the dream, their privacy fences tagged with graffiti, their roofs sprouting satellite dishes, often two at a time—a sign, my father said, that the family inside was Hispanic, since one dish would be for American television, a second for Latin American channels.

He often reads ethnicity in the details. After jimmying the front-door lock and taking a look around, he guessed that these owners must have been Hispanic, too, since nearly every square inch of floor was covered with white tile, a cooling system of sorts. In one corner of the back yard, another clue: a makeshift *caja china*—a box in which a pig is sealed and slowly roasted under coals piled atop the lid. This one had been discarded long ago and was little more than a tub for rainwater now, swarming with ants that had carried off the pig's drippings but still searched for more.

The house held curious loot: a pleather couch, a weightlifting set, empty liquor bottles. The garage had been used as a make-shift room but not altogether converted. In it were signs of a final effort to coordinate an exodus that must have failed, since there were half a dozen garbage bags sitting full, as if waiting.

"Here," my father said, kicking a headlight casing. "It's a motorcycle . . . thing."

I picked up a helmet, which felt creepily personal, tossed it aside, and dug into the bags. Every single one was crammed with toys, mostly stuffed animals and dolls.

In the rest of the junk, a profile came together: Sindy lived with Robert, but they didn't share a last name. Perhaps she was a stepdaughter, or a roommate, because in the back bedroom, split by veloured light, SINDY & CHRI$ was stenciled on the wall in black, with a devil's tail whipping underneath. So Sindy, just twenty-five, judging by the birthday card left behind, loved Chris deeply, but other than the stenciled dedication there wasn't a trace of him. My bet was that Robert had something to do with it, but it was hard to say. Information only fueled speculation.

The one indisputable fact was their indiscriminate taste in booze. The bottles scattered throughout the tiny kitchen—Seagram's, Crown Royal, Hine, Hennessy, Bacardi, Holland Vodka (in a bong-shaped bottle), and Brugal rum—suggested either a slovenly habit of keeping empties or a blowout near the end; and the way the padded dining chairs were angled against the window-side table, with the bottles knocked over, lent some credence to the rager theory, in which Sindy and Robert and whoever else—bags full in the next room, their sofa too heavy to keep, the sheriff on his way—drank up their courage, kicked aside a box or two, and headed out into an unpredictable future.

·　　·　　·

Between addresses, we made a quick stop at a nearby Cuban *panadería*, a ritual of my visits home. We hovered over cartoonishly bright pastries until called upon, then ordered a couple of *cafés con leche*, and, while waiting, admired the fried stuff—pork skins, ham croquettes, minced-meat pies, bronze and garish and sultry under the heat lamp. Salsa music played softly above us. The doorbell dinged. The crowd swelled and ebbed with regulars dedicated to this brave motherland diet, in a tiny room packed with the odors of hot oil and coffee and sugar and warm bread. And sure, pork skins for breakfast might mean fewer days in the long run, but they added a weird vigor to the morning. If anything, the grease is sentimental.

We took turns rummaging through the bag of food on the way to the next house, passing through Odessa's thick stretches of cypress and oak, the last rural stronghold against Tampa's sprawl. The city's rate of expansion meant that my father's work had expanded too. Logging a hundred miles a day had become common, leaving plenty of time for window-gazing and small talk.

On the way to Anaheim Avenue, we lit on the subject of breaking into a house. My father's preferred method, which he had used back on Centennial, was to slide a flathead screwdriver between door and frame, then leverage the cylinder out of the lock as he twisted the doorknob with a clamp wrench. "You're bending the insides," he said. "All you need is about a quarter of an inch. It's got a shaft, and the shaft is connected to the cylinder, so if you pull it back enough—"

"What did you do before that?"

"Bang it with a hammer. But that messed up the door. This is more surgical. And if it fails, you use a drill and open holes in it so you can get to it. Drill directly into the deadbolt. Those things are cheap, the deadbolts. Once you open three or four holes, it falls apart."

"So it's pretty easy to break into a house."

"Oh, yeah," he said. "We've never failed to get into a house. There is *always* a way."

Out the window, I could see a subdivision frozen in an early phase of construction. A handful of bright nouveau-Victorian town houses stood lifeless, surrounded by empty plots. There was no activity whatsoever—no earth diggers, no foremen, not even a pickup truck darting across a street. Just a ghost town starting at $200 a square foot. Nearer to us, along the shoulder of the road, the power company was laying lines for future works.

"If not," my father said, "you take the sliding doors, lift them up off the track, and they come out."

I didn't get it.

"Well, typically, those doors, people never adjust them, so they settle, to a point where there's enough room on top so that you can lift them higher than the track and pull them out. People use them for years without adjusting them. At the bottom, that little wheel can be adjusted up and down. Over time, it wears down. That's all you need."

.   .   .

The truck's GPS device guided us to Anaheim Avenue but couldn't tell us where the house was exactly. Three lawns down, though, we saw it: a pair of white wicker chairs, one crushed, leaning against the trunk of a bedraggled live oak, as if pitched there by a wind. A few feet away, iron patio chairs lay facedown like drunks passed out on the lawn. The house was a mid-century ranch, maybe a little more recent, with tall windows stretching between the bushes and the eaves.

We got out. The lawn was carpeted with the live oak's brittle, mustard-colored leaves—months of shedding, if not a year's worth. An elderly couple walked past and stared, and I waved. The breeze picked up. The air was lush. Nimbus clouds sauntered high behind the roof.

We walked around to the back of the house, past a futon frame cradling a pile of branches, through a picket fence, and into a small yard, with a bird fountain at the fence's edge and beyond that a pond with houses along the far bank. In the yard, to the left, was an aluminum shed. My father moved past it and walked up to the screen door of the sunroom. He pressed his face against the glass and humphed. "I know I can get into this one," he said.

Circling back around, we checked the front door—locked—and peeked through the living-room windows. The curtains were missing. In the middle of the living room, on the carpet, sat an electric stove and a wicker shelf for menagerie toppled on its side.

"You sure this is unoccupied?" I said.

"Mena thinks it is," he said.

A small yellow notice taped to the window, stuck there by an agent of Fidelity Information Services, confirmed that the house was vacant. The window screen leaned on the ground, and we figured this must have been how Fidelity's agent slipped in. I was busy reading the rest of the notice as my father bent down and yanked the window open, the springs cracking—*the mortgage holder has the right and duty to protect this property accordingly. It is likely that the mortgage holder will have the property*—and let the window slam shut.

"See," my father said, muted behind the glass. "There's always a way."

Inside, surrounded by half-full boxes, I began scribbling down a partial inventory:

1 wicker throne
1 walkie-talkie
The White Album
Masterplots (6 volumes)
15 pairs of women's shoes
Mother's Day card, signed, "Love, Us"
Glasses, one pair

The owner's name was Sue, a fact gleaned from the pile of bills and letters left on the bedroom floor. The paper trail told that she had inherited money from a will, apparently, then spent it, and was collecting Social Security by the time she lost the house. She had lived in Maine for a while. She scribbled epigrams and lyrics on index cards and coupons: "Words express both the best & worse of life. Let the words you choose express the life you wont to live"—"Send me a man that Reads"—"She walked across his heart like it was Texas"—"He was on the morning side of the mountain, She was on the twilight side of the hill."

She struggled with work. Birthday and Mother's Day cards and letters included encouragements and best wishes in finding jobs, be it in 1999 or 2002. One birthday card had a basset hound on the cover, which made me guess she had owned one. Turns out she owned two, Hanzel and Gretel, whose vet bills were in the pile, and against whom an injunction had been filed in court, for nuisance and trespassing. I couldn't find a picture of her or of anyone she knew. All the framed photographs that remained were of models in generic scenes, or a publicity still from *Titanic*, or a stock photo of the Golden Gate Bridge.

I could hear my father in another room, taking pictures with a disposable camera, cranking to the next frame, clicking. I followed the sound to the pine-paneled sunroom, through the windows of which I could see an egret alight on the edge of the pond. Bad guess—my father was elsewhere—but here was a set of boxes that suggested Sue was an ambitious reader with eclectic tastes: Huxley's *Brave New World*, several Sidney Sheldon titles, Danielle Steel, *Bartlett's Familiar Quotations*, a thesaurus, the *Irritable Bowel Syndrome Gastrointestinal Solutions Handbook*, Hemingway, a waterlogged *Don Quixote*, Salinger, I. F. Stone's *The War Years*, *Reader's Digest*, *Nine Steps to Financial Freedom*, *Love Handles for the Romantically Impaired*. Books on thinking positively, on self-hypnosis, on UFOs, on Darwinism. I found copies of *Dog Fancy* and a long outdated issue of *The Best and Worst Makeovers Ever*. There were boxes stuffed with monographs on Dalí, Toulouse-Lautrec, Picasso; books on Art Nouveau, on the Impressionists, on the painters of Montmartre. A stack of travel sections from the local newspaper, and an article on "Five Myths About Reagan."

I went to the shed out back and found more books—in boxes, lined up on a makeshift shelf, stacked in a pile among Christmas gift wrapping, lodged against picture frames swaddled in blankets. It was a shrine of sorts. Here, apparently, was everything that pertained to a late husband, Herb, whose effects had been stored long enough to dissolve in the Florida heat. Shelby Foote's Civil War trilogy rotted next to the Harvard Classics; millipedes chewed through John Jakes. The humidity had devoured Herb's yearbooks. His memory seemed to have been entombed in this shed for years and never visited. Even the stove had made it closer to an exit than Herb had.

My father called Mena to fill her in. One bedroom, unoccupied, with a two-car garage and central heat and air. The pond out back was a plus.

·　　·　　·

Hector, bronze and balding, his thick waist wrapped in a weightlifting belt, is the bullish half of my father's two-man crew. He stands a broad five foot eight, with forearms that seem divinely constructed for ripping things apart. Hector moved from Puerto Rico more than twenty years ago and began working with my father not long after. English still eludes him; only when he attempts it does he reveal a shyness. But speaking Spanish with him doesn't help much either, since his is gruffly muttered and loaded with idiom. Even my father shrugs at most of what Hector says, or asks him to repeat it, slowly. Hector is also furiously Christian, and given his penchant for talking constantly, with a drill sergeant's urgency, it is difficult to predict what topic will trigger some irritable call to Christ.

Ismael, also Puerto Rican, is Hector's Sancho Panza, and his English is only slightly less dysfunctional. He's in his early seventies but is so small and fumbling that he never wins the respect due the elderly. Hector merely barks at him, or corrects him, or berates him when he's klutzy. Ismael tends to stay quiet in Hector's presence. In truth, he despises Hector for his discourtesy, but he has been working with him for fifteen years now, and they have become grudgingly inseparable, like a marriage or a bitter vaudeville act. But they are mule-like in their constancy and fearlessness when it comes to digging through repugnant places.

Three in the truck, tiny Ismael in the middle, we were headed this morning to Sue's house to trash it out. The job would require three trips to a landfill another forty minutes away, convenient only because it wouldn't make us sort the trash ourselves; we could back up to the incinerator, unload the pile, and go.

Religious folk music blasted out of the speakers—Hector's favorite group: Spanish, melodic, and sweet, a family of singers, children and all. I asked him what he thought the difference was between the job now and in years past. Now, he said, everyone is mixed up in it, every race and every class. Now, he shouted, in Spanish and with an evangelical urgency, "it's *much* more than you think. *Son de todo! Todo, todo!*"

"All mix," Ismael muttered.

"You know why so many people are losing their houses?" Hector asked. "Yeah, sure, people lose their jobs, but the majority— thousands! hundreds of thousands!—they lost their homes because the people at the bank, many of them, are wicked! They don't tell you that the interest rates are going to go up. They just make you sign the papers. They cheat you!"

Ismael, inspired, blurted out: "You need to think about your resources, whether you have the means or not to pay for a house. That's why the Bible says, 'For which one of you, when he wants to build a tower, does not first sit down and calculate—'"

Hector cut him off: "No, that's different, that's not what I'm talking about."

"It's the same thing."

"No, totally different."

"Buy only what you—"

"We're talking about something else."

At Sue's house, we backed the trailer up to the garage and got to work, each of us tackling a different room, and from the bedroom I could hear Hector reprimanding Ismael for misunderstanding some direction on where to put what. Paint cans went along the south wall of the garage; anything metal went in the yard; items for the church went on the opposite side of the trailer. Whenever Ismael saw me after some heated exchange ("Leave the paint there." "But you told me to move the paint—" "Leave it!"), he'd mutter something and roll his eyes, already frustrated. Fast, gloveless, and without much curiosity, the two of them loaded the first trailer in half an hour. For one cabinet too heavy to drag, Hector grabbed the sledgehammer and brought down devastation upon it, then tossed it on the pile, piece by piece.

The house locked, we eased back onto the street and headed for the dump, chair legs jutting out, paper flying off behind us. After a quick stop at a hot-dog vendor in the parking lot of a defaulted store, we drove on to the Pasco County Solid Waste Resource Recovery Facility. It was a preserve of waste, almost sylvan if one took care not to breathe. We could pick up the stench of rot a quarter mile out. Having declined to buy a hot dog, I was getting hungry, and Hector knew it. "Smells like cake!" he shouted, and then in English barked: "Coffee cake!"

We drove up a hill and into a hangar that housed the main incinerator. A mountain of garbage rose about four stories high along the east wall, out of a pit that sank another six or so stories down into the earth. A crane glided along the top of the wall; its claw lowered, clamped shut, lifted a dripping, car-sized pile up as far as the lip of the wall, then let the pile drop behind it and out of sight, where it slid into the fire.

A cheery inspector signaled us into the proper slot, then observed what we dragged from the trailer. Clearly this was just a formality. We chatted. Across the hangar, the claw kept picking up and dumping garbage in the same spot, as if kneading the stuff. "To make it fluffy," the inspector said, because fluffy garbage burns better.

There, among the whines of reversing garbage trucks, the shriek and hiss of brakes, the groaning of horns, Sue's possessions slid down into a heap, got fluffed, and were carried over the wall to burn, dissolve, and compress, all traces of what she once prized dragged along the sludge and shoved over the edge into an ash pile so tidal in its proportions as to be barely comprehensible. Foreclosures, in their own way, regenerate: one family's loss is another's first home. But this was the colossal deposit left behind, and it was growing by the cubic foot, by the ton. Pulling out of the hangar, driving toward the landfill's exit, we could see the earth movers perched high up on the trash bluff, where their drivers awaited orders to till another layer, to massage that Kilimanjaro of garbage, and where—if they looked away from the incinerator—they would have had a pretty good view of the city from whose ruin that mountain grew, and into whose streets we now descended to fetch the next load.

.   .   .

When we weren't dragging trash—splintered speakers, hula hoops, mildewed fur coats—onto the trailer, or from the trailer onto a larger pile at the dump, we drove. For hours. We visited nearly every landfill in three counties, calculating which to use by balancing the cost of miles and fuel against the hassle of sorting the trash ourselves. Each landfill charges a different rate by the pound, and each uses some kind of discretion to determine what it will handle and what it won't. Our favorites, of course, were those that took it all, no questions asked.

With so many miles to cover, the truck became Hector's sweaty, Christ-soaked soapbox, but a kind of campfire tent, too, for weird yarns about what he and Ismael had seen during trash-outs.

"We went to one house," Hector said. "These people lived like cockroaches. They left everything, but nothing worked! Useless. The dogs had shit everywhere. In the laundry room, there was about three feet of clothing on the floor. And when we went into the garage? Same thing. It took us *four* days to clean that house, and I don't know how many trips to the dump!"

The squalor is a shock every time, each excavation a peek into a state of mind, like dismantling some diorama of dejection. Each one of us at this job has been desperate, despondent, lazy, and otherwise lacking, but the scattered depravity of these vanquished homeowners remains humbling. They seem to lose a little of themselves. I've come across traces of vanished pets, their dried piles in almost every corner of the house and in between. Then there are the refrigerators, tombs of rot trapped for long enough that when we happen to open them, they release a florid wretchedness, an odor never entirely contained within the box, so that sometimes creatures are drawn inside.

"*Chacho!*" Hector said. "We find snakes all the time. In refrigerators, snakes in luggage. One time we even found the skin of a—what do you call it—a python!"

Snakes and dog shit, curd and bees. Depressing as the rancid houses are, though, their desolation is rivaled by that of the houses left in a state of creepy tidiness. There were more clean homes among this generation of foreclosures. Like the house on Vanderbilt Drive, in a subdivision called Ashley Lakes: a six-bedroom, four-bathroom box with a second-story view of other roofs, a house new enough that it had been built, bought, lived in, and lost before the garage was even finished. In the kitchen, copies of *Martha Stewart Living* and *Real Simple* were stacked on the counter next to a Rolodex of index-card recipes, a cookbook (*365 Ways to Cook Pasta*), and more recipe cards with instructions on one side and a picture of the end result—curried coleslaw! fish crepes! etc.—on the back. Christmas decorations had been set neatly near the sliding-glass door. A handful of popcorn lay scattered on the carpet. Outside, the big-screen television had been set carefully at the edge of the driveway, next to a fern. Such conscientious neatness was strangely defiant, a declaration of dignity against any transgression.

In the driveway, after locking up, we waved to an elderly neighbor in a bikini, who was sunning in front of her screened-in garage patio. We would soon see her again, in the same position, when we returned for two more trash-outs on the same block—same square footage, same layout, same view, same fate.

.   .   .

For every ten or so notices my father tapes to a door or slips into a mailbox—guessing a soon-to-be-foreclosed home might be occupied but not willing to linger long enough to find out—he will take his chances and knock. Late one day, after hours of driving, we approached one such house just off I-275, in a neighborhood of cruddy single stories with gutted cars in the yard and enclosed patios, their screens ratty and casting an eerie kind of shade. An ice-cream truck squeezed a reggaetón ditty through a megaphone on its roof, and rednecks idled in jacked-up diesel pickups. Perhaps it was the dismissiveness with which they told my father that someone still lived in the house next door— whatever it was, he decided it was safe to knock. He went through the screen door and rapped politely. A woman's voice from inside resonated big and tough, and she came to the door in purple scrubs: a nurse.

The exchange was brusque but not tense, and when my father mentioned the bank, she mentioned Ronnie, that we were probably looking for him. My father gave her Mena's number, they thanked each other, and we assumed by her presence and Ronnie's absence that an unforeseen illness was the cause of Ronnie's predicament. "But see," my father said, turning around at a dead end, driving past the house again, "how did he get a mortgage on *that* house? That house doesn't pass FHA. It doesn't pass a lot of criteria."

"It's a piece of junk," I said.

"Loan shark," my father said. "He couldn't go anywhere to get a decent loan. A guy probably promised him a loan but said there's no way the bank would do it. So he gets a loan at 13 percent, five points."

Weeks went by before Ronnie called, and it wasn't until I heard the nurse's voice again, bleating through a speakerphone in Mena's home office, that the facts were parceled out. The nurse, Kay, had lived in the house for ten years, but somehow Ronnie owned it, and had refinanced it, and had lost it. Both she and Ronnie were on the line, confused about Mena's explanation of the foreclosure process, and even more confused by the cash-for-keys offer. And underneath that confusion was an undeniable desperation to keep the house.

He had tried to cover the risk of an adjustable-rate loan through a shell game of refinancing that finally caught up with him. He was vague with the numbers and spat out the names of the banks he'd dealt with—Ameriquest, Wells Fargo, et al.

Kay interrupted: "We been trying to finance, and we wish we could find somebody to finance so we won't *have* to *move*."

"I'm sorry about this," Mena said, "but this is already, you know, done. The bank already closed. The bank is the owner now. And unfortunately, you know, you guys don't have any other option but to accept the cash for keys or be evicted."

I could hear Ronnie moaning on the other end of the line.

"Is there no way that we can move out and then try to re-buy the house back again?" Kay asked.

"The only way that you might be able to buy the house back is maybe have your family purchase the house and, later on, they can do a deed to you, and you can be the owner. But if you had a hard time trying to get somebody to refinance the house, it's going to be more difficult now, because automatically your credit score dropped 200 points."

We couldn't figure out if the noises coming over the line were speakerphone glitches or noises of distress—voices broken, vowels dragging.

"So I'm sorry there aren't other solutions. Just trying to do the best on getting all the stuff together and trying to move, you know. But as I mentioned before, the condition with the cash for keys is that the house needs to be free of all debris. Do you have a lot of stuff?"

"Yeah. It'll take more than two weeks."

"Well, see, you told me you want $2,000 and you'd be out in two weeks. But now you're telling me that you're not sure you're going to be out in two weeks."

"We supposed—I don't want no eviction notice," Kay said, pleading. "You know, I got enough pride in myself, I don't want to go evicted. I don't want to go out like, you know, somebody comin' in and the sheriff comin' up here and stuff like that. I been livin' in this neighborhood for *ten years* and never had a problem. I want to go out in class. I wanted to stay here. It's breakin' my heart, you know. You know?"

It occurred to Mena that Kay had never been listed on any of the paperwork for the house—not the deed, not a single one of Ronnie's refinancings—and that, since her name had stayed off the books, her lack of credit history was their only chance. Kay could, in theory, qualify for a loan that would allow her to buy the house after it went back on the market. She brought home $1,400 a month. Mena guessed the house was now worth about $80,000, "which would make your payments around $1,000 a month. Can you afford that?"

Kay burst out. "Yes, ma'am, we'll do it! Yes, ma'am! Yes, ma'am! We'll do it! Won't miss a damn payment. You don't have to worry about it, the thousand dollars will be there every month—*every month*. I don't want to move from this house, ma'am. I will do anything. The bank will get their thousand dollars every month. *On time.*"

It wasn't an offer, it was a scenario, and Mena spent the next several minutes explaining that the house was already gone, but that—without making any promises—she would ask if the bank would be willing to postpone the eviction while Kay sought financing to buy the house herself.

"Don't put Ronnie on the loan," Mena reminded her. "Ronnie, you're on the blacklist now."

I left the room and stepped outside for a minute, overwhelmed, knowing we'd likely see Kay and Ronnie again, with a sheriff in front of us. Even if Kay could get a loan, there wasn't a single institution in this economic climate that would lend her a cent for that shabby house. Hearing Kay's panicked voice, one could understand the depth of this crisis in a way that the business pages failed to convey. One could simply multiply her desperation by tens of thousands—leagues upon leagues of homeowners trapped in pathetic confusion, having been upended by their desire, taught as a tenet of good citizenship in America, to own something permanent; in this case, a house that was now practically worthless, that merely marked a spot for bulldozers when it came time to widen the interstate.

$$\cdot \qquad \cdot \qquad \cdot$$

After a couple of weeks and no response from the owner on Hillsborough Lane, Mena's cash-for-keys offer there was off the table. The time had come for eviction. Arrangements were made, the sheriff posted a note, and a couple of days later we arrived to follow through.

Eviction is a worst-case scenario for good reason. The sheriff is steeled and armed for this kind of thing. We are not, nor are we eager to act as muscle for Citibank or Ocwen or Countrywide. And yet, by default, that is exactly what we do when we arrive with the sheriff on eviction day, waiting for an owner to be escorted off his property so he can watch us set his belongings on the curb.

I had worked only one eviction prior to this, during my first stint, in '98. I was changing the front-door lock when the owner snuck up behind me, after I thought he had left, shuffling along the concrete walk and with his hand outstretched. I wasn't sure exactly what was in it, and maybe he saw I was startled, because he paused, and shook a set of keys, and apologized about surprising me like that—but would I be interested in buying his car, a rusted-out Oldsmobile on blocks in the driveway? Six hundred? I said thank you, *thank you*, but no, I didn't really need it, and the disappointment merely flitted across his face before he turned and walked off, not upset or saddened but thinking, it seemed, about his next move, and ever so humble, a humility that infuriated me for holding the lock that shut him out of his own house, a job I finished in a nervous sweat.

My father, on the other hand, has witnessed much worse. Mena, heeding a strange premonition, had come along with the crew one eviction day, which she'd never done before, and as they approached the house, they weighed giving the owner more time. But the sheriff insisted, and knocked. A middle-aged man answered and seemed unsurprised at the news; he asked for just a moment to retrieve a few things. He ducked back inside and to the bedroom, where he sat on the edge of the bed, put a pistol in his mouth, and pulled the trigger.

This time, it was a cold-snap morning. Hector was home with a bad toe, and the job was left to the three of us—Ismael, my father, and me. With Ismael at five feet and ninety pounds, and my father's vertebrae just waiting to disable him, that meant I was the muscle if anything should go down. So the odds were against us. We arrived early and parked up the street. A jackhammer rattled a few blocks away; the interstate sighed. We walked through the gate and across the yard, over the chain that snaked and hooked to the buried dumbbell, past the empty plywood doghouse, and up to the door.

My father whispered, "What do you think?"

Ismael, somewhat oblivious, opened the screen door as if to get started.

"No, no, no, no," my father said.

Ismael read a sign on the door: "Be-ware off de doch."

"*Esperemos por el sheriff*," my father told him, and we moved away from the door.

"Why don't we just knock?" I said, irritated by both the weather and the suspense.

"Because *he* will," my father said of the sheriff. "We don't want to get shot. He has a gun. We don't."

"*Mi madre, qué frío!*" Ismael said.

I felt a pinch on my ankle and slapped at it, and saw Ismael slapping at his own leg, and noticed my father, too, reaching for his shin, and all of a sudden we realized that fleas, starving, were beginning to feast on us. Within seconds, it felt like we were walking through a skillet of popping grease.

The sheriff arrived to find us all with our pants rolled up, bending groggily up and down in a sort of scratching calisthenics. He laughed. "I walked in there to stick the notice up the other day and they just crawled all over me," he said, passing by us into the yard. He was tall and pale and didn't look especially athletic or even all that tough. He was rather pear-shaped, really, but he was cold-tempered, and didn't seem like the kind of fellow who repeated himself too often.

His knock was loud and simple, with a short salutation: "Sheriff's office. Eviction." We waited ten seconds. "All right," he said, "go do your thing."

My father kneeled at the door and shoved the flathead on the shaft, slipped the scraper in, pried, and it was that easy, door open.

"Very good," the sheriff said, slightly impressed, and he slipped into a darkness backlit by a kitchen window, veiled in gossamer, and splotched with shadows as the sun crawled through branches, then through the curtains, to just barely touch the dull linoleum.

A dank warm funk wafted out as he moved around inside. He took less than a minute.

We followed him inside, adjusting to the lack of light, creeping past an enormous television that blocked the front window. All we could make out at first were shadowy mounds and piles, and then I could see the short distance to the kitchen and noticed white plastic jumbo cups scattered across the counter, dishes piled up, cabinets flung open, and suddenly saw why, despite the open front door, the light failed in here: the walls, once white, were leopard-spotted in black and green. My father passed me with his camera and began clicking, and the brief pulse of the flash snapped the rooms into view. The deeper we waded toward the back, the more rancid the air became. There were boxes half packed in the bedrooms, amid standing fans and clothes and papers on the floor, amid unshaded lamps, giant stuffed tigers, framed photos of babies and other loved ones, lightbulbs, stuffed sheep, Bibles, boxes of mothballs and red high heels, portraits of panthers, a typewriter stuffed with neckties. It was as if in the preparation for escape, the thoughts had piled up and suffocated the mind.

The fleas were incredible. We were being devoured by them. We didn't know it then, but it would take four attacks with several gallons of poison to destroy them, an exhausting discovery each time we returned ready to work, and each time realizing, not ten steps onto the property, that another wave of bloodsuckers had hatched. For now, we were simply relieved to have avoided a confrontation.

•   •   •

After a stop at Home Depot, and then at the Krispy Kreme nearby, Ismael and I returned to eradicate the fleas. I handed Ismael a sprayer, with orders to soak the yard, which he began doing, and I dragged my socks up over my jeans and went back inside to set the fumigators.

George, eighty-seven, who lived next door, came out to observe what we were up to. Under the small shade of his New York Giants cap, from behind thick glasses, he filled me in on the man who had lived here. "He a deacon," George said. "Been in prison but cleaned up. He come over and we talk Christ talk." He wasn't sure when he'd see him next. He was surprised to see that his neighbor had lost the house. "I knew he borrowed a little bit of money, but we didn't talk too much about that."

I left my number with him on a scrap of paper, and in our small talk learned that George had been raised nearby, when this end of Tampa was still mostly rural. He left at sixteen, he said, a departure prompted by a white boy half-blinding him with an avocado pit ("This eye is cooked," he said, pointing to the left one). There was nothing the law would do for him, so he fled to New York, where, already good at the saxophone, he started gigging with the musicians on the bop scene and shortly wound up in James Brown's first band. Was he sure about that? He promised it was true. When the band hit the Chitlin' Circuit, George, terrified of the South, quit. He moved upstate instead, janitored, got a music-teaching gig, retired, and came home again. He bought a condo from a friendly Jewish guy, he said, who gave him good advice; he sold it when the time was right, and used the profit to buy this house, nothing extraordinary, and not all that different from the deacon's except that it was freshly painted, with a tight roof, a trim yard with a flower-bed, and paid for in full. He didn't owe anyone a penny, he said, and because of this freedom was the envy of his debt-saddled children.

Just then, Pops, the neighbor from across the street, walked over and asked me if I would save for him whatever metal we found inside. "He had a washin' machine or somethin' he said he was going to give 'fore he leave," he said. Pops was a junkman who made his living on recycling, and it was all but a blessing to let him haul the metal away: one load less for us to carry. Fine, I said. We would toss the metal in the yard, where the dumbbell was. He could have at it.

Pops had a lady friend with him who observed the flea situation. "Sevin dust," she said. "It chokes 'em. It kills 'em out. And if you got fresh oranges and you throw that dust and you cut some oranges up and throw it—"

"The peel is what kill 'em," Pops said. "My grandmama used to put a bunch a orange peel—*hey! George!* Where you *been,* man!" Pops had been standing next to George this whole time and only just now noticed him. They lived just twenty yards from each other, but you'd have thought it was a homecoming.

I looked over at Ismael, who was busy soaking the ground with that poison, and every time he felt a pinch he'd spray himself—his legs, his hands, even his torso, and in the breeze I could see the poison, lit by sunlight, waft toward his head. "Keep it down!" I told him, but by the time he was done, he was dizzy, and in pain, and mumbling that he needed a nap.

"Pops wants first dibs on that metal," the lady friend said.

I nodded. "He'll get it."

•   •   •

A day off, and with Hector and Ismael assigned to errands, I went to visit the Remax office in Palm Harbor. Mena was out when I showed up, so another agent, Joe Koebel, agreed to bring me along to inspect a few foreclosed properties. His office sat halfway down a long, bleached-white hallway lined with county maps. He had two desks, one near a window and piled with manila folders, the other set against the opposite wall, where Koebel sat hunkered over a laptop while talking on his cell phone, using an earpiece that allowed him to type with both hands.

It was midmorning, but Koebel, a fast talker and hyperactively friendly, already looked haggard. He squeezed our conversation between the incoming calls as he darted between the desks, shuffling papers with the busy poise of a knife juggler. Behind me, a greaseboard was covered with addresses, top to bottom, of the thirty or so foreclosures—both houses and condos—he had in rotation, their progress marked by green, blue, or red ink. Green meant closed, meant money, and there was precious little green on the board that day.

The real estate culture in Florida had pushed profiteering to new levels, in large part because of its condominium economy. "The condo market was such a craze here for the past five years," Koebel told me, once he was off the phone, "that if you bought in 2001, put $20,000 down, and the condo was built in late 2002 or early 2003, you made a hundred grand before you even closed. People were selling their escrow—'double closing.' They were closing their loan in the morning, selling to a new buyer for $100,000 more by the afternoon. The fuckin' *mayor* did it."

He grabbed a folder. "These people," he said, running his finger down the sum column of a single page on a thick stack, "they paid $728,000 for this condo in 2006. Look at the loan history. Here's a loan for $70,000 from American Brokers; here's a loan for $582,000, which makes $650,000 of loan. Now, they must have refinanced here for $671,000 through Lehman Brothers. They took out another fuckin' loan for $224,000, so they owed $895,000 on $728,000." He rolled his chair back. "I can't speak for these people, but do the math. Looks like they probably put in maybe a hundred grand . . . they took the equity out . . . they got their hundred grand back, and they probably walked because they couldn't sell it. That's a total guess on my part. But look at the numbers. It's a foreclosure, a ding on their credit. But they don't give a shit because they're from New York State"—meaning that the home in question was a second property, and ultimately expendable. "They're untouchable," he said.

His handyman called: a condominium was ready for inspection, and afterward Koebel needed to see if another house was still occupied. We drove through fast traffic for forty minutes to a Tuscan-themed apartment complex that had become condos during the boom. The property on our list was on Chianti Place. "Until just about last year," Koebel said, "you had developers buying apartments, converting them to condos, and selling them for outrageous prices. These things sold for $240,000 back then. Now they're worth about $130,000."

The place was empty, and clean, with only the occasional chirp of the dying smoke alarm to interrupt us. Koebel shuttled from room to room, taking pictures. I asked him if he'd ever run into awkward situations, confrontations, anything of that sort. "Strangest thing I came across," he said, "I got to this one house, every piece of furniture was intact. The closets were filled, the baby's room had everything in it. The bed was in the master bedroom. Even the table was set. I open up the stove, gnats come flying out." He called the sheriff's office and asked a detective to track down the previous owners, to see if they still wanted any of what they'd left behind. "They were somewhere in Canada," he said. "A lady calls me back, and I asked her what she wanted me to do with all the stuff. She said, 'Let me ask my husband, I'll call you back.'" And that was it. "Gave it all away," Koebel said. "Dining room set, gold jewelry, all of it."

He took another call: an assistant from the office was asking about a foreclosure on Loquat Avenue. It would be going to auction, Koebel said, and available for viewing that Saturday. He gave her the lockbox code and address, then hung up.

Koebel had just a handful of houses registered with the auction, most of which had received "short sale" offers—meaning offers at their current value rather than for what they had been worth, say, a year ago. A short sale tends to fall well below what the owner owes the bank, but it's an offer in an otherwise frozen market and spares a bank the tens of thousands of dollars required to file a foreclosure with the court. Still, banks often turn these offers down.

"This is the greed I'm talking about," Koebel said, "and the auction is a big part of it. I had two houses. One was purchased for $400,000. One was purchased for $395,000. I had offers on both of them prior to them going to auction, one for $220,000, one for $218,000. The bank turned them both down. At the auction, one sold for $175,000, the other sold for $180,000. They lost about $40,000 collectively on those houses, when I had *real human being* buyers—not investors—wanting to buy these homes to live in them. They ended up selling them to investors for $40,000 less at the auction. Because the money is tied into a portfolio or a package, so they just dump it."

Who was to blame for the insanity in this kind of decision making? Banking officials, mortgage brokers, buyers' agents, overanxious consumers—all were guilty parties. Parceling out which foreclosures were the consequences of scams, bad luck, or fiscal recklessness was a nearly impossible task. In the end, no matter the math, the numbers could never fully divulge the motives. Koebel saw it all as a reckoning that was overdue.

"When a mortgage guy comes to you and says, 'Look, your ratios are a little big, but don't worry about it. I'll get you the loan.' The guy might fib and say your payments are going to be $1,200, and you think, 'Oh, I can afford that.' But he doesn't tell you that after you add the taxes and insurance, it's $1,700. And then you're sitting there at closing, and what are you going to do? You're not going to be a *man* and not close? Or are you gonna close?"

•   •   •

George must have followed through on his promise to share my number, because the deacon called. His name was Joe Logan. I explained who I was, that I was writing about foreclosures, that

I'd been in his house with a crew to clean it out, that I wanted to meet. He suggested a Denny's not too far from the house. I sat and waited, ordered coffee, then saw him: a black man near middle age, not big but solid, and clean-headed, his thick glasses fighting back the daylight coming in from outside. It wasn't until he sat down opposite me that I noticed the stillness in his eyes, as if some heaviness had settled his stare. His voice was grizzled and gentle. He didn't want food, only coffee. A baby squawked in the booth across the room.

I couldn't bring myself to ask him about what I'd found—the spots, the piles, the chaos in there. I asked very few questions, in fact, and instead let him walk me through what had happened, interrupted now and then by the waitress.

"When I bought my home, I had just got out of prison, after doing eighteen years. I was sentenced for drugs in the federal system. Distribution, cocaine. I was raised up in a good home. It had nothing to do with parents. Men are just gonna be men. I chose that life and I had to pay that price.

"But when I got out, things changed. I got saved, and after about two years I was set aside to be a deacon. My pastor brought me before the church, and they approved me. People notice you, your faithfulness, the way you've changed. Even my parole officer did. He went to my pastor and said they was going to put me up for early termination. So they took me off parole.

"So I got a job and, you know, I always wanted my own home. It meant that I was trying to do the right thing, not only in society but to myself. I never owned a home, and to have worked and accomplished this *by yourself—to buy a home*: that means a lot. And the day you get a key to your own house, you feel like you have accomplished something, you know what I'm saying?

"So I worked, and I worked, and I looked around, and I kinda . . . some kinda way they gave me a . . . a voucher . . . to buy a house. Something in the mail. It was like somebody was saying that I could get a house worth fifty thousand dollars.

Preapproval, that's what it was. It was legit. So I went out lookin' for a house. They gave me an agent and he showed me the houses within that range, but the houses he showed me was all beat up. So I continued lookin', and I was just driving by and I seen it. I went to the guy. They said after a year it would go from $650 to five-something a month because I was a first-time buyer. But it didn't. It went up.

"When I tried to refinance it, I told the guy that I wanted a thirty-year fixed. We did all the paperwork, talked on the phone. And when the lady came out there to do the signing, I'm looking at it and it said two-year adjustable something. I said, 'I didn't ask for this. The man told me it was going to be a thirty-year. I don't need a two-year.' She said, 'Well, you call him.' I called him, and asked him why he sent a two-year when I asked for a thirty. He said, 'No, you told me this and told me that.' I said, 'No, I got witnesses.' 'Cause when I was doing it, my boss man told me a two-year will hurt you unless you're gonna sell.

"So the *lady*. By the lady understanding me—she knew I was a God man—she said, 'Son, I'm gonna tell you this here and this off the record: Don't buy it. Don't sign those papers.' She said, 'I get paid for this, but I'm telling you 'cause you seem like a person who's bein' beat 'cause you don't know. Don't sign.'

"But within a year, I was going through a lot of turmoil. Job went under—I was a fabricator, you know, those glass mechanics that do sliding doors, windows, big company. I had a car and a truck, and they came to me with a refinance deal, saying, you know, you could combine all that and make one price. You know, it sounded good, but it wasn't good.

"The thing I'm trying to find out is how bad the foreclosures affect my economy. I got to read up on all that. I know it messed my credit up. But I got to find a way to try and establish it back. I can't sit down, I'm not that type. I learn from my mistakes, it teaches me to grow. Matter of fact, they just put the lock on it, what, a week ago? Yeah, Monday. So now I wanna find out: Is there anything else they can do to me, as an individual? I know the house is gone, but say, for instance, in the next six months something blessed happens to me, I get some money. Can they come and get it?"

They could, though I didn't say it. He didn't seem to understand that I had helped them put that lock on his door on Monday. And I had trouble telling him that most of what he owned was gone now, and that he should set aside any plans to buy another home, because with his income, and a foreclosure on his record, he will not own another house for a long time, if ever.

We walked out into the parking lot, to my car, the heat stifling by now, and I tried to explain again who I was and my purpose, and that I was at his home with the crew. I told him that most of his stuff was gone, thrown away, but that I grabbed what I could so I could learn about him and maybe track him down. I reached for the Bible with phone numbers scribbled in the back—parole officers, friends, pastors. "And anyway, I grabbed this and I brought it in case you wanted it."

And he laughed and laughed.

"I guess that's your Bible?"

"Yes," he said, and the laugh was laced with—*pity.* "That's part of my ex-wife's stuff. Yeah, this is nice."

"If I find out if there's anything left in the house—"

"No. I don't want nuthin'. I'm through with it."

"But you left so much. Pictures and letters and—"

"It's trash."

.   .   .

Saturday morning, cool and humid, my last day home. A hundred and fifty properties were set to go on the auction block at the convention center in downtown Tampa, the first stop of the Real Estate Disposition Corporation's eight-city tour, during which about a thousand homes and condos would be rattled off like livestock to mostly tepid crowds. For the past month, people had been combing the city with REDC's catalogue in hand, nosing through it, following the signs. Some houses were tended to by an agent, some by a neighbor's boy, whoever had the time to sit there for eight hours while investors and the merely curious walked through, grabbed the paperwork, and checked their lists. Most of these were low-priority properties that weary agents couldn't move themselves, or didn't want to. Some were bargains, if the market held steady and the bidder didn't get trigger-happy; others seemed like slogs of repairwork; the rest were eyesores.

The main hall of the convention center was packed. Joe Koebel was there, along with a few of his clients. He looked distracted. "My guy forgot his cashier's check," he said. "I had to call a buddy of mine and do a bait and switch." The buddy was a man named Jeff, linebacker tall but with a voice that sounded like some parody of a grandmother from New Jersey. Jeff knew a lot about property, enough that it had become profitable for him, and I couldn't help but admire his type—an industrious fellow who had mastered the complexities of the business, and who could tear a wall down, and who had a bored swagger about it all. Even this mind-boggling crisis seemed just barely entertaining to him.

Jeff flipped through the book. "Is this your house, Joe, on Thirteenth Avenue?"

"No."

"Oh, this one was. This was the one that little kid who couldn't speak English was at."

"Yeah, Alex. The Russian kid. I paid him to sit my houses for me."

"His handwriting was phenomenal."

Inside the ballroom, the auctioneer's podium was flanked by two giant screens on which rotated the planet Earth with REDC superimposed upon it, a sun rising in the galactic distance. The Commodores' "Brick House" thumped from the PA system.

Chris Chamberlain, the executive vice president of REDC, waltzed up to give the crowd a pep talk. "You have the perfect storm right now," he said. "Remember, folks, this is the perfect buying opportunity. If you look at real estate cycles in the last hundred years in the United States of America, every time we go into a low—which we are in the low portion of that real estate cycle right now—that represents a great buying opportunity for you. And remember, that low is not as low as the previous cycle's low. However, over a hundred years, every time the market comes storming back, the next peak has always—I repeat, *always*—exceeded the peak of the last real estate cycle. That's how money's made in real estate, folks. Buy in the low part of the cycle."

Was it an opportunity? Or just a primer for the next disaster? The lessons of the Great Depression had been lost on the baby boomers and must have seemed unnecessary to the generations since. Chamberlain's history lesson worked as revival-tent homily, but it ignored what was changing in America's economic condition. It assumed this low part of the cycle was like any other, and it wasn't. The collapse of corporate giants like Bear Stearns does not happen during a lull; the housing lifelines Fannie Mae and Freddie Mac had never been as threatened. The "low part of the cycle" grossly understated how widespread the damage was, and how quickly it was spreading. That planet on the big screen seemed appropriate enough, given the global fallout from America's collapse; just a month earlier, 6,000 angry shareholders had filled a soccer arena in Switzerland after UBS, the Swiss financial juggernaut, wrote down $37 billion in losses from securities propped up by the same sort of Florida real estate that was on auction today.

The auction began. Property No. 1, a condominium in Palm Harbor, worth $150,000 six months ago, opened at $1,000, and the emcee leapt through tens of thousands of dollars with shivering speed, reaching $60,000 in half a minute. When he reached $70,000 he chopped the bidding down to increments of $5,000 but didn't slow his blubbering, only repeated the bid until a card went up and a spotter, dressed in a cheap tux, shrieked and did his jog across the room; and when the emcee hit $80,000, the crowd got careful, the spotters grew restless and waved their hands and flicked their fingers, goading, but no one bit, and the condo went for $75,000 in just under a minute and forty-three seconds, to the gentleman in a middle seat. The crowd applauded. The spotter guided him to the stage. Financing was just down the hall.

And it went on like this for hours, through 140 more properties. Afterward, Joe and Jeff shook their heads at some of the bids, at how auction fever had led to some questionable decisions.

"This is the one I thought was a joke," Jeff said, pointing. "Tangerine Street. Fifty-five thousand, it went for! I mean, it's a beautiful, brand-new home, but you can't get to or from the house without risking your life. Right across the street is the number-one drug-dealing section in Clearwater—right across the street! I went to look at it this morning, couldn't get out of the car. Fifty-five thousand and I couldn't get out of the car! If you rent it out as Section 8 housing, it might be a good deal. But you can't go there. They literally tackled my car trying to sell me drugs."

"The one on Belcher," a stranger piped in. "*Somebody* overpaid for that."

"That one I liked," Jeff said. "It was very clean. New windows, new tile floor. Built-in pool."

"Yeah, but that kitchen! And there was all that mold behind that wall."

"No, it was a cute little home. All you got to do is a little work on it. What'd it go for?"

"$135,000."

Jeff tilted his head and cocked a brow.

•   •   •

On the morning of my flight out, we swung by the deacon's house one last time to photograph it, to document its progress for the bank. Just a block away, on North Elmer Street, Hector and Ismael were handling another foreclosure. The snore of Hector's chain saw razzed the block as he lopped off the limbs of a stubborn oak that had fallen against the house's freestanding clapboard garage. Ismael, meanwhile, busied himself in the yard, cramming the leftovers—dominoes, toy-wagon wheels, an ironing board, a lamp—into a black lawn bag he dragged behind him.

On Hillsborough, directly across the street from the deacon's house, a real estate agent and her subcontractor boyfriend had just finished cleaning out a foreclosure. Now ready for market, it would compete with the one we had just finished, as would the house next door, a new shotgun modular with a sale sign promising $895 DOWN BUYS THIS HOUSE NO BANK NEEDED. Other than a gaggle of small children a couple of doors down, George and Pops were just about the last people left on the block.

The grass in the deacon's yard had filled out; it seemed to thrive despite the gallons of pesticide we'd dumped on it. Breezes played with the screen door, a rhythmic creak. Inside, not a scrap of paper was left: Ismael had cleaned the place out single-handedly. The only traces of the deacon that hadn't been stuffed into the plastic bags were the names and phone numbers scribbled on the walls of the bathroom, the bedroom, the kitchen. The uncurtained windows made the place a little brighter. Even the carpet had been ripped out. Funny how the house showed a little promise now.

My father didn't say much, except to marvel at the tenacity of those fleas that remained. After taking a few pictures and locking up, he grabbed a can of repellent and sprayed his shoes with it. "Want some?" he offered.

I declined. But back in the truck, with Hillsborough Lane well behind us, the salsa music turned up, I felt a needling on my ankle. I lifted a pant leg, picked off the flea, and worried it between my fingernails, which were dirty and in bad need of a trimming but long enough, at least, to clip the vile pest.

And so I pinched, and saw just the slightest dab of blood.

The New Yorker

WINNER—REVIEWS AND
CRITICISM

In his reviews and essays, James
Wood brings a human approach
to thinking and writing about
literature, parsing both the latest
novels and world classics with
passion, good humor, and
all-too-rare precision.

James Wood

The Homecoming

Growing up in a religious household, I got used to the sight of priests, but I always found them at once fascinating and slightly repellent. The funereal uniform is supposed to obliterate the self in a shroud of colorlessness, even as it draws enormous attention to the self; humility seems to be cut from the same cloth as pride. Since the ego is irrepressible—and secular—it tends to bulge in odd shapes when religiously straitened. The priests I knew practiced self-abnegation but had perfected a quiet dance of ego. They were modest but pompous, gentle but tyrannical (one of them got angry if he was disturbed on a Monday, the vicar's day off), pious but knowing. Most were good men, but the peculiar constrictions of their calling produced peculiar opportunities for unloosing.

This is probably one of the reasons—putting the secular antagonism of novelists aside—that in fiction priests are usually seen as comical, hypocritical, improperly worldly or dangerously unworldly, or a little dim. Another reason is that fiction needs egotism, vanity, venality, in order to produce drama and comedy; we want our sepulchers craftily whited. The seventy-six-year-old Reverend John Ames, who narrates Marilynne Robinson's second novel, *Gilead*, is gentle, modest, loving, and above all good. He is also a bit boring, and boring in proportion to his curious lack of ego. At home in the Iowa town of Gilead, in the mid-1950s, and aware of his imminent demise, he writes a long letter to his seven-year-old son, which is presented as a series of diary entries. (Georges Bernanos's novel *Diary of a Country Priest* seems to have been one model.) Mellowly resigned, tired but faithful, he is a man who can serenely exclaim, "How I have loved this life!" or inform us that he has written more than 2,000 sermons "in the deepest hope and conviction." The reader may roll his eyes at this, and perhaps think of Fielding's Parson Adams, in *Joseph Andrews*, who tries to pawn his sermons, and who falls into argument with another parson about who is the better writer. Fielding seems closer to the human case, and more novelistically vivid.

But Robinson skirted this potential objection by making her novel swerve away from the traditionally novelistic. Ames's calm, grave diary entries contain almost no dialogue, shun scenes, seem to smother conflict before it has taken a breath. Very beautifully, *Gilead* becomes less a novel than a species of religious writing, and Ames's entries a recognizable American form, the Emersonian essay, poised between homily and home, religious exercise and naturalism:

> This morning a splendid dawn passed over our house on its way to Kansas. This morning Kansas rolled out of its sleep into a sunlight grandly announced, proclaimed throughout heaven—one more of the very finite number of days that this old prairie has been called Kansas, or Iowa. But it has all been one day, that first day. Light is constant, we just turn over in it. So every day is in fact the selfsame evening and morning. My grandfather's grave turned into the light, and the dew on his weedy little mortality patch was glorious.

The result was one of the most unconventional conventionally popular novels of recent times.

Robinson describes herself as a liberal Protestant believer and churchgoer, but her religious sensibility is really far more uncompromising and archaic than this allows. Her essays, a selection of which appeared in *The Death of Adam* (1998), are theologically tense and verbally lush in a manner that is almost extinct in modern literary discourse, and which often sounds Melvillean. She is a liberal in the sense that she finds it difficult to write directly about the content of her belief and shuns the evangelical childishness of gluing human attributes onto God. She writes that as a child she "felt God as a presence before I had a name for him," and adds that she goes to church in order to experience "moments that do not occur in other settings." In a way that many Americans, and certainly her liberal readers, would find palatable, her Protestantism seems born of a love of religious silence—the mystic, quietly at prayer in an unadorned place, indifferent to ecclesiastical mediation.

But Robinson is illiberal and unfashionably fierce in her devotion to this Protestant tradition; she is voluble in defense of silence. She loathes the complacent idleness whereby contemporary Americans dismiss Puritanism and turn John Calvin, its great proponent, into an obscure, moralizing bigot: "We are forever drawing up indictments against the past, then refusing to let it testify in its own behalf—it is so very guilty, after all. Such attention as we give to it is usually vindictive and incurious and therefore incompetent." We flinch from Puritanism because it placed sin at the center of life, but then, as she tartly reminds us, "Americans never think of themselves as sharing fully in the human condition, and therefore beset as all humankind is beset." Calvin believed in our "total depravity," our utter fallenness, but this was not necessarily a cruel condemnation. "The belief that we are all sinners gives us excellent grounds for forgiveness and self-forgiveness, and is kindlier than any expectation that we might be saints, even while it affirms the standards all of us fail to attain," Robinson writes in her essay "Puritans and Prigs." Nowadays, she argues, educated Americans are prigs, not Puritans, quick to pour judgment on anyone who fails to toe the right political line. Soft moralizing has replaced hard moralizing, but at least those old hard moralists admitted to being moralists.

I do not always enjoy Robinson's ecstasies, but I admire the obdurateness with which she describes the difficult joys of a faith that will please neither evangelicals nor secularists. Above all, there is the precision and lyrical power of her language, and the way it embodies a struggle—the fight with words, the contemporary writer's fight with the history of words and the presence of literary tradition, the fight to use the best words to describe both the visible and the invisible world. Here, for instance, is how the narrator of *Housekeeping*, Robinson's first novel, describes her dead grandmother, who lies in bed with her arms wide open and her head flung back: "It was as if, drowning in air, she had leaped toward ether." In the same novel, the narrator imagines her grandmother pinning sheets to a clothesline, on a windy day— "Say that when she had pinned three corners to the lines it began to billow and leap in her hands, to flutter and tremble, and to glare with the light, and that the throes of the thing were as gleeful and strong as if a spirit were dancing in its cerements." "Cerements," an old word for burial cloth, is Robinson in her Melvillean mode, and is one of many moments in her earlier work when she sounds like the antiquarian Cormac McCarthy. But stronger than that fancy word is the plain and lovely "the throes of the thing," with its animism and its homemade alliteration.

Her new novel, *Home* (Farrar, Straus and Giroux), begins simply, eschewing obvious verbal fineness, and slowly grows in luxury—its last fifty pages are magnificently moving, and richly pondered in the way of *Gilead*. *Home* is not a sequel to that novel but more like that novel's brother, since it takes place at the same narrative moment and dovetails with its happenings. In *Gilead*,

John Ames's great friend is the Reverend Robert Boughton, a retired Presbyterian minister (Ames is a Congregationalist). The two men grew up together, confide in one another, and share a wry, undogmatic Protestantism. But where Ames married late and has only one son, Boughton has eight children, one of whom, Jack, is a prodigal son. In the earlier novel, Ames frets over Jack (now in his forties), who has been difficult since he was a schoolboy: there has been petty theft, drifting, unemployment, alcoholism, and an illegitimate child, now deceased, with a local woman. Jack walked out of the Boughton home one day and stayed away for twenty years, not returning even for his mother's funeral. After all that time, we learn, Jack has unexpectedly returned. In the last part of *Gilead*, Jack comes to Ames for a blessing—for the blessing he cannot get from his own father—and spills a remarkable secret: he has been living with a black woman from Memphis named Della and has a son with her.

Home is set in the Boughton household at the time of Jack's sudden return, and is an intense study of three people: the Reverend Boughton, the old, dying patriarch; his pious daughter Glory; and the prodigal Jack. Glory has her own sadness: she has come back to Gilead after the collapse of what she took to be an engagement, to a man who turned out to be married. Like Princess Marya in *War and Peace*, who does daily battle with her father, the old Prince Bolkonsky, she is the dutiful child who must submit to the demands of an aging tyrant. She is fearful of Jack, whom she hardly knows, and is in some ways envious of his rebellious freedom. Robinson evokes well the drugged shuffle of life in a home dominated by the routines of an old parent: how the two middle-aged children hear "a stirring of bedsprings, then the lisp lisp of slippered feet and the pock of the cane." There are the imperious cries—for help getting dressed; a glass of water—and the hours distracted by the radio, card games, Monopoly, meals, pots of coffee. The very furniture is oppressive, immovable. The numerous knickknacks are displayed only "as a courtesy to their givers, most of whom by now would have gone to their reward." For Glory, who is in her late thirties, there is the dread that this will be her final home:

> What does it mean to come home? Glory had always thought home would be a house less cluttered and ungainly than this one, in a town larger than Gilead, or a city, where someone would be her intimate friend and the father of her children, of whom she would have no more than three. . . . She would not take one stick of furniture from her father's house, since none of it would be comprehensible in those spare, sunlit rooms. The walnut furbelows and carved draperies and pilasters, the inlaid urns and flowers. Who had thought of putting actual feet on chairs and sideboards, actual paws and talons?

Much of *Home* puzzles out the mystery of Jack Boughton's rebellion, his spiritual homelessness. From his earliest years, he had seemed a stranger to his relatives. The family had been waiting for him to walk out, and he did, and then this story became their defining narrative: "They were so afraid they would lose him, and then they had lost him, and that was the story of their family, no matter how warm and fruitful and robust it might have appeared to the outside world." Even now that he has returned, Glory reflects, there was "an incandescence of unease about him whenever he walked out the door or, for that matter, whenever his father summoned him to one of those harrowing conversations. Or while he waited for the mail or watched the news." In the course of the book, we discover a little of what he has been doing in those twenty years away—as in *Gilead*, we learn about the early illegitimate child, and about his eight-year relationship with Della, herself a preacher's daughter.

Jack is a suggestive figure—a highly literate nonbeliever who knows his Bible backward but finds it hard to do theological battle with his slippery father. Back home, he dresses formally, putting on his threadbare suit and tie, as if to do his reformed best; but he has a perpetually wary expression and a studied politesse that suggest an existential exile. He tries to conform to the habits of the childhood home—he tends the garden, does the shopping, fixes up the old car in the garage—but almost every encounter with his father produces a tiny abrasion that smarts and festers. The novel quietly mobilizes the major biblical stories of father and son: Esau, denied his birthright, begging for a blessing from his father; Joseph, reunited, finally, with his father, Jacob; the Prodigal Son, most loved because most errant.

·　　·　　·

What propels the book, and makes it ultimately so powerful, is the Reverend Boughton, precisely because he is not the soft-spoken sage that John Ames is in *Gilead*. He is a fierce, stern, vain old man, who wants to forgive his son and cannot. He preaches sweetness and light, and is gentle with Jack, like a chastened Lear ("Let me look at you for a minute," he says), only to turn on him angrily. There are scenes of the most tender pain. Robinson, so theologically obsessed with transfiguration, can transfigure the most banal observation. In the attic, for instance, Glory finds a chest of her father's shirts, ironed "as if for some formal event, perhaps their interment"; and then the novelist, or poet, notices that the shirts "had changed to a color milder than white." (Those cerements again.) Father and son clash while watching television news reports of the racial unrest in Montgomery. Boughton swats away his son's anger with his bland, milky prophecy: "There's no reason to let that sort of trouble upset you. In six months nobody will remember one thing about it."

As the old man palpably declines, an urgency sets in. The imminence of death should conduce to forgiveness, but the father cannot allow it. He knows that his son has not returned for good. "He's going to toss the old gent an assurance or two, and then he's out the door," he complains. Nothing will change, because the family situation rests on a series of paradoxes, which interlock to imprison father and son. Jack's soul is homeless, but his soul is his home, for, as Jack tells his sister, the soul is "what you can't get rid of." He is condemned to leave and return. If the prodigal son is the most loved because most errant, then it is his errancy that is secretly loved: perhaps a family needs to have its designated sinner? Everyone longs for restoration, for the son to come home and become simply good, just as everyone longs for Heaven, but such restoration, like Heaven itself, is hard to imagine, and in our lack of imagination we somehow prefer what we can touch and feel—the palpability of our lapses.

Behind all of Robinson's work lies an abiding interest in the question of heavenly restoration. As she puts it in *Housekeeping*, there is a law of completion, requiring that everything "must finally be made comprehensible. . . . What are all these fragments for, if not to be knit up finally?" But will this restoration ever be enough? Can the shape of the healing possibly fit the size of the wound? You see a version of this concern in *Home*, in the way the novel ponders the question of return. The Boughton children come home to a strange, old-fashioned Iowa town, but the return is hardly the balm it promises to be, for home is too personal, too remembered, too disappointing. Eden is exile, not Heaven:

And then their return to the *pays natal*, where the same old willows swept the same ragged lawns, where the same old prairie arose and bloomed as negligence permitted. Home. What kinder place could there be on earth, and why did it seem to them all like exile? Oh, to be passing anonymously through an impersonal landscape! Oh, not to know every stump and stone, not to remember how the fields of Queen Anne's lace figured in the childish happiness they had offered to their father's hopes, God bless him.

So old Boughton is dying, and nothing changes. "What I'd like to know is why you didn't love us," he petulantly chides his son. "That is what has always mystified me." He continues a little later, "You see something beautiful in a child, and you almost live for it, you feel as though you would die for it, but it isn't yours to keep or to protect. And if the child becomes a man who has no respect for himself, it's just destroyed till you can hardly remember what it was." Early in the novel, the reverend seemed to want his son to call him something other than the customary, rather estranged "sir"—Papa or even Dad. Late in the novel, when Jack calls him Dad, he bursts out, "Don't call me that. I don't like it at all. Dad. It sounds ridiculous. It's not even a word." When he is not rebuking his son, he is complaining about old age: "Jesus never had to be old." He is calm only when asleep: "His hair had been brushed into a soft white cloud, like harmless aspiration, like a mist." In a final encounter of devastating power, Jack goes to his father to tell him that he is going away again. Jack puts out his hand. "The old man drew his own hand into his lap and turned away. 'Tired of it!' he said." They are the last words that the Reverend Boughton says to Jack, an angry inversion of the last, tired words of the serene John Ames in *Gilead*: "I'll pray, and then I'll sleep."

Esquire

WINNER—LEISURE
INTERESTS

Often politically incorrect but totally delicious, steak moves most men. "The Esquire Almanac of Steak" is a generous platter that's full of beef—including Tom Chiarella's evocative account of the art of being a butcher.

Tom Chiarella

Butcher

The sink is full of tongues. Beef tongues, each as big as a man's shoe, frozen into one icy clump the size of a propane canister, defrosting for an afternoon pickup. There's a lot of mouth, too, I guess, or palate—I'm not sure, because the top tongue is unfrozen enough that I can see a bone that looks like a little saddle. But right now the guys in back are breaking cows—sawing the hindquarters down with a handsaw, cutting the hip on the band saw, then the shank, thumbing out the ribs for short loin. Short loin is their money cut. No one is particularly worried about the tongues. You don't have to rush the tongues, they tell me.

"Who ordered tongues?" I ask. Sometimes it's loud in a butcher shop. The grinding saws or the clattering, the cuber, the vacuum sealer, the hasp and slam of the walk-in-refrigerator door, the radio. Not a cruel, industrial noise—no one wears earplugs. This is the loudness of commerce, the fail-safe cadence of call-in orders, the rattling meter of the morning butcher-shop routine.

So far today I've hung three bone-in rib roasts for aging, trimmed and trayed out eighty boneless-skinless chicken breasts, retrayed the rib eyes and the pork chops—rotate the meat, replace the green paper between the layers, restack the cuts on narrow, slide-in aluminum trays, which are notched, edge to edge, into the store-length glass counter—and collected a shop's worth of trim for cut-down and grinding. I've wiped the blocks with bleach water twice. And I'm doing the least of it.

"Who ordered the tongues?" I say again.

"A doctor," Dennis calls out. He's head-down, working his six-inch blade into a tenderloin, shaving the blade along the broadside, steadily pulling the tissue. Trimming with the grain, they call it. "Some surgeon."

"Why so many?" I can only think: tongue sandwiches. A whole lot of them.

Dennis shrugs. He's got a little kid's haircut, the demeanor of a philosophy professor, and hands glossy with the tiny scars that come with fifteen years of cutting meat. Butcher. "Uses them to demonstrate some new instrument," he says. "I guess they're about the size of a uterus." I can't tell if he's serious. But no one laughs, which, with these guys, may well be another way to break my balls.

And then they point me to the counter, where a woman has edged up to the deli, in front of the ham loaves. The day's first customer. I rinse and towel off my hands, then turn to her.

Butchering is propelled by time. The entire morning is one terrific act of preparation. There are only so many hours to sell, and so many hours to prepare for the selling. The meat never waits. But customers never come into a butcher shop to browse. They are there to buy. There's always something they need, something they must have, or something they don't know about yet. So you give them a little time—you rinse your hands, you make eye contact, you touch your hat, you show a little focus even as you're moving through the ritual.

It's simple enough: They want answers, and they want meat. A butcher has to have a lot of each. So that's when I lean in, against the solidity of the counter, into the skin of the apron. I've been there long enough to be a guy with some answers, a guy with trusted skills. Butcher.

I ask her, "How can I help you?"

•   •   •

Several Christmases ago, I decided to cook a standing rib roast. I had some dim idea I wanted to make Yorkshire pudding with it. My local supermarket had recently moved its butchers out of the stores to a central processing plant. In order to make my request, the kid behind the meat counter handed me the phone so I could speak directly with the regional manager. I read aloud what I had written at the top of a shopping list, weight and cut. A suggestion, frankly, from Julia Child. I had no idea where it came from in the cow, even how big it would be.

"I can have it out to you in three days," the regional manager said.

"Is there any special way to cook it?" I asked.

There was a long pause, and then I could picture what I was up against, speaking into a gap like that. The guy had what I wanted, he just didn't know what I needed. Maybe he was looking something up for me on the Internet, a recipe or a tip. More likely he was looking out his window at a dumpster in the parking lot. The pause made me quit it. I needed someone with a little knowledge.

I live in a small town where the butchers have mostly folded up their tents. So that day, I drove into the city, to an old-timey shop a friend had told me about called Kincaid's. It was, he said, the best butcher shop in America. Or the last. Worth the drive, he said. Nested in a residential neighborhood soggy with old trees on the north side of Indianapolis, it looked the part—little storefront, wooden butcher blocks, rolls of white freezer paper hovering in their brackets, handmade signs in the window advertising various pork chops. And big, chockablock guys in aprons, Sharpies tucked in shirt pockets, wrists like baseball bats.

Even a week before Christmas, requesting a rib roast in a joint like Kincaid's didn't make anyone blink. And when I asked for help on how to cook it, the owner stepped forward. He was a bag of cement with a bad haircut named Dave, who regarded me with dark eyes, as if uncertain I was paying attention. Butcher. The guy was the physical representation of his job—muscular, stern, sore, maybe just a little too aware that the world was changing. I deserved his doubt, if that's what this was. I was about to buy a $120 cut of meat, and I had no clue what I was doing.

"First of all, nice, nice, nice, nice, nice meat," he said. Five *nices*. I remember it like it was a day ago. "Here's the thing. Put your oven on high. Superhigh. All the way. Get it as hot as you can. Then put this in there for ten minutes. That'll seal it right up. Brown the whole outside. That's the only trick. Then go ahead and follow old Julia Child." I asked him about Yorkshire pudding and he reached under the counter, pulled out a handwritten recipe from a pile of Xeroxes. "I like a little more salt than this recipe calls for," he says. "But I'm not a skinny man and I do have some habits." The store bustled, but I'll be damned if he was thinking about anything but my roast, my skills, my meal. He raised his eyebrows, nodded, and told me it would be great.

•   •   •

At a bakery, the bread is finished when they hand it to you. At a grocery store, you assume all the risk once the boxed-up food is in your car. A butcher shop is unlike any other retail venue, because the parties on both sides of the counter are at work on the same process. The butcher is a kind of partner. Somehow the prime rib you serve belongs in equal measure to him as it does to you.

You can ask butchers anything and they will deconstruct your need. Ask for a porterhouse and trust that they will pick through the T-bones to get you a good one. Or ask what a porterhouse is and they will take out a T-bone to explain that if the short-loin portion is a good bit thicker than an inch, it's a porterhouse. Or ask if a porterhouse is what you want in the first place. They'll ask how you're cooking it, what you're serving with it, how much room you have on your cooking surface. They'll find the answer. And whether it's the apron or the smudges of blood or the enormous weight of the counter or the sheer mass of the product, you believe a butcher. He knows.

A man should have a butcher.

I became a Kincaid's loyalist. Year after year, I watched them work the room—thorough, efficient, a little fussy. They took all orders—a single burger or a dozen chops— seriously. They called the women dear and honey but never pissed them off. They called the men sir but still managed to pal around. They looked you in the eye and remembered your last order. Generous in their curiosity and professional in their detachment, they took all comers—the exacting and the simply curious—with equal zeal. They knew things, but you had to ask. They were butchers, the last monks of the town square. They had answers.

I want to be a guy with answers. So it was that one day earlier this year, I asked them if I could give it a try.

I showed up wearing a hat, a threadbare T-shirt, some old pants, and a decent pair of sneakers. When I stood at the two little saloon doors that hung between the work area and the back of the shop, Dave looked at me from head to toe.

"Okay," he said. "You look like a butcher. Get in here."

The manager, Shawn, pole-armed and heavy-bellied, with a sheen of sweat on his brow, huffed. Immediately he regarded me with sidelong disdain, leaning against the metal table, his weight on brisket he'd just cut and towel-dried. "I got orders coming in," he said. "I don't have anything for this guy."

It's cool, I wanted to say. I can just watch. But watching a butcher was not the point. Dave understood as much. He pointed to the front of the store, up the narrow passage between the counter and the walk-in, enough room there for one man to stand and another to pass, wrenched sideways. "Just put him on chickens today," Dave said. "Get him used to the knives. Lori can set him up."

So I settled in with Lori, the only female butcher in the shop, a skinny little hardass who knew every price in the store without looking. Butcher. She slid a knife across the block to me. "Always leave your knife closed—facing the wall—when you're done," she said. She lay a chicken leg on the block, tugged a handful of skin, then cut it. "You gotta use your judgment about how much to take off, but we ain't here to sell people chicken skin."

I was a cook once, and a dishwasher before that. I've hung Sheetrock and laid roofing. There is a coziness to manual work that I understand. Repetitive tasks—pulling the gummy viscera from the breast of a chicken, trimming out the little ridge of fat, cutting off ragged edges—that stuff was some comfort to me that first morning. The knife they gave me was so sharp that it required almost no downward pressure at all. "You just move the knife forward," Lori said. "One move only. And if you drop it, don't try to trap it or break the fall. Just jump back with your hands up. That thing will stick in your foot just as good as it will a boneless-skinless."

During a lull, with Lori in the walk-in dealing with a plastic bucket full of leg quarters, a woman approached the counter. The others were in the back inspecting an order. And I figured: No time like the present. The meat was right there in front of me. How hard could it be?

She was sixty years old, with a Fendi purse on her shoulder and a little piece of paper pinched between her fingers like a baby mouse. I stepped forward.

"I need just a quarter pound of lean ground beef," she said. And before I could tell her, "You got it!" or "Good enough!" — the phrases I had picked on the drive in as my own personal signature to every transaction—she kept on. "Lean," she said. "How lean? What's the percentage? Only a quarter pound. I make only one hamburger. Nothing left over. And I need two flank steaks. Not the marinated ones." I glanced left and downward. "What sort of marinade do you use, anyway?" she went on. "I can marinate it myself, can't I? Can you sell me the marinade separately?"

"Okay," I said, looking for a place to start with the work of it, with the litany of questions. She was asking for a quarter pound of ground beef, but I didn't know which side of the hamburger case to reach for. The signs faced the customer. "Okay," I said again.

My first transaction, stymied by a question about hamburger. What *did* lean mean, anyway? When I couldn't answer, she narrowed her eyes and bore in. "And I want four center-cut, bone-in pork chops. And really, they have to be the same thickness," she said. I nodded and said okay again. "And be sure you chine the bone."

You can't be a butcher unless you know what you're selling, and I'll be damned if I knew what chining the bone meant. There was a piece of paper in my pocket on which I'd inscribed the various cuts, their names in rows as they were in the case. Along the top, it read, *Chuck-Rib-Short loin-Sirloin*. Below: *Round. Shank and brisket, plate and flank*. What good was that doing me now? Chining the bone? It sounded like some sex thing, or a music term. I didn't look like a butcher; I looked like a placeholder. A butcher moves in an informed, muscular fashion, slides the cooler doors with authority, plucks the product, an awkward arm's-length away, with some aplomb. I didn't know the first step of that dance. The woman looked left, then threw her head back, glancing at the rear of the store. "Is Shawn here?" she said. Then, blessedly, Lori came up beside me.

"Hello, sweetie. What'll it be today?"

Sweetie! The woman looked at me glassily, recentered on Lori, then went back to the top of her list. "Yes," she breathed, starting again. "I only need a quarter pound of lean ground beef. I make only one hamburger."

Lori moved before the sentence ended. One hand to the cooler door, the other to a piece of wax paper.

"How lean is that?"

"Ninety-three percent," Lori said without breaking stride.

"Is that what I want?"

"Some people like a little more fat." Steady.

The woman looked down into the cooler, placing a finger on her lip. "More fat," she repeated, puzzled. In the weeks to come I grew to understand that once a customer was looking in the case, the sale was in the hands of the butcher. You worked through the order methodically, answered one question at a time, and used the wrapping time to think a little, to write down prices and answer follow-ups. A little cajoling slowed people down. Praising a cut created pauses. The trick was to lay in an undercurrent of military orderliness, a sense that precision was pleasure, without being bossy or abrupt.

"It's just taste," Lori said. "If you don't cook it too long, lean is good, too." She was shoulder deep in the cooler, holding. I saw her foot tapping the linoleum. Too fast for me, the sale was, I could see, too slow for her.

．　　　．　　　．

One of them trims chicken, one butterflies pork chops, another trims out a special order of tenderloins. One person to a block, one block per type of meat. The space is tight, but each station is ample. It's a world constantly decorated with signs of the process. A stray thumbprint of blood, a blackening dust of sawed bones, smears of raw fat.

Sometimes Dave stands in the middle of this, wide-legged, proprietary, appearing a little dizzy, and cooks a small piece of lamb or sirloin on a plug-in griddle. It helps with the smell, he says.

There's a skinny kid they call Joe Mack. Sturdy, tanned, sometimes wears a little rope necklace, who favors a golf shirt under his apron and keeps it tucked in. Barely two years in, he takes classes at night. His father is a meat supplier, and maybe for Joe Mack this is a kind of apprenticeship. There is no part of the job he won't do, though he does nothing so well as work the counter, where the women poke into their own small line in front of him. He speaks politely and slowly, he broadens his smile with every answer so it's broadest as he finishes, at which point he bags the meat and offers to carry it to the car. "Meat makes people happy," he says. "Women like it when you don't get in the way of their happiness." Butcher, through and through.

James is thicker, just slightly older, arms dotted with tattoos, all business at the counter, working the front of the store, mostly preparing the expensive cuts. I ask him about the tattoos. "Believe it or not," he tells me, "I was a rocker. I was in a pretty solid band, and this was my part-time job. But this was something I knew I could get better at." He works the knife upward, with the grain. "It's not going to go away," he says. "People always need meat-cutters." Butcher.

Behind the counter is a thirty-foot-long walk-in, with two doors that swing open so slowly that anyone darting in with a tray of chops has to stop and wait. Shawn calls it the million-dollar walk-in, the irreplaceable fridge. It was built in the first Kincaid's family store across town eighty-seven years ago, moved here one cork-lined wall at a time when the store relocated in 1934. "There isn't enough cork left in the world for them to build this again," he said one day while we were standing in the cooler. The temperature is a rock-steady thirty-five degrees. The humidity is 70 percent, always. This produces a dry cold, and what I came to think of as a bloody air, ideal for the aging of beef. Meat can hang in this freezer for up to ninety days in the aging process. It blackens on the outside, but it does not rot.

Temperature and time break down the fibers in the meat as it dries.

At Kincaid's they laugh at the phenomenon of "wet aging," in which meat is vacuum-sealed for days or weeks. "It's bullshit," Shawn says.

"The whole key to aging is evaporation," Dave says. "You let dry air pass freely over the meat. That's why the walk-in is so valuable to us. We have a term here for wet aging."

"It's called old meat," Shawn says.

      •   •   •

On Tuesdays, they break beef. On Wednesdays, they break lamb. A quartered cow, or half a lamb, pulled clean of hide, flat on the metal tables in back, sawed into sections, then worked into cuts from there. On Thursdays, they concentrate on the specialty cuts. Fridays mostly they get ready for Saturday, because on Saturdays, well, they try to sell everything, so nothing sits until Monday, when they break everything down and start over again. Each of these days requires a different set of implements—the saw, the fillet knife, the cleaver, the sponge, mop, and towel.

I thought I would get sick of it, or disgusted. I'd sort of held my breath when I went in, expecting large pools of blood, tubs of kidneys, brains lying on a table. But there is nothing grim about working in a butcher shop. Even the sinkful of tongues made sense to me that day. People were using this stuff. And when meat has a use, a purpose, a destination, it doesn't seem like a wasteful cultural indulgence. To a butcher, a filet does not look like a cylinder of dark, wine-red flesh that runs beneath the spine of a cow; it looks like product to be cared for and tended. It looks like someone's dinner. And of course, it looks like money.

There is no waste. Lifting, toting, trimming, tying—remarkable economy in every step. Lamb trim gets cut for stew meat. Pork trim made into five different types of sausage. Beef trim: hamburger. The chicken bones are sold for soup stock, the beef bones packed for dogs. Ham and pork scraps are mixed with pineapple juice in tubs of mayonnaise for ham loaf. The basic compact: Weight is money.

Even the fat goes to a rendering house for grease and soap, though "there's not even any profit in that part," Dave's wife, Vicki, the store's bookkeeper, told me. "We actually pay for it to be taken away. You just can't throw old meat away. You just—" she turned her head at the thought; no one likes to think about rot. "Well, you just can't."

Everything I touched in the butcher shop was either cold, sharp, or both. Every surface in the freezer, the Cryo-packs, the meat itself: icy cold. My fingers ached, and I labored through some scut work, mashing gelid tubs of ground ham with my hands, making sausage in an ancient steel tub, vacuum-wrapping the frozen homemade meatballs. I stayed away from the counter. The prospect of those rapid-fire orders pretty much terrified me, and one thing I knew was you couldn't show uncertainty. No one likes a butcher who balks. It shakes the gut-level confidence in stewardship. I spent my spare time standing in front of the counter, on the customer side, trying to memorize cuts and prices, preparing for a time when I could flex some muscle.

. . .

Mark taught the lessons of the grinder. Twenty-six years in the business, arms like water mains, he was a former pastor who had lived in Alaska for more than a decade. Butcher. The grinder is a four-foot-long tray, tilted toward a hole in one end. You push the day's trimmings into the hole, where it feeds into a sixteen-inch corkscrew blade. Out the other end: hamburger or sausage. One morning, tossing trim onto the tray, he turned on the grinder and said: "Look, the rule is, if you feel anything tug, anything at all, you hit the button and run." He poked the rubber-covered stop button with his thumb. We stood in the walk-in, the compressors humming like a train. "You put your hands in the air and you run," he said, "like a little girl. I'm serious as a sock. This stuff will humble you. Get away from it. You always run away from trouble in a butcher shop."

I liked the knife work, learning to work the heart of the blade—that section where the knife curves, just where it begins to flatten out—rather than the tip. I learned not to saw the meat but to cut with a consistent pressure, a single change of direction. Sawing the blade left ragged edges, little pointy stubs of meat, ugly and prone to burning.

I figured I would get cut, and I figured it would be nasty. The knives, marvelously sharp at the start of the day, were sharpened by Lori during the lulls. One morning, while trimming chicken, I asked her if there was a pool on when I would get cut. She looked at me like I had just pissed myself. "Why would there be?"

"It's going to happen, isn't it? Butchers get cut, right?"

She just wouldn't talk, not about cuts. None of the butchers would, not while they worked, and especially not while holding knives. Catch them on a smoke break and they might begrudgingly tell you about the time they watched a guy clip off the top third of his ring finger on the meat saw, or about hunting for the tip of a thumb in a pile of pork fat in order to ice it down so it might be reattached.

Dave will talk about last year, when he got his hand caught in the cuber, a nasty mouthful of steel teeth designed to gnash the fibers and tendons in the toughest meat. He points to the bottom of his fingers, where the hand meets the first digit. "I was in up to here," he says, "and most of my fingers were no better than hamburger. We just unscrewed the fitting and took the whole thing straight into the hospital room. They wanted to pull it apart—they were wacky. I couldn't let them. Vicki unscrewed it for them with an Allen wrench. To them it looked like a monster. It's an old piece. I didn't want to lose it."

He's left with trenches down his middle fingers, straight up through the nails. He's unable to bend them much, and not without pain. Still, he thinks of himself as lucky. He squeezes them as if they were produce. "I think they set up pretty well," he says. "I can still cut meat—what choice do I have?"

.   .   .

You aren't a butcher if you can't deal with people. You're just a meat cutter. Eventually, I made myself work the counter. I spooned out the hamburger: one-pound, four-pound, nine-ounce orders. I stacked and wrapped pork tenderloins for a Moose Lodge cook-out. I took an order in French from an angry Quebecois who couldn't understand why we didn't have roulade ready just then. I rang up beef short ribs, after Shawn sawed them down, for a kid from Texas. I displayed T-bones, urged people to look hard at the weak little loin, then held up a porterhouse for comparison. I sold hanger steaks, flank steaks, chateaubriand, told people that a Delmonico was simply a rib eye, and that we had good ones to show them. I parsed out noxiously sticky ground turkey and shaved turkey breast for women toting their children to the swimming pool, and proffered the kids a free bite before I wrapped it. I sold six Kobe steaks to a German guy in for the Indianapolis 500, then up-sold him three buffalo rib eyes just by asking him to take a look at their leanness.

Sales are the punctuating event of a butcher's day. And the butchers themselves were like shape-shifters. In one moment, they shouldered hindquarters into the cooler, as punch-drunk with the weight of the task as any bricklayer, then straightened like attentive librarians the second the bells on the door rang.

They packaged their meats in white freezer wrap and carefully wrote the cut and the prices with a Sharpie, each in his own particular handwriting, a kind of butcher's font, eschewing the bar-coded labels printed at the scales. I was miserable at it before

I slowed to concentrate on the letters—before I realized this was a message that would speak to the customer from the refrigerator hours later, a reminder of the wealth and promise and exactitude of the butcher shop.

.   .   .

Shawn is breaking a beef quarter. I'm piling out the cuts, wiping off the bone dust with a towel and stacking them on a tray. While lamb meat is riddled with fat, which must be trimmed in small upward flicks, sometimes producing no more than a chunk of meat half the size of a cheeseball, beef is more fully assembled and of a piece. The fat has to go, but it comes off the blade in strips that you throw in the trim pile like old neckties.

Shawn presses a finger into the hip joint, looking for a spot to set his saw. He's been cutting meat for thirty years. He claims that I'm of some use now, and we pass the time talking about his life as a boy in Jersey, riding around the city in a car with his aunt, the nun.

"What'd you learn here?" he asks me during a lull. No follow-up. No filler. Butcher. I tell him I don't find myself very disturbed with what I've come across. I'd thought there would be organs, and blood, some hint of a larger misery. "It doesn't seem like a very miserable business," I tell Shawn.

He shrugs. "I ate raw calf brain on a dare once," he says. "That's pretty miserable. Don't do that." He works perilously fast, making one push with the knife every time, never sawing the meat. I can't help but admire it now. "And you gotta remember, this isn't the killing floor." He tilts his head on his huge neck, wipes the tips of his fingers on the breast of his apron, and holds a paw open in a gesture to the whole place. "That is a rough business right there. Right here, we're a long way from slaughter.

A shop like ours is an intermediate step. We humanize things a little, help them see the culture of—"

He pauses then. A guy in a baseball cap has approached the counter. "Counter!" Shawn shouts. Mark and Lori converge on the sale. Then he looks back to me. "The culture of meat, I suppose you'd call it," he says. "People don't have time to know everything about meat. That's what we do. And we don't have time to know anything else." Pause. "Counter," he says, softer now. This time he's talking to me.

I rinse my hands, towel off, and approach. I'm dealing with another of these women, the older ones, the ones with the crimped list and the precise order. I've been here a month now, and I've come to see how customers like this are notoriously fair in their expectations. This one is a regular. She likes chicken, boneless and skinless. Two breasts. No more.

She hands me two potatoes, which I put on the scale before she starts her order. I drop them into a paper sack and price it. I don't talk. It feels orderly and smart, for us both, I think. It allows her to think longer, to want the service more.

This one—well, she's a dame. Her hair is done up smart, her cheeks are rouged, and her jewelry is on the gaudier fringe of elegant. "There you go, dear," I say, placing the potatoes on the counter. "What else can I get you?" I stare straight at her. There is no need to concentrate on anything else. I know what's around me. I think I even know what she wants.

"My son wants a steak," she says, "but I never buy red meat. What do you suggest?"

I hitch my apron and lean forward, elbows out. I need to know a little about her plans. They're grilling, it turns out. They're drinking imported beer. They're eating on her balcony. She smiles telling me about it.

"I'm thinking rib eye," I tell her. "But big men always think that."

She laughs. "My son is big, too," she says.

"Then the eagle has landed," I say. She laughs once more. And I have her. "Rib eye it is," I say. I show her the meat, spread wide on my hand, then wrap it tight like a Christmas present. "Nice meat," I tell her as she pays. "Good choice."

And when she blushes, I ignore it. I'm a butcher. I'm only giving her what she needs.

New York

FINALIST—REVIEWS AND
CRITICISM

With elegant prose and deep cultural knowledge, Justin Davidson decodes and critiques the city's environment, bringing the stories of mute structures to boisterous life.

Justin Davidson

The Glass Stampede

Our city is molting.

Bricks flake away. So do brittle fire escapes, terra-cotta encrustations, old paint, cracked stoops, faded awnings, sash windows, and stone laurels fashioned a century ago by Sicilian carvers. New York is shucking off its aging walk-ups, its small and mildewed structures, its drafty warehouses, cramped stores, and idle factories. In their place, the city is sprouting a hard, glistening new shell of glass and steel. Bright, seamless towers with fast elevators and provisional views spring up over a street-level layer of banks and drugstores. In some cities, a building retains the right to exist until it's proved irredeemable. Here, colossal towers are merely placeholders, temporary arrangements of future debris. New York lives by a philosophy of creative destruction. The only thing permanent about real estate is a measured patch of earth and the column of air above it. The rest is disposable.

And the metamorphosis has sped up. In the past fifteen fat years, more than 76,000 new buildings have gone up, more than 44,000 were razed, another 83,000 were radically renovated—a rate of change that evokes those time-lapse nature films in which flowers spring up and wither in a matter of seconds. For more than a decade, we have awakened to jackhammers and threaded our way around orange plastic netting, calculating that, since our last haircut, workers have added six more stories to that high-rise down the block. Now that metamorphosis is slowing as the economy drags. Buildings are still going up, but the boom is winding down. Before the next one begins is a good time to ask, has this ferment improved New York or eaten away at the city's soul?

Some see this sustained spasm of building as an urban lobotomy, in which the city has sacrificed its eccentricities and variety to placid prosperity. I am more optimistic, but to test that feeling against unsightly reality, I decide to canvass the city, inventory the construction that so many New Yorkers revile, and see what is worth defending. The results of my tour (or fifty-four side-by-side comparisons, at least) appear on these pages. Half a century ago, similar upheavals resulted from urban-renewal campaigns and social housing planted on the scale of Midwestern corn. This time the boom has happened lot by lot. I see single-family houses on Staten Island and a vertical metropolis at Columbus Circle, juice-carton towers and displays of virtuoso design. In some cases, the same architects have built for sybarites (Polshek Partnership's Standard Hotel, which stands, Colossus-like, astride the High Line) and for the low-income, elderly, and disabled (Polshek's Schermerhorn House in Brooklyn). I hear the wails of those who mourn the city they knew decades, years, or weeks ago, but I come away satisfied that the boom has left us a better town.

I start my peregrinations at the corner of Bowery and Houston Street, which has rolled over from a rank and raffish past to a more sedate kind of glumness. Here, in the last few years, graffiti-encrusted storefronts have made way for a pair of hulking rental boxes by the suburban developer Avalon-Bay Communities. On the south side of Houston is the company's first Manhattan beachhead, Avalon Chrystie Place, which is marginally edgier than its usual pabulum. Paired with SLCE, Arquitectonica, the firm that brought you the gaudy Westin hotel in Times Square, has restrained itself to the point of invisibility, giving the façade a smattering of texture that does little to lighten the dumpy massing. A vast Whole Foods took most of the retail space, confirming fears of a middle-class takeover of the Lower East Side: The tofu's fine and the living is easy, but couldn't class warfare be waged with better design?

Leaping across Houston Street, Avalon-Bay leveled McGurk's, a rickety five-story dive that in the 1890s employed whores so desperate that the place came to be known as Suicide Hall. The glass block that went up instead—Avalon Bowery Place—might not oppress its residents quite that much, but its aggressive blandness has a way of chipping at the soul. A gimcrack look is nearly all that connects the reflective interloper to the dark, medieval dwellings all around. You don't have to be ancient to remember the Bowery's concordance of ravaged masonry and human ruins, who tottered from flophouse to dive to doorway. Now the closest thing to a den of sin is Bruce Willis's wine bar, Bowery Wine Company, which a few dozen neighbors welcomed with placards that read DIE HARD YUPPIE SCUM. The National Trust for Historic Preservation tried more-genteel tactics: It has put the area on its list of "Most Endangered Historic Places."

As I make my way up the new boulevard of Bowery toward the de-punked East Village, I think about the tradeoffs. As the grandchild of Lower East Side tenement dwellers, I sympathize with preservationist sentiments. We need to remember, if not actually to relive, the experience of this once colorfully impoverished neighborhood. And yet it's one thing to preserve the traces of history, as the Lower East Side Tenement Museum does; it's another to fetishize misery. This slum sucked in huddled masses who craved less putrid air, more abundant food, and a little more space between one person and the next. Is it right to romanticize what they wanted desperately to escape? Hasn't the birthplace of Gertel's and Katz's earned itself a place to buy organic spelt? Avalon's ersatz châteaux could have been more graceful, but is the transformation they've helped to wreak really so dismal? Bad architecture can be good for people, too.

Think of the alternatives. In the last twenty-five years, the city's population has increased by a million people, and another million will be here twenty-five years from now. The question is not whether to make room for them but how. We could, in theory, rope off most of Manhattan to new development and push new arrivals to the city's fringes. Had we done that years ago, we would have created a museum of shabbiness. Even doing so now would keep the city in a state of embalmed picturesqueness and let the cost of scarce space climb to even loonier heights than it already has. In its forty-three-year existence, the Landmarks Preservation Commission has tucked more than 25,000 buildings under its protective wing, which seems about right. Protect every tenement, and eventually millionaires can no longer afford them.

An abundance of new architecture comes with a concomitant amount of demolition, which is not necessarily a bad thing. The most admired, most architecturally resplendent cities are the products of major destruction: Paris, gutted by Baron Haussmann in the mid-nineteenth century, Chicago and London, leveled by fire; Rome, radically reorganized by Pope Sixtus V in the late 1580s; San Francisco, flattened by an earthquake in 1906. I'm not advocating growth through trauma, only pointing out that periods of rapid change can be spectacularly constructive and that the results outlast the pangs. As pieces of the city evaporate, they take our memories with them. It gets hard to remember which block that old Chock Full o'Nuts was on or what was next to a lamented laundromat. This chronic amnesia is part of the New York condition. In his 1962 poem "An Urban Convalescence," James Merrill captured the feverish yet methodical sacking of the city and the way it toys with our sense of comfortable familiarity.

As usual in New York, everything is torn down
Before you have had time to care for it.
Head bowed, at the shrine of noise, let me try to recall
What building stood here. Was there a building at all?

Among Merrill's disciples is one Jeremiah Moss, who maintains the engagingly gloomy blog Jeremiah's Vanishing New York, which he terms "an ongoing obituary for my dying city." His topic is the steady erosion of the city's texture. He is the defender of all the undistinguished hunks of masonry that lend the streets their rhythm and give people a place to live and earn a living: bodegas, curio stores, a metalworking shop in Soho, diners, and dingy bars.

The jaundiced view of the Lower East Side is that it can no longer be rescued from the sneaker boutiques, the bulbous Blue condo, or the guests at the Hotel on Rivington who sit at the bar and gaze at the diorama of quaint old tenements. But we should put this transformation in context. A century ago, when the neighborhood was among the most congested places on Earth, New York kept bounding beyond its three-dimensional borders. By the city's own standards, the current spasms of construction are not really so severe. What makes the current escalation feel so sharp is that it comes after a long period of decline. The fortysomething who grew up here knew a metropolis that was not just smaller but rapidly desiccating. Between 1970 and 1980, more than a million people leached out of the five boroughs, their numbers only partially offset by new immigrants and aspiring actors. Crime rose, property prices collapsed, and plenty of smart people began to write New York off as another Newark, Cleveland, or Detroit.

Urban nostalgists reserve their greatest animus for gentrification, which is a stark word for a complicated phenomenon. It does not describe only the relentless territorial expansion of the rich at the expense of everybody else: Gentrification eddies across the city, polishing formerly middle-class enclaves to an affluent shine, prettying up once-decrepit neighborhoods for new middle-class arrivals, and making awful slums habitable. In the intricate ecology of New York, each current triggers a dizzying series of countercurrents. Low crime rates make city life more desirable, so fewer middle-class families feel like they are being forced to flee to the suburbs. That causes real-estate prices to climb, which forces out some of those same middle-class families. Rising housing costs in low-income areas require the poor to spend a growing slice of their income on rent but also make it financially feasible for developers to build affordable housing.

The way to deal with this tangle of paradoxes is not to rail against gentrification or lunge to halt it but to mitigate its impact on the poor through activism, governance, and good design. New York has the country's largest municipal affordable-housing program, not just now but ever. It doesn't manifest itself in jerry-built towers of despair, because below-market housing is often mixed with the expensive kind; a quarter of the apartments in the Avalon complex are reserved for low-income families. That kind of housing, too, can rescue a neighborhood. The needle-strewn South Bronx seemed beyond redemption until a collective of developers, nonprofits, and city agencies built Melrose Commons, a low-rise, low-income housing complex that is safe, durable, and appealing. That, too, is gentrification.

Do the dedicated yearners who would roll back this tide look fondly on the charred South Bronx of the eighties? Would they stick by the most depressed and derelict expanses of Brooklyn, or the cracked-out squats around Tompkins Square Park, or the blocks of boarded-up windows in Harlem? *That* New York was not authentic or quaint; it was miserable and dangerous.

Intelligent preservation is precious, but nostalgia is cheap, and every era nurtures its own variety. Those late-nineteenth-century Upper West Siders who still thought of Broadway as the bucolic, elm-lined Bloomingdale Road of their youths resented the incursion of brownstones in the 1880s. Their children must have been horrified in turn when those same houses were wiped away by the now-classic apartment buildings that line West End Avenue. Bitterness springs eternal. So rail, if you must, at the forest of mediocrities sprouting furiously in every Zip Code, at the way they bleach out character and promote a bland parade of chain stores. But keep in mind that when all those buildings have begun to age, the architecture of our immediate future will get down to the task of becoming the past.

It would be wonderful if we could stem the Avalonization of New York simply by demanding better buildings. (*Good Design Now!*) The power to do that lies in the hand of the client at the top of the consumer chain, especially the condo buyer. We might wish that an aesthetically enlightened branch of government would commission masterpieces and mandate design standards for everyone else, but this is New York, where an adversarial system bludgeons designs into a collection of compromises. Craving a visionary government with the leeway to reshape large swaths of the city means forgetting a time when bureaucrats and politicians garlanded the Lower East Side with grim brown housing projects and Robert Moses smashed neighborhoods to ram highways through. To give officials such Sim City powers again would violate the spirit of New York, which since the days of the Dutch East India Company has evolved a sophisticated mechanism of controlled venality: Government sets the terms; developers take the risks. This partnership between public and private spheres is ancient and, for all its flaws, corruption, and obstacles to excellence, has nevertheless built a very fine city. The great advantage to top-down planning is that it can hatch and act on a Big Idea. It was not government alone, however, that brought Times Square back to life in the nineties; it was a convergence of planning, zoning, architecture, politics, entertainment, finance, commerce, preservation, and pure civic ambition.

If we don't want a New York frozen in recollection, and we don't really want politicians with the clout to strew master-pieces, then we must welcome a certain amount—okay, a large amount—of bland architecture. It's paradoxical, I know, to wrinkle my nose at Avalon's Bowery incursions and yet be gladdened by what they say. Much of what has gone up since the early nineties is anonymous and shoddy, but the same could be said for medieval Paris or Gilded Age Chicago—or virtually any of New York's own glorious eras. Most architecture in any age is crap, and today's crap isn't as bad as yesterday's. Fifty years ago, the sweeping attempts to house the city's burgeoning masses produced the alpine bulk of LeFrak City and Co-op City. In their day, our generic would have been considered luxe. "When you compare these new [residential] buildings to the red-brick or white-brick apartment houses that were standard in the fifties and sixties, they're far better," says Alex Garvin, a planner who has been tinkering with ways to improve New York since the Lindsay years. "Both the ordinary and the exceptional have increased in quality." One reason housing is so expensive is that even your basic rental is a better place to live.

I find myself on West Thirty-seventh Street at Tenth Avenue, where a pale gray rental by Handel Architects is under construction, its tower bending into a gentle chevron above a squared-off base. "Ten years ago, the developer would have said, *Why does it have to have that shape? It creates strange angles in every apartment. What's in it for me?*" the firm's principal Gary Handel says. "Now they understand that the formal gesture has a function on the skyline. There's a real change in the client's acceptance of architecture." By which he means not high-flown architecture-as-art, but rank-and-file buildings that are better than strictly necessary.

Few architects have responded more energetically to the tumescent market, or had greater impact on the fabric of New York City, than Costas Kondylis, the prolific Greek-born master of the semi-deluxe. Like a Johnny Appleseed of real estate, Kondylis has sprinkled Manhattan with buildings such as the Lyric, on Broadway at Ninety-fourth Street. The Lyric is a more or less typical specimen of New York residential architecture at the turn of the twenty-first century, and to anybody who had a fondness for an earlier incarnation of Upper Broadway—with its low-slung stores and ponderously corniced apartment buildings—it represented the homogenization of New York's most motley avenue. In truth, the Lyric is neither disgraceful nor excellent; it is the soul of adequacy. Symphony Space, a performance hall colorfully and admirably renovated by Polshek, sits under the north corner like a bright block inserted in the base. Above, the twenty-three-story tower does what the zoning says it must: rise a dozen stories to a setback before continuing on up to its allowable height. Red brick frames the obligatory picture windows, which wrap around the corners. A judicious smattering of Art Deco–ish fins makes a perfunctory nod to the glory days. The westward side of the tower extends the arms of a shallow U, offering wide-angle views of the Hudson.

Pleasant to live in, harmless to the skyline, equipped with all the standard luxuries, and practically invisible to the casual glance, the Lyric is a chorus member in the opera of New York architecture. But even unradical building has a powerful effect on life at street level. As required, Kondylis lined the Broadway side with glass-faced storefronts that should in theory keep the sidewalks lively. In practice, the economics exclude small businesses with meager credit histories in favor of companies that can back up a twenty-year lease. This block has a New York Sports Club, a Commerce Bank, and a Starbucks, feeding the triumvirate of upper-middle-class needs: fitness, money, and caffeine.

Nobody flat-out hates the Lyric, whereas the nine-story Avalon Bowery Place seems more egregious. That's partly because the Avalon flaunts its hide of metal and glass, and because its sole nod to its proletarian surroundings is in the crudeness of the design: Its curtain wall is so clumsily detailed that it appears to have been patched together out of bulletproof windows salvaged from subway token booths. To accuse a new building of being out of character with the neighborhood is the protest of first resort. But fitting in doesn't mean blending in. Donning red-brick camouflage is a cheap and thoughtless way for a building to assimilate. Truly contextual architecture starts a conversation with the block, the street, and the city.

When that happens, it can yield greatness, and the boom has given us some of that as well. One superb example of elegant context is the fanciful riff on the glass-and-steel fish tank that Winka Dubbeldam, the principal of Archi-Tectonics, bestowed on Greenwich Street. The glass in Dubbeldam's condo has both the liquidity of water, in ripples down the inclined façade, and the roughness and depth of masonry, which links it to the muscular workhorse buildings all around. Equally thrilling is the way the interloper throws an arm over the old brick warehouse next door, making it a partner in the block's modernization. Now *that's* how you transform a block without betraying it.

Dubbeldam's tour de force lends strength to the idea that the context of the city places healthy constraints on artistes of unlimited imagination and equally expansive ego. "The urbanism of the city dominates architecture," says Robert A. M. Stern, who is dean both of the Yale School of Architecture and of New York's traditionalist wing. "The intricacies of the street wall are unending, and the edges of the parks, the streets, the squares, create amazing architecture at the urban scale. I like the fact that European architects are adjusting their techniques so that their work becomes part of the city and not just a piece of Barcelona dropped in here."

In its awkward way, Avalon Bowery Place, too, attempts to absorb some local character. Squeezed along the Houston Street side is Liz Christy Community Garden, founded by the Green Guerrillas in the early seventies. Instead of ravaging it, Avalon paid to restore it, and it now provides a lush haven from the thundering traffic. Around the back of the building is Extra Place, an alley that served as CBGB's vomitorium. Avalon plans to line it with stores and cafés. In their tiny way, these two scraps of land embody New York's powerful urbanistic force.

But if Avalon Bowery Place was so keen on fitting in, what is that big glass paperweight thing doing here? The answer is that each era gives one or two materials a starring role, and our celebrity is a crystalline concoction of fused silica rolled into panes. Architects love glass for an assortment of technical reasons: It is relatively cheap, malleable, and lightweight; it can be used in tiny chips or vast sheets. It can be mounted on movable frames; it can take on a thousand forms, from the plain storefront to the baroque contortions of Gehry's IAC headquarters. It can be environmentally virtuous by letting in more light than heat. Its delicacy can set off an assertive frame, or it can be inconspicuously clipped to a hidden structure and appear to float in midair. But the chief allure of glass in this era of deceptive exhibitionism is its usefulness in crafting illusion. A glass wall carries with it the suggestion of obviousness; it is the architectural equivalent of a magician's rolled-up sleeve. Glass looks insubstantial and yet it keeps the weather out. It's brittle yet remarkably immune to age; weightless yet able to carry a load; revealing as it keeps secrets. If glass has become the material of our age, it's not because it keeps us honest but because it implies, falsely, that we have nothing to hide. The *New York Times* has moved from a fortress to a glass-walled headquarters, for example, but it has not for that reason become less Kremlin-like. It's still impossible to divine what's going on in a marriage, even if the couple lives in a zoolike pad. So the great glass wall has become an alternative to the ponderous luxuries of the prewar palais. It has also become our vernacular siding—what clapboard is to the Cape Cod saltbox.

You can't hold the material responsible for the architecture. To compare the ham-fisted use of glass by Avalon's designers to the wizardry of Dubbeldam is almost grotesque, but they are linked because one represents the vulgarization of the other, in the same way that brick furnished forth both the tenement and the Dakota. The Dakota of glass is Richard Meier's pair (and then trio) of condos in the West Village. When the Perry Street buildings went up in 2002, they were defiantly different from everything else in that bastion of old-time Jane Jacobean preservationism. Meier imported the pared-down, transparent office-building aesthetic of Mies van der Rohe and fused it with the sexy California aeries of Pierre Koenig, Richard Neutra, and John Lautner. The classic modernists shared a worship of visibility, but there was a huge difference in the sights they framed. In midtown, white-collar laborers toil in stacked modules, glancing out at each other from time to time. In Los Angeles and Palm Springs, residents of modern mansions gaze out on vistas of desert, city, or ocean. Meier's Perry Street buildings attempt a compromise between proximity and panorama. They look out on drivers and joggers who gaze right back, enjoying high-def views of the inhabitants and the backs of expensive sofas.

I have mixed feelings about these apartments' watery cool. Their austere beauty jangles with the distasteful look-at-me pose. Meier has fashioned exhibitionist paradises for the wide-screen age. Even when there's nobody home or nothing much to see, they broadcast the illusion that the lives being led within them qualify as public spectacles. How un–New York: What's the point of being a voyeur if everything is on display?

The glamour of living under glass spread quickly, evolving from Meier's impractical purity into both more nuanced and more plebeian uses. The fact that the rich crave it is good, because glass is becoming an ever more complex and flexible material. So long as clients will pay to live behind it, designers will keep finding new ways to bend it, toughen it, color it, coat it, cast it, etch it, fill it with light, and bake it full of ceramic frits. Avalon Bowery Place is a by-product of the market's boiling upper end.

So even here, standing before an icon of discontent, I am not inclined to inhale the nostalgia that thickens an atmosphere already dense with concrete dust. I am convinced that the boom has left New York better off: stronger, suppler, safer, better integrated, and better looking. Yes, it's grown stands of interchangeable rental towers, but it's also given Crown Heights prettier, more livable streets. The wealthy have their decorative bouquets of Tribeca condos; the commuting throngs benefit from an airy new subway terminal in Coney Island. In the rush to satisfy the voracious demand for square footage, the city has also rediscovered the pleasures of good architecture, an art that for years it had written off as a costly frill. We need new buildings just as much as we need the old. I hear in the cacophonic symphony of construction the sound of a still vigorous and hungry city. I see in all that moving of dirt and hoisting of concrete panels the New York I've always known: unsentimental and steadfast in its refusal to stay the same, yet vigilantly proud of its past.

Sports Illustrated

FINALIST—COLUMNS AND
COMMENTARY

Selena Roberts is not simply a sports journalist—she is a storyteller about modern life. In this deeply personal story, Roberts shares the ways in which sports helped to heal and bring her family together after the death of her older brother, Mike, at age nine.

Selena Roberts

The Healing Season

The play unfolded in our backyard, a rural patch of north Florida invaded by the occasional possum and dotted with Vesuvian anthills, which, if you used your imagination, would suffice as blockers.

My big brother, Mike, had explained all the angles to my four-year-old sensibilities, though I'm not sure how I heard him. He'd placed a helmet on my head that was so outsized, its ear holes rested atop my shoulders. Yet I was ready, a defender lined up in a three-point stance. With a shout of "Hut!" Mike, all of seven, picked up the football and churned toward me, moving with the slow, deliberate strides of a man on the moon. As my outstretched fingers brushed his belt loop, Mike collapsed in a heap of exaggeration: flat on his back, eyes closed, tongue out. I'd just made the greatest tackle in the history of Suwannee County.

I would become the best sprinter in the state when I beat Mike in races to the car door or the cookie jar. I would become the shrewdest Battleship player this side of Milton Bradley when I'd yell out B-9,099, and Mike would proclaim, "You sank my battleship!" even when there was no B-9,099. He protected me from bugs, bogeymen, and disappointment.

Our moments together are spliced in my memory from jerky home movies, Polaroids, and family tales. My first clear recollection of Mike is from sometime after my tackling primer, when he darted across the yard and, for no reason, tilted and fell.

I will never understand why my mind captured this instant and then held it as a lifelong keepsake. His tumble could have been just a screwy loss of balance. What I know is that my parents, Mike, and I soon moved to Jacksonville in early 1971 to be near a hospital that treated children with brain tumors.

By November, Mike was gone, at age nine. Grief stretched into months of silence at our house. The only sound at dinner was that of ice cubes settling in the tea. Car rides were quiet except when my dad mindlessly tapped his wedding ring against the steering wheel. I played Battleship alone, conditioned to whisper the coordinates of aircraft carriers. My parents sat apart on our couch, looking right through Sonny and Cher, lost in separate thoughts, in separate mourning.

Sadness rarely gave way to joy until well into 1972. I remember showing my dad a Crayola creation of mine: a Miami Dolphin, with a fish on the helmet that looked more like a slug. He laughed. That was a start.

My parents adored the Dolphins. My mom was a math junkie, so she loved the precision angles of Bob Griese's pass plays and coach Don Shula's perfectly square jaw. My dad believed there was no better football name than Nick Buoniconti and taught me to spell Larry Csonka without a z.

Every Sunday that fall another Miami victory provided another dose of lightness to help offset my parents' leaden emptiness. I wouldn't dare simplify sorrow by describing the undefeated '72 Dolphins as faith healers for my family—my parents' marriage didn't survive in the end—but I can recall how the team brought relief to our home if only as conversation filler, if only as a vehicle for the return of sound.

We talked about the Dolphins on car rides in our Plymouth Fury, at dinner in our kitchen nook and between commercials on TV. And with each win in '72—can you believe that Earl

Morrall? how about the moves of Mercury Morris?—the topic grew bigger, louder, more wonderful.

I'm still grateful for them—more than I ever understood, until Super Bowl XLII. From the press box in Glendale, Ariz., I watched the Giants' Eli Manning spin free from the Patriots' rush and rear back, his spiraling emergency flare to David Tyree with fifty-nine seconds left spelling the end to New England's bid to match Miami's unbeaten season.

A deadline tends to obstruct introspection, but about two days later, out of a nonobjective reflex in my soul, I had one reaction to the Patriots' loss: good. The thought surprised me. I didn't realize it, but I wasn't ready for a rival to the only team I'd known as flawless, to a period I wanted to preserve as singularly unspoiled. If nothing else, sports are placeholders of our pasts, marking moments and tipping points as we move from one life passage to the next.

The '72 Dolphins provided my family with sweet volume. Mike would have loved that team, how it never let anyone down, how it sustained its magic. But in our backyard, lined up between anthills, he would have played the role of a Washington Redskin and assigned me to be a perfect Dolphin, forever protecting his little sister from loss.

The Atlantic

FINALIST—FEATURE
WRITING

Hanna Rosin's empathetic examination of the dilemmas faced by parents whose young children believe they were born the wrong gender, uses the compelling and surprising case of Brandon, the eight-year-old son of two army veterans who's convinced that he is a she.

Hanna Rosin

A Boy's Life

The local newspaper recorded that Brandon Simms was the first millennium baby born in his tiny southern town, at 12:50 A.M. He weighed eight pounds, two ounces, and, as his mother, Tina, later wrote to him in his baby book, "had a darlin' little face that told me right away you were innocent." Tina saved the white knit hat with the powder-blue ribbon that hospitals routinely give to new baby boys. But after that, the milestones took an unusual turn. As a toddler, Brandon would scour the house for something to drape over his head—a towel, a doily, a moons-and-stars bandanna he'd snatch from his mother's drawer. "I figure he wanted something that felt like hair," his mother later guessed. He spoke his first full sentence at a local Italian restaurant: "I like your high heels," he told a woman in a fancy red dress. At home, he would rip off his clothes as soon as Tina put them on him, and instead try on something from her closet—a purple undershirt, lingerie, shoes. "He ruined all my heels in the sandbox," she recalls.

At the toy store, Brandon would head straight for the aisles with the Barbies or the pink and purple dollhouses. Tina wouldn't buy them, instead steering him to neutral toys: puzzles or building blocks or cool neon markers. One weekend, when Brandon was two and a half, she took him to visit her ten-year-old cousin. When Brandon took to one of the many dolls in her huge collection—a blonde Barbie in a pink sparkly dress—Tina let him bring it home. He carried it everywhere, "even slept with it, like a teddy bear."

For his third Christmas, Tina bought Brandon a first-rate army set—complete with a Kevlar hat, walkie-talkies, and a hand grenade. Both Tina and Brandon's father had served in the army, and she thought their son might identify with the toys. A photo from that day shows him wearing a towel around his head, a bandanna around his waist, and a glum expression. The army set sits unopened at his feet. Tina recalls his joy, by contrast, on a day later that year. One afternoon, while Tina was on the phone, Brandon climbed out of the bathtub. When she found him, he was dancing in front of the mirror with his penis tucked between his legs. "Look, Mom, I'm a girl," he told her. "Happy as can be," she recalls.

"Brandon, God made you a boy for a special reason," she told him before they said prayers one night when he was five, the first part of a speech she'd prepared. But he cut her off: "God made a mistake," he said.

Tina had no easy explanation for where Brandon's behavior came from. Gender roles are not very fluid in their no-stoplight town, where Confederate flags line the main street. Boys ride dirt bikes through the woods starting at age five; local county fairs feature muscle cars for boys and beauty pageants for girls of all ages. In the army, Tina operated heavy machinery, but she is no tomboy. When she was younger, she wore long flowing dresses to match her long, wavy blond hair; now she wears it in a cute, Renée Zellweger–style bob. Her husband, Bill (Brandon's stepfather), lays wood floors and builds houses for a living. At a recent meeting with Brandon's school principal about how to handle the boy, Bill aptly summed up the town philosophy: "The way I was brought up, a boy's a boy and a girl's a girl."

School had always complicated Brandon's life. When teachers divided the class into boys' and girls' teams, Brandon would stand with the girls. In all of his kindergarten and first-grade self-portraits—"I have a pet," "I love my cat," "I love to play outside"—the "I" was a girl, often with big red lips, high heels, and a princess dress. Just as often, he drew himself as a mermaid with a sparkly purple tail, or a tail cut out from black velvet. Late in second grade, his older stepbrother, Travis, told his fourth-grade friends about Brandon's "secret"—that he dressed up at home and wanted to be a girl. After school, the boys cornered and bullied him. Brandon went home crying and begged Tina to let him skip the last week.

Since he was four, Tina had been taking Brandon to a succession of therapists. The first told her he was just going through a phase, but the phase never passed. Another suggested that Brandon's chaotic early childhood might have contributed to his behavior. Tina had never married Brandon's father, whom she'd met when they were both stationed in Germany. Twice, she had briefly stayed with him, when Brandon was five months old and then when he was three. Both times, she'd suspected his father of being too rough with the boy and had broken off the relationship. The therapist suggested that perhaps Brandon overidentified with his mother as the protector in the family, and for a while, this theory seemed plausible to Tina. In play therapy, the therapist tried to get Brandon to discuss his feelings about his father. She advised Tina to try a reward system at home. Brandon could earn up to twenty-one dollars a week for doing three things: looking in the mirror and saying "I'm a boy"; not dressing up; and not wearing anything on his head. It worked for a couple of weeks, but then Brandon lost interest.

Tina recounted much of this history to me in June at her kitchen table, where Brandon, now eight, had just laid out some lemon pound cake he'd baked from a mix. She, Bill, Brandon, his half sister, Madison, and Travis live in a comfortable double-wide trailer that Bill set up himself on their half acre of woods. I'd met Tina a month earlier, and she'd agreed to let me follow

Brandon's development over what turned out to be a critical few months of his life, on the condition that I change their names and disguise where they live. While we were at the table talking, Brandon was conducting a kind of nervous fashion show; over the course of several hours, he came in and out of his room wearing eight or nine different outfits, constructed from his costume collection, his mom's shoes and scarves, and his little sister's bodysuits and tights. Brandon is a gymnast and likes to show off splits and back bends. On the whole, he is quiet and a little somber, but every once in a while—after a great split, say—he shares a shy, crooked smile.

About a year and a half ago, Tina's mom showed her a Barbara Walters *20/20* special she'd taped. The show featured a six-year-old boy named "Jazz" who, since he was a toddler, had liked to dress as a girl. Everything about Jazz was familiar to Tina: the obsession with girls' clothes, the Barbies, wishing his penis away, even the fixation on mermaids. At the age of three, Jazz had been diagnosed with "gender-identity disorder" and was considered "transgender," Walters explained. The show mentioned a "hormone imbalance," but his parents had concluded that there was basically nothing wrong with him. He "didn't ask to be born this way," his mother explained. By kindergarten, his parents were letting him go to school with shoulder-length hair and a pink skirt on.

Tina had never heard the word *transgender*; she'd figured no other little boy on Earth was like Brandon. The show prompted her to buy a computer and Google "transgender children." Eventually, she made her way to a subculture of parents who live all across the country; they write in to listservs with grammar ranging from sixth-grade-level to professorial, but all have family stories much like hers. In May, she and Bill finally met some of them at the Trans-Health Conference in Philadelphia, the larger of two annual gatherings in the United States that many parents attend. Four years ago, only a handful of kids had come to the conference. This year, about fifty showed up, along with their siblings—enough to require a staff dedicated to full-time children's entertainment, including Jack the Balloon Man, Sue's Sand Art, a pool-and-pizza party, and a treasure hunt.

Diagnoses of gender-identity disorder among adults have tripled in Western countries since the 1960s; for men, the estimates now range from one in 7,400 to one in 42,000 (for women, the frequency of diagnosis is lower). Since 1952, when army veteran George Jorgensen's sex-change operation hit the front page of the *New York Daily News*, national resistance has softened a bit, too. Former NASCAR driver J. T. Hayes recently talked to *Newsweek* about having had a sex-change operation. Women's colleges have had to adjust to the presence of "trans-men," and the president-elect of the Gay and Lesbian Medical Association is a trans-woman and a successful cardiologist. But nothing can do more to normalize the face of transgender America than the sight of a seven-year-old (boy or girl?) with pink cheeks and a red balloon puppy in hand saying to Brandon, as one did at the conference:

"Are you transgender?"

"What's that?" Brandon asked.

"A boy who wants to be a girl."

"Yeah. Can I see your balloon?"

Around the world, clinics that specialize in gender-identity disorder in children report an explosion in referrals over the past few years. Dr. Kenneth Zucker, who runs the most comprehensive gender-identity clinic for youth in Toronto, has seen his waiting list quadruple in the past four years, to about eighty kids—an increase he attributes to media coverage and the proliferation of new sites on the Internet. Dr. Peggy Cohen-Kettenis, who runs the main clinic in the Netherlands, has seen the average age of her patients plummet since 2002. "We used to get calls mostly from parents who were concerned about their children being gay," says Catherine Tuerk, who since 1998 has run a support network for parents of children with gender-variant behavior, out of Children's National Medical Center in Washington, D.C. "Now about 90 percent of our calls are from parents with some concern that their child may be transgender."

In breakout sessions at the conference, transgender men and women in their fifties and sixties described lives of heartache and rejection: years of hiding makeup under the mattress, estranged parents, suicide attempts. Those in their twenties and thirties conveyed a dedicated militancy: they wore nose rings and Mohawks, ate strictly vegan, and conducted heated debates about the definitions of *queer* and *he-she* and *drag queen*. But the kids treated the conference like a family trip to Disneyland. They ran around with parents chasing after them, fussing over twisted bathing-suit straps or wiping crumbs from their lips. They looked effortlessly androgynous, and years away from sex, politics, or any form of rebellion. For Tina, the sight of them suggested a future she'd never considered for Brandon: a normal life as a girl. "She could end up being a *mommy* if she wants, just like me," one adoring mother leaned over and whispered about her five-year-old (natal) son.

· · ·

It took the gay-rights movement thirty years to shift from the Stonewall riots to gay marriage; now its transgender wing, long considered the most subversive, is striving for suburban normalcy, too. The change is fueled mostly by a community of parents who, like many parents of this generation, are open to letting even preschool children define their own needs. Faced with skeptical neighbors and school officials, parents at the conference discussed how to use the kind of quasi-therapeutic language that, these days, inspires deference: tell the school the child has a "medical condition" or a "hormonal imbalance" that can be treated later, suggested a conference speaker, Kim Pearson; using terms like *gender-identity disorder* or *birth defect* would be going too far, she advised. The point was to take the situation out of the realm of deep pathology or mental illness, while at the same time separating it from voluntary behavior, and to put it into the idiom of garden-variety "challenge." As one father told me, "Between all the kids with language problems and learning disabilities and peanut allergies, the school doesn't know who to worry about first."

A recent medical innovation holds out the promise that this might be the first generation of transsexuals who can live inconspicuously. About three years ago, physicians in the United States started treating transgender children with puberty blockers, drugs originally intended to halt precocious puberty. The blockers put teens in a state of suspended development. They prevent boys from growing facial and body hair and an Adam's apple, or developing a deep voice or any of the other physical characteristics that a male-to-female transsexual would later spend tens of thousands of dollars to reverse. They allow girls to grow taller, and prevent them from getting breasts or a period.

At the conference, blockers were the hot topic. One mother who'd found out about them too late cried, "The guilt I feel is overwhelming." The preteens sized each other up for signs of the magic drug, the way other teens might look for hip, expensive jeans: a sixteen-year-old (natal) girl, shirtless, with no sign of breasts; a seventeen-year-old (natal) boy with a face as smooth as Brandon's. "Is there anybody out there," asked Dr. Nick Gorton, a physician and trans-man from California, addressing a room full of older transsexuals, "who would not have taken the shot if it had been offered?" No one raised a hand.

After a day of sessions, Tina's mind was moving fast. "These kids look happier," she told me. "This is nothing we can fix. In his brain, in his *mind*, Brandon's a girl." With Bill, she started to test out the new language. "What's it they say? It's nothing wrong. It's just a medical condition, like diabetes or something.

Just a variation on human behavior." She made an unlikely friend, a lesbian mom from Seattle named Jill who took Tina under her wing. Jill had a five-year-old girl living as a boy and a future already mapped out. "He'll just basically be living life," Jill explained about her (natal) daughter. "I already legally changed his name and called all the parents at the school. Then, when he's in eighth grade, we'll take him to the [endocrinologist] and get the blockers, and no one will ever know. He'll just sail right through."

"I live in a small town," Tina pleaded with Jill. "This is all just really *new*. I never even heard the word *transgender* until recently, and the shrinks just kept telling me this is fixable."

In my few months of meeting transgender children, I talked to parents from many different backgrounds, who had made very different decisions about how to handle their children. Many accepted the "new normalcy" line, and some did not. But they all had one thing in common: in such a loaded situation, with their children's future at stake, doubt about their choices did not serve them well. In Brandon's case, for example, doubt would force Tina to consider that if she began letting him dress as a girl, she would be defying the conventions of her small town, and the majority of psychiatric experts, who advise strongly against the practice. It would force her to consider that she would have to begin making serious medical decisions for Brandon in only a couple of years, and that even with the blockers, he would face a lifetime of hormone injections and possibly major surgery. At the conference, Tina struggled with these doubts. But her new friends had already moved past them.

"Yeah, it is fixable," piped up another mom, who'd been on the *20/20* special. "We call it the disorder we cured with a skirt."

•　　•　　•

In 1967, Dr. John Money launched an experiment that he thought might confirm some of the more radical ideas emerging in feminist thought. Throughout the 1960s, writers such as Betty Friedan were challenging the notion that women should be limited to their prescribed roles as wives, housekeepers, and mothers. But other feminists pushed further, arguing that the whole notion of gender was a social construction, and easy to manipulate. In a 1955 paper, Money had written: "Sexual behavior and orientation as male or female does not have an innate, instinctive basis." We learn whether we are male or female "in the course of the various experiences of growing up." By the 1960s, he was well-known for having established the first American clinic to perform voluntary sex-change operations, at the Johns Hopkins Hospital, in Baltimore. One day, he got a letter from the parents of infant twin boys, one of whom had suffered a botched circumcision that had burned off most of his penis.

Money saw the case as a perfect test for his theory. He encouraged the parents to have the boy, David Reimer, fully castrated and then to raise him as a girl. When the child reached puberty, Money told them, doctors could construct a vagina and give him feminizing hormones. Above all, he told them, they must not waver in their decision and must not tell the boy about the accident.

In paper after paper, Money reported on Reimer's fabulous progress, writing that "she" showed an avid interest in dolls and dollhouses, that she preferred dresses, hair ribbons, and frilly blouses. Money's description of the child in his book *Sexual Signatures* prompted one reviewer to describe her as "sailing contentedly through childhood as a genuine girl." *Time* magazine concluded that the Reimer case cast doubt on the belief that sex differences are "immutably set by the genes at conception."

The reality was quite different, as *Rolling Stone* reporter John Colapinto brilliantly documented in the 2000 best-seller *As Nature Made Him*. Reimer had never adjusted to being a girl at all. He wanted only to build forts and play with his brother's dump trucks, and insisted that he should pee standing up. He was a social disaster at school, beating up other kids and misbehaving in class. At fourteen, Reimer became so alienated and depressed that his parents finally told him the truth about his birth, at which point he felt mostly relief, he reported. He eventually underwent phalloplasty, and he married a woman. Then four years ago, at age thirty-eight, Reimer shot himself dead in a grocery-store parking lot.

Today, the notion that gender is purely a social construction seems nearly as outmoded as bra-burning or free love. Feminist theory is pivoting with the rest of the culture, and is locating the key to identity in genetics and the workings of the brain. In the new conventional wisdom, we are all prewired for many things previously thought to be in the realm of upbringing, choice, or subjective experience: happiness, religious awakening, cheating, a love of chocolate. Behaviors are fundamental unless we are chemically altered. Louann Brizendine, in her 2006 best-selling book, *The Female Brain*, claims that everything from empathy to chattiness to poor spatial reasoning is "hardwired into the brains of women." Dr. Milton Diamond, an expert on human sexuality at the University of Hawaii and long the intellectual nemesis of Money, encapsulated this view in an interview on the BBC in 1980, when it was becoming clear that Money's experiment was failing: "Maybe we really have to think . . . that we don't come to this world neutral; that we come to this world with some degree of maleness and femaleness which will transcend whatever the society wants to put into [us]."

Diamond now spends his time collecting case studies of transsexuals who have a twin, to see how often both twins have transitioned to the opposite sex. To him, these cases are a "confirmation" that "the biggest sex organ is not between the legs but between the ears." For many gender biologists like Diamond, transgender children now serve the same allegorical purpose that David Reimer once did, but they support the opposite conclusion: they are seen as living proof that "gender identity is influenced by some innate or immutable factors," writes Melissa Hines, the author of *Brain Gender*.

This is the strange place in which transsexuals have found themselves. For years, they've been at the extreme edges of transgressive sexual politics. But now children like Brandon are being used to paint a more conventional picture: before they have much time to be shaped by experience, before they know their sexual orientation, even in defiance of their bodies, children can know their gender, from the firings of neurons deep within their brains. What better rebuke to the *Our Bodies, Ourselves* era of feminism than the notion that even the body is dispensable, that the hard nugget of difference lies even deeper?

.   .   .

In most major institutes for gender-identity disorder in children worldwide, a psychologist is the central figure. In the United States, the person intending to found "the first major academic research center," as he calls it, is Dr. Norman Spack, an endocrinologist who teaches at Harvard Medical School and is committed to a hormonal fix. Spack works out of a cramped office at Children's Hospital in Boston, where the walls are covered with diplomas and notes of gratitude scrawled in crayons or bright markers ("Thanks, Dr. Spack!!!"). Spack is bald, with a trim beard, and often wears his Harvard tie under his lab coat. He is not confrontational by nature, but he can hold his own with his critics: "To those who say I am interrupting God's work, I point to Leviticus, which says, 'Thou shalt not stand idly by the blood of your neighbor'"—an injunction, as he sees it, to prevent needless suffering.

Spack has treated young-adult transsexuals since the 1980s, and until recently he could never get past one problem: "They are never going to fail to draw attention to themselves." Over the years, he'd seen patients rejected by families, friends, and employers after a sex-change operation. Four years ago, he heard about the innovative use of hormone blockers on transgender youths in the Netherlands; to him, the drugs seemed like the missing piece of the puzzle.

The problem with blockers is that parents have to begin making medical decisions for their children when the children are quite young. From the earliest signs of puberty, doctors have about eighteen months to start the blockers for ideal results. For girls, that's usually between ages ten and twelve; for boys, between twelve and fourteen. If the patients follow through with cross-sex hormones and sex-change surgery, they will be permanently sterile, something Spack always discusses with them. "When you're talking to a twelve-year-old, that's a heavy-duty conversation," he said in a recent interview. "Does a kid that age really think about fertility? But if you don't start treatment, they will always have trouble fitting in."

When Beth was eleven, she told her mother, Susanna, that she'd "rather be dead" than go to school anymore as a girl. (The names of all the children and parents used as case studies in this story are pseudonyms.) For a long time, she had refused to shower except in a bathing suit, and had skipped out of health class every Thursday, when the standard puberty videos were shown. In March 2006, when Beth, now Matt, was twelve, they went to see Spack. He told Matt that if he went down this road, he would never biologically have children.

"I'll adopt!" Matt said.

"What is most important to him is that he's comfortable in who he is," says Susanna. They left with a prescription—a "godsend," she calls it.

Now, at fifteen and on testosterone, Matt is tall, with a broad chest and hairy legs. Susanna figures he's the first trans-man in America to go shirtless without having had any chest surgery. His mother describes him as "happy" and "totally at home in his masculine body." Matt has a girlfriend; he met her at the amusement park where Susanna works. Susanna is pretty sure he's said something to the girl about his situation, but knows he hasn't talked to her parents.

Susanna imagines few limitations in Matt's future. Only a minority of trans-men get what they call "bottom" surgery, because phalloplasty is still more cosmetic than functional, and the procedure is risky. But otherwise? Married? "Oh, yeah. And his career prospects will be good because he gets very good grades. We envision a kind of family life, maybe in the suburbs, with a good job." They have "no fears" about the future, and "zero doubts" about the path they've chosen.

Blockers are entirely reversible; should a child change his or her mind about becoming the other gender, a doctor can stop the drugs and normal puberty will begin. The Dutch clinic has given them to about seventy children since it started the treatment, in 2000; clinics in the United States and Canada have given them to dozens more. According to Dr. Peggy Cohen-Kettenis, the psychologist who heads the Dutch clinic, no case of a child stopping the blockers and changing course has yet been reported.

This suggests one of two things: either the screening is excellent, or once a child begins, he or she is set firmly on the path to medical intervention. "Adolescents may consider this step a guarantee of sex reassignment," wrote Cohen-Kettenis, "and it could make them therefore less rather than more inclined to engage in introspection." In the Netherlands, clinicians try to guard against this with an extensive diagnostic protocol, including testing and many sessions "to confirm that the desire for treatment is very persistent," before starting the blockers.

Spack's clinic isn't so comprehensive. A part-time psychologist, Dr. Laura Edwards-Leeper, conducts four-hour family screenings by appointment. (When I visited during the summer, she was doing only one or two a month.) But often she has to field emergency cases directly with Spack, which sometimes means skipping the screening altogether. "We get these calls from parents who are just frantic," she says. "They need to get in immediately, because their child is about to hit puberty and is having serious mental-health issues, and we really want to accommodate that. It's like they've been waiting their whole lives for this and they are just desperate, and when they finally get in to see us . . . it's like a rebirth."

Spack's own conception of the psychology involved is uncomplicated: "If a girl starts to experience breast budding and feels like cutting herself, then she's probably transgendered. If she feels immediate relief on the [puberty-blocking] drugs, that confirms the diagnosis," he told the *Boston Globe*. He thinks of the blockers not as an addendum to years of therapy but as "preventative" because they forestall the trauma that comes from social rejection. Clinically, men who become women are usually described as "male-to-female," but Spack, using the parlance of activist parents, refers to them as "affirmed females"—"because how can you be a male-to-female if really you were always a female in your brain?"

●   ●   ●

For the transgender community, *born in the wrong body* is the catchphrase that best captures this moment. It implies that the anatomy deceives where the brain tells the truth; that gender destiny is set before a baby takes its first breath. But the empirical evidence does not fit this argument so neatly. Milton Diamond says his study of identical transgender twins shows the same genetic predisposition that has been found for homosexuality: if one twin has switched to the opposite sex, there is a 50 percent chance that the other will as well. But his survey has not yet been published, and no one else has found nearly that degree of correlation. Eric Vilain, a geneticist at UCLA who specializes in sexual development and sex differences in the brain, says the studies on twins are mixed and that, on the whole, "there is no evidence of a biological influence on transsexualism yet."

In 1995, a study published in *Nature* looked at the brains of six adult male-to-female transsexuals and showed that certain regions of their brains were closer in size to those of women than of men. This study seemed to echo a famous 1991 study about gay men, published in *Science* by the neuroscientist Simon LeVay. LeVay had studied a portion of the hypothalamus that governs sexual behavior, and he discovered that in gay men, its size was much closer to women's than to straight men's; his findings helped legitimize the notion that homosexuality is hardwired. But in the transsexual study, the sample size was small, and the subjects had already received significant feminizing hormone treatments, which can affect brain structure.

Transsexualism is far less common than homosexuality, and the research is in its infancy. Scattered studies have looked at brain activity, finger size, familial recurrence, and birth order. One hypothesis involves hormonal imbalances during pregnancy. In 1988, researchers injected hormones into pregnant rhesus monkeys; the hormones seemed to masculinize the brains but not the bodies of their female babies. "Are we expecting to find some biological component [to gender identity]?" asks Vilain. "Certainly I am. But my hunch is, it's going to be mild. My hunch is that sexual orientation is probably much more hardwired than gender identity. I'm not saying [gender identity is] entirely determined by the social environment. I'm just saying that it's much more malleable."

Vilain has spent his career working with intersex patients, who are born with the anatomy of both sexes. He says his hardest job is to persuade the parents to leave the genitals ambiguous and wait until the child has grown up, and can choose his or her own course. This experience has influenced his views on parents with young transgender kids. "I'm torn here. I'm very ambivalent. I know [the parents] are saying the children are born this way. But I'm still on the fence. I consider the child my patient, not the parents, and I don't want to alleviate the anxiety of the parents by surgically fixing the child. We don't know the long-term effects of making these decisions for the child. We're playing God here, a little bit."

Even some supporters of hormone blockers worry that the availability of the drugs will encourage parents to make definitive decisions about younger and younger kids. This is one reason why doctors at the clinic in the Netherlands ask parents not to let young children live as the other gender until they are about to go on blockers. "We discourage it because the chances are very high that your child will not be a transsexual," says Cohen-Kettenis. The Dutch studies of their own patients show that among young children who have gender-identity disorder, only 20 to 25 percent still want to switch gender at adolescence; other studies show similar or even lower rates of persistence.

The most extensive study on transgender boys was published in 1987 as *The "Sissy Boy Syndrome" and the Development of Homosexuality*. For fifteen years, Dr. Richard Green followed forty-four boys who exhibited extreme feminine behaviors, and a control group of boys who did not. The boys in the feminine group all played with dolls, preferred the company of girls to boys, and avoided "rough-and-tumble play." Reports from their parents sound very much like the testimonies one reads on the listservs today. "He started . . . cross-dressing when he was about 3," reported one mother. "[He stood] in front of the mirror and he took his penis and he folded it under, and he said, 'Look, Mommy, I'm a girl,'" said another.

Green expected most of the boys in the study to end up as transsexuals, but nothing like that happened. Three-fourths of the forty-four boys turned out to be gay or bisexual (Green says a few more have since contacted him and told him they, too, were gay). Only one became a transsexual. "We can't tell a pre-gay from a pre-transsexual at eight," says Green, who recently retired from running the adult gender-identity clinic in England. "Are you helping or hurting a kid by allowing them to live as the other gender? If everyone is caught up in facilitating the thing, then there may be a hell of a lot of pressure to remain that way, regardless of how strongly the kid still feels gender-dysphoric. Who knows? That's a study that hasn't found its investigator yet."

. . .

Out on the sidewalk in Philadelphia, Tina was going through Marlboro after Marlboro, stubbing them out half-smoked against city buildings. The conference's first day had just ended, with Tina asking another mom, "So how do you know if one of these kids stays that way or if he changes?" and the mom suggesting she could wait awhile and see.

"Wait? Wait for what?" Tina suddenly said to Bill. "He's already waited six years, and now I don't care about any of that no more." Bill looked worried, but she threw an army phrase at him: "Suck it up and drive on, soldier."

The organizers had planned a pool party for that night, and Tina had come to a decision: Brandon would wear exactly the kind of bathing suit he'd always wanted. She had spotted a Macy's a couple of blocks away. I walked with her and Bill and Brandon into the hush and glow, the headless mannequins sporting golf shorts with eighty-dollar price tags. They quietly took the escalator one floor up, to the girls' bathing-suit department. Brandon leaped off at the top and ran to the first suit that caught his eye: a teal Hannah Montana bikini studded with jewels and glitter. "Oh, I love this one," he said.

"So that's the one you want?" asked Tina.

Brandon hesitated. He was used to doing his cross-dressing somewhat furtively. Normally he would just grab the shiniest thing he saw, for fear his chance would evaporate. But as he came to understand that both Tina and Bill were on board, he slowed down a bit. He carefully looked through all the racks. Bill, calm now, was helping him. "You want a one-piece or two-piece?" Bill asked. Tina, meanwhile, was having a harder time. "I'll get used to it," she said. She had tried twice to call Brandon "she," Tina suddenly confessed, but "it just don't sound right," she said, her eyes tearing.

Brandon decided to try on an orange one-piece with polka dots, a sky-blue-and-pink two-piece, and a Hawaiian-print tankini with a brown background and pink hibiscus flowers. He went into a dressing room and stayed there a long, long time. Finally, he called in the adults. Brandon had settled on the least showy of the three: the Hawaiian print with the brown background. He had it on and was shyly looking in the mirror. He wasn't doing backflips or grinning from ear to ear; he was still and at peace, gently fingering the price tag. He mentioned that he didn't want to wear the suit again until he'd had a chance to wash his feet.

At the pool party, Brandon immediately ran into a friend he'd made earlier, the transgender boy who'd shared his balloon puppy. The pool was in a small room in the corner of a hotel basement, with low ceilings and no windows. The echoes of seventy giddy children filled the space. Siblings were there, too, so it was impossible to know who had been born a boy and who a girl. They were all just smooth limbs and wet hair and an occasional slip that sent one crying to his or her mother.

Bill sat next to me on a bench and spilled his concerns. He was worried about Tina's stepfather, who would never accept this. He was worried that Brandon's father might find out and demand custody. He was worried about Brandon's best friend, whose parents were strict evangelical Christians. He was worried about their own pastor, who had sternly advised them to take away all of Brandon's girl-toys and girl-clothes. "Maybe if we just pray hard enough," Bill had told Tina.

Brandon raced by, arm in arm with his new friend, giggling. Tina and Bill didn't know this yet, but Brandon had already started telling the other kids that his name was Bridget, after the pet mouse he'd recently buried ("My beloved Bridget. Rest With the Lord," the memorial in his room read). The comment of an older transsexual from Brooklyn who'd sat behind Tina in a session earlier that day echoed in my head. He'd had his sex-change operation when he was in his fifties, and in his wild, wispy wig, he looked like a biblical prophet, with breasts. "You think you have troubles now," he'd yelled out to Tina. "Wait until next week. Once you let the genie out of the bottle, she's not going back in!"

·　　·　　·

Dr. Kenneth Zucker has been seeing children with gender-identity disorder in Toronto since the mid-1970s, and has published more on the subject than any other researcher. But lately he has become a pariah to the most vocal activists in the American transgender community. In 2012, the *Diagnostic and Statistical Manual of Mental Disorders*—the bible for psychiatric professionals—will be updated. Many in the transgender community see this as their opportunity to remove gender-identity disorder from the book, much the same way homosexuality was delisted in 1973. Zucker is in charge of the committee that will make the recommendation. He seems unlikely to bless the condition as psychologically healthy, especially in young children.

I met Zucker in his office at the Centre for Addiction and Mental Health, where piles of books alternate with the Barbies and superheroes that he uses for play therapy. Zucker has a white mustache and beard, and his manner is somewhat Talmudic. He responds to every question with a methodical three-part answer, often ending by climbing a chair to pull down a research paper he's written. On one of his file cabinets, he's tacked up a flyer from a British parents' advocacy group that reads: "Gender dysphoria is increasingly understood . . . as having biological origins," and describes "small parts of the brain" as "progressing along different pathways." During the interview, he took it down to make a point: "In terms of empirical data, this is not true. It's just dogma, and I've never liked dogma. Biology is not destiny."

In his case studies and descriptions of patients, Zucker usually explains gender dysphoria in terms of what he calls "family noise": neglectful parents who caused a boy to overidentify with his domineering older sisters; a mother who expected a daughter and delayed naming her newborn son for eight weeks. Zucker's belief is that with enough therapy, such children can be made to feel comfortable in their birth sex. Zucker has compared young children who believe they are meant to live as the other sex to people who want to amputate healthy limbs, or who believe they are cats, or those with something called ethnic-identity disorder. "If a five-year-old black kid came into the clinic and said he wanted to be white, would we endorse that?" he told me. "I don't think so. What we would want to do is say, 'What's going on with this kid that's making him feel that it would be better to be white?'"

Young children, he explains, have very concrete reasoning; they may believe that if they want to wear dresses, they are girls. But he sees it as his job—and the parents'—to help them think in more flexible ways. "If a kid has massive separation anxiety and does not want to go to school, one solution would be to let them stay home. That would solve the problem at one level, but not at another. So it is with gender identity." Allowing a child to switch genders, in other words, would probably not get to the root of the psychological problem, but only offer a superficial fix.

Zucker calls his approach "developmental," which means that the most important factor is the age of the child. Younger children are more malleable, he believes, and can learn to "be comfortable in their own skin." Zucker says that in twenty-five years, not one of the patients who started seeing him by age six has switched gender. Adolescents are more fixed in their identity. If a parent brings in, say, a thirteen-year-old who has never been treated and who has severe gender dysphoria, Zucker will generally recommend hormonal treatment. But he considers that a fraught choice. "One has to think about the long-term developmental path. This kid will go through lifelong hormonal treatment to approximate the phenotype of a male and may require some kind of surgery and then will have to deal with the fact that he doesn't have a phallus; it's a tough road, with a lot of pain involved."

Zucker put me in touch with two of his success stories, a boy and a girl, now both living in the suburbs of Toronto. Meeting them was like moving into a parallel world where every story began the same way as those of the American families I'd met, but then ran in the opposite direction.

When he was four, the boy, John, had tested at the top of the gender-dysphoria scale. Zucker recalls him as "one of the most anxious kids I ever saw." He had bins full of Barbies and Disney princess movies, and he dressed in homemade costumes. Once, at a hardware store, he stared up at the glittery chandeliers and wept, "I don't want to be a daddy! I want to be a mommy!"

His parents, well-educated urbanites, let John grow his hair long and play with whatever toys he preferred. But then a close friend led them to Zucker, and soon they began to see themselves as "in denial," recalls his mother, Caroline. "Once we came to see his behavior for what it was, it became painfully sad." Zucker believed John's behavior resulted from early-childhood medical trauma—he was born with tumors on his kidneys and had had invasive treatments every three months—and from his dependence during that time on his mother, who has a dominant personality.

When they reversed course, they dedicated themselves to the project with a thoroughness most parents would find exhausting and off-putting. They boxed up all of John's girl-toys and videos and replaced them with neutral ones. Whenever John cried for his girl-toys, they would ask him, "Do you think playing with those would make you feel better about being a boy?" and then would distract him with an offer to ride bikes or take a walk. They turned their house into a 1950s kitchen-sink drama, intended to inculcate respect for patriarchy, in the crudest and simplest terms: "Boys don't wear pink, they wear blue," they would tell him, or "Daddy is smarter than Mommy—ask him." If John called for Mommy in the middle of the night, Daddy went, every time.

When I visited the family, John was lazing around with his older brother, idly watching TV and playing video games, dressed in a polo shirt and Abercrombie & Fitch shorts. He said he was glad he'd been through the therapy, "because it made me feel happy," but that's about all he would say; for the most part, his mother spoke for him. Recently, John was in the basement watching the Grammys. When Caroline walked downstairs to say good night, she found him draped in a blanket, vamping. He looked up at her, mortified. She held his face and said, "You never have to be embarrassed of the things you say or do around me." Her position now is that the treatment is "not a cure; this will always be with him"—but also that he has nothing to be ashamed of. About a year ago, John carefully broke the news to his parents that he is gay. "You'd have to carefully break the news to me that you were straight," his dad told him. "He'll be a man who loves men," says his mother. "But I want him to be a happy man who loves men."

The girl's case was even more extreme in some ways. She insisted on peeing standing up and playing only with boys. When her mother bought her Barbies, she'd pop their heads off. Once, when she was six, her father, Mike, said out of the blue: "Chris, you're a girl." In response, he recalls, she "started screaming and freaking out," closing her hand into a fist and punching herself between the legs, over and over. After that, her parents took her to see Zucker. He connected Chris's behavior to the early years of her parents' marriage; her mother had gotten pregnant and Mike had been resentful of having to marry her, and verbally abusive. Chris, Zucker told them, saw her mother as weak and couldn't identify with her. For four years, they saw no progress. When Chris turned eleven and other girls in school started getting their periods, her mother found her on the bed one night, weeping. She "said she wanted to kill herself," her mother told me. "She said, 'In my head, I've always been a boy.'"

But about a month after that, everything began to change. Chris had joined a softball team and made some female friends; her mother figured she had cottoned to the idea that girls could be tough and competitive. Then one day, Chris went to her mother and said, "Mom, I need to talk to you. We need to go shopping." She bought clothes that were tighter and had her ears pierced. She let her hair grow out. Eventually she gave her boys' clothes away.

Now Chris wears her hair in a ponytail, walks like a girl, and spends hours on the phone, talking to girlfriends about boys. Her mother recently watched her through a bedroom window as she was jumping on their trampoline, looking slyly at her own reflection and tossing her hair around. At her parents' insistence, Chris has never been to a support group or a conference, never talked to another girl who wanted to be a boy. For all she knew, she was the only person in the world who felt as she once had felt.

The week before I arrived in Toronto, the Barbara Walters special about Jazz had been re-aired, and both sets of parents had seen it. "I was aghast," said John's mother. "It really affected us to see this poor little peanut, and her parents just going to the teacher and saying 'He is a "she" now.' Why would you assume a four-year-old would understand the ramifications of that?"

"We were shocked," Chris's father said. "They gave up on their kid too early. Regardless of our beliefs and our values, you look at Chris, and you look at these kids, and they have to go through a sex-change operation and they'll never look right and they'll never have a normal life. Look at Chris's chance for a happy, decent life, and look at theirs. Seeing those kids, it just broke our hearts."

•   •   •

Catherine Tuerk, who runs the support group for parents in Washington, D.C., started out as an advocate for gay rights after her son came out, in his twenties. She has a theory about why some parents have become so comfortable with the transgender label: "Parents have told me it's almost easier to tell others, 'My kid was born in the wrong body,' rather than explaining that he might be gay, which is in the back of everyone's mind. When people think about being gay, they think about sex—and thinking about sex and kids is taboo."

Tuerk believes lingering homophobia is partly responsible for this, and in some cases, she may be right. When Bill saw two men kissing at the conference, he said, "That just don't sit right with me." In one of Zucker's case studies, a seventeen-year-old girl requesting cross-sex hormones tells him, "Doc, to be honest, lesbians make me sick . . . I want to be normal." In Iran, homosexuality is punishable by death, but sex-change operations are legal—a way of normalizing aberrant attractions.

Overall, though, Tuerk's explanation touches on something deeper than latent homophobia: a subconscious strain in American conceptions of childhood. You see it in the hyper-vigilance about "good touch" and "bad touch." Or in the banishing of Freud to the realm of the perverse. The culture seems invested in an almost Victorian notion of childhood innocence, leaving no room for sexual volition, even in the far future.

When Tuerk was raising her son, in the 1970s, she and her husband, a psychiatrist, both fell prey to the idea that their son's gayness was somehow their fault, and that they could change it. These were the years when the child psychologist Bruno Bettelheim blamed cold, distant "refrigerator mothers" for everything from autism to schizophrenia in their children. Children, to Bettelheim, were messy, unhappy creatures, warped by the sins of their parents. Today's children are nothing like that, at least not in their parents' eyes. They are pure vessels, channeling biological impulses beyond their control—or their parents'. Their requests are innocent, unsullied by baggage or desire. Which makes it much easier to say yes to them.

Tuerk was thrilled when the pendulum swung from nurture toward nature; "I can tell you the exact spot where I was, in Chevy Chase Circle, when someone said the words to me: 'There's a guy in Baltimore, and he thinks people are born gay.'" But she now thinks the pendulum may have swung too far. For the minority who are truly transgender, "the sooner they get into the right clothes, the less they're going to suffer. But for the rest? I'm not sure if we're helping or hurting them by pushing them in this direction."

It's not impossible to imagine Brandon's life going in another direction. His early life fits neatly into a Zucker case study about family noise. Tina describes Brandon as "never leaving my side" during his early years. The diagnosis writes itself: father, distant and threatening; mother, protector; child overidentifies with strong maternal figure. If Tina had lived in Toronto, if she'd had the patience for six years of Dr. Zucker's therapy, if the therapy had been free, then who knows?

Yet Zucker's approach has its own disturbing elements. It's easy to imagine that his methods—steering parents toward removing pink crayons from the box, extolling a patriarchy no one believes in—could instill in some children a sense of shame and a double life. A 2008 study of twenty-five girls who had been seen in Zucker's clinic showed positive results; twenty-two were no longer gender-dysphoric, meaning they were comfortable living as girls. But that doesn't mean they were happy. I spoke to the mother of one Zucker patient in her late twenties, who said her daughter was repulsed by the thought of a sex change but was still suffering—she'd become an alcoholic and was cutting herself. "I'd be surprised if she outlived me," her mother said.

When I was reporting this story, I was visibly pregnant with my third child. My pregnancy brought up a certain nostalgia for the parents I met, because it reminded them of a time when life was simpler, when a stranger could ask them whether their baby was a boy or a girl and they could answer straightforwardly. Many parents shared journals with me that were filled with anguish. If they had decided to let their child live as the other gender, that meant cutting off ties with family and friends who weren't supportive, putting away baby pictures, mourning the loss of the child they thought they had. It meant sending their child out alone into a possibly hostile world. If they chose the other route, it meant denying their child the things he or she most wanted, day after day, in the uncertain hope that one day, it would all pay off. In either case, it meant choosing a course on the basis of hazy evidence, and resolving to believe in it.

•   •   •

About two months after the conference, I visited Brandon again. On Father's Day, Tina had made up her mind to just let it happen. She'd started calling him "Bridget" and, except for a few slipups, "she." She'd packed up all the boy-clothes and given them to a neighbor, and had taken Bridget to JC Penney for a new wardrobe. When I saw her, her ears were pierced and her hair was just beginning to tickle her earlobes. "If it doesn't move any faster, I'll have to get extensions!" Tina said.

That morning, Tina was meeting with Bridget's principal, and the principal of a nearby school, to see if she could transfer. "I want her to be known as Bridget, not Bridget-who-used-to-be-Brandon." Tina had memorized lots of lines she'd heard at the conference, and she delivered them well, if a little too fast. She told the principals that she had "pictures and medical documentation." She showed them a book called *The Transgender Child*. "I thought we could fix it," she said, "but gender's in your brain." Brandon's old principal looked a little shell-shocked. But the one from the nearby school, a young woman with a sweet face and cropped curly hair, seemed more open. "This is all new to me," she said. "It's a lot to learn."

The week before, Tina had gone to her mother's house, taking Bridget along. Bridget often helps care for her grandmother, who has lupus; the two are close. After lunch, Bridget went outside in a pair of high heels she'd found in the closet. Tina's stepfather saw the child and lost it: "Get them damned shoes off!" he yelled.

"Make me," Bridget answered.

Then the stepfather turned to Tina and said, "You're ruining his fucking life," loud enough for Bridget to hear.

Tina's talk with Karen, the mother of Bridget's best friend, Abby, hadn't gone too smoothly, either. Karen is an evangelical Christian, with an anti-gay-marriage bumper sticker on her white van. For two years, she'd picked up Brandon nearly every day after school, and brought him over to play with Abby. But that wasn't going to happen anymore. Karen told Tina she didn't want her children "exposed to that kind of thing." "God doesn't make mistakes," she added.

Bridget, meanwhile, was trying to figure it all out—what she could and couldn't do, where the limits were. She'd always been a compliant child, but now she was misbehaving. Her cross-dressing had amped up; she was trying on makeup, and demanding higher heels and sexier clothes. When I was over, she came out of the house dressed in a cellophane getup, four-inch heels, and lip gloss. "It's like I have to teach her what's appropriate for a girl her age," says Tina.

Thursdays, the family spends the afternoon at a local community center, where both Bridget and her little sister, Madison, take gymnastics. She'd normally see Abby there; the two of them are in the same class and usually do their warm-up together, giggling and going over their day. On the car ride over, Bridget was trying to navigate that new relationship, too.

"Abby's not my best friend anymore. She hits me. But she's really good at drawing."

"Well, don't you go hitting nobody," Tina said. "Remember, sticks and stones."

When they arrived at the center and opened the door, Abby was standing right there. She looked at Bridget/Brandon. And froze. She turned and ran away. Madison, oblivious, followed her, yelling, "Wait for us!"

Bridget sat down on a bench next to Tina. Although they were miles from home, she'd just seen a fourth-grade friend of her stepbrother's at the pool table, and she was nervous.

"Hey, we need to work on this," said Tina. "If anybody says anything, you say, 'I'm not Brandon. I'm Bridget, his cousin from California. You want to try it?'"

"No. I don't want to."

"Well, if someone keeps it up, you just say, 'You're crazy.'"

Tina had told me over the phone that Brandon was easily passing as a girl, but that wasn't really true, not yet. With his hair still short, he looked like a boy wearing tight pink pants and earrings. This meant that for the moment, everywhere in this small town was a potential land mine. At the McDonald's, the cashier eyed him suspiciously: "Is that Happy Meal for a boy or a girl?" At the playground, a group of teenage boys with tattoos and their pants pulled low down did a double take. By the evening, Tina was a nervous wreck. "Gosh darn it! I left the keys in the car," she said. But she hadn't. She was holding them in her hand.

After gymnastics, the kids wanted to stop at the Dairy Queen, but Tina couldn't take being stared at in one more place. "Drive-thru!" she yelled. "And I don't want to hear any more whining from you."

On the quiet, wooded road leading home, she could finally relax. It was cool enough to roll down the windows and get some mountain air. After high school, Tina had studied to be a travel agent; she had always wanted to just "work on a cruise ship or something, just go, go, go." Now she wanted things to be easy for Brandon, for him to disappear and pop back as Bridget, a new kid from California, new to this town, knowing nobody. But in a small town, it's hard to erase yourself and come back as your opposite.

Maybe one day they would move, she said. But thinking about that made her head hurt. Instead of the future, she drifted to the past, when things were easier.

"Remember that camping trip we took once, Brandon?" she asked, and he did. And together, they started singing one of the old camp songs she'd taught him.

> Smokey the Bear, Smokey the Bear,
> Howlin' and a-prowlin' and a-sniffin' the air.
> He can find a fire before it starts to flame.
> That's why they call him Smokey,
> That's how he got his name.

"You remember that, Brandon?" she asked again. And for the first time all day, they seemed happy.

Automobile

WINNER—COLUMNS AND
COMMENTARY

Jamie Kitman's ornery industry column for Automobile *magazine unflinchingly puts the screws to Detroit's Big Three for their sputtering finances, bad decisions, and stalled creativity—all from the exasperated perspective of a car enthusiast who expected much better.*

Jamie Kitman

They Fought the Laws (of Supply and Demand), and the Laws Won

G ame over. After almost half a century of fighting battles, America's Big Three—the Moderately Large Three, if you prefer—have at long last lost the war. Yes, it's official. From this day forward, fuel economy matters. From now on, judicious use of fossil fuels trumps road-hugging weight. Too bad Detroit carmakers weren't prepared. They only had fifty years to get ready.

Of course, many said the same thing—mileage is the new, eternal bogey—during the energy crises of the 1950s and the 1970s, and they were wrong. They failed to recognize that, given enough encouragement, Americans would use too much fuel again. The captains of Detroit professed their blamelessness: Americans love big, thirsty machines. Gas is cheap. What could we do?

But now that gas isn't cheap, this is the part that's important to remember. Detroit didn't have to encourage profligacy, it chose to. And some will argue that the power of advertising dollars could and should have been used to encourage efficiency. The American industry could have played the same patriotic card it deployed following 9/11 to advocate fuel conservation instead of throwing around billions of dollars to make sure there were large SUVs in every garage. It didn't have to spend some four decades fighting safety, emissions, and fuel-efficiency standards.

By way of justification, the men from the Motor City have maintained that America's large cars—virtually unique in the world for their heft—were safer. This didn't explain the big spike in deaths in single-car rollover accidents that accompanied the shift to SUVs. Or why these same companies were selling all those unsafe small cars to Europeans and Third Worlders. (Don't their lives count, too?) And it ignored the hazard large SUVs posed to occupants of normal cars, cyclists, and pedestrians. In a war between a Ford Excursion and a Focus, the Excursion wins. But only sometimes. The Focus can outmaneuver an Excursion, and it takes up less room, two keys to avoiding accidents in the first place. The truth is, if you're going to get hit by an 80,000-pound Peterbilt running late and full up, it makes no difference whether you're in a 7,000-pound Excursion or a 2,600-pound Focus. It's kind of like asking whether you would rather die in a fire at 1,000 degrees Fahrenheit or 2,200. Myself, I think I'd go with the 2,200-degree fire.

As I write, gasoline costs more than four dollars a gallon, and several noninsane analysts have predicted it may hit as much as twelve dollars, which would place it barely a hair above current world pricing. Scary as hell, it's probably inevitable and, on some level, hard to argue against. Was this what American exceptionalism—an idea, first forwarded by Alexis de Tocqueville, that America is unique among nations—was supposed to be all about? Surely, we stand for something besides cheap gasoline . . . for Americans. Anyone?

Unlike rough patches in the past, Detroit isn't making any money now—and that's after it's closed plants, squeezed suppliers, slashed waste, jammed the union, and laid off workers. Excepting executive salaries, more generously supersized than ever, what's left to cut? (Alongside a bold $38.7 billion loss in 2007, General Motors turned over a new leaf by approving a 64 percent increase in chairman and CEO Rick Wagoner's annual compensation, to $15.7 million, among other raises it handed out to top execs. Imagine if the company actually turned a profit.)

It is chilling to remember that GM spent a fair part of the last century fighting to keep its market share below 50 percent for fear of triggering antitrust intervention. And it seems like only yesterday that GM executives wore "29" buttons on their expensive lapels. That represented the percentage of market share GM was going, as their bold exhortative prophecy indicated, to reclaim. Whoops. GM's market share has just sunk below 20 percent, its lowest showing since the 1920s. Will we see "19" buttons this year? Or should we go straight to "16"? Recently, the company announced plans to close four factories, lopping a substantial 35 percent off its light-truck production capacity—about 700,000 units—in one fell swoop.

Just as grave, GM says it's thinking of selling the Hummer division, on which it has surely lost billions and its dealers millions. Or perhaps the company will just shutter it. GM has a point. Who would be foolish enough to buy Hummer? Besides GM, that is. It probably shouldn't bother. Unless what's in the cards is a radical recasting of Hummer as a maker of low-volume, high-tech, alt-energy off-roaders. But GM is too broke to make Hummer relevant, much the way it's too broke to aggressively market the desirable cars it does sell. May's disappointing total of 1,091 Saturn Astras sold is a picture worth 1,091 words.

How violent is the sea change for Detroit? In May, Ford's F-150, which hadn't been outsold by a car since October 1991, skydived to fifth spot behind a couple of Hondas (Civic and Accord) and two Toyotas (Corolla and Camry). The Civic is now the best-selling car in America, with 53,299 sold in May alone. By contrast, Chrysler sales are off 25 percent, and as I sit down to write, Dodge has just announced plans to darken its Ram facility in Saltillo, Mexico, for what it said would be only two weeks.

We'll see about that.

Clearly this is not just a down year, it's a total paradigm shift. Honestly, it's hard to think about cars in the same way anymore. Cars that seemed like pretty good ideas—say, Pontiac's six-cylinder G8, headed in the right direction with twenty-five-mpg EPA highway mileage—suddenly seem less inspired with only seventeen-mpg city. Cars that appeared bad ideas before now seem like the worst ideas ever. The Hummer brand, for instance, is on target to sell fewer than 35,000 units this year, or about 12 percent the number of Oldsmobiles GM was selling when it decided to shut that venerable brand to concentrate on . . . Hummer.

Mercifully for our domestic makers, they're not the only ones whose affection for American gluttony is reflected in suddenly ridiculous products and plans. Audi has been talking about setting up a factory in the States. But instead of building the A3, the second-highest-mileage model in its lineup, Audi talked about building large SUVs, possibly to share with Volkswagen. It goes without saying that VW has been given a golden opportunity by the oil potentates—not to sell Americans more crap-mileage, me-too SUVs, but rather a production version of its tempting Up! show car, the one with the two-cylinder, rear-mounted engine that promises to be both highway-ready and incredibly green. It would be perfect for marketing to Americans at a semi-premium price, with currency-exchange woes excised if the car is built in the United States. Porsche, reclaiming the old formula, should conjure something wondrous based on it.

The point is, the peace following the war that the carmakers have lost doesn't have to be a bad thing. Let the new game begin.

The New Yorker

FINALIST—ESSAYS

With astonishing intimacy, wit, and poignancy, Roger Rosenblatt captures his family's pain after his daughter's death and chronicles how the minute details of daily living may be the secret to surviving their ordeal.

Roger Rosenblatt

Making Toast

The trick in foraging for a tooth lost in coffee grounds is not to be misled by the clumps. The only way to be sure is to rub each clump between your thumb and index finger, which makes a mess of your hands. For some twenty minutes this morning, Ginny and I have been hunting in the kitchen trash can for the top left front tooth of our seven-year-old granddaughter, Jessica. Loose for days but not yet dislodged, the tooth finally dropped into a bowl of Apple Jacks. I wrapped it for safe-keeping in a paper napkin and put it on the kitchen counter, but it was mistaken for trash by Ligaya, Bubbies's nanny. Bubbies (James) is twenty-three months and the youngest of our daughter Amy's three children. Sammy, who is five, is uninterested in the tooth search, and Jessie is unaware of it. We would prefer to find the tooth, so that Jessie won't worry about the Tooth Fairy not showing up.

This sort of activity has constituted our life since Amy died, last December 8. The night of her death, Ginny and I drove from our home in Quogue, on the south shore of Long Island, to Bethesda, Maryland, where Amy and her husband, Harris, lived. With Harris's encouragement, we have been there ever since. "How long are you staying?" Jessie asked the next morning. "Forever," I said.

•   •   •

Amy Elizabeth Rosenblatt Solomon, thirty-eight years old, pe-
diatrician, wife of the hand surgeon Harrison Solomon, and
mother of three, collapsed on her treadmill in the downstairs
playroom at home. "Jessie discovered her," our oldest son, Carl,
told us on the phone. Carl lives in Fairfax, Virginia, not far from
Amy and Harris, with his wife, Wendy, and their two boys,
Andrew and Ryan. Jessie had run upstairs to Harris and told
him, "Mommy isn't talking." Harris got to Amy within seconds,
and tried CPR, but her heart had stopped and she could not be
revived.

Amy's was ruled a "sudden death due to an anomalous right
coronary artery"—meaning both her coronary arteries fed her
heart from the same side. Her combined arteries could have
been squeezed between the aorta and the pulmonary artery,
which can expand during physical exercise. The blood flow was
cut off. Her condition, affecting less than two-thousandths of 1
percent of the population, was asymptomatic; she might have
died at any time in her life.

Amy would have appreciated the clarity of the verdict. She
was a very clear person, even as a small child, knowing intui-
tively what plain good sense a particular situation required. She
had a broad expanse of forehead, dark, nearly black hair, and
hazel eyes. Both self-confident and selfless, when she faced you
there could be no doubt you were the only thing on her mind.

Her clarity could make her harsh with her family, especially
her two brothers. Carl and John, our youngest, withered when
she excoriated them for such offenses as invading her room. She
could also be slightly cutting in her wit. When she was about to
graduate from N.Y.U. Medical School, her class had asked me to
be the speaker. A tradition of the school allows a past graduate
to place the hood of the gown on a new graduate. Harris, who
had graduated the previous year, was set to "hood" Amy. At

dinner the night before the ceremony, a friend remarked, "Amy, isn't it great? Your dad is giving the graduation speech, and your fiancé is doing the hood." Amy said, "It is. And it's also pretty great that I'm graduating."

Yet her clarity contributed to her kindness. When she was six, I was driving her and three friends to a birthday party. One of the girls got carsick. The other two girls backed away, understandably, with cries of "Ooh!" and "Yuck!" Amy drew closer to the stricken child, to comfort her.

.   .   .

Ginny and I moved from a five-bedroom house, with a den and a large kitchen, to a bedroom with a connected bath—the in-law apartment we used to occupy whenever we visited. We put in a dresser and a desk, and Harris added a TV and a rug. It may have appeared that we were reducing our comforts, but the older one gets the less space one needs, and the less one wants. And we still have the house in Quogue.

I found I could not write and didn't want to. I could teach, however, and it helped me feel useful. I drive from Bethesda to Quogue on Sundays, and meet my M.F.A. writing classes at Stony Brook University on Mondays and Tuesdays. Then back to Bethesda on Wednesdays. The drive takes more than five hours and a tank of gas each way. But it is easier and faster than flying or taking a train.

Road rage was a danger those first weeks. I picked fights with store clerks for no reason. I lost my temper with a student who phoned me too frequently about her work. I seethed at those who spoke of Amy's death in the clichés of modern usage, such as "passing" and "closure." I cursed God. In a way, believing in God made Amy's death more, not less, comprehensible, since the God I believe in is not beneficent. He doesn't care. A friend was visiting Jerusalem when he got the news about Amy. He kicked the Wailing Wall, and said, "Fuck you, God!" My sentiments exactly.

What's Jessie's favorite winter jacket? The blue, not the pink, though pink is her favorite color. Sammy prefers whole milk in his Froot Loops or Multigrain Cheerios. He calls it "cow milk." Jessie drinks only soy milk. She likes a glass of it at breakfast. Sammy prefers water. Such information had to be absorbed quickly. Sammy sees himself as the silver Power Ranger, Jessie is the pink. Sammy's friends are Nico, Jonathan, and Kipper. Jessie's are Oana, Danielle, and Luxmi. There were playdates to arrange, birthday-party invitations to respond to, school forms to fill out. Sammy goes to a private preschool, Jessie to the local public school. We had to master their schedules.

I reaccustomed myself to things about small children I'd forgotten. Talking toys came back into my life. I will be walking with the family through an airport, and the voice of a ventriloquist's dummy in a horror movie will seep through the suitcase. Buzz Lightyear says, "To infinity and beyond!" Another toy says, "I'm a pig. Can we stop?" A talking phone says, "Help me!"

In all this, two things were of immeasurable use to us. First, a friend of Amy's created a Web site inviting other friends to prepare dinners for our family. Participants deposited dinners in a blue cooler outside our front door. Food was provided every other evening, with enough for the nights in between, from mid-December to the beginning of June.

The second was a piece of straightforward wisdom that Bubbies's nanny gave Harris. Ligaya is a small, lithe woman of about forty-five. I know little of her life except that she is from the Philippines, has one grown son here who is a supervisor in a restaurant, and has a work ethic of steel and the flexibility to deal with any contingency. She also shows a sense of practical formality, by calling Bubbies James, to insure that name for his future. Ligaya altered her schedule to be with us twelve hours a day, five days a week—an indispensable gift, especially to her small charge, who giggles with delight when he hears her key in the front door. No one outside the family could have felt Amy's death more acutely. Yet what she said to Harris, and to the rest of us, was dispassionate: "You are not the first to go through such a thing, and you are better able to handle it than most."

·   ·   ·

It is late December. Bubbies looks around for Amy, says "Mama" when he sees her pictures, and clings to his father. Bubbies has blond hair and a face usually occupied by observant silences. When I am alone with him, he plays happily enough. I've taught him to give me a high five, and when he does I stagger across the room to show him how strong he is. He likes to take a pot from one kitchen cabinet and Zone bars from another, drop the bars in the pot, and put back the lid. He'll do this contentedly for quite a while. When Harris enters the kitchen, Bubbies drops everything, runs to him, and holds him tight at the knees.

Jessie is tall, also blond, with an expression forever on the brink of enthusiasm. Amy used to say that she was the most optimistic person she'd ever known. She is excited about her hip-hop dance class; about a concert her school is giving in Amy's name, to raise money for a memorial scholarship set up at the N.Y.U. School of Medicine; about going to *The Nutcracker*. "Do your *Nutcracker* dance, Boppo," Jessie says. (Ginny is Mimi, I am Boppo.) I swing into my improvised ballet, the high point of which is when I wiggle my ass like the dancing mice. Jessie is also excited about our trip to Disney World in January, the adventure that Amy and Harris had planned months before Amy died. We speak of distant summer plans in Quogue. Jessie is excited.

Sammy is tall, too, with dark hair and wide-set, ruminative eyes. He brings me a book to read, about a caterpillar. He brings another, which just happened to be in the house, called *Lifetimes: The Beautiful Way to Explain Death to Children*. The book says, "There's a beginning and an end for everything that is alive. In between is living." The book illustrates its lessons with pictures of birds, fish, plants, and people. I lean back on the couch with Sammy tucked in the crook of my arm, and read to him about the beauty of death.

.   .   .

While Ligaya and Ginny look after Bubbies and Sam, I take Jessie to the bus stop. We stand together at the corner of our street on a gray, damp morning in January. One by one, down the hill come the mothers of the neighborhood, their kids running beside them. An impromptu soccer game develops. Jessie joins in. The scene passes for pleasant and ordinary, unless one notes the odd presence of the lone grandfather.

With luck, Ginny and I will live to see all three children grow into adults, and Jessie will become a teen-ager and throw fits about boyfriends and stamp her feet and yell that we don't understand a thing, not a thing. But today I help her with her oversized pink backpack and her little umbrella with pink butterflies before she boards the school bus. And I stand looking as the bus drives off, and tell the mothers to have a good day.

.   .   .

I wake up earlier than the others, usually around 5 A.M., to perform the one household duty I have mastered. After emptying the dishwasher, setting the table for Jessie and Sam's breakfast, and pouring the Cheerios or Apple Jacks, or Special K or Froot Loops, I prepare toast.

I take out the butter to allow it to soften, and I put three slices of Pepperidge Farm Hearty White in the toaster oven. Bubbies and I like plain buttered toast; Sammy prefers it with cinnamon, with the crusts cut off. When the bell rings, I shift the slices from the toaster to plates, and butter them.

Harris usually spends half the night in Bubbies's little bed. When I go upstairs, around 6 A.M., Bubbies hesitates, but I give him a knowing look and he opens his arms to me. "Toast?" he says. I take him from his father, change him, and carry him downstairs to allow Harris to sleep for another twenty minutes.

.   .   .

The house that Amy and Harris bought in 2004 was a sand-yellow Colonial, built in the 1960s, and it had substance—a family home for a lifetime. The walls were thick, the hardwood floors level, the oak, black walnut, and poplar trees in the back yard old.

Whenever Ginny and I drove down, we phoned Amy from the car when we were a few minutes away. She would stand framed by the dark-red doorway, holding a child or two. Everyone smiled.

She practiced medicine only two days a week, to be with the children. Her household was like her—lighthearted and full of play, but careful. In the storage area downstairs, there was always a surplus of bandages and paper towels and light bulbs, as well as batteries of every size. To this day, we have not run out of Advil.

She had a gift for custom and ceremony—the qualities Yeats wished for in "A Prayer for My Daughter." Last Thanksgiving, seventeen family members arrived. There were many cooks, not too many, all toiling under Amy's supervision. Harris, his dad, Wendy's dad, Carl, John, and I watched as much football as we were permitted. The hand surgeon carved the turkey, his skill with a knife impressive and creepy. We took our seats at the table. We clasped our glasses. During the previous year, Harris's dad had had a heart valve repaired, and I was treated successfully for prostate cancer and melanoma. Harris raised a toast to the family's renewed health.

.   .   .

Harris's stoicism is undemonstrative. A strong man, built wide and powerful, he easily carries all three children at once in his arms up the stairs. But the sight of his back makes me sad. He performs surgery two days a week and heads orthopedics at Holy Cross Hospital. At home, his few remaining hours are devoted to playing Twister and watching SpongeBob with the kids. He bathes them and tucks them in.

He rarely speaks about Amy, or his feelings. He and I were friends before Amy died, and we talk comfortably about sports and the nonsense of politicians. And we talk a lot about the children. Ginny tells me that when I am away, and she and Harris sit down to their late dinner in the kitchen, her heart breaks for him. "This should be his wife sitting across the table," she says.

He says he doubts that he'll remarry. Self-sufficient, he tends to be a world within himself. He fixes lamps and toilets. He sews. He solves problems with the toys. He makes the hands of others work again. And he has done everything one can do in his situation—encouraging the children to talk about Amy whenever they feel like it, and not to hold back tears. Whenever necessary, he and the children visit a psychologist who specializes in grief counseling. He keeps in close contact with Jessie's and Sam's teachers. But he also deserves a life. He is thirty-nine years old.

Still, he embraces the demands of his life with a gusto that dispenses cheer, and in the lulls we try to keep one another afloat. One night in February, Jessie and Sam had a meltdown as they were going to bed. Ginny and I sat in the living room, listening to Harris's steady voice in the intermissions of the children's wailing. Eventually, they were quieted. He came downstairs and sat staring vacantly at his laptop. "Look," I said, going over to him. "We're never going to get over this. That's a given. But the children will. I promise you. I've seen it elsewhere."

"I'm a scientist," he said. "It's hard for me to deal with things that aren't facts."

.   .   .

Ginny taught kindergarten and first grade in the early years of our marriage. Now she volunteers in the children's schools. She helps Jessie with her homework. I watch them at the kitchen table, bent over a book, and overhear their soft talking. Ginny asks, "How does the chrysalis protect itself against predators?" Jessie says, "It shakes to scare them off."

I do puzzle books with Jessie, and Sammy peppers me with questions about animals and the stars and planets. I can't answer most of his questions. "What are afternoons like on Jupiter?" he asks me. I have to look that up.

I am often confounded by something else I'd forgotten about children: they have no respect for sequential thought. Responding to one of their relentless questions, I will go as deep as I can into an explanation of, say, a solar eclipse. Sammy will ask, "What's the biggest number in the world?" At the same time, Jessie will ask, "How tall will I be, Boppo?" Then Sammy: "Do marlins have lips?"

"So when the moon moves between the earth and the sun . . ."

"What are you talking about, Boppo?"

Bubbies has been attending to his own education—proceeding from one word, to several, to two-word sentences, to three and more. Some say that children learn to speak in order to tell the stories already in them. An early word of his was "back." He wanted reassurance that when any of us left the house, or even a room, we were coming back. He has always used one-word sentences to his advantage, his vocabulary consisting mainly of references to things he favors—the mower, the stove, birds, bananas.

The single words suit his despotic streak. "Outside" means "Let's move it, Boppo!"

Jessie's teacher occasionally invites me to visit her first-grade class. They ask about writing. But the first graders seem to know at least as much as I do. Ms. Carone asks me how a character is developed. I bumble through an answer. She asks the children to write a story with a main character, then list his or her qualities—loyal, jealous, brave, generous. Each child stands before the class to answer questions. Arthur writes about a superhero.

"Anything you'd like to ask Arthur?" Ms. Carone says to the others.

One girl asks, "Does your superhero tell the truth?"

Arthur thinks and says yes.

"Always?" the girl asks.

•　　•　　•

In a rare tranquil moment on a March afternoon, I sit on the green couch in the lower-level play area, reading Alice McDermott's *After This*. It is around four-thirty, and the light has gone from the day. Jessie comes downstairs and asks why I am so quiet. "I'm reading," I tell her. She takes one of her own books from the coffee table and sits beside me, extending her long legs over the front of the couch. We sit in silence, reading, five feet from where Amy collapsed and died. I look up from time to time, then return to my book.

Sammy hurtles downstairs and demands to know where his knight outfit is. Amazingly, I spot the outfit, which consists of silver pants, a shirt of mail, a shield, a sword, and a helmet with a visor. Sammy puts it on at once, lowers the visor over his face, and parades back and forth before the couch.

Jessie drops her book and plays a song from *High School Musical 2* at full blast on the stereo. She dances in front of the couch as Sir Sam marches. Bubbies climbs down the stairs, Ligaya trailing behind him. He dances, too.

• • •

Throughout the winter and the spring, there is hardly a moment for anything but play, caretaking, schooling, chauffeuring, and, by 9 P.M., sleep. Jessie has soccer; Sammy has a party; Jess and Sam have tennis; Sammy has a playdate; Bubbies has "gym" (an hour in which babies waddle around a large, highly polished floor, heedless of the commands of an "instructor," and bump into one another); Jessie starts piano.

We lived in Washington, D.C., in the 1970s, when I worked at *The New Republic* and wrote a column for the *Washington Post*. One column, called "No Sleep-Overs," was a father's complaint about what was then the recent practice of overstuffing a child's day with lessons and social life. I received more hate mail in response to that piece than to anything I wrote against capital punishment or in favor of gun control. Clearly, I was out of touch, as usual.

These days, I am grateful for the children's crammed schedules. Between December and June, Sammy and Jessie had birthdays, advancing to five and seven, and Bubbies went from fourteen months to twenty-one. His transformation seemed like one of those time-lapse tricks in movies. In April, we celebrated Amy's birthday, too. When we blew out the candles, Harris asked Sammy what he thought Mommy would wish for. "To be alive," Sammy said.

He looks more like his father now, with a face that mixes independence and innocence. Jessie has perfected the ironic smile of a grown woman. When Sammy was going over the invitation list for his birthday party, which consisted of everyone in his class, he was asked if he was sure he wanted to include the class bully. "Yes," he said. "I wouldn't want him to cry." When, in a terrible coincidence, the mother of a girl in Jessica's class died suddenly, Jessie said, "She can live with us."

.   .   .

All the grandchildren came to Quogue for the month of August—Jessie, Sam, Bubbies, Andrew, and Ryan. A year earlier, Ginny and I had begun to convert our garage to a playhouse. We wanted a place where the grandchildren could paint, work with clay, race cars, and fight over games. Amy had been in on the plans, and after she died the project became a kind of therapy. I cleaned out junk closets, gave order to a chaotic shelf of DVDs, and cleared an ivy-choked area of the back yard.

We built a small stage, and one of the children's early productions was a reenactment of *American Idol*. I played Paula. Another was a play based on Sammy's imagined utopia of Moseybane. We called it "The King of Moseybane." Harris ordered costumes online for Sammy (the King), Ryan (the Prince), Jessie (the Wizard), and Andrew (the Knight). Boppo (the Dragon) and Bubbies (the Narrator) required no costumes.

On opening night (which coincided with closing night), Ryan appeared onstage with his mother, Wendy. Andrew would not appear at all at first, but, when coaxed, delivered his lines from memory. Jessie's over-the-top Wizard was indistinguishable from her *American Idol* audition. The King looked stunned with his own power. Bubbies decided that his one line, "Dookies"— his word for his favorite cookie—would be more effective if delivered from the driveway, fifty feet from the stage, with Harris beside him. The Dragon had to read all the parts, except Andrew's. But the audience—my brother Peter, two friends, and the remaining grownups—was appreciative. The bewildered cast received a standing ovation.

.   .   .

Amy and Harris were married in our Quogue house on one of those fiercely bright June days which draw artists to eastern Long Island. We rented a big white tent, which billowed in the wind on the front lawn. Amy and Harris chose a band from New York that played mostly sixties music. There were blue blazers and red ties and navy-blue dresses with white trim, and many white roses. The sky was clear as glass.

We had asked Amy what sort of ceremony she and Harris wanted, and she said they'd like a friend of ours, a well-known cartoonist, to marry them. After making inquiries, we learned that New York State does not permit cartoonists (or any other layperson, for that matter) to perform wedding ceremonies, so we had two ceremonies—one by the cartoonist and a legal one performed by another family friend who actually was a minister. The   oonist said many beautiful things to the couple, before telling the assembled that he was marrying Amy and Harris with the power vested in him "by the State of Euphoria."

·   ·   ·

Bubbies sits in my lap in the den, in Quogue. He locks his hands behind his head when he relaxes. I do the same. We sit there in a lopsided brown leather chair—same pose, sitting in tandem, like luge drivers.

One evening, he points to the shelf to his left and says, "Book." He indicates *The Letters of James Joyce*, edited by Stuart Gilbert. It seems an ambitious choice for a twenty-three-month-old boy, but I take down the book and prop it up before us.

"Dear Bubbies," I begin. "I went to the beach today and played in the sand. I also built a castle. I hope you will come play with me soon. Love, James Joyce."

Bubbies seems content, so I "read" another: "Dear Bubbies, Went to the playground today. Tried the slide. It was a little scary. I like the swings better. I can go very high, just like you. Love, James Joyce."

Bubbies turns the pages. I occasionally amuse myself with an invented letter closer to the truth of Joyce's life and personality: "Dear Bubbies, I hate the Catholic Church, and am leaving Ireland forever. Love, James Joyce."

It tickles me that Bubbies has chosen to latch on to a writer who gladly would have stepped on a baby to get a great review.

I try to put back the book, but he detects an implicit announcement of his bedtime, and he protests. "Joyce!" he says. Eventually, he resigns himself to the end of his day. He puts the book back himself, and quietly says, "Joyce."

.   .   .

Late in August, we return to Bethesda for the first days of the children's schools. Bubbies begins preschool. School for someone thirty inches high—it seems preposterous. Jessie starts second grade, Sammy kindergarten. He is excited, mainly about taking the school bus. The first day, Sammy's bus runs out of oil on the way home.

"What was your favorite part of the day?" I ask him later.

"When the school bus couldn't move," he says. Harris says that might turn out to be Sam's favorite part of the whole year.

On the weekend, we visit the cemetery. Each time, I go with a mixture of need and trepidation, because I know I may break down at the sight of the small rectangle of earth, the boxwood outlining it, the conical brass receptacle for flowers, and the marker, which is so definite. When we chose this spot, in December, the nearby office buildings showed through the shorn trees. Since spring the area has burgeoned with dogwoods and magnolias.

Jessie has brought white carnations; Sammy a Washington Redskins balloon in the shape of an oversized football, which he plans to release into the air. He seems fragile these days—drifting into faraway stares and silences. When we went bowling a week earlier, I took him to the men's room. Walking out, he forgot to pull up his pants.

Yet he talks more about Amy's death. Yesterday morning, he asked me again how Mommy died: "The heart stopped. Right?" His first day of kindergarten, when the children were asked to draw pictures of their families, Sam's drawing included Amy lying dead on the floor.

At the gravesite, Harris asks him if he has something to say. He stands behind the marker and says, "I miss you, Mommy." He tells Amy about Bubbies's first teacher in preschool, Ms. Franzetti, and about Jessie's second-grade teacher, Mrs. Salcetti, and about his own, Ms. Merritt. He tells Amy about the balloon, and predicts that the Redskins will win the Super Bowl. Jessie has no message for Amy today.

Sammy asks Harris if he can be buried next to Mommy. Harris says yes, but tells him it's a very long way off.

Ginny and I take turns holding Bubbies, who carries a small plastic penguin. When you squeeze its "trigger," its beak opens and shuts, its little wings flap, and the penguin squawks. On an earlier visit to the cemetery, Bubbies refused to be taken from his car seat, and cried out, "No, no, no!" Today he has his penguin, and is content simply to look around.

Jessie places the carnations in the conical vessel. Harris writes "We love you, Mommy" on the football balloon. The children let it go. It flies up in the heavy air and snags on a distant tree. We assure the children that the wind will free it eventually.

•   •   •

Once in a while, Ginny is brought low by a photograph of Amy or by another artifact attached to a memory. I am felled more often by mundane problems and momentary concerns, such as choosing a shirt to wear or remembering to take a vitamin—since nothing will ever be normal again. Harris moves forward.

One of the few pieces of writing I have done in the year since Amy died was a book review for the *Washington Post Book World*. The novel was David Lodge's *Deaf Sentence*—about a retired linguistics professor, Desmond Bates, who is losing his hearing and who is also deaf to life until, against his will, he visits Auschwitz, where the silence teaches him to hear. He reads a letter from a prisoner in the camp to his wife, discovered in a pile of human ashes. One sentence rises up to Desmond: "If there have been, at various times, trifling misunderstandings in our life, now I see how one was unable to value the passing time." As far as I can tell, this is how to live—to value the passing time.

•   •   •

It is early September. Shortly before 6 A.M., the morning is dark—black clouds, black sky. On TV, the newscasts speak of Hurricane Gustav lumbering toward New Orleans. I hear Bubbies over the monitor, go upstairs, and take him from Harris.

We look out the glass door. "Raining," Bubbies says.

"Not yet," I tell him. "But it's dark."

"Raining."

"Yes, it'll probably rain, Bubs. Grapes?"

"Toast," he says.

I put him in his booster seat. He buckles up. I bring his grapes and toast, along with my own toast and coffee. We eat.

Backpacker

WINNER—ESSAYS

Tracy Ross marches her father back to the physical and emotional wilderness—a place of beauty, love, and pain—where he first began to molest her as a child. A tour de force of courage and insight, Ross's essay reveals her ordeal with a clarity and compassion that's unsparing and cathartic.

Tracy Ross
_____

The Source of
All Things

A ll my dad has to do is answer the questions.
Just four simple questions. Only they aren't that
easy, because questions like this never are. We're almost to The Temple, three days into the craggy maw of Idaho's
Sawtooth Mountains, and he has no idea they're coming. But I
have them loaded, hot and explosive, like shells in a 30-30.

It's July, and hotter than hell on the sage-covered slopes,
where wildfires will char more than 130,000 acres by summer's
end. But we're up high, climbing to 9,000 feet, and my dad thinks
this heat feels cooler than the heat in Las Vegas, where he lives.
Four days ago, he met me in Twin Falls, a town 140 miles south
of here where I grew up, after driving north across Nevada, past
other fires, including one on the Idaho border. The air is thin,
the terrain rugged, and his body—sixty-four years old, bow-
legged, and fifteen pounds overweight—seems tired and heavy
to me. He struggled the last half-mile, stopping every few feet to
catch his breath, adjust his pack, and tug on the big, wet circles
that have formed under the armpits of his shirt, which reads
Toot My Horn.

At sunrise this morning, we slid out of our bags, washed up,
made breakfast, and caught a few fish. When we finally starting
hiking, we climbed out of one basin and into another, inching
up switchbacks sticky with lichen and loose with scree. When

we came to the edge of one overlook, we saw smoke rising on the horizon from a fire that was crowning in the trees. And when we arrived at the lake with the dozen black frogs, we called it Holy Water Lake, because it was Sunday and we did feel a bit closer to God.

I know my dad is hurting, because I'm hurting, too—and not just my legs and lungs, or the blisters on the bottoms of my feet. We have barely spoken since we left the dock at Redfish Lake three days ago, left the boat and the worried Texans who looked at our forty-pound packs and said, "You're going where?" I'm sure we seemed an odd pair: an old man and his—what was she? Daughter? Lover? Friend? When we stepped off the boat, I wanted to turn back. But The Temple was out here somewhere, and, besides, I still hadn't decided if I was going to kill him outright or just walk him to death.

We continue climbing above Holy Water Lake until, a few hundred feet from a pass, we turn off the trail. In front of us is a cirque of smooth granite towers, sharp and fluted, like the turrets on the Mormon Tabernacle. The Temple shoots out of a giant boulder field. Loose rocks slide down vertical shafts and clatter to the ground. Quickly but carefully, my dad and I crabwalk across the jumbled blocks, insinuating ourselves into tight slots and willing our bodies to become lighter, so the boulders won't shift beneath us and break our legs.

When we get to the wide, flat rock that looks like an altar, we stop. He slumps over, sips water, and chokes down a few bites of food. His eyes, the color of chocolate, begin to melt, and the corners of his mouth tremble, like he's fighting off a frown.

Hunching next to him on the granite slab, I squint into his red-brown, sixteenth-Cherokee face. I dig into my pack and take out my tape recorder.

That's when the questioning begins.

.   .   .

If we'd thought about it, back when I was a kid and my dad first joined the family, we might have nominated him for an award. Idaho Dad of the Year. Or the Elks Club Father's Day prize. In the mid-1970s, after he married my mom and before the trouble set in, he built us an Idaho dream.

We had a RoadRunner camper, and every Friday between Memorial Day and the end of hunting season, my dad would leave his job at Van England's store in Twin Falls, change into his camping clothes, and load his new family into his bright yellow Jeep Cherokee. While we sipped root beers and adjusted our things, he'd grease the ball on the tail of the Jeep, pull up the trailer steps, and ease us back until the hitch on the RoadRunner took hold. By the time the other dads on Richmond Drive were cracking their first weekend beers, we'd be chugging across the Perrine Bridge, past the lava flats with their searing heat, and approaching the cool, clean air of the Stanley Basin, where the Sawtooth Mountains top out at 10,800 feet.

If my dad loved being outside—hunting, hiking, and fishing Idaho's pristine mountains and streams—he quickly taught me to love it, too. I was four and my brother was eight the year my parents married, following a blistering whole-family courtship that included picnics at Shoshone Falls, ski trips to Soldier Mountain, and drive-in movies watched from bean bags in the back of my future dad's 1949 Willys Jeep.

My real dad, a U.S. Navy man who held a kegger outside my mom's hospital window the day I was born, died when I was seven months old after an aneurysm exploded in his brain. My brother and I were too young to feel the gut-punch of his death— the disorienting, life-sucking loss that shook my mom so violently the doctors sedated her. But when lanky, bell-bottomed Donnie Lee walked through the door of our military-pension house, it was as if we remembered to miss something we'd never known. By the time my parents were married, the family honeymoon was already in full swing.

My new dad's pride and joy—after his new family—was the RoadRunner he bought in 1976. On Thursdays, and sometimes as early as Wednesdays, he'd start loading it with supplies: bags of chips, Tang mixed with tea, and twelve-packs of mini-cereals for my brother and me. One spring, he painted a yellow swoosh on the side to match his Cherokee. It came out looking like a streak of mucous, but we all told him we liked it anyway.

During the winter, when the roads were too snowy to pull the trailer, we feasted on elk steaks and venison stew made from the bucks my dad had harvested near Rock Creek and Porcupine Springs. But come mid-June, we were in full summer-camping mode.

In the long shadows of the Sawtooths, we built castles in the freshwater sand and swam out to a giant rock a few hundred feet from shore. Sometimes, other families came with us, and all the kids would hike together, searching for bird nests along wooden walkways that stretched over primordial wetlands, or climbing on top of beaver lodges before taking off our clothes and jumping into the murky ponds. At the time, the streams pouring out of Redfish Lake teemed with sockeye salmon on their way home from the mouth of the Pacific Ocean, 900 miles away.

As a little girl, I stared down at their rotting bodies, the wild look in their bulging eyes, and the long, hooked jawlines dotted with razor-sharp teeth. Though I couldn't have articulated it then, I wondered what demon drove them to travel so far inland—without food or rest, for weeks—to decompose and die at Redfish Lake.

•   •   •

It's early June, dusk, and the whole family is naked. We've stopped off at Russian John hot spring on our way to Redfish Lake.

Our clothes—my mom's silk bra next to my size-six flowered panties, big jeans and little jeans in a heap, a kid's down vest, and a grown man's hunting cap—are piled near the steaming pool that's just past the ranger station on Highway 75. One by one, we slip into water that smells less like sulfur and more like infused sage. My parents slide down the algae-covered rock and laugh—at the urgency, the cold air, and the slight, acceptable indiscretion we are committing, uphill and just out of range of the car beams passing below.

We soak until the last rays of sun paint the mountains pink. We all scan the hillsides for deer. Spot one, and you earn a dollar: my new dad's rule. A star—my new dad points it out—burns itself into view. "Wish on it," he says, and we all do. When we begin to prune, we get out, tug on underwear and shirts, and rush back to the Jeep, where our black lab, Jigger, awaits.

When I think back to those early moments, I see a family, newly formed and on the front end of a great adventure. I see the four of us, back on the road after soaking in the springs. We are dried off and warming up, the blast of the heater drowning out Lynyrd Skynyrd on the radio. It's dark now, and I have moved into the front seat. My dad and I are calling truckers on the CB using our handles, Pinky Tuscadero and Coyote. Outside the window, the Sawtooths rise into the night.

•　　　•　　　•

In my last, best memory of 1979, autumn light reflects off a golden Redfish Lake. Decaying aspen leaves smell good, in a sad, slowed-down way. Though I am only eight, these trips to the mountains have already become a foundation upon which I will build my identity. I'm telling my dad how I want to go into the Sawtooths, next summer maybe, on a real backpacking trip. He stomps out a cigarette and puts it in his pocket, then smiles tenderly. Because I don't know what's coming, I think this is how it will always be.

He takes my hand and leads me back to the trailer, where my mom and brother are fixing dinner. We crunch hard-shell tacos and guzzle cups of milk. Later, at the foldout table, we play cards—Spoons or Go Fish. My dad drinks beer and my brother begs for a sip. When I go to bed, my mom does, too, on the foldout couch directly below my foldout bunk. She reads for a while, then drifts off. I listen to my dad and brother. "Pair of jacks," says my dad. And I fall asleep.

When I wake up, sandpaper is crawling on my skin. At least that's what I think it is, until I feel hot breath against my cheek. The bunk bed where I am sleeping is two feet from the camper ceiling, and it's coffin-dark. I can't sit up, so I lay perfectly still, while my eight-year-old mind tries to understand sandpaper and beer-soaked breath. At first, I think someone has broken into the trailer. I must be alone, or my mom would jump up and scream. My dad would grab his rifle and start shooting. My brother would run out of the trailer and hide in the trees.

The sandpaper keeps moving, five round pieces the size of dimes. It scrapes my stomach, sliding along the top of my pajama pants, where it hesitates, then dips down. Completely disoriented, I try to scream, but no sound comes out. Holding my breath, I force myself to buck—away from the beer and abrasion, into the tightest ball I can make. The sandpaper stops moving. The breath grunts away from my face.

I'm swimming in tar. I will suffocate. I lay awake listening to the wind beat the trailer for hours.

The next morning, my dad and I walk to Fishhook Creek. I lead, he follows. I find a log, whitewashed and slippery, and inch across it to the center. My dad scoots behind me, lights a Camel, and sits down so that the soles of his black work boots just skim the ripples, which are metallic and bright.

I feet itchy and sick to my stomach, like I've been sunburned from the inside out. My dad puffs on his cigarette, exhaling streams of smoke that hang in the frosty air.

"I know what you're thinking," he says. "I know what you think that was."

I consider asking him what he thinks I'm thinking, because what I am really wondering is how the salmon, struggling against the current below my feet, breathe in the murky eddies that disappear under the grassy bank. I am imagining, in some abstract and childish way, that I will dive in the river and let it flush me downstream. I hold my breath and let my dad continue. He puffs on his cigarette, then throws the butt into the creek.

"I mean it, Tracy," he says. "I was only tucking you in."

.   .   .

"What's a pretty girl like you doing hiking alone?"

The guide at the cash register asks this when I step up to pay for my maps. It's early October 2006, and the thermometer reads 41°F. I'm standing at the counter at River One Outfitters in Stanley, Idaho, a tiny town at the base of the Sawtooths. Two months earlier, a congressman's kid had gone missing on a solo hike. A search was mounted: helicopters, volunteer ground crews, and rangers all picking and flossing the granite teeth. There'd been no sign of him until a couple of days ago, when a corpse dog got onto—and then lost—a scent. This afternoon, I will hike eight miles into the Sawtooths.

"I'm prepared and conservative," I tell the man as he rings up the maps. But it's only a brave front. Two days ago, I flew to Boise, rented a car, and started driving east. On the freeway, the early October sun seemed too bright. But as I wound through Lowman, big stands of trees diffused the light, until the air took on a golden hue that I associate only with southern Idaho.

I didn't plan to be driving down this road, concealing an open beer, listening to Zeppelin on the radio. I have a husband and two kids at home. It's coming on three decades since my dad put his hands down my pants in the family trailer at Redfish Lake. I've been to therapy—years of it—and energy workers, astrologists, and priests. I've even been back to the Sawtooths, including once with my parents and kids. I thought it would be romantic to show the boys my favorite childhood place. They were babies, and they dug in the sand near the dock. We took off their diapers and let them wade among tiny flickering minnows that flashed like silver paperclips between their chubby legs.

Yesterday, I drove out of Sun Valley and pulled off the road at Russian John hot spring. I walked to the small, steaming pool where my family used to soak, and stood there imagining us naked under the stars. I didn't get in. After an hour, I walked back to the car and drove toward Redfish Lake. I stopped at our favorite campsite near Fishhook Creek. And I found the spot where my dad and I once balanced on a log in the early autumn light.

Some people say you can heal yourself just by returning to the scene of a crime. They do that at the World Trade Center: put roses on the approximate spot a husband or sister landed after jumping out a window a hundred stories up. I sat on the bank of Fishhook Creek for maybe half a day, thinking about the sandpaper, the cigarette in the water, and the chance my dad had to fess up.

He could have done it, told the truth right then and there, and avoided this whole damned mess. But he chose to pretend I was out of my head, a little girl confused by a scary dream. I can't remember if he tried to hug me after we talked, but I know I instantly stopped trusting him.

Sometimes, I take out a picture of myself from the early days at Redfish Lake. I am pigtailed and pink-cheeked, holding a

Dixie Cup with a tadpole inside. I am beaming into the camera, proud of the new life I cradle in my hands.

I became a sad kid after that picture was taken. I've been a sad kid ever since.

I pack up my things and head toward the Sawtooths, where I hope to hike some happiness back into myself.

·   ·   ·

Looking back, there were no signs or indications to tell us my dad's desire was unraveling inside him, dragging him away from my mother, toward me. For a long time after we stood on the log across Fishhook Creek, he didn't touch me. But at age twelve, as I began to climb the wave of puberty, he came back.

At first, he really was tucking me in—just *thoroughly*. But later, he let his hands wander. Sometimes, he watched me undress through the blinds he half-opened after dinner, when he went outside to smoke. When I sensed him in the backyard pretending to rake the grass, I would crouch and freeze, like a deer that tries to become invisible in broad daylight. Night after night, he ranged across my body, exploring this place and that. And sometimes he sat in a corner shining his flashlight on my exposed abdomen and thighs. The effect was so bewildering, I stopped knowing what to think.

For the growing-up victims of sexual abuse, every day becomes a test of personal perception. According to Darkness to Light, an international nonprofit dedicated to child sexual-abuse awareness and prevention, one in four girls and one in six boys are sexually abused in the United States annually, and only 30 percent of all cases are reported. Most girls are molested by their fathers or stepfathers, and almost always inside the family home.

Even if my dad had stopped molesting me after that first night in the trailer, I would still carry wounds. Incest victims suffer from a wide range of maladjustments, including alcoholism, drug addiction, and promiscuity. Some experts believe that a child's emotional growth is stunted at the age of the first attack, and that he or she will not begin to recover until adulthood, if ever. As adults, many survivors (or "thrivers," as they're now being called) find themselves unable to trust. They suffer from low or nonexistent self-esteem. And they almost always have deeply conflicted feelings about sex.

As my dad frequented my bedroom, a creeping disintegration set in. It attacked my self-image, then spread, disease-like, to my sense of morality, ambition, and trust. I now think my entire family felt ill, though no one acknowledged why. We stopped camping, drew the curtains, and hardly ventured outside. Any connection I may have felt—to the mountains, my own potential, the world—began to erode.

．　　　●　　　●

Stacey, Tina, and I are speeding down Highway 75, passing a giant bottle of peach wine cooler between us and cranking Depeche Mode. I'm the only one old enough to drive. As we pass the turnoff for Fairfield and seventy-mph wind rips through our hair, I turn to Tina and say, "Who're you gonna screw tonight?"

It's early fall. We take acid and smoke cigarettes. We lie to our parents and drive to Ketchum, across the Perrine Bridge, away from the dairy farms of Twin Falls, to a place where nobody knows us, except for the guys who've heard.

We wait outside a gas station begging people to buy us beer. In a couple of hours, we'll go to a guy's house whose name I don't know, but who we met the last time we were here. I'll stand outside on the porch, smoking a Camel Straight. Someone named Sam will walk out the door, push me against the wall, and smash his mouth against mine. By the end of the night, I will have consented to a certain kind of rape.

•   •   •

I started contemplating suicide on a regular basis when I was fourteen, as it dawned on me that no one was going to help—no matter what I said or did. My grandmother, a stoic with her own skeletons, refused to get involved. She listened to my reports at her kitchen table while she prepared elaborate duck or pheasant dinners for her hunting friends. But she never confronted my dad. And my mom, who'd already lost one husband, wore her denial like a heavy coat.

I can still remember the look on her face when I handed her a poem I'd written, one morning after my dad had been in my room. She read half of it—I can't remember what it said—then folded the paper over. My dad was standing close enough in the kitchen to intercept the missive, but he didn't see it. Why I didn't give her the poem in private, I don't know. But when she peered up, her eyes burned their own message back. "Please, please stop telling me this," they said. And so, one night in the middle of August 1985, I ran away.

It's late, and I'm lying stomach-up on the living room floor, with one leg sticking out of a faded yellow nightgown with Tweety Bird on the front. I'm pretending to sleep as the wind screams across the lava flats, rattling the windows of our house. And my dad, dressed in a terrycloth robe and reeking of Old Spice, hovers a couple of inches above me, so that I can feel the heat coming off his chest.

I squirm, and he backs off. I roll over; he inches on. I jerk my head and lurch my body—still pretending to sleep, but showing him that I know what he's doing and that it's making me sick. My dad and I twist around like this until he decides I'm too restless to lay on top of tonight.

He gets up and stares at me, then goes outside for a smoke. When he comes in, he turns out the lights and heads to bed. I listen. Teeth brushed. Covers back. A little moan. Asleep.

When I hear him snoring, I put on my pink-and-black Vans and slip out the front door, careful not to let the wind slam it shut. I run to the end of our driveway and turn north, toward the Perrine Bridge. This is the night, I think, that everyone will remember, but no one will understand. I am running to the bridge, which stretches across the Snake River, nearly 500 feet in the air. When I get there, I will walk to the very center. I will climb on top of the railing. And I will jump.

· · ·

The nights I was abused have become like dreams, some locked in a vault and others softened around the edges so that they sometimes seem almost tender. But there are others, terrifying aftershocks that flash out of nowhere—visceral as if they'd happened yesterday.

Lying in my sleeping bag a half-mile below Sawtooth Lake, I can't get the bridge, the Tweety Bird nightgown, or my desperate fourteen-year-old face out of my head. It's three A.M., and I'm staring at the roof of my tent. A thin layer of condensation has turned to ice, which keeps shearing off into my face.

Yesterday, I'd left the trailhead near Stanley and headed north, out of the showering aspen leaves and past the hillsides covered in scree. Even if I couldn't find answers at Redfish Lake, I thought, I would still hike into my favorite mountains to clear my head. When I got to the dead ponderosa overlooking the limestone pipes, I'd taken a picture of myself and my pack. And when I reached the lake surrounded by snow-capped peaks, I'd tried to pitch my tent, but it was slushy and muddy and I started to cry.

Around 6 P.M., I packed up my things and turned down the trail. *It's okay to go to pieces*, I thought, and then I started to run. I ran until I reached the lower basin, where I found strangers camped by a lake. Their closeness soothed me, so I laid out my gear, cooked some oatmeal, and went to bed. An ice cloud formed around the moon. The next twelve hours felt endless, like how I imagine solitary confinement would be.

The summer of 1985, I stood in the middle of the Perrine Bridge and didn't jump. It might have been that the wind was howling so hard I couldn't balance on the rail. I might have remembered the cat my brother told me he threw over, after he dipped it in gas—how it didn't light on fire but seemed to scream. I stood there for a long time, and then I turned around and walked to the house of a friend whose mother was dating a cop.

The next day, the police knocked on my parents' door and asked them for my things. When I later testified against my dad, I learned he had denied everything, then refused to take a lie-detector test. At the hearing, my mother wept quietly in the second row. I was moved into a foster home and became a ward of the state. My dad, who continued proclaiming his innocence, was sentenced to a year of abstinence—from me.

Somehow, in those darkest days when I was being shuttled from home to home and finally back to my mother, my parents decided that it would be best if they got back together. I moved to Oregon to live with a relative so my dad could go home. Several months later, when the year of our separation was over, my parents came to pick me up.

They thought they could jump-start our family and forcibly undo the damage that had been done. On the eve of their arrival in Oregon, my dad granted me a sparse admission over the phone—something like, "I did it. I'm sorry." But it felt half-hearted, and I knew he was holding out. For the next year, I unleashed my hatred upon him, daring him to touch me so I could have him locked up. I mocked him for being an Idaho hick. And I meant it when I told him I'd kill him if he weren't such a worthless fuck. A year after we reunited, when I was sixteen, I used my military pension to pay for boarding school in Michigan, planning never to return.

It almost worked. In following years, I extricated myself from my family by disappearing for months at a time. I went to places that didn't have phones, like the Utah desert and Mexico. I enrolled in college several times—and dropped out when the urge to disappear became stronger than the need to fit in. But through it all, I continued to fragment.

·   ·   ·

Some people fall into the snakepit of their lives and reach their arms, like a baby, toward God. Others discover long-distance running or opium on a back street in Bali. When I realized that there was no escaping my pain, I turned my compass north and followed it until I reached a place where it was light all day.

Alaska. I went there after a friend told me that people in the forty-ninth state partied till dawn in the endless gloaming of the Arctic summer. Our plan was to hike up glaciers and hang out on the banks of rivers loaded with salmon rumored to be as big as small dogs. We might work; we might not. The town we were headed to, McCarthy, didn't have phone service and was accessible during the winter only by plane. It was a place where nobody knew you or cared if your story was true.

I took to Alaska like I'd been born there. By December 1994, my first winter, I was living in a twelve-by-sixteen-foot cabin, just off the McCarthy road in Wrangell–St. Elias National Park. The cabin was eight hours northeast of Anchorage near the Canada border, with 10 million acres of wilderness out the front door. I was twenty-four years old—a baby. Even if they'd known where to look, my parents couldn't have found me.

In the mornings, I wake up, stoke the barrel stove, and haul water from a pond after chopping a foot-thick hole in the ice. All day, I ski giant loops through stands of birch and black spruce on waxless cross-country boards. I glide along the moraine of a wide glacier that recedes at a geologic pace, skiing so hard my body sweats—even in thin layers when it's −20°F. The miles rack up: fifteen, thirty, one hundred. When I ski, some of the rage and sorrow seeps out of me.

Throughout the winter, I meet people who don't care where I've come from, how long I'm staying, or when I'll move on. My neighbors share homemade bread, store-bought cheese, and other prized possessions. We sit in wood-fired saunas drinking nearly brewed beer, planning climbing trips, and watching the northern lights. I stare into their winter-rough faces and think I see something I can trust.

After McCarthy, I move to Fairbanks, the coldest spot on earth, to work for a sprint musher who spends $30,000 a year on seventy huskies that never win. I am in charge of something— four litters of puppies—for the first time in my life. I will make big decisions, like who will lead us out of the dog yard, who will get extra food, and who will live or die.

Solstices and equinoxes pass. By June 1996, I'm living in Talkeetna, on the southern edge of Denali National Park. I am building a cabin on two acres of land with a dog trail out back. I make friends who admire my tenacity. I start to believe they might be right. One day, a neighbor asks me to help with her dogs as she trains for the Iditarod. She, too, is brave and afraid; her boyfriend is dying of cancer. When I meet her at the start of another long race, she is crying, but she pushes 150 miles to the Kuskoquim River, then turns around and brings her dogs across the finish line. When I get home, I write a story about her on the back of a grocery bag, then take it to the local radio station and read it over the air. Weeks later, on the eve of the Iditarod, my story is broadcast on radio stations across the state, and months later wins an award. A light goes on in my head.

When I look back on the years I spent in Alaska, I see a more perfect version of myself emerging. I am stronger, more trusting, and kind. In 1997, I score a job as a backcountry ranger in Denali. I roam the park protecting grizzlies from people and people from bears. Against all odds, the hikers trust my advice. I'm promoted. One day, I find myself hiking with Bruce Babbit's secretary, talking about the power of wilderness and how it changes lives—how it's saving mine. Mid-conversation, I flash to a moment my dad would have loved: soaking in the kettle ponds hidden in the muskeg below 20,320-foot Mt. McKinley. Maybe I think of him out of gratitude, for showing me how wilderness can shape and define. Maybe it's just the hazy mellowing of distance and time. But by September, when I leave Alaska for the Lower 48, I am ready to embrace the world—and perhaps even my father.

· · ·

It would be great if a few years in the wilderness could wipe away our pain. But of course it isn't that easy. For a long time, through my late twenties and into my thirties, my dad and I airbrushed the abuse out of our family photo. We got so good at pretending, we almost convinced ourselves that we had moved on.

Truth is, my dad and I got on well together—in part because he tried hard to be good and normal again. He flew to Anchorage once, when I needed a partner to drive with down the Alcan Highway, too scared of the frost heaves and endless stretches of road between gas stations to do it alone. Over the years, he has given me cash and cosigned on cars. He has picked up the phone when I called to talk about my loneliness—or the weather—at 3 A.M. And it is he, not my mother, who has saved all of my stories, in big, black binders at home.

We have, as they say in psychotherapy circles, reconstructed our house of relationship. In 2000, he came to see the ultrasound of my first baby. When Scout was born, and sixteen months later, Hatcher, my dad found a new reason to live. Indeed, my sons have become the brightest spot in his diminished life, and they love him acutely. He even babysits when my husband and I go skiing at Whistler for a week.

This easing of relations was good for my dad, and easy for me. But I still didn't trust him—not completely.

.   .   .

"I can't do this," I tell my husband. "I can't hold up the weight." I am lying on a trail with my legs twisted in my mountain bike, and I can't force myself to get up.

It's Memorial Day, 2006. We are riding down Winiger Ridge when I miss a turn and grind into the dirt. The sun is shining on tight blue buds that will soon flower across hillsides covered in sage. The boys are at home with a babysitter. I am falling apart.

"What happened?" my husband asks. "You were flying back there. You looked good."

Most things are looking good these days. After Alaska, I moved to Winter Park, Colorado, and skied five days a week. I kept writing, too, and landed a position at a big magazine. I live on two wooded acres at 8,500 feet on the outskirts of Boulder. My family hikes out the front door. On summer nights, we sit on our deck and watch satellites cross the sky, and in the winter, with snow blanketing the ground, we listen to a quiet so vast it creates its own sound.

And yet the weight had crept back, so heavy I felt it would crush me.

It started last spring, after an exhausting stretch of work-related travel. I felt wretched and broke out in cold sores. When I went for a check-up, a physician's assistant prescribed the antidepressant Lexapro, and I took it even though I wasn't depressed.

Instead of making me feel better, the pills made me groggy, irritable, and profoundly morose. After a week, I stopped sleeping almost completely and couldn't concentrate. I laid in bed staring at the ceiling. A bobcat wandered through the backyard; I didn't try to get up. I couldn't understand why I was feeling so down. I kept saying, *My life is a million times better than it should have been.* And then I thought about my dad, and my head began to hurt.

In recent years, his apologies had become more frequent, though he still talked euphemistically about "hurting me" or "making my life hard." He suffered openly when I refused to let him give me away at my wedding, and has cried man-size tears while we've sat at breakfast joints and bar stools across the West. But he never truly came clean—to me or anyone else in the family—about the extent of my abuse. No one knew the capacity for incest he still had. I couldn't be sure he didn't harbor fantasies about me. And I began to worry about what he could do to my kids.

In the haze of my antidepressant detox, I decided I had to go back to the Sawtooths. I believed I could find answers there, at the scene of the crime.

It didn't work. I laid in my sleeping bag at Sawtooth Lake. I waited for the ice cloud to burn off the moon. By the time the sun spread over the peaks, I knew I couldn't reconstruct the past by myself. I needed my dad to complete the story. And I knew we could only do it in the one place that had formed us both.

·　　·　　·

My dad was born on March 12, 1943. His mom was seventeen. One day, her husband went deer hunting in the mountains above their Colorado home. She wanted to go with him; she'd bring the baby. He said, "No, a woman's place is in the home," and she divorced him because of that.

A year later, my grandmother married Baby Donnie a new father. He worked as a wire-stringer for the phone company. The entire family—Les, Lorraine, and little Donnie Lee—traipsed up and down the Rockies eavesdropping on people's conversations zzztzing through the line. By the time my dad was six, his family had lived in seven states, moving across the country like well-dressed gypsies.

Life was good on the road. My dad slept in hotels and ate out every night. He was resourceful and obedient. He made boats that he floated down gutters along empty backroads in New Mexico, Arizona, and Idaho. And when he was five, he was sodomized.

It was an older cousin at a family gathering. My dad says the kids were just being kids. And besides, it only went on for a couple of years. He doesn't think he was mentally scarred, but admits it formed his attitude toward sex. "It showed me sex wasn't something you should be afraid of," he told me once. "It was how you showed your love."

.　　.　　.

I'm afraid. My dad and I sit at the picnic table on the far side of Redfish Lake. The boat has left, and so have the worried Texans, who didn't offer to help with our packs but waved as they motored away.

Today, we will hike through the yarrow and sage, stopping every ten minutes for my dad to catch his breath. When we get to the slippery rocks in the river, I'll take off my boots and slide fifty feet into the emerald pool. And when we pass the giant face under the Elephant's Perch, I'll realize that this is going to take more out of us than I had expected.

After the Lexapro, and the vision, and the truncated solo that ended with a sleepless night, I called my dad and asked, "Will you come to the Sawtooths with me?" I was in the loft, at home, and felt overheated, confused, and slightly brave. He said, "Yes. Of course. I think so. Let me think about it."

Now we are heading into a mountain range that looks impos-
ing and mean. When I called my dad months ago, this trip
seemed noble, necessary, and in a twisted way, fun. This will be
the first and last time we go on a multiday backpacking trip, just
the two of us, in the place we love most on earth.

I'm scared because when I am with my dad I am eight years
old. We will walk for days up forested valleys. We will camp in
places so lovely we'll want to weep. Fish will rise to the surface of
a dozen glassy lakes. And he might try to lie on top of me when I
fall asleep.

"I've made some rules for myself," he announces, then rattles
them off. "I won't ask questions. I won't speak out of turn. I
won't be vulgar or too descriptive. I won't get pissed off at you." I
stare at him. *You won't get pissed at me? What the hell is wrong
with you?* Then I check off the questions I will ask him when we
get to The Temple, three days from here.

When did it start?
When did it end?
How many times did you do it?
And why?

•   •   •

Two hours later, we are inching our way up the dusty switchbacks through spruce trees and lodgepole pine. My dad drags
his legs. A week ago, at a party in Utah, he tried dangling from a
rope swing that hung out of a tree. When he caught the edge of
his shoe on a root, he held on and scraped himself over some
rocks, rubbing the flesh off of his knees. Now the scabs are deep,
dark red, and crack open when he walks.

We continue like this until we reach the sign for Alpine Lake,
where we'll spend our first night. We've hiked five miles and
gained just 1,000 feet, but our campsite is still a mile away and
another 800 feet higher. My dad looks weary, like he could lie

down right here with his pack on and sleep until morning. I make him eat a Clif Bar and we load up, the trail becoming steeper with every step.

At the fifth switchback, my dad has fallen ten minutes behind. I consider waiting, then clip along at my own pace. I know my dad is getting older and is out of shape, and that in his condition he could be back there somewhere having a heart attack. I keep walking until I reach Alpine Lake.

That night, after dinner, I change my clothes and worm into my sleeping bag. My dad heads to the lake and casts for rainbows. I scoot my sleeping pad as far from his as possible, until I'm lying in the corner of the tent.

I know it's weird that we didn't bring two tents, but this is my dad, my *father*, who took up the job of caring for us voluntarily when he married my mom. Like most little girls, I worshiped my dad. We snuggled in my parents' double-wide Cabela's sleeping bag. He let me brush and blow-dry his hair. And I don't know how many hours I watched him load shotgun shells in the basement of our house.

I do know that any self-respecting woman would demand her own space. And yet my weakness isn't just a longing for simpler times. As I have learned about my dad's abuse, I've begun to see him in a different light. Once, after a bluegrass show when he imbibed too much, he cried in the car and told me that he would give anything if he could go back and make things right. For better or worse, I believed him. And before all that—before everything—there were the years at Redfish Lake. I hold those early memories carefully, like pressed wildflowers that, if jostled, would crumble to dust.

Still, the tent is an uncomfortable place, and so this too becomes a crime. One of backpacking's greatest virtues is that it makes instant bedfellows out of strangers and friends. When else do we lie under a star-filled sky separated by a few cubic inches of down? In the tents of my past, I have fallen in love and whispered my greatest longings and dreams. My tentmates and I have laughed until we peed our pants, knowing that in the morning, we will have created a shared history at 10,000 feet. Herein lies one of backpacking's true beauties, beyond the stunning vistas and close encounters with wildlife: It creates an intimacy that transcends normal friendship and even eludes some of the best marriages.

This is the first time my dad and I will lie shoulder-to-shoulder since I was a teenager in Twin Falls. I will wear all of my clothes and never really fall asleep.

The next morning, we pack up, eat breakfast, and head back down the switchbacks, which murder our knees. As we walk, my dad fills the silence I create. He reminisces about bird hunting with his friend Gary Mitchell and fishing for the eight-pound trout that used to feed on freshwater shrimp in Richfield Canal.

He sifts through his better memories, until we come to a big log on the side of the trail, where we break out our lunch. Then this:

"I was sixteen the first time I killed a deer," he says. A four-point buck "that would have been an eight-point by Eastern standards" walked into the crosshairs of his gun. When he pulled the trigger, he got so excited he started shaking uncontrollably. It was buck fever, and he had it bad.

"You can hardly grab your breath," he says, grinning mischievously. "Just knowing that you can actually kill something, it's the height of excitement. It makes you weak in the knees."

My dad scans the trees, inhales deeply, and smiles. I realize that I haven't seen him in this setting, surrounded by rivers and trees, in years. In 1990, my parents moved to Nevada. They sold the camper and packed my dad's shot-loading equipment in a box. One summer a few years later, he came to visit while I was living in Jackson, Wyoming. He said he'd bring his fly rod and camping stuff. When he arrived, he was underdressed in a light wind shell and braced himself against the cold. We went to the Snake River and he sat down in a heap.

"Break out your rod, Dad," I said. But he couldn't. He'd forgotten to pack it.

My dad looks up the trail. "I got away from shooting does," he says, "after I killed one with a fawn." The fawn's cries echoed through the South Hills, and he couldn't stand the sound. So he put a bullet in its head.

We chat, nibble on sausage, and dry our sweaty shirts in the breeze.

Two hours later, we take off our boots and wade into a bottom-clear lake. The silence is back, bigger than it has been all week. A giant rock leads into the water, then drops off like a cliff. The fish are rising now, and my dad follows the ripples out to the edge of the lake. Watching him, I rehearse different ways to interrogate.

So, Dad. When was the first time you . . . abused me? (Too clinical. This isn't an after-school special.)

. . . touched me? (Too real-time.)

. . . completely fucked up my bearings? Yes, that's it. That's how I'll start the conversation when we get to The Temple and he's so tired he can't defend himself. I join him by the water. He looks up and smiles. "Feels warm enough to swim."

.   .   .

My dad collapses the second we reach the altar. We're in the middle of the boulder field that threatened to break us in half. Sweat drenches his entire torso. His face looks punched and weak. Before we left the trail, he stopped to peer up at the stone minarets surrounding The Temple. I heard the bones cracking as he craned his neck. "Beautimus," he whispered.

I crouch down, slightly behind him, and dig in my pack. This is the moment I've been waiting for: when the truth will shine down upon us and the heavens break open under the weight of a million dirty-white doves. I take out my dictaphone, test the battery, and push record. The entire conversation will last thirteen minutes.

The Truth (A One-Act Play)

[The lights come up on a rock in the middle of a boulder field. Don, an attractive man in his mid-sixties, sits slightly in front of his daughter, Tracy. She holds a reporter's tape recorder in front of his face.]

TRACY:	*[Fidgeting; tugging at her shorts.]* So . . . this is going to be hard.
DON:	It's okay.
TRACY:	*[Hands spread on the rock, absorbing its heat.]* All I have are four questions. And I don't want to know details. Because I know. I was there. And so what is important to me is to know your version of the truth.
DON:	*[Nodding, looking down.]*
TRACY:	Okay. When did it start?
DON:	*[Clearing his throat, composed.]* On a camping trip up here at Redfish. I had been drinking. I lied. I was tucking you in. My hands went to a spot, which surprised me, and I kept them there. But the severity—it wasn't that often at that age. Just periodically.
TRACY:	*[Agitated.]* But I was eight. Couldn't you see what that did to me and say, "Oh my God, oh my God, I did that. That was a mistake"?
DON:	*[Calmly; choosing his words.]* A person who does what I did . . . you make things up. You don't think of the other person. You just need that closeness. If I had ever known how it

would have affected you, I probably would done something completely different.

TRACY: *[Still agitated.]* So . . . that day on the log. I wasn't upset?

DON: I don't think so. I don't remember. I was trying to cover things up. I had feelings for you. I thought of you as my fishing buddy. The only thing I could do was lie. I wasn't thinking of you.

TRACY: Just so you know . . . in case you were wondering . . . I was thinking about what would happen if I jumped in the river and died. *[Starting to cry.]* I was eight. That's so fucked up.

DON: *[Tenderly.]* No, it isn't.

TRACY: *[Sadly.]* Yes, it is. When you're eight years old, you're a little kid. It wasn't a physical thing?

DON: Not then, but later I was put in a position where you were going through puberty. This was your teen years, you were probably twelve or thirteen. Your mother stopped being intimate. I leaned to you for closeness.

TRACY: *[Putting her hands up as if to say "stop."]* Okay, okay. So mom wasn't interested in being intimate? Why didn't you go have an affair?

DON: *[Nodding.]* That's what I shoulda done. By all means.

[A break. Tracy takes a drink of water, shakes her head. Stands up, sits down. Don looks across the valley. A hawk skims the trees.]

TRACY: Okay. *[Sigh.]* Now, how many times did it happen? In various degrees of whatever it was. Coming into my room . . . whatever that was. Till it ended.

DON:	Between twenty-five and fifty times maybe. You know, I never kept track. *[A long silence.]*
TRACY:	*[Fighting tears.]* You must have felt like shit about that, right? I mean, I didn't want that, right? *[Sitting down, hugging her legs to her chest.]* I wasn't a willing accomplice . . . right?
DON:	You weren't a willing accomplice. I didn't expect you to be willing. I really felt screwed up. Why would I jeopardize my family like that? And I'm not using this as an excuse, but I was abused when I was real young.
TRACY:	Did you do it to Chris?
DON:	No, no. It's never boys.
TRACY:	*[Her eyes squeeze shut, her face registering fear.]* Who else then?
DON:	I haven't had those feelings for anybody, ever since.
TRACY:	Since when?
DON:	Since you. It ended when you left, when you ran away. *[They're both crying now. The wind has picked up.]*
TRACY:	So one day it was just . . . over?
DON:	No, it's never over. You have those feelings, but they're just like this tape. It replays but you learn how to stop it. You learn how.

•　　　•　　　•

Some people believe the truth will set you free. I think that's too easy. When my dad made his confession at The Temple, a weight lifted, but only long enough for me to take a deep breath.

After twenty years of second-guessing my own memory, feeling ashamed of my sexuality, and aching for the confirmation that others have always denied, I finally had proof. But the victory wasn't entirely sweet. My dad's confession also horrified me. I'd always hated that he put his twisted desire before a small girl's suffering. Now that I had learned how often it had happened—fifty nights lost, never to be regained—a new sadness gripped me. And yet, things had changed for the better at The Temple. By confessing, my dad has given me something back—power, the anticipation of a fuller future, maybe even my life. And finally, after all of these years in the wilderness, I'm might find the strength to truly forgive him.

•   •   •

In the dry, wild heart of southern Idaho, past Russian John hot spring and the ranger station on Highway 75, there is a small wooden sign, barely visible from the overlook on Galena Pass. Through a camera lens you might not even notice it, dwarfed as it is by the Sawtooth Mountains, which spread out before you and fall away somewhere in Utah. But if you know where to look, you'll find the sign, and below it, a tiny spring buried in overgrown grass. These are the headwaters of the River of No Return, a creek that seeps out of the earth, gathers volume and speed, and becomes so fierce a hundred miles from here that it cuts a trench in the earth 1,000 feet deep.

People say the river was named this because the current is so strong it's impossible to travel upstream. But when I was a little girl, I stood on the banks watching sockeye struggling toward their ancient spawning grounds at Redfish Lake. Nine hundred miles from their starting point in the Pacific, they arrived redder than overripe tomatoes, their flesh already breaking apart.

In the early 1970s, thousands of fish returned here to lay their eggs and die. Then we put in dams along the Columbia and

Snake Rivers. By 1975, eight concrete barriers stood between the Pacific Ocean and Redfish Lake, and by 1995, the sockeye population had dwindled to none.

Many people took this as a sign: that the world had become too corrupt for something so pure as native salmon to exist. I might have believed that, too, until last summer, when four Snake River sockeye made it home.

The Antioch Review

FINALIST—ESSAYS

Maureen McCoy's father, a troubled war vet and alcoholic, lived in a shadow world revealed to her thirty years after his death. This nuanced essay, told with no trace of false sentimentality, stands as a testament to the healing powers of time, acceptance, and love.

Maureen McCoy

Vickie's Pour House: A Soldier's Peace

The envelope addressed to Mrs. Johnny McCoy tips me off that the writer was an old bar friend of my father. I have discovered the cache of sympathy cards thirty years after my father's death, in my mother's bottom dresser drawer. Clearing the house is an ongoing process, still, two years since my mother died: sorting, remembering, and making new connections from doing both. My mother had stashed mementos willy-nilly, and the bedroom dresser yields up surprising gems. I have discovered a pin that belonged to her father, who raised his family on the Minnesota Iron Range: Catholic Forester. Did such foresters sing out "Hail Mary!" as they whacked trails, hauled logs, and baited bears in the Superior National Forest?

The saying goes "give time time" and, sure enough, the sympathy cards for my father waited mute as death in a little white cardboard box buried by cheerful workday scarves, requiring loads of time to pass and, sadly, my mother's life, too, before they could play their part in letting new light shine in my brain and shape a fuller picture of my father.

Like the cards, much of my father's life had lain out of reach, in an unexamined silence. He had engaged in a secret life, a necessary life of companionable and destructive drinking too generative of pain for us to acknowledge, ever, or ask about, in a place or places left unnamed. A bigamist could not have separated his worlds more concisely. That other, shadow world, the one we shunned and denied, lay vividly before me now, in this letter to Mrs. Johnny McCoy and, I was yet to discover, some of the cards bundled with it. I believe we had not allowed, in imagination or fact, that the other world was peopled by real humans perhaps as needful of the shadow community as was my father. The letter to Mrs. Johnny McCoy starkly asserted the essentials: strangers from the tavern life loved and missed my father. The return address indicated an unremarkable residential street across town.

Dear Mrs. Johnny McCoy,
It seems odd that we've known Johnny so long, and yet never met you. At least I don't think we ever met?

My John and your Johnny and me go back at least 24 years—that's our next wedding anniversary. I think your John was driving a Reed's ice cream truck—or a meat truck? Gee, I seem to get more vague with each passing day!

Anyway, our men were always shooting pool in those days. And in those days wherever John went, I went too. So we both became very fond of Johnny. And he was a good friend, through the years.

I know how much you and the children meant to him. (I don't know how many times he told me that he didn't deserve *you*—and I'd wish my John would feel that way!) And how many times he said, later, that if he could just hold out until the kids were through school . . ."

I don't know how either of you found the strength and the courage for these past years. I suppose one does what one has to do. But how well would I have handled the same situation?

That's why I felt I should write this note to you. Just to tell you how much John and I have admired you, and what you did for Johnny. And to tell you that we were very fond of Johnny and shall miss him, too.

I hope that knowing you did all that one human being can do for another will help ease the pain of today.

We are proud to have called Johnny "friend."

Sincerely—"Mary" Hippen

One of the eerie aspects of my father's absence in death was the undisturbed sameness of our house. At a glance, minus his corporeal being, how little in it specifically suggested his presence in our family years. His few things hailed from life before our time; before he left home; before World War II.

Our house was a jumble of antique and contemporary furniture, but in one living room corner stood a small black octagonal end table that my father made in high school carpentry class. Its place was immutable, and his matching knick-knack shelf hung on the wall above. We are a sentimental family for whom history beats a brass band every chance it gets, and these talismans of my father's youthful industry anchored imagination as well as the heirloom lamp and a fine caned rocker. My father's life, their presence suggested, had once run along lines as clean and simple as plank wood. He had been a boy, after all.

On my parents' closet door a wooden tie rack shaped and painted to look like an owl spilled dozens of silk ties from my father's former life, a young man's life that came after the carpentry phase, though before us. In 1969 when, unbelievably— who in Des Moines *could* believe such fortune?—Janis Joplin came to town and performed at Vets Auditorium, I threaded my bellbottoms' waistband with one of my father's ties that seemed to catch the mood of those days: swirling blue and cream and mauve. My mother encouraged me; we picked out the tie together and off I went to worship Janis feeling ready and hip because of that belt. My father smiled his bashful smile when told about the transformative role his tie played.

Only our bathroom medicine chest held evidence of the afterwar, his time with us: prescription vials, pills that might keep him alive; and these, unnervingly, were not disturbed for quite a while after his death. Perhaps two years went by during which I would come to visit, peek in the medicine cabinet even as I dreaded the sight of those pills. Then they vanished. Finally my mother had dumped that hard evidence of the fatal illness she had been made to realize was already churning in my father's blood, way back, when they met as young people at Drake University in a business class. My father attended on the GI Bill, courtesy of the jungle warfare years that destroyed him in keen and subtle ways; my mother had followed her older sister down from northern Minnesota. At that time—and my mother liked telling us this—she and her friends were called "bobby-soxers." They wore loose white men's shirts, jeans rolled to mid-calf, bobby sox and loafers. She implied a carefree time: Some adults disapproved! Some adults said, "Oh, those bobby-soxers!"

Sifting through the sympathy cards and letters I find some from my mother's work colleagues, others from friends and relatives. But I am socked thirty years back in time, blushingly hot all over again, when I come across the small cards that indicate flowers and condolences were sent from Vickie's Pour House, The Uptown Tap, and Joe's Place. I relive fleeting waves of shame and the smidgen of defensive pride that rattled me as we toured the effulgent bouquets at the funeral home. My mother, who considered funereal flowers to be nonsense, glanced at the cards, made no comment, and moved on, but who knows what mix of emotion played out for her and again when tucking these cards away in the dresser? What must she have thought of a couple of cards sent to the house signed only with an unfamiliar first name, or an expression of sympathy offered by strangers who, though they signed full names, did not identify their connection to my father?

The downtown corner bars such as Vickie's Pour House were places that literally poured away my father's paychecks. Vickie's *Poor* House, indeed. Vickie's and the others were joints my mother sometimes called on the nights my father got paid and was obviously not coming straight home. "Is John McCoy there? I have to speak with John McCoy." But he had either "just left" or had not been seen. Whoever answered, however, knew him, a regular. Just as we understood from the riot of ties stuffed onto the owl rack that my father had lived a mysterious (but only vaguely conceived by me and thus only mildly interesting) former life as a vibrant young man, we knew and did not dwell on the fact that in our lifetimes his drama played out in an alternate arena that nourished even as it sickened him. Because his drinking at the bars caused grief at home, we would not have understood the nourishment aspect. His drinking cowled secrecy and silence over us, which forbade our asking, or even thinking too much about that world or the comrades therein. Let all that remain a dark isolated void, otherwise we would have to consider why he would spend evenings with people not us. What was so great about them?

On a good day, a Sunday evening, with my father there at the dinner table, he might entertain us with bits of odd news from that world. He began, always: "The other day a guy told me a funny story." Occasionally something wonderful would materialize from that universe, such as our first dog. One day our father alighted from a taxi at the foot of Monona and tenderly carried an armload of large gangly puppy up the hill to us. We all stood at the windows, watching, and my mother gasped: "Look at those feet. He's not a beagle!" Other offerings, such as a television set, came our way as mysteriously, and only vague mention was made of provenance.

In these twelve-step days, people may disbelieve or mistrust that my mother managed a shattered war veteran husband with no outside help, nor did she ever disparage our father to us, or shrivel into a dry leaf of victimhood. She did not give it all over to religious fate, either. Unlike Adam, my mother did not feature naming all things in this world. She emphasized the positive in life; as for the negative, that which hurt us seemed to have no name, or was just too much to explain. It existed in silence and, therefore, might, if we were lucky, slip away. In silence lay a walloping dread, but to name its source might kill you.

Agony kept us silent, but of course what comes through to a child is hugely different from the adult's understanding of a situation or a person, and that, as simple and true as it is in general, has perhaps taken me thirty years to embrace—a jolt of illumination—on my own family's account, now reading the cards. My mother had her reasons as well as her strength that kept her from breaking down or ever ranting to us. We saw what we saw, heard what we heard; explicit interpretation was left hanging. Meanwhile, on she went: working, sewing, singing carols as we put up the tree, keeping to birthday cake-and-party rituals, getting her requisite six books—the limit allowed—from the book mobile every week, and looking beautiful. She took care of the family and fed her inner life with reading and craft projects. My sister and I went off to school wearing fabulous clothes she ran up on the Singer Featherweight, often without bothering to use a pattern—designer clothes, indeed. Upholstering furniture, caning chairs, nothing was beyond her craft eye and hand and enthusiasm to imagine or fix, except of course our father. Perhaps her artistic gifts flourished all the more, set against that knowledge. I think of the combination of the two of them: my mother's sturdy constitution and bright curiosity, humor and dexterous creativity that would not be quashed for anything; my father's fragile self that could not psychologically withstand his war experience, with or without money, and despite his gentle humor. To learn later, from a medical diagnosis, that his physical fate was sealed by the war must have secured his sense of defeat.

From Friends at the Uptown Tap I find a card with an earnest list of patrons, the names Bud, Bea, and Earl; Archie, one Evie Garcia, and a Billie Smith; a couple named Don and Ginger, and more, with the message scrawled in: *We all miss our friend Johnny very much. Sympathy to you & family.*

From Vickie's Pour House came an equally long list of comrades, probably written out by Vickie herself. (A Vickie Walk is listed—possibly the owner? I wonder.) Most have first and last names but a few are listed singly: Cliff and Gary L. and Willie. These are all genial names, common names, nothing to indicate swagger or outsized personalities.

An oversized card accompanied flowers sent from Joe's Place. A steady hand had managed to cram twenty-three names onto the card: some couples, a Mel, an Elmo; Sammy, Charlie, Johns and Jims. The list is topped with Mr. and Mrs. Joe Harris, owners perhaps.

I value the record, lists put down determinedly, in the best penmanship, for a serious occasion. For these folks, a setting down of name boldly said it all. I am most heartened by Mary Hippen's letter, though. I go back and back to it. I thank Mary Hippen for going further. I note that her writing is at ease with formality: "we were very fond of Johnny and *shall* miss him too"; "... I suppose *one* does what *one* has to." Also, the conversational "Gee ..." and "My John and your Johnny and *me* go back, ..." Mary had placed quotes around her first name, a strangeness perhaps meant to emphasize or echo my father's calling her by her first name only.

That address had caught my eye: Mrs. Johnny McCoy. Someone else had sent a card to Mrs. Sully McCoy, "Sully" being my father's nickname for our mother whose family name was Sullivan. Of course he would speak of her, to his close buddies, as Sully. I imagine that the young bobby-soxer, down from the Minnesota Iron Range, might have felt posh being renamed affectionately by a man, an older man who had, in fact, been to war. "Sully" meant love.

At home, when someone phoned for my father (pretty rarely), we could peg the realm of life he or she called from, a kind of carbon dating. Asking for John McCoy signaled some kind of business; John Robert meant that an older elegant relative from his small hometown of Indianola was calling; anyone who asked for Johnny spoke from the dark void of nighttime mystery, whipping my mind with a ribbon of fear and thrill.

On The Uptown Tap's list someone signed for Ginny Bognanno, evidently after advisement: above, rather wildly crossed out, was "*Jennie* Bognanno." He or she wanted to get it right, to be precise in who mourned our father, and in what context. At the end of the list the proprietor wrote Uptown Tap, 1323 Locust, Des Moines. Bud Burmeiser.

From each of these taverns someone had emerged into the light of day and gone to the florist. Someone had picked out flowers and a card. In the case of Joe's Place, which sent flowers and card to the funeral home, nothing to our house, the person in charge would have requested or sought out a card large enough to contain a long list of names. This designated person would have collected money at the bar, possibly taken time out of work, perhaps entered a flower shop as if it were a place as fantastical as the moon, and penned in all the names from the list in hand. These people and places sheltered my father and saw him through the years (and years) of illness and the changes it caused: shingles, for one; and sometimes thin Johnny McCoy would blimp out due to new medication. His absences (time in the VA hospital) would be noted and his return to the fold welcomed. Here, I like to think, lay stress-free friendship, camaraderie however blurred or exalted by the drink. At last, in his death, the comrades came forward to reveal themselves.

I called his drinking holes old-man corner bars. My parents called them taverns. They stood as small shelters whose wooden façades were painted in sensible colors. (Anything fancy and you'd drive away the people who needed you most.) The taverns plied their trade in the lively auto parts-and-repair section of the western edge of downtown that recently has been decimated in favor of green space as an entry to the city. Garage-size doors opened onto sidewalks; tires rolled; tools clanged; new and vintage cars gleamed behind plate-glass windows. Specialty shops, thriving before chain outfits for muffler and lube jobs, worked on transmissions and other components. A coffee shop, Grace's Tee-Pee, served nickel cups and sandwiches. The taverns each had a window blackened for privacy yet permanently aglow with a neon beer sign: Hamm's, Schlitz, Pabst Blue Ribbon. Additional entice-ment was painted on the glass: *Grill Special* or *Chili.*

In my early twenties, years before my father's death, I was pleased to discover bars whose names excited me into imagining experiences, and even promises, as distinct from one another as Frank's Pizza House and King Ying Lo's restaurants. In Denver I took to The Satire Lounge, The Lemon Tree, Cloud Nine, and, the real coup, Butch & Daddy Pine's Sportsman's Club, an after-hours dive I had even less business poking around in than the others. Never mind the bullet holes studding the doorway to The Sportsman's Club, youth is the age of immortals, and my immor-tal companions and I ran past danger, hungering for flash and dancing until dawn. I maintained that my bars were not the sad places of my father's time. I felt a triumph over my father: I was not like him.

No, I had not fought his war.

Returning from the South Pacific, a month-long journey by ship, my father saw in a heightened compressed way the raving lunatic results of the war: men gone mad and howling, scalded bodies, physically twisted bodies, and men missing parts that ren-dered them as grasping caricatures. He saw torment that would not subside. Both my parents referred to the experience—rarely, vaguely, and never in the company of the other—as wielding enormous impact. The unrelenting ravings and woe, displaced from the jungles and packed into unavoidable close quarters, were enough to tip toward the deep end a fragile soul journeying home. All that time heading toward the United States, my father had to think *this is who we are now.* He had nothing to do those weeks aboard ship but smell, hear, and see human wreckage, without escape; tell himself he was lucky; and carry it all in his head as he looked out on an indifferent sea. The only prewar time he had seen an ocean, this same Pacific, he had driven his roadster from Iowa on a boisterous teenage trip to California. He and his friends ran whooping into the water. Now that ocean, like the men cargoed aboard ship, had lost all trace of mirth.

And what did his small-town faux-genteel family imagine and want for him on V-J Day, but to meet at Younkers Tea Room for a celebratory outing. His mother would have worn a little hat with the veil crimped high, good jewelry, the works—the costume of the respectable lady lunching at one of the downtown's major tea rooms. His father would have arrived in suit and tie. His sister would be seasonally dressed in a fabulous outfit. All would be bursting with love and utter incomprehension. The nightmare was over, now please resume—life! Surely affecting a semblance of normalcy might speed a return to it. My grandparents had not known for forty-four months the location of their son except in the vaguest terms—somewhere in New Guinea, the odd respite in Australia—every day praying that he still walked the earth; and from that paralysis of dark time they would forever peer at him, their shaken boy, and ache with love made cautious. The toll of waiting, the miracle of his survival, and the slow dawning of his alteration would gently rock them back and back into memory, to the sweet hopes of "before." On that day, though, I picture his family: clinking tea cups, waiting; shifting a bit in their seats; touching napkins to lips; placating the solicitous waiter; finally ordering club sandwiches. Meanwhile, my father had joined the packs of soldiers who roamed the downtown streets drunk as skunks and demented by freedom. Therein lay the balm my father would always need. Bars, not the golf course, where he had excelled before the war, would supply it. *He could have gone pro* became the wistful family refrain. The unspoken followed: *if not for the War.*

The tea room mentality and the bumptious daily life of my father's own growing family, however fondly observed, allowed for little salving of his torment. I imagine that his bar friends were especially needed after he had been diagnosed with the fatal blood disease that doctors acknowledged had resulted from his enduring malaria thirteen times in New Guinea. He sought relief, hardly an ambition to fault. He found companions, gentle or roaring souls, or gentle-turned-roaring, perhaps, as the drinking nights wore on. In Vickie's Pour House, The Uptown Tap, Joe's Place, and perhaps other beer joints, he found acceptance of himself for exactly who he helplessly revealed himself to be: a broken man, scared, funny, compassionate, interested, and likable, a GI vet who could not fathom his family, and needed to talk, talk, talk to his own kind and drink himself to a nub.

Wounds seek air, all right. It all had to come out somehow, somewhere, in an effort to grasp at healing. Mary Hippen's letter asserts that my father needed to talk about his fears, and somehow deal with the grief he felt he rained down on my mother, on us, the innocents who inexplicably went forward, thriving, achieving, despite his contrary needs. He was in love with my mother until the end, and he told the world, *his* world. His bar confidences did not relieve us of his deep private harm, but they must have assuaged him some. He loved, dammit. Let someone know that he loved. This is what I have come to understand. He loved faithfully, truly, if incapably. To grasp and believe this, I have to step outside of the popular and somewhat sniffy saying: *Love is an action.* Not always so, I contend. Love is first and always a soul yearning. Before all else it is the shock felt within that affects body and soul forever. The most wretched or blameworthy poor sap who never makes it off the mark toward peace, responsibility, comfort, or whatever else could allow for some smooth going ahead, some clarity and so acceptance, might rightly insist *and still, I love.*

Of course we knew this in our hearts and, in truth, helplessness ran both ways. We could not help my father out of his fix.

Along with the sympathy letters and flower cards I find my father's wallet. I cry when I see that, forever, he carried small photos of my mother, young and lovely from their Drake University courting days. He never opened his wallet and said, "Look, kids. Look at your mom back then." He also carried a photo of what was then a family of four, before my brother's birth. In this photo my father and mother are holding up my sister and me, babies in snowsuits. Both parents are smiling hugely. I wonder if my mother knew he carried these photos. Grasping at his wallet, mad to find money, did she ever notice? The wallet is crusted and curled over on itself. It is slim, as if money was not meant to take up a berth there anyway. Rather, it contains fragments of biography, reference to my father's years with us.

A frayed orange library card belies my memory; I have no recollection of my father frequenting a library, ever. The card expired in 1970, the same year that another card acknowledges him as being a Boy Scout committee member for my brother's Troop 29. Whatever his involvement—slight, I'm guessing; my brother cannot recall—it was more than I knew of. I note the charge cards issued from department stores I cannot imagine my father entering; Amvets membership, of course; a notice of honorable withdrawal from the International Brotherhood of Teamsters. My father's last driver's license issued June 4, 1974, would expire two years after his death. He was pegged at 5 feet 8 inches, weight 144, and eyes, wrongly, GRY. He had green eyes. We are a family of green-eyed people.

I have just found a tiny square of newspaper in the wallet, cut from a longer article:

After modifying the combination treatment, Djerassi treated 12 more. Six of the 12, or 50 percent, are alive after 4-1/2 to 8-1/2 years after being diagnosed. All were under 14 years of age and five of the six had the most advanced form of the disease.

Dejerassi [newspaper's spelling or misspelling] uses an old anti-cancer drug called methotrexate in combination with a compound called citrovorum.

Surely my father carried that scrap in earnest to the Veterans' Hospital at some point, offering it as proof of hope: Can't something be done? Perhaps he sat before a discouraging doctor and silently slipped the paper back into his wallet, to have something to do as his ears burned with heartache.

Another card, a black one bordered in brown plastic, announces Army of the United States and my father's honorable discharge. He was a technician, fifth grade. CO 1 and 186 Infantry. On the back: Separation Center: Jefferson Barracks, MO. Date: June 8, 1945—two weeks before his twenty-eighth birthday; two years before marrying my mother.

On the Emergency Medical Identification Card, under *My Doctor is*: Veteran's Hospital, no actual doctor's name. On the back he filled in Present Medical Condition thus: Leukemia and lymphosarcoma. Line two: Cancer of the lympathic system. Then: Dangerous allergies: horse serum as in tetanus antitoxin.

Which was it, then; how could it be both lymphosarcoma and leukemia? His diagnosis was eventually switched to Hodgkin's Disease, but when, I wonder? What difference did it make?

I am so ignorant, so long without a father.

Evidence of all three children follows: My brother Mark's social security number written upside down on a clinic prescription note that reiterates: *John McCoy is allergic to all medications with horse serum*; a little photo of my sister Katy taken for her junior high graduation; a ragged slip with my name and Denver address: 475 South Depew, Lakewood, Colo. 80226. That was my last address in Denver, the lavish gingerbread house whose walls were insulated with old newspapers that reported on the antics of Butch Cassidy and the Sundance Kid. From that house I was called home by my mother for what turned out to be my father's last month. Before going, I sat on my bed clutching the spread and thought, "I don't want to be a girl without a father."

Back behind all this waits a note folded onto a piece of paper with the Frank Paxton Lumber Company logo. *I Here By owe Johnnie $20.00. Bert Anderson. Witness George*—somebody. I cannot read the last name. A tavern transaction, no doubt sworn to in a moment of great need.

My father died on Leap Year Day, February 29, 1976. Just as his "doctor" card lacked the name of a doctor and our house retained only slight evidence of his existence, so my father lacked even a solid day on which to perish. His anniversary of death passes invisibly most years, as if even the Roman calendar colludes with some higher powers that foretold my father's always being more spirit than body, just a presence of baffled light on earth. He died in the Bicentennial year, and I remember deciding that his service life and death were ironically acknowledged by all that red, white, and blue.

At the time of my father's death the Des Moines sky hung insufferably dark and low. I had grown used to Denver's thin bright air and moved sluggishly, with humidity sinking chillingly into my body. I was reluctant to leave my mother—I had no job in Denver—so I stayed on for months. I returned to Colorado only to perch in the mountains for a summer, then gather my things and get back to Des Moines, to live at home for a spell.

At the end of summer I stood outside with my mother and the dogs, looking at flowers in the far back yard. After a while, I headed back into the house, probably to get a drink of water or to use the bathroom. I walked in to a ringing phone. I answered and heard in the question "Is this Mrs. McCoy?" a tentative, even a somewhat trembling female voice—if a chain saw can tremble. This voice had been raked and rusted, doused and corrugated with years of double-barrel living. I identified myself, and this woman hesitated before saying that she was Vickie, from Vickie's Pour House, a friend of my father. She struggled on, and I grew hot in her pauses as she sought, haltingly, to impress upon me just how much my father had meant to her and to many other people, how brave these people knew he was; what he suffered—uncomplainingly. She knew about all of us; he had always spoken of us with pride.

I remember the tone and rhythm of Vickie's voice and her heavy-breathing silences. I gripped the receiver tightly as she spoke. Here was a direct connect to the taboo world, a voice from its darkness thickly smoked with need and kind words, hesitancies and slight gulps that did not successfully hold back the sobs. I wasn't used to hearing any adult women of her generation cry. I had never seen or heard my mother cry. I believe she trained herself to swallow pain down to some solid flooring, some cellar part of the heart that locked away the risk of it. In deep summer, Vickie's grieving was still, or again, fresh and salty. I wonder now about the courage it took, and what awful pressing need she bore for months, finally daring to call up my mother, meaning to unburden herself, by giving color and humanity to the world that she knew had anguished us. Then, possibly to Vickie's relief, she found me on the phone instead of my mother and switched into a maternal gear, trying to say what a daughter could not yet comprehend: that her father was a full human being. A daughter must know this—and trust. Vickie, I remember, called me "honey."

After Vickie trailed off and said goodbye, I went back outside to my mother and the flowers and the dogs. I did not mention the call. I believed as I had so often believed in childhood, foolishly no doubt, that I protected my mother by saying nothing.

Of course, my father's life was more nuanced than the family, his children especially, could have understood. Away from us, in his other world, he was not a shadow in a dark void, rather a real man in the company of other real people. I could not quite comprehend the import of this, the grace revealed in Vickie's call, as the thrill of shame still wrestled my heart. A sense of the emotional texture of my father's life was not available to me then. Now it is so urgently upon me, as I read the sympathy cards, lighting on that one from Mary Hippen to Mrs. Johnny McCoy and seeing the words *Vickie's Pour House*. Mary Hippen knew him twenty-four years, since I had been a baby. How long did Vickie know him? I wish my father could have told us, "I have friends, as you do, and I go talk to them. I need friends, as well as my family." And were he able to manage both worlds, indeed I am sure he would have done so with generous aplomb.

About a year after Vickie called—high summer now—again my mother and I ranged around the back yard, the dogs in tow as usual. I lived in Iowa City by then, two hours away, and had bussed to town to tell my mother of a dream I had had of my father:

He stood outside and, sure enough, the sky was somewhat informed by old Hollywood miracle-movies in its luminous blue and yellow, its gilt-edged clouds; but my father wore a loose shirt that would have been absurd in his day, or ever in his life, and not derivative of the movies: a V-necked thing the weave and color of Wheat Chex. I described the abashed smile I had known all my life, the look on my father's face as he spoke to me. He said, "I parked the car."

"Parked the car," my mother repeated. "Parked the car." Then, laughing: "Odds Bodkins, wouldn't you know."

Death has the power to free the living in unexpected ways, but I was floored, delighted by the way my no-nonsense mother seized on this dream. She embraced it as nothing less than a visitation—and she wanted to get the goods. She asked the kinds of questions one asks of someone who has seen one's long-lost love: again, describe the clothes, the surroundings; his voice saying, "I parked the car." She especially wanted to know about the expression on my father's face. "He had that little smile," I said.

Until then we had been stuck in the downside of my father's death, the sorrow of a long illness, a predetermined death. We had not yet allowed ourselves to relax into celebratory memories. By way of my dream—what other recourse did he have?—my father jumped in the driver's seat and took the wheel of grief to pry us loose of our unspoken confusions and hesitations. *It's ok to laugh—at me! He* was at peace, now get a move on. The man had always had a good sense of humor, and now he was offering a clear straightaway to acknowledging connection and appreciation—love. *I parked the car.* Get it?

We did. My mother and I varoomed right into car stories, the safe and obvious opening he had given us. Had we forgotten that cars and driving were a great joy to my father and, so, pleasing to us? Had we really not yet acknowledged that car business, buying us cars and teaching his children to drive, was the high sovereign province of my father's parenting? For this important passage he had gathered himself into fatherly duty and wisdom and patience. Cars, their purchase, maintenance, and our education of them, these were feats repeated through three cycles of children turning sixteen. He found exquisite '57 Chevys for my sister and me—great gleaming tanks of finned chrome beauty—and then brought one home for himself. I am betting that the tavern neighborhood, with its drinkers and car shop camaraderie, played its part in the magnificent conjury. We measured oil together, fiddled with the carburetors and put on new air filters; I learned about the rear axle and the V-8 engine. (It needed to be "opened up" regularly.) His meticulous instructions included what to do in case of specific emergencies, such as the brakes going out: "Don't jump out of the car," which is exactly what I imagined doing and told him so. He had suspected as much. "That's why I'm telling you, don't jump," he repeated.

His caution, I decide now, also serves as a retrospective take on his life's milestones: family; driving emergencies; jungle warfare: he did not jump. From what I have read now of the New Guinea jungles and the impossible "campaign" there, the miracle is that any man survived. About one-third of the foot soldiers simply lost their minds; many died from disease and others from face-to-face combat. Malnutrition, thanks to a horrible shortage of rations early on, claimed a mean share of lives. Self-inflicted wounds and even allowing jungle rot to claim one's feet were all-too-common acts of desperation, a means to getting out. The terrain was unknown to the bigwigs who sank soldiers into its depths, along some stretches considered impassable to native residents. Few infantrymen came home to speak openly to their loved ones about slogging day after day through dark jungle cover in torrential rains, with no sense of escape or conclusion or peace, and no real sleep in the foxholes. Combat was overwhelmingly hand-to-hand; enemy soldiers leaped forth as if from the twenty-yard line, then the ten-yard line, distances my father and others judged accurately from having played high school football.

And yet: In remarkably elegant cursive my father sent home from New Guinea outright cheerful V-mails, philosophically upbeat, even wise little messages to his family. With magnifying glass I have begun deciphering these little missives that underwent a heat-transference process to seal the ink, yet blurred it in the process. My father asked for cigarettes and mentioned sending money home, stressing that his mother and grandmother were to buy new dresses. He alluded, always, to coming home. I have read enough accounts to know that U.S. and Australian soldiers mired in the New Guinea jungles overwhelmingly assumed they would die there. My father wrote about eating a great turkey dinner or playing cards by flashlight, and then might add, "If you don't hear from me for the next five weeks, don't worry!" He would be going back into combat.

Struck happy by my dream, my mother and I continued to reel around in our memories and the pleasures of our lush summertime yard. Oaks leafed out, and cicadas sang like mad. By way of conclusion to this episode, my mother took in the details of the dream once more, and said gently, "You were always the fey one"—in touch with the other side.

Two years ago, when her death was imminent, my mother did not speak of it openly to me except to toss off, "I know *I have a rendezvous with death*, they're just trying to delay it, and by the way, you should read that poem." But by the time she was bedridden, with just days left, and still she had conceded only, "I know what's happening," I approached her at her bedside, yearningly. We had always taken our cues from her silence and optimism; now inspiration and need led me to break silence and push optimism, happily rush my words as she had done quoting the Alan Seeger poem.

"I just want to make sure we're on the same wavelength here and can make a deal," I said. "You might get there before I do, but we know—let's promise—that some day we'll carry on together as wild women in the Celtic Otherworld."

The grace of my parents' deaths, the gentle side of that inevitability, comes to me proffered, of course, by love, a new reverence for its nature and reach. Indeed, love lifts the veils between worlds, and there we all find ourselves, witting or not, in its boundlessness. I exult.

2009 National Magazine Award Finalists

Note: All nominated issues are dated 2008 unless otherwise specified. The editor whose name appears in connection with finalists for 2009 held that position, or was listed on the masthead, at the time the issue was published in 2008. In some cases, another editor is now in that position.

General Excellence

This category recognizes overall excellence in magazines in six circulation categories. It honors the effectiveness with which writing, reporting, editing, and design all come together to command readers' attention and fulfill the magazine's unique editorial mission.

Under 100,000 circulation

The American Scholar: Robert Wilson, editor, for Spring, Summer, Autumn issues.

Aperture: Melissa Harris, editor-in-chief, for Spring, Summer, Fall issues.

Bidoun: Lisa Farjam, editor-in-chief, for Winter, Spring/Summer, Fall issues.

Print: Joyce Rutter Kaye, editor-in-chief, for February, April, October issues.

The Virginia Quarterly Review: Ted Genoways, editor, for Winter, Summer, Fall issues.

100,000 to 250,000 circulation

Foreign Policy: Moisés Naím editor-in-chief, for January/February, March/April, May/June issues.

Los Angeles Magazine: Kit Rachlis, editor-in-chief; Mary Melton, executive editor for February, May, November issues.

Mother Jones: Monika Bauerlein and Clara Jeffery, editors, for March/April, May/June, November/December issues.

Paste: Josh Jackson, editor-in-chief, for July, August, October issues.

Time Out New York: Michael Freidson, editor, for June 12–18, December 11–17, December 18–31 issues.

250,000 to 500,000 circulation

The Atlantic: James Bennet, editor, for July/August, November, December issues.

Backpacker: Jonathan Dorn, editor-in-chief, for June, October, November issues.

New York: Adam Moss, editor-in-chief, for March 24, June 23, October 6 issues.

Texas Monthly: Evan Smith, president and editor-in-chief, for May issue; Evan Smith, president and editor-in-chief, Jake Silverstein, editor, for November, December issues.

W: Patrick McCarthy, chairman and editorial director, for September, October, November issues.

500,000 to 1,000,000 circulation

The Economist: John Micklethwait, editor-in-chief, for October 4, November 1, December 20 issues.

Fast Company: Robert Safian, editor and managing director, for June, September, November issues.

GQ: Jim Nelson, editor-in-chief, for July, September, November issues.

Runner's World: David Willey, editor-in-chief, for May, September, October issues.

Wired: Chris Anderson, editor-in-chief, for February, April, November issues.

1,000,000 to 2,000,000 circulation

Bon Appétit: Barbara Fairchild, editor-in-chief, for September, October, December issues.

Field and Stream: Anthony Licata, editor, for May, June, December/January issues.

The New Yorker: David Remnick, editor, for February 11 and 18, May 26, November 17 issues.

Popular Science: Mark Jannot, editor-in-chief, for July, September, November issues.

Vogue: Anna Wintour, editor-in-chief, for March, April, August issues.

Over 2,000,000 circulation

Martha Stewart Living: Martha Stewart, founder; Michael Boodro, editor-in-chief, for August, October, November issues.

National Geographic: Chris Johns, editor-in-chief, for May, July, September issues.

Reader's Digest: Peggy Northrop, editor-in-chief, for June, August, September issues.

Real Simple: Kristin van Ogtrop, managing editor, for February, September, December issues.

Time: Richard Stengel, managing editor, for April 7, September 15, September 29 issues.

Single-Topic Issue

This category recognizes magazines that have devoted an issue to an in-depth examination of one topic. It honors the ambition, comprehensiveness, and imagination with which a magazine treats its subject.

Atlanta Magazine: Rebecca Burns, editor-in-chief, for "King: 40 Years Later," April.

IEEE Spectrum: Susan Hassler, editor-in-chief, for "Special Report: The Singularity," June.

New York: Adam Moss, editor-in-chief, for "The Birth of the Modern City: 1968–2008," October 6.

Newsweek: Jon Meacham, editor, for "How He Did It," November 17.

Saveur: James Oseland, editor-in-chief, for "A World of Breakfast," October.

Magazine Section

This category recognizes excellence of a regular, cohesive section of a magazine, either front- or back-of-book, and composed of a variety of elements, both text and visual. Finalists are selected based on the section's voice, originality, and unified design and packaging.

Best Life: David Zinczenko, editorial director; Stephen Perrine, editor-in-chief, for "It Works for Me" section, February, September, October.

Golf Digest: Jerry Tarde, chairman and editor-in-chief, for "The Digest" section, March, April, May.

Newsweek: Jon Meacham, editor, for its "Periscope" section, February 25, June 30, December 29/January 5.

O, The Oprah Magazine: Oprah Winfrey, founder and editorial director; Amy Gross, editor-in-chief, for its "Reading Room" section, February, May, October.

Wired: Chris Anderson, editor-in-chief, for its "Start" section, September, October, December.

Reporting

This category recognizes excellence in reporting. It honors the enterprise, exclusive reporting, and intelligent analysis that a magazine exhibits in covering an event, a situation, or a problem of contemporary interest and significance.

Fast Company: Robert Safian, editor and managing director, for "China Storms Africa," by Richard Behar, June.

GQ: Jim Nelson, editor-in-chief, for "Papa," by Sean Flynn, April.

GQ: Jim Nelson, editor-in-chief, for "The Longest Night," by Sean Flynn, December.

The New York Times Magazine: Gerald Marzorati, editor-in-chief, for "Right at the Edge," by Dexter Filkins, September 7.

The New Yorker: David Remnick, editor, for "Making It," by Ryan Lizza, July 21.

Public Interest

This category recognizes journalism that sheds new light on an issue of public importance and has the potential to affect national or local debate or policy.

Bicycling: Loren Mooney, editor-in-chief, for "Broken," by David Darlington, January/February.

BusinessWeek: Stephen J. Adler, editor-in-chief, for "Do Cholesterol Drugs Do Any Good?" by John Carey, January 28.

Mother Jones: Monika Bauerlein and Clara Jeffery, editors, for "Torture Hits Home," by Peter Bergen, Michael Mechanic, Justine Sharrock, Eric Umansky, and JoAnn Wypijewski, March/April.

Newsweek: Jon Meacham, editor, for "We Fought Cancer . . . and Cancer Won," by Sharon Begley, September 15.

Vanity Fair: Graydon Carter, editor, for "The Green Light," by Philippe Sands, May.

Feature Writing

This category recognizes excellence in feature writing. It honors the stylishness and originality with which the author treats his or her subject.

The Atlantic: James Bennet, editor, for A Boy's Life, by Hanna Rosin, November.

Esquire: David Granger, editor-in-chief, for "The Things That Carried Him," by Chris Jones, May.

GQ: Jim Nelson, editor-in-chief, for "The Long Shadow of War," by Kathy Dobie, January.

Harper's Magazine: Roger D. Hodge, editor, for "Bleak Houses," by Paul Reyes, October.

The New Yorker: David Remnick, editor, for "Up and Then Down," by Nick Paumgarten, April 21.

Profile Writing

This category recognizes excellence in profile writing. It honors the vividness and perceptiveness with which the writer brings his or her subject to life.

Esquire: David Granger, editor-in-chief, for "Steve Jobs and the Portal to the Invisible," by Tom Junod, October.

GQ: Jim Nelson, editor-in-chief, for "Let God Love Gene Robinson," by Andrew Corsello, July.

The New York Times Magazine: Gerald Marzorati, editor-in-chief, for "Chris Matthews, Seriously . . . ," by Mark Leibovich, April 13.

Rolling Stone: Jann Wenner, editor and publisher; Will Dana, managing editor, for "The Lost Years and Last Days of David Foster Wallace," by David Lipsky, October 30.

Vanity Fair: Graydon Carter, editor, for "Robert Frank's Unsentimental Journey," by Charlie LeDuff, April.

Essays

This category recognizes excellence in essay writing on topics ranging from the personal to the political. Whatever the subject, emphasis should be placed on the author's eloquence, perspective, fresh thinking, and unique voice.

The Antioch Review: Robert S. Fogarty, editor, for "Vickie's Pour House: A Soldier's Peace," by Maureen McCoy, Winter.

Backpacker: Jonathan Dorn, editor-in-chief, for "The Source of All Things," by Tracy Ross, February.

Glamour: Cynthia Leive, editor-in-chief, for "I Want My Life Back," by Andrea Coller, June.

Harper's Magazine: Roger D. Hodge, editor, for "Mandela's Smile," by Breyten Breytenbach, December.

The New Yorker: David Remnick, editor, for "Making Toast," by Roger Rosenblatt, December 15.

Columns and Commentary

This category recognizes excellence in short-form political, social, economic, or humorous commentary. It honors the eloquence, force of argument, and succinctness with which the writer presents his or her views.

Automobile: Jean Jennings, president and editor-in-chief, for three columns by Jamie Kitman, "They Fought the Laws (of Supply and Demand), and the Laws Won," September; "Lease Me to the Moon: The Rise and Fall of Consumer Finance?" November; "Bailout Time for the Big Three. None Dare Call Them Republicans," December.

The Nation: Katrina vanden Heuvel, editor and publisher, for three columns by Naomi Klein, "Disowned by the Ownership Society," February 18; "Obama, Being Called a Muslim Is Not a Smear," March 17; "Obama's Chicago Boys," June 30.

The New Republic: Franklin Foer, editor, for three columns by Jonathan Chait, "Obama Nation," February 13; "Popular Will," May 7; "Scared Yet?" December 31.

The New Yorker: David Remnick, editor, for three columns by Hendrik Hertzberg, "Foreigners," August 4; "Like, Socialism," November 3; "Eight Is Enough," December 1.

Sports Illustrated: Terry McDonell, editor, for three columns by Selena Roberts, "Missing Masters of Augusta," April 21; "Time for Some Horse Sense," May 26; "The Healing Season," September 1.

Reviews and Criticism

This category recognizes excellence in criticism of art, books, movies, television, theater, music, dance, food, dining, fashion, products, and the like. It honors the knowledge, persuasiveness, and original voice that the critic brings to his or her reviews.

The Atlantic: James Bennet, editor, for three columns by Sandra Tsing Loh, "Tales Out of School," March; "I Choose My Choice!" July/August; "Should Women Rule?" November.

The Nation: Katrina vanden Heuvel, editor and publisher, for three columns by William Deresiewicz, "Foes," February 25; "Homing Patterns," October 13; "How Wood Works," December 8.

New York: Adam Moss, editor-in-chief, for three columns by Justin Davidson, "Reconstructionist Judaism," January 14; "The Glass Stampede," September 15; "One's Huge, the Other's Crazy," September 22.

New York: Adam Moss, editor-in-chief, for three reviews by David Edelstein, "Play It Again," May 19; "Bat Out of Hell," July 21; "'Tis the Season . . . ," December 22–29.

The New Yorker: David Remnick, editor, for three columns by James Wood, "Say What?" April 7; "The Homecoming," September 8; "Wounder and Wounded," December 1.

Fiction

This category recognizes excellence in magazine fiction writing. It honors the quality of a publication's literary selections.

The American Scholar: Robert Wilson, editor, for "Royal Blue," by Charles Baxter, Spring; "Happy with Crocodiles," by Jim Shepard, Summer.

The New Yorker: David Remnick, editor, for "Clara," by Roberto Bolaño;August 4; "The Dinner Party," by Joshua Ferris, August 11 and 18.

The New Yorker: David Remnick, editor, for "Them Old Cowboy Songs," by Annie Proulx, May 5; "The Noble Truths of Suffering," by Aleksandar Hemon, September 22.

The Paris Review: Philip Gourevitch, editor, for "Departure," by Alistair Morgan, Summer; "The Lover," by Damon Galgut, Winter.

The Virginia Quarterly Review: Ted Genoways, editor, for "Asal," by Sana Krasikov, Summer; "Tale of the Teahouse," by Kanishk Tharoor, Summer.

Personal Service

This category recognizes excellence in service journalism. The advice or instruction presented should help readers improve the quality of their lives in areas that are core to their personal well-being.

Esquire: David Granger, editor-in-chief, for "Retool, Reboot, Rebuild," by Mehmet Oz, M.D., and Michael Roizen, M.D., May; "Seventy-Five," by Susan Casey, May.

Family Circle: Linda Fears, editor-in-chief, for "Power Play," by Scott Alexander, November 1.

Health: Ellen Kunes, editor-in-chief, for a three-part series, "Read This Before You Go to the Hospital," by Lorie A. Parch, July/August; "Danger at Your Doctor's Office," by Lorie A. Parch, September; "Warning: This Rx May Be Harmful to Your Health," by Cara Birnbaum, November.

More: Lesley Jane Seymour, editor-in-chief, for "The Endangered Uterus," by Peg Rosen, December/January.

Prevention: Liz Vaccariello, senior vice president/editor-in-chief, for "Is Your Parent Over-medicated?" by Siri Carpenter, December.

Leisure Interests

This category recognizes excellent service journalism about leisure-time pursuits. The practical advice or instruction presented should help readers enjoy hobbies or other recreational interests.

Esquire: David Granger, editor-in-chief, for "The Esquire Encyclopedia of Sandwiches," by Scott Raab, March.

Esquire: David Granger, editor-in-chief, for "The Esquire Almanac of Steak," September.

Field & Stream: Anthony Licata, editor, for "Best of Summer Fishing," by John Merwin, June.

The New Yorker: David Remnick, editor, for three columns by Patricia Marx, "Buy Shanghai!" July 21; "Sole Sisters," September 1; "The Price Is Right," December 8.

Texas Monthly: Evan Smith, president and editor-in-chief, for "BBQ08," June.

Design

This category recognizes excellence in magazine design. The award honors the effectiveness of overall design, artwork, graphics, and typography in enhancing a magazine's unique mission and personality.

Bon Appétit: Barbara Fairchild, editor-in-chief; Matthew Lenning, design director, for July, August, December issues.

Good: Zach Frechette, editor-in-chief; Scott Stowell, design director; Casey Caplowe, creative director, for January/February, March/April, May/June issues.

GQ: Jim Nelson, editor-in-chief; Fred Woodward, design director; Jim Moore, creative director, for June, November, December issues.

New York: Adam Moss, editor-in-chief; Chris Dixon, design director, for March 24, June 9, October 6 issues.

Wired: Chris Anderson, editor-in-chief; Scott Dadich, creative director; Wyatt Mitchell, design director, for February, June, November issues.

Photography

This category recognizes excellence in magazine photography. It honors the effectiveness of photography, photojournalism, and photo illustration in enhancing a magazine's unique mission and personality.

Bon Appétit: Barbara Fairchild, editor-in-chief; Matthew Lenning, design director; Elizabeth Mathews, photo editor, for August, September, October issues.

GQ: Jim Nelson, editor-in-chief; Fred Woodward, design director; Jim Moore, creative director; Anton Ioukhnovets, art director; Dora Somosi, director of photography, for August, November, December issues.

National Geographic: Chris Johns, editor-in-chief; David Griffin, director of photography; Kurt F. Mutchler and Susan A. Smith, deputy directors, photography, for May, July, November issues.

T: The New York Times Style Magazine: Gerald Marzorati, editor-in-chief; Stefano Tonchi, editor; Janet Froelich, creative director; David Sebbah, art director; Kathy Ryan, director of photography; Judith Puckett-Rinella, photo editor, for August 17, September 7, December 7 issues.

W: Patrick McCarthy, chairman and editorial director; Dennis Freedman, creative director; Edward Leida, group design director; Nathalie Kirsheh, art director; Nadia Vellam, photo editor, for March, April, September issues.

Photojournalism

This category recognizes the informative photographic documentation of an event or subject in real time. Photo essays accompanied by text are judged primarily on the strength of the photographs.

Harper's Magazine: Roger D. Hodge, editor; Stacey D. Clarkson, art director, for "Life and Death," photographs by Lynsey Addario, November.

National Geographic: Chris Johns, editor-in-chief; David Griffin, director of photography; Kurt F. Mutchler and Susan A. Smith, deputy directors, photography, for "Who Murdered the Virunga Gorillas?" by Mark Jenkins, photographs by Brent Stirton, July.

The New York Times Magazine: Gerald Marzorati, editor-in-chief; Kathy Ryan, director of photography; Janet Froelich, creative director; Arem Duplessis, art director, for "A Cutting Tradition," by Sara Corbett, photographs by Stephanie Sinclair, January 20.

The New York Times Magazine: Gerald Marzorati, editor-in-chief; Kathy Ryan, director of photography; Janet Froelich, creative director; Arem Duplessis, art director, for "Children of God," by Sara Corbett, photographs by Stephanie Sinclair, July 27.

Time: Richard Stengel, managing editor; Arthur Hochstein, art director, for "The Forgotten Plague," by Alice Park, photographs by James Nachtwey, October 13.

Photo Portfolio

This category honors creative photography and photo illustration.

Bon Appétit: Barbara Fairchild, editor-in-chief; Matthew Lenning, design director; Bailey Franklin, photo editor; Robert Festino, senior art director, for "A Heritage Feast," by Nancy Oakes and Pamela Mazzola; photography portfolio by Tim Morris, November.

GQ: Jim Nelson, editor-in-chief; Fred Woodward, design director; Jim Moore, creative director; Dora Simosi, director of photography; Anton Ioukhnovets, art director; Krista Prestek, senior photo editor, for "Who It Takes," photographs by Jeff Riedel, November.

Gourmet: Ruth Reichl, editor-in-chief; Richard Ferretti, creative director; Erika Oliveira, art director; Amy Koblenzer, photo editor, for "Out of Sight," recipes by Shelley Wiseman; photographs by Romulo Yanes, December.

The New Yorker: David Remnick, editor; Elisabeth Biondi, visuals editor, for "Service," portfolio by Platon, September 29.

W: Patrick McCarthy, chairman and editorial director; Dennis Freedman, creative director; Edward Leida, group design director; Nathalie Kirsheh, art director; Nadia Vellam, photo editor; Anita Bethel, photo and imaging director, for "Come on Down to Nawlins," photographed by Bruce Weber; styled by Karl Temper, April.

General Excellence Online

This category recognizes excellence in magazine Web sites, as well as online-only magazines that publish original content. The site must convey a distinct editorial identity and create a unique magazine environment on the Web.

Fewer than 1,000,000 average monthly unique visitors

Backpacker.com (www.backpacker.com): Jonathan Dorn, editor-in-chief; Anthony Cerretani, online editor.

MotherJones.com (www.motherjones.com): Clara Jeffery and Monika Bauerlein, editors.

Parenting.com (www.parenting.com): Rachel Fishman Feddersen, director.

RunnersWorld.com (www.runnersworld.com): David Willey, editor-in-chief; Mark Remy, executive editor; George Vlahogiannis, executive producer.

Triple Canopy (www.canopycanopycanopy.com): Sam Frank and Alexander Provan, editors; Caleb Waldorf, creative director.

At least 1,000,000 average monthly unique visitors

BusinessWeek.com (www.businessweek.com): Stephen Adler, editor-in-chief.

Chow.com (www.chow.com): Jane Goldman, editor-in-chief.

NationalGeographic.com (www.ngm.com): Chris Johns, editor-in-chief; Rob Covey, creative director and managing editor, ngm.com.

Nymag.com (http://nymag.com): Adam Moss, editor-in-chief; Kelly Maloni, director of P.D. and editorial operations; Ben Williams, editorial director, nymag .com.

Time.com (www.time.com): Josh Tyrangiel, editor, *Time.com*; assistant managing editor, *Time*.

Personal Service Online

This category recognizes excellent service journalism on the Web. The practical advice or instruction presented should help readers either improve the quality of their personal lives or enjoy recreational pursuits. The category honors a site's effective use of multimedia technology that users can act on.

Backpacker.com—"Maps Project" (www.backpacker.com/hikes): Jonathan Dorn, editor-in-chief; Anthony Cerretani, online editor; Kris Wagner, map editor.

CNNMoney.com—"Ultimate Guide to Retirement" (http://money.cnn.com/ retirement/guide): Craig Matters, managing editor, *Money*; Chris Peacock, editor and vice president, *CNNMoney.com*.

Gourmet.com—"Favorite Cookies: 1941–2008" (www.gourmet.com/recipes/cookies): Ruth Reichl, editor-in-chief; Adam Houghtaling, editorial director

Health.com—"Journey" (www.health.com): Scott Mowbray, editorial director

RunnersWorld.com—"Half-Marathon Challenge" (www.runnersworld.com): David Willey, editor-in-chief; Mark Remy, executive editor; George Vlahogiannis, executive producer

Interactive Feature

This category recognizes an outstanding feature or section of a Web site that uses multimedia technology, tools, community platforms, or other interactive formats to deliver or share content such as news, information, and entertainment, rather than practical instruction or advice.

AARP The Magazine Online—"1968: The Year That Rocked Our World" (www .aarpmagazine.org/people/1968): Nancy Perry Graham, editor-in-chief; Julie Feiner, online content producer; Marilyn Milloy, features editor

Epicurious.com—"Recipe Box" (www.epicurious.com): Tanya Wenman Steel, editor-in-chief

NationalGeographic.com—"Your Shot" (www.ngm.com): Chris Johns, editor-in-chief; Rob Covey, creative director and managing editor, ngm.com

Salon Magazine—"Open Salon" (www.salon.com): Joan Walsh, editor-in-chief; Kerry Lauerman, Open Salon director

Wired.com—"iPhone3G" (www.wired.com): Evan Hansen, editor-in-chief

Judges, 2009

* Indicates judging leader
NOTE: affiliations listed are at the time of the judging

Stephen J. Adler	*BusinessWeek*
Benjamin Anastas	*Author*
Miriam Arond	*Good Housekeeping Research Institute*
Amy Astley	*Teen Vogue*
Richard Babcock	*Chicago Magazine*
Florian Bachleda	*FB Design*
Glenda Bailey	*Harper's Bazaar*
Lisa Bain	*Parenting*
Jenny Barnett	
Dirk Barnett	*Blender*
Elizabeth Barr	*Time Out New York Partners, LP*
Jennifer Barr	*Travel +Leisure*
Seth D. Bauer	*National Geographic's Green Guide*
Maria Baugh	*Glamour*
Julie Belcove	*W*
Melina Gerosa Bellows*	*National Geographic Kids*
Keith Bellows*	*National Geographic Traveler*
Gary Belsky	*ESPN The Magazine*
Giselle Benatar	*ConsumerReports.org*
Lisa Benenson	*Hallmark*
James Bennet	*The Atlantic*
Elisabeth Biondi	*The New Yorker*
Debra Birnbaum	*TV Guide*
Deborah Bishop	*More*
Kent Black	*Outside's Go*
Janet Bodnar	*Kiplinger's Personal Finance*
Michael Boodro	
Dana Bowen	*Saveur*
Arabella Bowen	*Sherman's Travel*
Richard Bradley	*Worth*
Millie Martini Bratten	*Brides*
Nicola Bridges	*Prevention.com*
Douglas Brod	*Spin*

Daniel Brogan	*5280 Magazine*
Peter Brown	*Scientific American*
Merrill Brown	*NowPublic.com*
Johanna Buchholtz-Torres	*Siempre Mujer*
James Burnett	*Boston Magazine*
Rebecca Burns	*Atlanta Magazine*
Angela Burt-Murray*	*Essence*
Gayle Butler*	*Better Homes and Gardens*
John Byrne	*BusinessWeek*
Michael Carroll	*Institutional Investor*
Karen Carroll	*Southern Accents*
Michael Caruso	*TheDailyTube.com*
Catherine Cavender	*Diversion*
Andrea Chambers	*New York University*
Janet Chan*	
Bob Cohn	*The Atlantic Online*
Roger Cohn	*Yale Environment 360*
Joanna Coles	*Marie Claire*
Amy Conway	*Consumer Reports*
Jennifer Cook	*Good Housekeeping*
Corynne Corbett	*Chic Jones Media, LLC*
Evan Cornog	*Columbia Journalism Review*
Dana Cowin	*Food & Wine*
Jennifer Crandall	*O, The Oprah Magazine*
Jonathan Dahl	*SmartMoney*
Will Dana	*Rolling Stone*
Lucy Danziger*	*Self*
Greg Daugherty	*Consumer Reports*
Maxine Davidowitz	
Hugh Delehanty	*AARP The Magazine*
Paula Derrow	*Self*
Ben W. Dickinson	*ELLE*
Karen Dillon	*Inc.*
Jonathan Dorn	*Backpacker*
Stephen Drucker	*House Beautiful*
Arem Duplessis	*The New York Times Magazine*
Alfred Edmond Jr.*	*BlackEnterprise*
Eric Effron	*The Week*
Rosemary Ellis*	*Good Housekeeping*
Sid Evans	*Garden & Gun*

Maryjane Fahey	*Maryjane Fahey Design*
Ellen Fair	
Kate Ferguson	*Real Health*
Dan Ferrara	*Inc.*
Paul Fichtenbaum	*SI.com*
Peter Flax	*Runner's World*
Ariel Foxman	*InStyle*
Janet Froelich	*The New York Times Magazine*
Mary Gannon	*Poets & Writers Magazine*
Ted Genoways	*Virginia Quarterly Review*
Pilar Gerasimo	*Experience Life*
Betsy Gleick	*People*
Klara Glowczewska	*Condé Nast Traveler*
Jon Gluck	*New York Magazine*
Thomas Goetz	*Wired*
Amy Goldwasser	*ELLE*
Susan Goodall	*Glamour*
Lisa Gosselin	*Eating Well*
Kellie Gould	*SheAndMe.com*
Nancy Perry Graham	*AARP The Magazine*
David Granger	*Esquire*
Sam Grawe	*Dwell*
Charles Green	*National Journal*
Jodie Green	*Waterfront Media*
Freddi Greenberg	
Edward Grinnan	*Guideposts*
Pilar Guzmàn	*Cookie*
Larry Hackett*	*People*
Rachel Hager	
Ann Hallock	*Disney Publishing Worldwide*
Tish Hamilton	*Runner's World*
Douglas Harbrecht	*Kiplinger's Personal Finance*
Melissa Harris	*Aperture Magazine*
Susan Hassler	*IEEE Spectrum*
Roseann Henry	*Waterfront Media*
Jill Herzig	*Glamour*
Lindy Hess	*Columbia University*
Hylah Hill	*This Old House*
Roger D. Hodge	*Harper's Magazine*
Vanessa Holden	*Martha Stewart Weddings*

William Horne	*World War II & MHQ Magazines*
Gail Horwood	*Martha Stewart Living Omnimedia, Inc.*
Michael Hoyt	*Columbia Journalism Review*
Laura Hughes	*Elite Traveler*
Adi Ignatius	*Harvard Business Review*
William Inman	*Bloomberg News Online*
Robert Ivy	*Architectural Record*
Josh Jackson	*Paste*
Andrzej Janerka	*Andrez Janerka Design*
Mark Jannot	*Popular Science*
Clara Jeffery	*Mother Jones*
Christopher Johns	*National Geographic*
Dorothy Kalins	*Dorothy Kalins Ink, LLC*
James Kaminsky	*Maxim*
Susan Kane	*The Parenting Group*
Janice Kaplan	*Parade*
Eliot Kaplan	*Hearst Magazines*
Lucy Kaylin	*Marie Claire*
Bruce Kelley	*San Francisco Magazine*
James Kelly	*Time Inc.*
Christopher Keyes	*Outside*
Kimberly Kleman	*Consumer Reports*
Sally Koslow	
Laurie Kratochvil	*Reader's Digest Development*
Ellen Kunes	*Health*
Diana La Guardia	
Steven Lagerfeld	*The Wilson Quarterly*
Frank Lalli	*Reader's Digest Association, Inc.*
Julie Lasky	*ID Magazine*
Kate Lawler	*Parents*
Cynthia Leive*	*Glamour*
Nicholas Lemann	*Columbia University*
Jacqueline Leo*	*The Peter G. Peterson Foundation*
Ellen Levine	*Hearst Magazines*
Carla Levy	*Self*
Anthony Licata	*Field & Stream*
Joanne Lipman	*Condé Nast Portfolio*
Emily Listfield	
Robert Love	*Best Life*
Susan Lyne	*Gilt Groupe*

Stephen Madden	*Rodale International*
Paul Maidment	*Forbes*
Paul Martinez	*Men's Journal*
Gerald Marzorati	*The New York Times Magazine*
Valerie May	*AARP The Magazine*
Pamela McCarthy*	*The New Yorker*
Terry McDonell*	*Sports Illustrated*
Kevin McKean	*Consumer Reports*
Jon Meacham	*Newsweek*
James B. Meigs*	*Popular Mechanics*
Francesca Messina	*McGraw-Hill Construction*
Sarah Gray Miller	*Country Living*
Keija Minor	*Uptown Magazine*
Peg Moline	*Fit Pregnancy/Mom & Baby*
Terence Monmaney	*Smithsonian*
Loren Mooney	*Bicycling*
Lisa Moran	*BabyTalk*
Kitty Morgan	*Better Homes and Gardens*
Stacy Morrison	*Redbook*
David Morrow	*TheStreet.com*
Marcy O'Koon Moss	*Arthritis Today*
Adam Moss*	*New York Magazine*
Cullen Murphy*	*Vanity Fair*
Moisés ;Naím	*Foreign Policy*
Christopher Napolitano	*Playboy*
Silvana Nardone	*Every Day with Rachael Ray*
Victor Navasky	*Columbia University*
Deborah Needleman	*Domino*
Jim Nelson	*GQ*
Robert Newman	*Newman Design*
Judith Nolte	*American Baby*
Peggy Northrop	*Reader's Digest*
Nancy Novogrod	*Travel +Leisure*
Barbara O'Dair	*Reader's Digest*
Melissa O'Neil	*Self*
Stacy Palmer	*The Chronicle of Philanthropy*
John Papanek	*ESPN Digital Media*
Jeannie Park	
Deborah Paul	*Emmis Communications*
Chee Pearlman	*Chee Company*

Abe Peck	*Northwestern University*
Jodi Peckman	*Rolling Stone*
Robert Perino	*Fortune*
Stephen Perrine	*Best Life*
Stephen L. Petranek	*Weider History Group*
George Pitts	*Parsons The New School for Design*
Larry Platt	*Philadelphia Magazine*
Sean Plottner	*Dartmouth Alumni Magazine*
Dana Points	*Parents*
Michele Promaulayko	*Women's Health*
Debra Puchalla	*Martha Stewart Living*
Kaitlin Quistgaard	*Yoga Journal*
Kit Rachlis	*Los Angeles Magazine*
John Rasmus*	*National Geographic Adventure*
Susan Reed	*O, The Oprah Magazine*
John Rennie	*Scientific American*
Evelyn Renold	
Laura Rich	*CNN Money/RecessionWire.com*
Susan Strecker Richard	*Caring Today*
Suzanne Riss	*Working Mother*
Paul Ritter	*ELLE*
Kerry Robertson	*O, The Oprah Magazine*
Meredith Kahn Rollins	*Lucky*
Caitlin Roper	*The Paris Review*
Mark Rozzo	*Men's Vogue*
Margaret Russell	*ELLE Decor*
Geoff Russell	*Golf World*
Robert Safian	*Fast Company*
Ina Saltz	*Saltz Design*
Diane Salvatore	
Chad Schlegel	*Entertainment Weekly*
David Schonauer	*American Photo*
Cynthia Hall Searight	*Self*
David Seideman	*Audubon*
Ellen Seidman	*Glamour*
Philip Semas	*The Chronicle of Higher Education*
Andrew Serwer	*Fortune*
Shannon Sexton	*Yoga +Joyful Living*
Lesley Jane Seymour	*More*
Bill Shapiro	*Time Inc.*

Stephen Shepard	*City University of New York*
Linda Shiner	*Air & Space/Smithsonian Magazine*
Ann Shoket	*Seventeen*
Thomas Shoop	*Government Executive*
Mitch Shostak	*Shostak Studios, Inc.*
Jake Silverstein	*Texas Monthly*
Anne Simpkinson	*Guideposts*
Margot Slade	*Bloomberg Markets*
Steve Slon	
Gretchen Smelter	*Brides*
Todd Smith	*Outdoor Life*
Courtenay Smith	*Prevention*
Larry Smith	*SMITH Magazine*
Nancy Soriano*	
Robin Sparkman	*American Lawyer Media*
Mark Spellun	*Plenty*
Sreenath Sreenivasan*	*Columbia University*
Mike Steele	*Us Weekly*
Lisa Stiepock	*Wondertime*
Cyndi Stivers*	*Entertainment Weekly*
Richard David Story*	*Departures*
Jay Stowe	*Cincinnati Magazine*
Katie Tamony	*Sunset*
Casey Tierney	*Real Simple*
Sheryl Hilliard Tucker	*Time Inc.*
Susan Ungaro	*The James Beard Foundation*
Mimi Valdés Ryan	*Latina*
Antonia van der Meer	*Modern Bride, Elegant Bride, Your Prom*
Kristin van Ogtrop*	*Real Simple*
Norman Vanamee	*Sherman's Travel*
Victoria von Biel	*Bon Appétit*
Donna Warner	*Metropolitan Home*
Mark Warren	*Esquire*
Ben Wasserstein	*The New Republic*
Jacob Weisberg*	*Slate*
Matt Welch	*Reason*
Linda Wells	*Allure*
Charles Whitaker	*Northwestern University*
Brad Wieners	*Men's Journal*
Emil Wilbekin*	*Giant*

David Willey*	*Runner's World*
John Willoughby	*Gourmet*
Robert S. Wilson	*The American Scholar*
Patti Wolter	*Northwestern University*
Betty Wong	*Fitness*
Jay Woodruff	*Alpha Media Group*
David Zinczenko	*Men's Health*
David Zivan	*Indianapolis Monthly*

National Magazine Award Winners, 1966–2009

Best Interactive Design

2001   SmartMoney.com

Columns and Commentary

2002   New York
2003   The Nation
2004   New York
2005   National Journal
2006   The New Yorker
2007   Vanity Fair
2008   Rolling Stone
2009   Automobile

Design

1980   Geo
1981   Attenzione
1982   Nautical Quarterly
1983   New York
1984   House & Garden
1985   Forbes
1986   Time
1987   Elle
1988   Life
1989   Rolling Stone
1990   Esquire
1991   Condé Nast Traveler
1992   Vanity Fair
1993   Harper's Bazaar
1994   Allure
1995   Martha Stewart Living
1996   Wired
1997   I.D.
1998   Entertainment Weekly

1999   ESPN The Magazine
2000   Fast Company
2001   Nest
2002   Details
2003   Details
2004   Esquire
2005   Kids: Fun Stuff to Do
        Together
2006   New York
2007   New York
2008   Wired
2009   Wired

Essays

2000   The Sciences
2001   The New Yorker
2002   The New Yorker
2003   The American Scholar
2004   The New Yorker
2005   National Geographic
2006   Vanity Fair
2007   The Georgia Review
2008   New Letters
2009   Backpacker

Essays and Criticism

1978   Esquire
1979   Life
1980   Natural History
1981   Time
1982   The Atlantic
1983   The American Lawyer
1984   The New Republic

1985	*Boston Magazine*			

1985   *Boston Magazine*
1986   *The Sciences*
1987   *Outside*
1988   *Harper's Magazine*
1989   *Harper's Magazine*
1990   *Vanity Fair*
1991   *The Sciences*
1992   *The Nation*
1993   *The American Lawyer*
1994   *Harper's Magazine*
1995   *Harper's Magazine*
1996   *The New Yorker*
1997   *The New Yorker*
1998   *The New Yorker*
1999   *The Atlantic Monthly*

Feature Writing

1988   *The Atlantic*
1989   *Esquire*
1990   *The Washingtonian*
1991   *U.S. News & World Report*
1992   *Sports Illustrated*
1993   *The New Yorker*
1994   *Harper's Magazine*
1995   *GQ*
1996   *GQ*
1997   *Sports Illustrated*
1998   *Harper's Magazine*
1999   *The American Scholar*
2000   *Sports Illustrated*
2001   *Rolling Stone*
2002   *The Atlantic Monthly*
2003   *Harper's Magazine*
2004   *The New Yorker*
2005   *Esquire*
2006   *The American Scholar*
2007   *GQ*
2008   *Atlanta*
2009   *Esquire*

Fiction

1978   *The New Yorker*
1979   *The Atlantic Monthly*
1980   *Antaeus*
1981   *The North American Review*
1982   *The New Yorker*
1983   *The North American Review*
1984   *Seventeen*
1985   *Playboy*
1986   *The Georgia Review*
1987   *Esquire*
1988   *The Atlantic*
1989   *The New Yorker*
1990   *The New Yorker*
1991   *Esquire*
1992   *Story*
1993   *The New Yorker*
1994   *Harper's Magazine*
1995   *Story*
1996   *Harper's Magazine*
1997   *The New Yorker*
1998   *The New Yorker*
1999   *Harper's Magazine*
2000   *The New Yorker*
2001   *Zoetrope: All-Story*
2002   *The New Yorker*
2003   *The New Yorker*
2004   *Esquire*
2005   *The Atlantic Monthly*
2006   *The Virginia Quarterly Review*
2007   *McSweeney's*
2008   *Harper's Magazine*
2009   *The New Yorker*

Fiction and Belles Lettres

1970   *Redbook*
1971   *Esquire*

1972	*Mademoiselle*		*Parents*
1973	*The Atlantic Monthly*		*The Sciences*
1974	*The New Yorker*	1989	*American Heritage*
1975	*Redbook*		*Sports Illustrated*
1976	*Essence*		*The Sciences*
1977	*Mother Jones*		*Vanity Fair*
		1990	*Metropolitan Home*

General Excellence

			7 Days
			Sports Illustrated
1973	*BusinessWeek*		*Texas Monthly*
1981	*ARTnews*	1991	*Condé Nast Traveler*
	Audubon		*Glamour*
	BusinessWeek		*Interview*
	Glamour		*The New Republic*
1982	*Camera Arts*	1992	*Mirabella*
	Newsweek		*National Geographic*
	Rocky Mountain Magazine		*The New Republic*
	Science81		*Texas Monthly*
1983	*Harper's Magazine*	1993	*American Photo*
	Life		*The Atlantic Monthly*
	Louisiana Life		*Lingua Franca*
	Science82		*Newsweek*
1984	*The American Lawyer*	1994	*BusinessWeek*
	House & Garden		*Health*
	National Geographic		*Print*
	Outside		*Wired*
1985	*American Health*	1995	*Entertainment Weekly*
	American Heritage		*I.D. Magazine*
	Manhattan, Inc.		*Men's Journal*
	Time		*The New Yorker*
1986	*Discover*	1996	*BusinessWeek*
	Money		*Civilization*
	New England Monthly		*Outside*
	3-2-1-Contact		*The Sciences*
1987	*Common Cause*	1997	*I.D. Magazine*
	Elle		*Outside*
	New England Monthly		*Vanity Fair*
	People Weekly		*Wired*
1988	*Fortune*	1998	*DoubleTake*
	Hippocrates		*Outside*

Preservation
Rolling Stone
1999   Condé Nast Traveler
Fast Company
I.D. Magazine
Vanity Fair
2000   National Geographic
Nest
The New Yorker
Saveur
2001   The American Scholar
Mother Jones
The New Yorker
Teen People
2002   Entertainment Weekly
National Geographic
Adventure
Newsweek
Print
Vibe
2003   Architectural Record
The Atlantic Monthly
ESPN the Magazine
Foreign Policy
Parenting
Texas Monthly
2004   Aperture
Budget Living
Chicago Magazine
Gourmet
Newsweek
Popular Science
2005   Dwell
Glamour
Martha Stewart Weddings
The New Yorker
Print
Wired
2006   ESPN The Magazine
Esquire

Harper's Magazine
New York
Time
The Virginia Quarterly
Review
2007   Bulletin of the Atomic
Scientists
Foreign Policy
National Geographic
New York
Rolling Stone
Wired
2008   Backpacker
GQ
Mother Jones
National Geographic
The New Yorker
Print
2009   Field & Stream
Foreign Policy
Print
Reader's Digest
Texas Monthly
Wired

General Excellence in New Media

1997   Money
1998   The Sporting News Online
1999   Cigar Aficionado
2000   BusinessWeek Online

General Excellence Online (Formerly General Excellence in New Media)

2001   U.S. News Online
2002   National Geographic
Magazine Online
2003   Slate

2004   CNET News.com
2005   Style.com
2006   National Geographic
            Online
2007   Beliefnet.com
2008   RunnersWorld.com

**General Excellence Online
(Fewer than 1 million average
monthly unique visitors)**

2009   Backpacker.com

**General Excellence Online
(At least 1 million average
monthly unique visitors)**

2009   nymag.com

Interactive Feature

2007   nymag.com
2008   Bicycling.com
2009   AARP the Magazine Online

Interactive Service

2007   BusinessWeek.com

**Personal Service Online
(Formerly Interactive Service)**

2008   BusinessWeek.com
2009   Backpacker.com

**Leisure Interests
(Formerly Special Interests)**

2002   Vogue
2003   National Geographic
            Adventure

2004   Consumer Reports
2005   Sports Illustrated
2006   Golf
2007   O, The Oprah
            Magazine
2008   New York
2009   Esquire

Magazine Section

2005   Popular Science
2006   Backpacker
2007   New York
2008   Condé Nast Portfolio
2009   Wired

Personal Service

1986   Farm Journal
1987   Consumer Reports
1988   Money
1989   Good Housekeeping
1990   Consumer Reports
1991   New York
1992   Creative Classroom
1993   Good Housekeeping
1994   Fortune
1995   SmartMoney
1996   SmartMoney
1997   Glamour
1998   Men's Journal
1999   Good Housekeeping
2000   PC Computing
2001   National Geographic
            Adventure
2002   National Geographic
            Adventure
2003   Outside
2004   Men's Health
2005   BabyTalk

2006	*Self*
2007	*Glamour*
2008	*Popular Mechanics*
2009	*Esquire*

Photography

1985	*Life*
1986	*Vogue*
1987	*National Geographic*
1988	*Rolling Stone*
1989	*National Geographic*
1990	*Texas Monthly*
1991	*National Geographic*
1992	*National Geographic*
1993	*Harper's Bazaar*
1994	*Martha Stewart Living*
1995	*Rolling Stone*
1996	*Saveur*
1997	*National Geographic*
1998	*W*
1999	*Martha Stewart Living*
2000	*Vanity Fair*
2001	*National Geographic*
2002	*Vanity Fair*
2003	*Condé Nast Traveler*
2004	*City*
2005	*Gourmet*
2006	*W*
2007	*National Geographic*
2008	*Gourmet*
2009	*GQ*

Photojournalism

2007	*The Paris Review*
2008	*National Geographic*
2009	*National Geographic*

Photo Portfolio

2007	*City*
2008	*Vanity Fair*
2009	*The New Yorker*

Photo Portfolio/Photo Essay

2004	*W*
2005	*Time*
2006	*Rolling Stone*

Profile Writing

2000	*Sports Illustrated*
2001	*The New Yorker*
2002	*The New Yorker*
2003	*Sports Illustrated*
2004	*Esquire*
2005	*The New Yorker*
2006	*Esquire*
2007	*New York*
2008	*Vanity Fair*
2009	*Rolling Stone*

Public Interest (Formerly Public Service)

1986	*Science85*
1987	*Money*
1988	*The Atlantic*
1989	*California*
1990	*Southern Exposure*
1991	*Family Circle*
1992	*Glamour*
1993	*The Family Therapy Networker*
1994	*Philadelphia*
1995	*The New Republic*

1996	Texas Monthly		1974	The New Yorker
1997	Fortune		1975	The New Yorker
1998	The Atlantic Monthly		1976	Audubon
1999	Time		1977	Audubon
2000	The New Yorker		1978	The New Yorker
2001	Time		1979	Texas Monthly
2002	The Atlantic Monthly		1980	Mother Jones
2003	The Atlantic Monthly		1981	National Journal
2004	The New Yorker		1982	The Washingtonian
2005	The New Yorker		1983	Institutional Investor
2006	The New Yorker		1984	Vanity Fair
2007	Vanity Fair		1985	Texas Monthly
2008	The Nation		1986	Rolling Stone
2009	Bicycling		1987	Life
			1988	The Washingtonian

Public Service

				and Baltimore
				Magazine
1970	Life		1989	The New Yorker
1971	The Nation		1990	The New Yorker
1972	Philadelphia		1991	The New Yorker
1974	Scientific American		1992	The New Republic
1975	Consumer Reports		1993	IEEE Spectrum
1976	BusinessWeek		1994	The New Yorker
1977	Philadelphia		1995	The Atlantic Monthly
1978	Mother Jones		1996	The New Yorker
1979	New West		1997	Outside
1980	Texas Monthly		1998	Rolling Stone
1981	Reader's Digest		1999	Newsweek
1982	The Atlantic		2000	Vanity Fair
1983	Foreign Affairs		2001	Esquire
1984	The New Yorker		2002	The Atlantic Monthly
1985	The Washingtonian		2003	The New Yorker
			2004	Rolling Stone
			2005	The New Yorker
			2006	Rolling Stone

Reporting

			2007	Esquire
1970	The New Yorker		2008	National Geographic
1971	The Atlantic Monthly		2009	The New York Times
1972	The Atlantic Monthly			Magazine
1973	New York			

Reviews and Criticism

2000	Esquire
2001	The New Yorker
2002	Harper's Magazine
2003	Vanity Fair
2004	Esquire
2005	The New Yorker
2006	Harper's Magazine
2007	The Nation
2008	The Atlantic
2009	The New Yorker

Service to the Individual

1974	Sports Illustrated
1975	Esquire
1976	Modern Medicine
1977	Harper's Magazine
1978	Newsweek
1979	The American Journal of Nursing
1980	Saturday Review
1982	Philadelphia
1983	Sunset
1984	New York
1985	The Washingtonian

Single Awards

1966	Look
1967	Life
1968	Newsweek
1969	American Machinist

Single-Topic Issue

1979	Progressive Architecture
1980	Scientific American
1981	BusinessWeek

1982	Newsweek
1983	IEEE Spectrum
1984	Esquire
1985	American Heritage
1986	IEEE Spectrum
1987	Bulletin of the Atomic Scientists
1988	Life
1989	Hippocrates
1990	National Geographic
1991	The American Lawyer
1992	BusinessWeek
1993	Newsweek
1994	Health
1995	Discover
1996	Bon Appétit
1997	Scientific American
1998	The Sciences
1999	The Oxford American
2002	Time
2003	Scientific American
2004	The Oxford American
2005	Newsweek
2006	Time
2007	Departures
2008	The Virginia Quarterly Review
2009	Saveur

Special Awards

1976	Time
1989	Robert E. Kenyon Jr.

Special Interests

1986	Popular Mechanics
1987	Sports Afield
1988	Condé Nast Traveler
1989	Condé Nast Traveler

1990	Art & Antiques
1991	New York
1992	Sports Afield
1993	Philadelphia
1994	Outside
1995	GQ
1996	Saveur
1997	Smithsonian
1998	Entertainment Weekly
1999	PC Computing
2000	I.D. Magazine
2001	The New Yorker

Specialized Journalism

1970	Philadelphia
1971	Rolling Stone
1972	Architectural Record
1973	Psychology Today
1974	Texas Monthly

1975	Medical Economics
1976	United Mine Workers Journal
1977	Architectural Record
1978	Scientific American
1979	National Journal
1980	IEEE Spectrum

Visual Excellence

1970	Look
1971	Vogue
1972	Esquire
1973	Horizon
1974	Newsweek
1975	Country Journal National Lampoon
1976	Horticulture
1977	Rolling Stone
1978	Architectural Digest
1979	Audubon

Permissions

Contributors

TOM CHIARELLA is writer-at-large for *Esquire* magazine, where he also serves as fiction editor. He is currently visiting professor of creative writing at DePauw University. His book, *The Proposition*, is upcoming from Crown.

DAVID DARLINGTON is the Berkeley-based author of the books *In Condor Country, Angels' Visits* (later retitled *Zin*), *The Mojave*, and *Area 51*. Winner of the 2008 James Beard Foundation Award for magazine writing about wine, his forthcoming book about the California wine industry will be published by Harper Collins.

JUSTIN DAVIDSON joined *New York* magazine as its classical music and architecture critic in September 2007, having previously worked as *Newsday*'s classical music critic since 1996. In 2002, he won a Pulitzer Prize for criticism and that year added the architecture beat to his portfolio. He has written about both music and architecture for *The New Yorker* and has also contributed to the *Los Angeles Times, Slate, Salon*, and *Opera News*. He is a regular columnist for the Web site E-music.com and a periodic guest on the WNYC music talk show *Soundcheck*.

SEAN FLYNN is a correspondent for *GQ* and has written three books, including *3000 Degrees: The True Story of a Deadly Fire and the Men Who Fought It*. He received the National Magazine Award for reporting in 2000 and was a finalist twice this year in that same category. His work also has been anthologized in *Best American Sports Writing, Best American Travel Writing*, and *Best American Crime Reporting*.

CHRIS JONES is a writer at large for *Esquire*. Before joining the magazine in 2002, he was a sports writer for the *National Post*, where in 2000 he was named Canada's Outstanding Young

Journalist. In 2005, he won a National Magazine Award in feature writing for his *Esquire* story "Home," about astronauts aboard the international space station. In the fall of 2009, Jones will teach nonfiction writing at the University of Montana School of Journalism.

JAMIE KITMAN, a lawyer and Grammy Award–winning rock band manager (They Might Be Giants, OK Go) is a columnist and New York bureau chief for *Automobile* magazine, as well as U.S. editor of England's *Top Gear*. Winner of the IRE medal for investigative magazine reporting for "The Secret History of Lead," which appeared in *The Nation*, he has contributed as well to *GQ*, *Harper's*, and the *New York Times Magazine* and is preparing a book for Simon and Schuster on the history of lead in gasoline.

NAOMI KLEIN is an award-winning journalist, a syndicated columnist, and the author of the *New York Times* best-seller *The Shock Doctrine: The Rise of Disaster Capitalism* (September 2007). The six-minute companion film to this book was downloaded more than one million times. Klein's previous book *No Logo: Taking Aim at the Brand Bullies* was also an international best-seller. A collection of her work, *Fences and Windows: Dispatches from the Front Lines of the Globalization Debate*, was published in 2002. Klein's regular column for *The Nation* and *The Guardian* is distributed internationally by the New York Times Syndicate. In 2004 her reporting from Iraq for *Harper's* won the James Aronson Award for Social Justice Journalism. The same year, she released a feature documentary about Argentina's occupied factories, *The Take*, coproduced with director Avi Lewis.

DAVID LIPSKY is a contributing editor for *Rolling Stone*. He has written for the *New Yorker*, the *New York Times*, and *Harper's*, among other publications. His fiction has appeared in the *New*

Yorker and *The Best American Short Stories*, and his novel, *The Art Fair*, won acclaim from the *New York Times Book Review, Newsweek, People,* and others. His book about West Point, *Absolutely American,* was a *New York Times* best-seller and won *Time* magazine's "Best Book of the Year." His honors include a MacDowell fellowship, a Lambert fellowship, and a Henry Hoyns fellowship.

RYAN LIZZA is *The New Yorker's* Washington correspondent. He covered the 2008 presidential election. Lizza joined *The New Yorker* after working at *The New Republic,* where he was a political correspondent from 1998 to 2007, covering the White House and presidential politics. He was formerly a correspondent for *GQ* and a contributing editor for *New York.* He has also written for the *New York Times, Washington Monthly,* and the *Atlantic.*

SANDRA TSING LOH is a writer and performer whose previous books include *A Year in Van Nuys; Depth Takes a Holiday; If You Lived Here, You'd Be Home By Now;* and *Aliens in America.* Her new book, *Mother on Fire: A True Motherf%#$@ Story About Parenting!* was published by Crown Publishers in August 2008. Her off-Broadway solo shows include *Aliens in America* and *Bad Sex with Bud Kemp.* She has been a regular commentator on NPR, and has her own weekly radio commentary series "The Loh Life," as well as a daily show "Loh Down on Science" (syndicated). Her awards include a Pushcart Prize in fiction and two National Magazine Award nominations for her writing in *The Atlantic.*

MAUREEN MCCOY is the author of four novels: *Walking After Midnight, Summertime, Divining Blood,* and, most recently, *Junebug.* She is a professor in the English Department at Cornell University. The short story "How Tiny Tim Entered the Witness Protection Program" appeared in *Epoch;* the *Mississippi Review* has recently published a series of her short-short fictions.

PAUL REYES is editor-at-large of *The Oxford American*, where his writing has appeared since 2001. He's also written for *Details*, *The Manchester Guardian Weekly*, the *Mississippi Review*, *Slate*, and the *Los Angeles Times*. Reyes lives in Little Rock, Arkansas.

SELENA ROBERTS is one of the most recognizable voices in sports journalism. She joined *Sports Illustrated* in January 2008 as a senior writer and is one of the magazine's "Point After" columnists. She also works on investigative projects. Before joining *Sports Illustrated*, Roberts worked at the *New York Times* for twelve years. There she had a variety of assignments covering sports. Previously, she was the Minnesota Vikings beat writer and a sports projects writer at the *Minneapolis Star-Tribune*. Before that, Roberts worked at the *Orlando Sentinel* and the *Tampa Tribune*. She started her professional career as an intern at the *Huntsville Times*. Roberts has received numerous honors including five Associated Press Sports Editors honors (1999, 2001, 2003, 2004, and 2006). Roberts is the author of two books: *A Necessary Spectacle: Billie Jean King, Bobby Riggs, and the Match That Leveled the Game* (2005) and *A-Rod: The Many Lives of Alex Rodriguez* (2009).

ROGER ROSENBLATT'S pieces for *Time* magazine have won numerous awards, including two George Polk Awards. His television essays for the *NewsHour with Jim Lehrer* on PBS have won a Peabody and an Emmy. His *Time* cover essay, "A Letter to the Year 2086," was chosen for the time capsule placed inside the Statue of Liberty at its centennial. He is the author of twelve books, including the national best-seller *Rules for Aging*; three collections of essays; and *Children of War*, which won the Robert F. Kennedy Book Prize. His first satirical novel, *Lapham Rising*, also a national best-seller, was published in 2006 by Ecco/HarperCollins. His second novel, *Beet*, was published in 2008. *Making Toast*, a family chronicle, portions of which appeared in *The New Yorker* in December 2008, will be published in 2010. He has written six off-Broadway plays, including *Ashley Montana Goes Ashore in the Caicos*, which was produced in 2005 at New York's Flea Theater. His play *I Must Be Off* was produced at the Flea in the spring of 2009. His comic, one-person show, *Free Speech in America*, which he performed at the American Place Theater, was cited by the *New York Times* as one of the ten best plays of 1991.

HANNA ROSIN splits her time writing longer stories for the *Atlantic* and shorter ones for *DoubleX*, the new women's magazine she cofounded this year as part of the Slate group. This year, she was nominated for a National Magazine Award for a story about transgendered children, and roundly attacked for another story about breast-feeding. She got her start in journalism at *The New Republic* writing contrarian essays and more recently worked at the *Washington Post*, reporting mostly on politics and religion. She has written for *The New Yorker*, the *New York Times*, and *GQ*. She is the author of *God's Harvard: A Christian College on a Mission to Save the Nation*.

TRACY ROSS is a senior editor at *Backpacker*. Her work has been recognized by *Best American Travel Writing* and *Best American Sports Writing* and has appeared in *Backpacker, Outside, Skiing*, and *Powder*. She's currently working on a book based on "The Source of all Things," to be published by Free Press in 2011.

JAMES WOOD has been a staff writer and book critic at *The New Yorker* since 2007. He was the chief literary critic at the *Guardian*, in London, from 1992 to 1995 and a senior editor at *The New Republic* from 1995 to 2007. His critical essays have been collected in two volumes, *The Broken Estate: Essays on Literature and Belief* (1999) and *The Irresponsible Self: On Laughter and the*

Novel (2004), which was a finalist for the National Book Critics Circle Award. He is also the author of a novel, *The Book Against God* (2003), and a study of technique in the novel, *How Fiction Works* (2008). He lives in Boston and teaches half-time at Harvard University, where he is Professor of the Practice of Literary Criticism.